Plains Histories

John R. Wunder, *Series Editor*

ALSO IN PLAINS HISTORIES

America's 100th Meridian: A Plains Journey, by Monte Hartman

American Outback: The Oklahoma Panhandle in the Twentieth Century, by Richard Lowitt

As a Farm Woman Thinks: Life and Land on the Texas High Plains, 1890–1960, by Nellie Witt Spikes; edited by Geoff Cunfer

Children of the Dust: An Okie Family Story, by Betty Grant Henshaw; edited by Sandra Scofield

The Death of Raymond Yellow Thunder: And Other True Stories from the Nebraska–Pine Ridge Border Towns, by Stew Magnuson

Flood on the Tracks: Living, Dying, and the Nature of Disaster in the Elkhorn River Basin, by Todd M. Kerstetter

Food, Control, and Resistance: Rationing of Indigenous Peoples in the United States and South Australia, by Tamara Levi

Free Radical: Ernest Chambers, Black Power, and the Politics of Race, by Tekla Agbala Ali Johnson

From Syria to Seminole: Memoir of a High Plains Merchant, by Ed Aryain; edited by J'Nell Pate

"Help Indians Help Themselves": The Later Writings of Gertrude Simmons Bonnin (Zitkala-Ša), edited by P. Jane Hafen

"I Do Not Apologize for the Length of This Letter": The Mari Sandoz Letters on Native American Rights, 1940–1965, edited by Kimberli A. Lee

Law at Little Big Horn: Due Process Denied, by Charles E. Wright

Nikkei Farmer on the Nebraska Plains: A Memoir, by The Reverend Hisanori Kano; edited by Tai Kreidler

The Notorious Dr. Flippin: Abortion and Consequence in the Early Twentieth Century, by Jamie Q. Tallman

Oysters, Macaroni, and Beer: Thurber, Texas, and the Company Store, by Gene Rhea Tucker

Railwayman's Son: A Plains Family Memoir, by Hugh Hawkins

Rights in the Balance: Free Press, Fair Trial, and Nebraska Press Association v. Stuart, by Mark R. Scherer

Route 66: A Road to America's Landscape, History, and Culture, by Markku Henriksson

Ruling Pine Ridge: Oglala Lakota Politics from the IRA *to Wounded Knee*, by Akim D. Reinhardt

A Sacred People: Indigenous Governance, Traditional Leadership, and the Warriors of the Cheyenne Nation, by Leo K. Killsback

Trail Sisters: Freedwomen in Indian Territory, 1850–1890, by Linda Williams Reese

Urban Villages and Local Identities: Germans from Russia, Omaha Indians, and Vietnamese in Lincoln, Nebraska, by Kurt E. Kinbacher

Where the West Begins: Debating Texas Identity, by Glen Sample Ely

A Witness to History: George H. Mahon, West Texas Congressman, by Janet M. Neugebauer

Women on the North American Plains, edited by Renee M. Laegreid and Sandra K. Mathews

A Sovereign People

A Sovereign People

Indigenous Nationhood, Traditional Law, and the Covenants
of the Cheyenne Nation

LEO K. KILLSBACK

Texas Tech University Press

Copyright © 2020 by Leo K. Killsback

All rights reserved. No portion of this book may be reproduced in any form or by any means, including electronic storage and retrieval systems, except by explicit prior written permission of the publisher. Brief passages excerpted for review and critical purposes are excepted.

This book is typeset in EB Garamond. The paper used in this book meets the minimum requirements of ANSI/NISO Z39.48-1992 (R1997). ∞

On the cover and frontis: *Buffalo Dancers—Annual Dance—Cheyenne*. Nov. 16, 1927, Edward S. Curtis, 1868–1952. National Anthropological Archives, Smithsonian Museum Support Center, Suitland, Maryland.

Library of Congress Cataloging-in-Publication Data is on file.
ISBN: 978-1-68283-037-6

Printed in the United States of America
19 20 21 22 23 24 25 26 27 / 9 8 7 6 5 4 3 2 1

Texas Tech University Press
Box 41037
Lubbock, Texas 79409-1037 USA
800.832.4042
ttup@ttu.edu

For Maela, Leon, and Tasbah

Contents

Illustrations xi
Tables xiii
Preface xv
Acknowledgments xix
Introduction xxi

Part I
Ma'heónėstónestôtse: Sacred Covenants 1

Chapter 1
Ma'heónohéstanove: A Sacred Nation 5

Chapter 2
The Communal Ceremonies 21

Chapter 3
The Covenant Ceremonies 39

Chapter 4
Ma'heónetanohtôtse: The Sacred Way of Thinking 65

Part II
Noónêho'emanestôtse: Traditional Law 75

Chapter 5
Tsėhéstanove naa Nevo'êstanémaneo'o: The Cheyenne Way and Kinship 79

Chapter 6
Tsėhéstanove naa Ho'emanestôtse: The Cheyenne Way and Law 95

| ix |

CHAPTER 7
Tsėhéstanove naa Nééʼéve: The Cheyenne Way and Marriage   115

CHAPTER 8
Maʼhëöʼo Hestoʼemanestôtse: Sacred Laws   133

PART III
Néstaxeoʼo: Allies   159

CHAPTER 9
Tsėhéstáno naa Xamaevoʼêstaneoʼo:
The Cheyenne Nation and Indigenous Peoples   163

CHAPTER 10
Hoʼóhomoʼeoʼo: The Lakota Nation   181

CHAPTER 11
Xamaevoʼêstaneoʼo Hoʼemanestôtse:
Indigenous Nations Law   191

CHAPTER 12
Tsėhéstanove and War   203

PART IV
Colonizing the Tsėhéstáno   215

CHAPTER 13
Véʼhóʼe: The White Man   219

Conclusion: Decolonizing the Tsėhéstanove   237

Notes   247

Bibliography and Suggested Readings   269

Index   283

Illustrations

The ten bands of the United Cheyenne Nation and
the two sacred covenants   11

The balance of power and authority between
the Véhoo'o and Nótâxeo'o   13

The balance of power and authority between the four sacred entities   14

The ceremonial calendar of the United Cheyenne Nation   26

Bull Thigh, Keeper of Sacred Arrow, 1910   49

Buffalo Dancers—Annual Dance—Cheyenne, 1927   62

*Oivit (Scabby) or Baldwin Twins, His Wife Amitsehei,
and Their Daughter, Nakai*, 1908   83

Traditional laws and the responsible authority figures   98

Aquqavenuts (Crossed Feathers) with Wife and Daughter, 1908   109

Young Man and Wife, 1893   118

Man and Woman inside Tipi, 1893   124

The worldview of Tsėhéstanove   155

Kamxwiwiyaxtah (Wooden Leg), 1913   166

Woir-Oqtuimanists (Man on a Cloud), 1892   201

Tables

2.1. Traditional Cheyenne Dances and Dance Societies Identified in 1910   22

2.2. Other Dances Identified by White Bull/Ice in 1910   23

2.3. Other Dances Identified by American Horse in 1910   24

5.1. Basic Cheyenne Kinship Terms   82

5.2. Cheyenne Kinship Terms for the Extended Family   86

5.3. Cheyenne Kinship Terms for the Nuclear Family   88

5.4. Cheyenne Kinship Terms for In-laws   90

5.5. Cheyenne Kinship Terms for Citizenship   92

9.1. Indigenous Nations Identified in 1910   164

9.2. Indigenous Nations Commonly Known to the Cheyennes   168

Preface

One of the reasons I authored *A Sovereign People* is to attempt to explain how traditional Cheyenne teachings like fairness and balance laid the foundations for peacemaking and nation building among the Cheyennes. Historically, such traditional teachings allowed smaller Cheyenne bands to unify until the Cheyenne "tribe" grew and matured into the Cheyenne Nation. The Cheyenne Nation then created alliances with other Plains Indian nations following the same principles. Traditional teachings like fairness and balance are embedded in the Cheyenne oral tradition and are reinforced in nearly every facet of Cheyenne life. For example, the concept of héveseónematsestôtse, brotherhood, is found in numerous stories, as it is a foundation of peacemaking and building alliances. From the Cheyenne perspective, héveseónematsestôtse is better understood as the sacred relationship that siblings, regardless of sex, have with one another. Siblinghood, therefore, may be a better translation of héveseónematsestôtse. The most notable stories of héveseónematsestôtse are in the epic of the Hestáhkeho, the holy hero twins. The epic of the twins is recorded in my previous book, *A Sacred People: Indigenous Governance, Traditional Leadership, and the Warriors of the Cheyenne Nation*, yet I reiterate the foundational concepts of the epic in *A Sovereign People*.

A second reason I authored this book is to initiate a much-needed discussion on nation building in my home community. I strongly believe that traditional teachings in the home can significantly contribute to the rebuilding and restoration of our Indigenous nation. I grew up on the Northern Cheyenne Indian Reservation in a single-parent household. Until my younger sisters were born eight and ten years later, I was the youngest of four boys and my mother worked full time to provide for our family. My brothers and I were all close in age: first there were "the twins," the two oldest, then "the middle child," who was a year younger, and then me, "the youngest," who was another year younger. It is common for brothers to argue and fight with one another, and it was common for us as well. Sometimes we fought over trivial things like chores. At times, my brothers and I would spend more energy arguing who was going to wash the dishes or sweep the floor than it would have taken to do it. From time to time, we would need lecturing from an uncle, especially when we grew into manhood and my mother focused more on raising our younger sisters.

PREFACE

My mother followed traditional customs, and in times of need, she invited an uncle to our house to "set us straight," especially when our fighting became too much for my mother to handle. One uncle in particular lectured us frequently. His lectures were more successful than were those given by others, probably because he also had a family with numerous sons. My uncle was also a ceremonial and spiritual leader. But even after his lectures, and as expected of siblings, sometimes we were at each other's throats again just days or weeks later. After numerous arguments, fistfights, and bloody noses, and more visits from uncles, my mother decided that we needed an intervention of greater proportion than before. I specifically remember the time that things were so bad among us fighting brothers that my mother took us all on a trip to visit the highest spiritual leader of our nation, the Sacred Hat Keeper. I was ten years old at the time. We did not know the significance of her intentions then, but when we reached adulthood we appreciated what she had done for us for the sake of our futures and, more important, for her health as a single parent living on the reservation.

The Sacred Hat Keeper is a man of considerable stature in our community. Before our visit, we prepared for a special trip to see "our medicine man": we dressed nicely, ate a wholesome breakfast, crammed into my mother's small car, and were on our way. Before we arrived, my mother instructed us to behave in a "respectful manner" because the person we were visiting was responsible for the spiritual well-being of "everyone in the tribe." My mother told us that the lodge of the Hat Keeper was "ma'heoneve," sacred. I had never heard her emphasize that term in the manner she did that day. Before that day, I had only heard the term in prayers, most of which were Christian prayers. And although I had entered many churches and other formal meetings with my mother, I had never entered the "sacred" lodge of the Sacred Hat.

After hearing her instructions, my brothers and I were on our best behavior out of fear and respect for the sacred unknown. We arrived. Before we entered the lodge of the Sacred Hat my mother and the Hat Keeper further instructed us on proper behavior in the presence of the Sacred Hat. None of us risked challenging either of their instructions. This leads to my third reason for authoring this book: the foundations of Cheyenne sovereignty and law lie in rituals and ceremonies. By following through with the proper protocols and adhering to traditional laws of ceremony, we were participating in the unwritten rules of traditional Cheyenne due process. As I understood then and now, these were sacred protocols that remained unchanged from their founding centuries ago among the Cheyenne people.

We sat patiently and quietly as the Hat Keeper and my mother spoke in Cheyenne. When it was our turn to talk, I distinctly remember that my brothers and I had shed all of the images that we created for ourselves and one another. In this lodge, there was no "eldest brother," no "middle brother," and no "youngest brother." We were all equal and our concerns were of equal importance.

PREFACE

Furthermore, there were no individuals. We were all one family and we all had a role in contributing to our problems, but we also had responsibilities in improving our shared situation. My brothers and I were counseled on how to be "better siblings," "better brothers," and "better sons." My mother spoke last, and the Keeper closed the meeting with a prayer, a blessing ceremony, and other rituals that involved lighthearted conversation and joking. We departed in silence: not gleeful, but content; not somber, but calmed. And this explains my fourth reason for authoring this book: that all humans seek and desire balance with one another and the unseen spiritual powers. Although there will always be conflict, everyone can agree that peace is much better.

To this day, I never forgot that experience because it seemed the sibling rivalries among us brothers came to a close. We seldom became jealous of one another, and we did not desire the material possessions of one another. Even if we lapsed, we did not let our jealousy fester into resentment or bitterness, and we did not let our desires turn into greed or thievery. My mother instituted family rules that we held sacred, which is my fifth purpose for authoring this book: the family is the most important institution in building healthy individuals and a healthy nation. The Hat Keeper recommended some of our family's rules, while others were my mother's creation or re-creation from her upbringing. For example, we could not use the word "hate" or "death" when talking or arguing with one another. We could not be jealous of one another. We could not lie or cheat one another. We could not gossip. We had to be fair and had to share when the moment was appropriate. As difficult as these rules were, it seemed that all four of us boys agreed to abide by them. This agreement was our promise to one another but also, more important, a promise to our mother and the Sacred Hat Keeper, which is my sixth purpose for authoring this book: that humans must make and keep sacred promises to sustain the peace and balance that we desire.

Not long after our meeting with the Sacred Hat Keeper, my mother sat us all down again and created a system in which every brother was assigned one or two household tasks every day. The schedule of tasks rotated so that each day every brother completed a different task and all the household chores would be done in a timely manner. This system of balance minimized conflict. The focus shifted from individual chores to the maintenance of the household that we all shared. There were no individuals, only the individual household. Although we continued to argue and fight from time to time, we never brought our conflicts beyond a certain level of respect and we most certainly did not violate the rules set by our mother. After our visit to the Hat Keeper we talked more and were willing to hear each other's point of view. We relearned how to be brothers, while my mother could focus on being our provider and raising our then baby sisters, among other motherly duties and responsibilities as the sole provider.

It was not until I grew older that I learned that my mother and her three sisters were raised in a similar situation. The person of authority in their household was their grandmother, Hattie Killsback. She bestowed upon my mother, Jackie, and her sisters—Nancy, Barbara, and Cheryl—traditional teachings of fairness and balance. Today these teachings were and are valuable in sustaining the health of their families. Those simple household rules were the foundation for our proper behavior in public. Traditionally, Cheyenne teachings of fairness and balance were to be carried into adulthood, thus creating fair and reasonable adults. Children who learn and practice the values of fairness and balance, however challenging and difficult, will likely apply the same values into adulthood. After all, if one can be fair and reasonable to relatives, they are more likely to be fair and reasonable to others. I have come to find that the teachings for proper behavior within Cheyenne family households are also the foundation for traditional concepts of law, sovereignty, and nationhood.

The Cheyenne Nation's autonomy as a sovereign entity relies heavily on the sanctity of the traditional concepts of law, sovereignty, and nationhood. Héveseónematsestôtse (brotherhood) is just one of many concepts that make up the fabric of traditional Cheyenne views of sovereignty. *A Sovereign People* is an attempt to explain the Cheyenne concepts of law, sovereignty, and nationhood as understood by the Cheyenne people. The Cheyenne Nation depended primarily on the strength, survival, and perseverance of the Cheyenne family system. The Cheyenne spiritual way of living was reinforced through ceremonial practices extended beyond the family and into traditional Cheyenne concepts of diplomacy and building alliances. The stories and traditional teachings of "the Cheyenne spiritual way" are more than family teachings; they are teachings for an entire nation, since the Cheyenne Nation is philosophically and spiritually a nation of families. I explore these traditional concepts in *A Sovereign People* in an effort to reclaim the original identity of the Cheyenne people. It is a journey toward decolonization and not necessarily a destination. I welcome you on this journey, vá'öhtáma!

Acknowledgments

Thanks to my past, present, and future spiritual advisers and ceremonial instructors. During the course of my authoring, editing, and publishing the two-volume book several people who contributed to the survival of the Cheyenne spiritual and cultural ways of life passed away. Some of these special people were influential to my formal and traditional education as a Cheyenne "sacred scholar." To them I say, "I am forever indebted to your contributions and hope that our generation and future generations continue to honor your legacy."

Introduction

Whose sovereignty, i.e., power, are we talking about? Does sovereignty belong to property owners, as John Locke proposed, or to political parties and competing economic interests, as is held in modern U.S. political theory? Or does it belong to future generations? Is the purpose of an Indian nation, when it acts as a collective in the name of all, to enrich one person, a few persons, or to enhance the well-being of every member, even the members yet unborn? What does sovereignty mean when it finds its roots in Indian traditions and not in the courts and congresses of the United States and Canada? What does it look like when the "Indian" in Indian sovereignty is alive and well? Can an Indian nation exercise sovereignty when it is torn into warring factions, each of which refused to cooperate with the others for the benefit of the whole? When the idea of sovereignty is not supporting a dictatorship, is it not supporting an egalitarian society?

—John Mohawk (Seneca)[1]

A Sovereign People is authored from a Cheyenne perspective, but it is by no means the one and only Cheyenne perspective. I am an enrolled member of the Northern Cheyenne Tribe of Montana, and I was raised on the Northern Cheyenne Indian Reservation and grew up in "the village" in Busby. Family and community members told my siblings and me traditional stories, and my mother and older relatives spoke Cheyenne fluently. Although my brothers and I are not completely fluent in the Cheyenne language, we certainly gained the fundamentals of the language as well as the teachings and meanings behind words, phrases, concepts, and stories. Our foundations in Cheyenne culture, language, and philosophy were beneficial to us, since we began participating in traditional ceremonies and rituals at early ages. Eventually we participated in fasting and Sun Dance ceremonies and joined traditional dance societies and ceremonial guilds. Like most Indigenous people in our generation, we are in a struggle to preserve and protect everything that is part of the Cheyenne spiritual way of living and to pass it on to our children. *A Sovereign People* is on no account the exclusive method for preserving and protecting the Cheyenne spiritual way of living, but I hope that it can be a vital contribution. My sentiment of *A Sovereign People* extends in preserving and protecting the abstract but

INTRODUCTION

formidable Cheyenne Nation as a whole. The Cheyenne Nation, as I demonstrate, is a much larger ideology and philosophy when compared to the "tribes" in which we are enrolled. In short, the Cheyenne Nation is best understood as our grandmother. As members, we are its grandchildren who must maintain a sacred relationship. This is not an easy task.

As I am an American Indian scholar, my experiences have certainly shaped my intentions and goals for *A Sovereign People*. Like most people who have grown up on an Indian reservation, I was conditioned to perceive the world through a colonized lens. It was not until I grew older that I realized our perceptions were the product of years of assimilation, of spiritual and mental colonization. For example, the concepts of sovereignty, nationhood, and law are assumed to be exclusively of European origin and application, yet American Indian and Indigenous peoples had these concepts long before the arrival of Europeans. I believe that American Indians have been relying on the European definitions of sovereignty, nationhood, and law for too long, especially since Indians have come to replicate the Western view of sovereignty and the ruthless exercises of it. In some cases, Indian leaders have used the concept of sovereignty against their own citizens and to exploit their own Indigenous lands.[2] It is time that American Indian and Indigenous nations begin to deconstruct and decolonize the term and concept of sovereignty. Mohawk scholar Taiaiake Alfred's discussion on sovereignty provides a backdrop for my intentions for this book:

> Sovereignty. The word, so commonly used, refers to supreme political authority, independent and unlimited by any other power. Discussion of the term "sovereignty" in relation to indigenous peoples, however, must be framed directly within an intellectual framework of internal colonization. Internal colonization is the historical process of political reality defined in the structures and techniques of government that consolidate the domination of indigenous peoples by a foreign yet sovereign settler state. While internal colonization describes the political reality of most indigenous peoples, one should also note that the discourse of state sovereignty is and has been contested in real and theoretical ways since its imposition.

The history of the colonization and assimilation of the Northern Cheyennes in particular has generated a cycle of internal colonization. Through this internal colonization the Northern Cheyennes have also internalized oppression and used the tools of the oppressor against one another. These tools are unseen forces in our communities, yet they are the driving force that impedes nation-building, diminishes traditional laws, and stifles the exercise of sovereignty. I have witnessed and experienced the destructive forces of internal colonialism and oppression firsthand. For example, Cheyennes tend to view each other as threats, even though we belong to the same nation, live in the same community, and share the same challenges. We are united by a shared history, culture, and ancestral language. We share kinship relationships with each other and we share a homeland that was secured by our ancestors. Despite our similarities,

INTRODUCTION

our small community has numerous factions, which are sometimes not clearly defined and may change depending on the political landscape. Some divisions may be based on family loyalties, while others are based on economics or professions like ranching or mining. Similarly, some divisions may exist because of historic family feuds, an unresolved disagreement among neighbors, or just plain jealousy and resentment. While such conflicts may be commonplace in any community, these "tribal" conflicts seem extraordinary because most Indian people seem to know that Indian people were traditionally united under sacred teachings of unity, respect, and cooperation. It is these sacred teachings, among others, that are the foundation of Indigenous concepts of sovereignty, law, and nationhood. And it is my goal to present and resurrect such concepts from the Cheyenne perspective.

With all of the petty political divisions, whether small or large, ultimately the most disenfranchised people in our communities are impoverished, undereducated, and marginalized "tribal" members and their families. These folks are primarily "full-blooded Indians": those who "look" more Indian, who are "dark," who typically are non-Christian traditionalists who speak English with an improper "rez" (reservation) accent, and who likely speak the Cheyenne language. Blood quantum has nothing to do with the term "full-blood," because the term is primarily based on color and how the colonial system has historically marginalized, discriminated against, and disenfranchised "Indians of color." This longstanding division that has continued to destroy our community is race based. "Indians of color" are typically mistreated by the racially and economically privileged minority, the "mixed-blood" or "half-breed Indians." The only way to effect any positive change is to confront and deconstruct the race-based paradigms that have dominated the social and political landscape among the Northern Cheyenne since the establishment of the reservation. I conclude in this book that once tribal members begin viewing themselves as citizens of a sacred Indigenous nation, that Indigenous nation can begin to heal itself. Citizens and leaders will see that they are part of a larger unified sovereign entity and that they are responsible to it and the lives and well-being of all its citizens.

The decolonization of "tribal sovereignty," however, is going to take more than dismantling the race-based paradigms of division and the complete deconstruction of concepts like "tribal membership" and labels like the so-called "full-bloods" and "half-breeds." To decolonize "tribal sovereignty," citizens and leaders of Indigenous nations must also strive to protect their nation against outside entities that threaten their nation's sovereignty. While internal conflict and race-based divisions are the immediate threats to sovereignty, Indigenous nations must understand that outsiders and outside entities tend to hold contempt toward Indian reservations. Further, such negative views of Indian homelands are used to justify the exploitation, mistreatment, and marginalization of Indigenous lands. Outside of the reservation, for example, the majority of people, who are white, tend to hold racist views of all Indians regardless of which petty faction said Indians belong to. The "reservation" in general is perceived by outsiders as the wasteland that harbors the primitive and unruly Indians, and outsiders freely apply these negative stereotypes to all Indians, their enterprises, their organizations, and their governments. This book is an effort to reclaim an Indigenous concept of nationhood based on traditional and historic concepts, not on racial or colonial ones.

When I was growing up, I was perplexed when I began to see how we as Cheyenne "tribal members" held race-based and, at times, racist views about our own people and our own institutions, especially about our government and homeland. I found that both Indians and whites held contempt for "rezers" and resented the "rez," yet only the Indians resided on the reservation. I began to unravel the intricacies of internal colonization, to track our people's mental and spiritual colonization, and to seek an alternative perspective. In this book I present a decolonized lens that aims to break the cycle of internal colonization so the Cheyennes and others can see how the Cheyenne people historically viewed themselves as a sovereign people, who honor sacred laws. I found that the concept of a "tribe" is nothing compared to the Cheyenne view of itself as a "nation," which is why I will use the term sparingly. Furthermore, the "rez" is nothing short of a derogatory term used to devalue and disempower Indian nations, yet it is a term that has been redefined and is now used commonly in Indian communities.

The Cheyenne Nation can be viewed metaphorically as our grandmother, thus our relationship to it is a sacred one, sustained through honoring sacred laws. Conversely, the "rez" is not our grandmother, and our relationship to it is not a sacred one, which is why we tend to devalue it. Through our colonized eyes, the "rez" is viewed as a place of lawlessness, disorder, pettiness; it is a refuge run amok by unruly and unpredictable "savages." This is the perception that upset me once I saw it for what it was. We hold resentment for the "rez" the same way an abused child holds resentment toward an abusive stepparent.

The perception was and continues to be reinforced by some community members and leaders who contribute to disorder and unruliness for personal gain or to advance an agenda that benefits a select few. In this view, the "rez" is the place where the uncivilized Indians live; it is the place where the "Wild West" remains wild. As the perception holds, the "rez" is where criminals live freely and without restraint and where the elite abuse power. It is the place of violence, thievery, and corruption and where nepotism and greed dominate all aspects of government and society. Through this lens, the "rez" is unclean, littered with trash, "rez" cars, and unclean people. Through this lens, the children live in poverty at the fault of their lazy parents. If you are from the "rez" and you are an Indian man you are branded a criminal; if you are an Indian woman you are branded promiscuous.

INTRODUCTION

In the end, the "rez" is not a sovereign nation, nor is it worthy of any respect or recognition beyond those of a ghetto. What little progress or structure that is present on the "rez" exists and persists thanks to the compassionate and resilient whites who have dedicated their lives to saving these "heathen" people from themselves. Through this colonial lens, the "white way" is the best way. And although the Indians have their culture and traditional practices, these are mere glimpses of once-noble "savages" from a time before the heroes of "white civilization" brought law, religion, and government. This view is wrong and destructive, yet it is merely a mental construct. The concept of "the rez" needs to be reinforced with negativity in order for it to remain, and this is its weakness. Time is due to deconstruct, dismantle, and decolonize this destructive term and concept.

Indigenous people should not underestimate the power and force of the colonial lens and its terms. For example, I have witnessed citizens rally to confront persisting problems on the reservation, yet almost every problem and its potential solutions were viewed through this colonial lens. I find the colonial lens itself to be the very root of the Indigenous struggle for sovereignty, nationhood, and self-determination. Indigenous people must be prepared to replace the colonial lens with an Indigenous one, or at least one that best suits the needs of their community. *A Sovereign People* is an effort to dismantle the colonial lens that has caused so much pain and suffering among the Cheyennes. It is an effort to re-create an Indigenous lens and use history and traditional knowledge to confront modern challenges through an Indigenous paradigm, rather than the same colonial one that has yielded few to no results.

At its core, *A Sovereign People* is a historical study of the Tsėhéstáno (the Cheyenne Nation) and the Cheyenne people, culture, and society with an approach to history unlike any previous study. In this book I aim to accomplish two tasks: first to examine and explain the Cheyenne concepts of sovereignty, law, and nationhood, and second to do this from a decolonized Cheyenne perspective. Colonization, the process and its resulting effects, dramatically changed how Plains Indian people view themselves as sovereign entities. Assimilationist policies further degraded and devalued traditional views of sovereignty, and since then others have determined the purpose and direction of American Indian and Indigenous nations. For the most part, "tribal sovereignty" and Indian "tribes" have been defined through colonial lenses that rely heavily on Western legal canons and principles of capitalism and economic development that emphasize resource extraction. Today Indian "tribes" continue to operate under these unstable and fragile systems in crisis mode, making it challenging for them to reexamine or change the enduring legacies of colonization and assimilation.

Today, "tribes" like the Northern Cheyenne and others on the Great Plains do not necessarily have a complete understanding of how their nations built and sustained themselves throughout history. American Indians must invest the time and effort in revealing, recovering, and reintroducing traditional histories from their perspectives. *A Sovereign People* aims to accomplish this for the Cheyennes in hopes that the next generations will gain a sense of an Indigenous national identity that is more akin to those of the "old ones"—those who lived before the establishment of the reservation system.

Since *A Sovereign People* is one of the first efforts to provide an in-depth analysis of an Indigenous view of sovereignty, nationhood, and nation-building, I also highlight the alliances that the Cheyennes created with other Indigenous nations of the Great Plains. *A Sovereign People* features the Cheyenne and other Plains Indian nations, and I believe that my discussion about Indigenous nationhood, traditional law, and sacred covenants certainly extends beyond the Great Plains. In fact, the principles I discuss, such as Indigenous brotherhood, sacred covenants, and unification, can be found in Indigenous cultures throughout the United States, Canada, and Central America.[3] *A Sovereign People* is especially significant to those Indigenous nations that continue to face enduring challenges of colonialism and in their commitments to decolonization. *A Sovereign People* represents a new genre in the study of Indigenous governance and law that can be applied to the modern discourse of Native American and Indigenous studies.

INDIGENOUS METHODOLOGIES

Although there have been numerous perspectives on American Indian and Indigenous histories, most do not come directly from the American Indian and Indigenous people or community themselves. Indigenous scholars have found that the lack of the Indigenous presence in the academy is more than just a missing perspective: "The result has been, and continues to be, that Indigenous communities are being examined by non-Indigenous academics who pursue Western research on Western terms."[4]

For *A Sovereign People* I have relied not only on traditional Cheyenne beliefs and customs but also on the ongoing efforts to bring Indigenous people into the forefront. Opaskwayak Cree scholar Shawn Wilson describes this effort:

> An important aspect of this emerging style of research is that Indigenous peoples themselves decide exactly which areas are to be studied. It is time for research that is conducted by or for Indigenous people to take another step forward. An integral part of Indigenous identity for many Indigenous people includes a distinct way of viewing the world and of "being." Indigenous people have come to realize that beyond control over the topic chosen for study, the research methodology needs to incorporate their cosmology, worldview, epistemology and ethical beliefs.[5]

I represent the new generation of American Indian and Indigenous academics whom I call "sacred scholars."[6] Sacred scholars are not merely enrolled members of an Indian nation. Rather, they also culturally and spiritually identify as Indigenous people and are formally trained in the academy. Using "sacred scholarship" as an approach to history will provide better representations of American Indian and Indigenous peoples, their cultures, and their histories.

INTRODUCTION

Sacred scholarship is an approach that will produce a fairer and more balanced American Indian and Indigenous perspective than those previously presented. In my community alone, there are several books and histories that have been authored by non-Cheyennes and non-Indians who claim, either directly or indirectly, they represent the Cheyenne voice, or at least an underrepresented Cheyenne voice. Yet there remains not one peer-reviewed book authored solely by a Northern Cheyenne scholar, let alone a sacred scholar.

A Sovereign People meets a Cheyenne studies research model that is a foundation of "sacred scholarship."[7] First, sacred scholarship is related to "being Cheyenne"; second, it is connected to Cheyenne philosophy and principles; third, it emphasizes, validates, and legitimizes the significance of Cheyenne language and culture; and fourth, it is concerned with the struggle for autonomy over our own cultural well-being. Finally, sacred scholars are the ones who primarily conduct sacred scholarship as they can apply the appropriate traditional and spiritual knowledge.

The Cheyennes continue to be the subject of numerous studies, ranging from health care to history, yet for some the Cheyenne perspective remains a mystery, nonexistent, or unimportant, even to some of the so-called experts in the field of Cheyenne studies. *A Sovereign People* reveals the Cheyenne world as they perceived it and as they lived it. I do so without violating the restrictions set forth by Cheyenne tradition and custom and with respect to the sovereign rights of the Northern Cheyenne Tribe.[8]

A Sovereign People highlights the fabric of the Cheyenne spiritual way of living, but I am not ambitious or overconfident to believe that this book is a blueprint for complete and actual decolonization. Instead, I am fully aware that this book is best perceived as a body of knowledge that was once practiced and lived. Reintroducing and reinstating some or all of the institutions or cultural practices detailed in *A Sovereign People* to a modern setting would be futile; besides, some of these institutions and practices are ongoing and remain unchanged even though they are under threat of extinction. The goal of *A Sovereign People* is not to erase the existing systems in place but to provide insight and guidance so that the Cheyenne people can remain Cheyenne. To what degree they and future generations want to remain Cheyenne is up to each individual. If the collective whole—that is, if one or both of the Northern Cheyenne or Cheyenne-Arapaho Tribes—decided to decolonize by reinstating and reintroducing traditional concepts of sovereignty, nationhood, and law, I would have to assert that this book is not the best blueprint for that change. Another sacred scholar or group of scholars would have to undertake that specific task at another time.

In the end, attempts to replicate or mimic the sophistication of our ancestors would be offensive and disrespectful. Any true attempts for effective, meaningful, sincere, and long-term Cheyenne national decolonization would require a figurative and literal rebirth of a nation, with the figurative rebirth of new leaders and the literal rebirth of citizens who can navigate and thrive as modern warriors. Indigenous national decolonization is a task that would be best achieved by the generations yet unborn. Realistically, those living today would not and could never be the ones up for such an arduous task. We certainly would not be the ones to enjoy this decolonized dream, but it does not mean we cannot plant some seeds.

The intellectual and cultural concepts that I present should not be mistaken for our people's continuing traditional ceremonial practices. These are not the primary subjects of this book. Instead, I emphasize values and principles that we have nearly lost; moreover, although they can be translated into the English language and recorded, they may have lost meaning to those who learned them in traditional households and through firsthand experience. To ensure that I do not violate any of our traditional ethics, I left out numerous components that can only be learned and taught growing up among the people and on the land, through our ceremonial practices, and by a commitment to the Cheyenne spiritual way of living and the continuation of the Cheyenne Nation. Our cultural and spiritual ways have been pirated for too long, and wannabes and thieves have taken advantage of our elders and traditional leaders for personal gain. I am mindful of the losses, but I am also aware of the efforts of numerous Indian people and leaders who strive to reawaken and rekindle their traditional ways. Traditional teachings should be learned and experienced in the traditional setting if true learning is to occur. Simply reciting or replicating them from a source, including mine, would only cause confusion and generate misunderstandings. Traditional Indian cultural ways are ongoing, and newcomers cannot replace these ways, but dedicated and sincere students of decolonization can certainly appreciate and help protect them.

HISTORY AND STORYTELLING

Most Cheyennes do not have access to published articles and books about their history, and only a few can access archival material if they wish to learn from older unpublished records. Chief Dull Knife College, in Lame Deer, Montana, has only begun to seek, retrieve, preserve, and utilize such materials. The archival material exists, but it needs close evaluation. For *A Sovereign People* I rely on the Truman Michelson collection from the National Anthropological Archives. This collection is composed of numerous unpublished stories recorded in English and the Cheyenne language. A challenge arose when I tried to match differing oral traditions—ones that I learned in the household, among my ceremonial instructors, family members, and traditional elders—with archival materials and published accounts from previous generations of Cheyenne studies scholars. Following the principles of "sacred scholarship," I privilege the oral tradition since the oral tradition is still alive. I believe that the storytellers adapted these stories or teachings to fit the conditions of the Cheyenne people and Cheyenne Nation of their time, but always within the confines set by Cheyenne philosophy.

INTRODUCTION

In short, the root meaning of the stories and their cultural and spiritual significance did not change. For example, some stories included horses or the presence of White Man, the trickster, while others did not. In the case of the Sweet Medicine stories, numerous Cheyenne informants and storytellers often place him as the main protagonist in stories that may have been originally about a previous generation's culture hero. The Cheyenne Nation was made up of numerous bands, and each possessed a unique oral tradition, which is why there may be numerous versions of the same stories. For example, when I discussed this idea as a seasoned historian graduate student with seasoned historian Margot Liberty, I noticed some resistance to the entire conversation, but I am glad she published the complete interviews in *A Cheyenne Voice* to provide better context to her previous work *Cheyenne Memories*.

Another challenge arose when I read through unpublished records that were recently made available through digital and electronic means. In these records I found minor inconsistencies from the first generation of Cheyenne studies scholars mentioned earlier to those of the second generation (Hoebel, Llewellyn, Liberty and Stands In Timber, Powell). For example, traditional Cheyenne elders assert that Sweet Medicine did not kill a man, when numerous documented sources, from reliable authorities, state otherwise. Other examples of inconsistency include the era and process in which the Tsétsêhéstâhese and Só'taeo'o united, the era and process in the creation of the warrior societies and Council of Forty-four Chiefs, and which bands were original and which were pseudodivisions. As a historian, I was trained to rely heavily on documented sources, often prioritizing the oldest above the most recent. But as an American Indian studies scholar, I was also trained to be cognizant of other factors. For example, these records were translated from the Cheyenne language, primarily by non-Cheyennes, some over a hundred years ago, and they report on events that may have occurred another hundred or more years earlier. To put this into perspective, a scholar who reads and studies a four-hundred-year-old story or narrative must choose whether to value its content above other narratives or whether to contextualize its significance to extant ceremonial practices, spiritual beliefs, and cultural norms. I had to confront similar dilemmas and chose to organize and prioritize data in a way that I believe the old storytellers, sacred protectors, and prophets would have done following the principles of sacred scholarship.

My method of choosing and prioritizing certain stories over others was not shallow or simplistic. For example, from 1910 to 1934, Michelson recorded numerous stories told by some of the most knowledgeable informants, whose ages ranged from fifty to eighty. Grasshopper was recorded to be fifty-four years old at the time of his interview, age seven at the time of the Sand Creek Massacre (1864), and not yet born at "the time the stars fell" in 1833. He could identify eight of the original Cheyenne bands, while other informants could identify more. His lack of knowledge is not necessarily a flaw because it reveals the circumstances of the Southern Cheyenne people of his generation: since 1869, many of the people were living within a reservation and under paternalistic conditions. For the majority of Grasshopper's life, he did not live as his older relatives had, who were likely more knowledgeable about the traditional bands of the Cheyenne Nation. When other scholars identified the ten principal bands and the warrior societies of the Cheyenne Nation, it appears they had to choose among the varying data provided by numerous informants. I made similar choices in identifying and highlighting data and concepts but did so in a manner that best matches the oral tradition and culture of current Cheyenne traditionalists.

THE CHAPTERS

Since the beginning of this project and earlier, I have worked with several traditional Cheyenne people including elders and spiritual leaders. Following the oral traditions and customs of my people, I organized the chapters and their content to follow the traditional concepts that underlie the development of the human mind and spirit. My organization may seem confusing and inconsistent at first, but as you read you will understand why I introduce some topics briefly then expound on them later. *A Sovereign People* focuses on the precontact autonomy of the Cheyenne Nation (Tsėhéstáno) and the Cheyenne concept of sovereignty, ma'xenėheto'stôtse (high authority). Indian nations have inherent rights and privileges that predate any European or American affirmations through treaties or legislation. Probably the most misunderstood concept is "tribal sovereignty," and the first chapter is dedicated to defining *sovereignty* as the Cheyenne perceived, exercised, and preserved it.

Part I is titled "Ma'heónėstónestôtse: Sacred Covenants" and comprises four chapters, each discussing the origins of the Cheyenne Nation's sovereignty and how it is sustained through ceremonial practices. Chapter 1, "Ma'heónohéstanove: A Sacred Nation," is a traditional Cheyenne conception of how they viewed their nation. This chapter highlights the spiritual concept of sovereignty and traditional Cheyenne views of sovereignty, which are primarily understood from a ceremonial and philosophical point of view. This chapter lays the foundation for the entire book. Chapter 2, "The Communal Ceremonies," focuses on how the Cheyenne concepts of sovereignty and their origins are preserved and sustained through the teachings and oral traditions of several minor ceremonies. Indigenous nations like the Cheyennes were deeply connected with nature and the spiritual world and therefore held a responsibility over the Earth as protectors. Chapter 3, "The Covenant Ceremonies," continues this discussion by highlighting the major ceremonies that reaffirmed the relationships and responsibilities of the people's spiritual identity in relation to the Earth. Ceremonies also reminded the people of what it meant to be part of a nation. Chapter 4, "Ma'heónetanohtôtse: The Sacred Way of Thinking," highlights guiding principles that were essential to the Cheyenne spiritual identity.

INTRODUCTION

Part II of *A Sovereign People* is titled "Noónêho'emanestôtse: Traditional Law" and also comprises four chapters. This section highlights internal, cultural sovereignty and emphasizes the significance of the traditional laws and customary practices. From the Cheyenne perspective, this concept of sovereignty, or ma'xenéheto'stôtse, is better understood as internal, cultural sovereignty: the right and authority for the nation to handle the affairs of its citizenry and the foundation of a nation's self-determination.[9] Chapter 5, "Tséhéstanove naa Nevo'êstanémaneo'o: The Cheyenne Way and Kinship," highlights the traditional Cheyenne kinship system. Chapter 6, "Tséhéstanove naa Ho'emanestôtse: The Cheyenne Way and Law," examines the basic structure of Cheyenne law, discussing the customs and traditions that promoted model behavior but also prohibited unacceptable conduct. Chapter 7, "Tséhéstanove naa Néé'éve: The Cheyenne Way and Marriage," is a close examination of traditional Cheyenne courtship, marriage, and divorce practices. Chapter 8, "Ma'hëö'o Hesto'emanestôtse: Sacred Laws," closely examines the highest traditional laws of the Cheyenne Nation. Enforcing such laws allowed for a nation to remain autonomous and healthy. The citizenry adhered to a body of laws that not only guided their behavior but also promoted unity and civility.

Part III, "Néstaxeo'o: Allies," examines the international customary laws that allowed leaders of the nation to negotiate peace with or declare war on other Plains Indian nations, like the Arapaho and Lakota. This section highlights the Cheyenne concept of ma'xenéheto'stôtse that the state exercises: the Cheyenne perspective of external sovereignty. Plains Indian nations exercised "Indigenous nation sovereignty," which is the right and authority of a nation to engage in diplomacy and build relationships with other nations.[10] The Tséhéstáno secured alliances that proved to be more than mere military and political alliances; the peaceful unifications transcended into "sacred unions" where each nation also shared cultural and spiritual practices to maintain long-lasting relationships. Chapter 9, "Tséhéstáno naa Xamaevo'êstaneo'o: The Cheyenne Nation and Indigenous Peoples," provides a general overview of how the Cheyenne people viewed other Indigenous peoples. Chapter 10, "Ho'óhomo'eo'o: The Lakota Nation," as the title implies, focuses on how the Cheyenne people viewed the Lakota people and how the Tséhéstáno united with this much larger nation. Chapter 11, "Xamaevo'êstaneo'o Ho'emanestôtse: Indigenous Nations Law," examines the laws, customary and traditional, that most Plains Indian nations followed when engaging in diplomacy and war. Chapter 12, "Tséhéstanove and War," focuses on the Cheyenne customs and laws of war. The Indigenous-nation identity and exercises of sovereignty of the Tséhéstáno reveal, at its height, a truly healthy and sophisticated society composed of dedicated and loyal citizens who honored humanity and nature. This is the legacy of the Cheyenne Nation.

Part IV, the final section, includes chapter 13, "Vé'hó'e: The White Man," and briefly discusses the major challenges that the Tséhéstáno endured while

INTRODUCTION

treating with the United States government. This discussion is important to understanding how the Tséhéstáno split into two sovereign entities: the Northern Cheyenne Tribe of Montana and the Cheyenne-Arapaho Tribes of Oklahoma. I conclude *A Sovereign People* with a brief discussion on decolonizing the Tséhéstanove and provide some recommendations for reviving and reinvigorating Cheyenne traditional and spiritual practices and beliefs. I take full responsibility for any unforeseen misinterpretations or misrepresentations of Cheyenne culture and law. My knowledge of Cheyenne language and culture may be advanced, but it is still developing when compared to that of the old Cheyennes. As we begin to decolonize we must also have the time and patience to relearn. We merely need to give ourselves a chance.

PART I

Ma'heónėstónestôtse: Sacred Covenants

The Great Plains environment determined how the Cheyenne Nation survived as a living-nation. The environment also determined whether or not the Cheyenne Nation prospered. The Cheyennes had come to respect and to live in balance and harmony with this environment, and their ceremonial cycle reveals the intricacies of a delicate spiritual relationship. The Cheyennes had come to depend heavily on hunting and gathering, and their ceremonial cycle coincided with the seasons. Time was measured by the migrations of herds, the blooming of plants and flowers, and movements of star constellations. The spring and summer were the seasons of plenty for the Plains Indians. The Cheyennes welcomed the arrival of spring when they noticed a shift in the position of the sun, the change in weather, and the return of migratory birds. The sun is at its highest at midday but begins to awaken the beauty and life of the new day as soon as it crests the horizon. This spring morning brings about the best in the Cheyenne people as they begin their days with a ritual offering and smoke from their pipes to greet the gift of power felt in the heat of the sun. While grandmothers and grandfathers brew some hot herbal tea, fathers and mothers awaken their children before the sun touches their skin: "Wake up, children! The day is half over!"

As spring days pass, the morning skies begin to glow of bright reds and oranges, colors that the young men try to capture in their paints and finest clothing. The animals have long shed their winter coats and look fluorescent as they stand out in the morning light and against the green hillsides. Birds sing, flowers are in bloom, and thick green grass covers the prairies. All of the creeks, rivers, and ponds are full of cool, clear water, and their banks are sheltered with thick brush and bright greens and blues from cottonwoods and other sacred trees. The prairies are dotted with purple, white, and yellow wildflowers. Pine trees in the distance appear navy blue but shift into shades of purple and black. The skies are turquoise at midday and sometimes filled with thick, fluffy, white clouds. The late spring days are never too hot for a Cheyenne person. They slowly end as the sun sets and fills the sky with bright purples and pinks, colors that the women try to emulate in their quillwork, dresses, and accessories of beauty and womanhood. The cool evening air soothes and calms the warmth left from the day, returning the night to the stars and a full moon. In the end, the Earth is the ultimate authority and determines the time to begin the ceremonial cycle.

CHAPTER 1

Ma'heónohéstanove: A Sacred Nation

Our existence in these lands has not been one of absolute peace and tranquility. We have had to work hard to develop the civilization we enjoy. There was a time when our lands were torn by conflict and death. There were times when certain individuals attempted to establish themselves as the rulers of the people through exploitation and repression. We emerged from those times to establish a strong democratic and spiritual Way of Life.

—*A Basic Call to Consciousness*[1]

Life for the Cheyenne people was quite different before they established the Véhoo'o (Council of Forty-four Chiefs) and the elaborate Nótâxeo'o (warrior society) system of governance. These institutions formed the foundation of the Cheyenne national government, leadership, and citizenship. Before the establishment of these two systems, the Cheyennes lived in small villages that were governed by one chief. The health and well-being of these small bands depended heavily on the decisions of the chief. Sometimes the small bands suffered because of the poor decisions of their leaders, and sometimes the people suffered directly from the rule of tyrants. During the prenation times, the Cheyenne people were disorganized, and the tragic events and poor leaders were memorialized in stories to prevent history from repeating itself. More important, these stories prevented the proliferation of poor leadership values. Out of the chaos and dysfunction, however, rose prophets and spiritual leaders, like Sweet Medicine and White Buffalo Woman, who brought new philosophies and ways of living based on spiritual principles. The Cheyenne Nation was then able to rebuild itself out of the ashes of previous, failed societies. Eventually the Cheyenne Nation reached prime and pinnacle under sacred teachings, unity, justice, and brotherhood. By the time whites arrived, the Cheyenne Nation operated under a refined system of governance and sacred laws.

PART I: MA'HEÓNÈSTÓNESTÔTSE: SACRED COVENANTS

PLAINS INDIAN SOVEREIGNTY AND NATIONHOOD

In 1803, Lewis and Clark acted as representatives of the United States to proclaim supremacy over lands acquired through the Louisiana Purchase. For the next one hundred years, the United States and its citizens sought to take Indian lands through force, political deception, and violence, even after the supposed purchase and outlandish claims of ownership. The United States was then still an undeveloped nation, yet it was ambitious and its leaders sought dominion over the West. The Indian nations of the Great Plains, as history reveals, were not going to give up their lands and ways of living so easily. The history of the wars for the West, however, is for another time.

The assaults on Plains Indian nationhood and sovereignty began with Lewis and Clark. In 1805 William Clark reported in his journals that the Sioux had "no fixed laws" and that "all the other nations have no other laws."[2] His assessment was inaccurate and contradictory. He had already described the Sioux and other Plains Indians as "nations." By definition, nations are independent political states with defined territorial boundaries and organized under a single government, and governments are made of political institutions, laws, and customs that serve, protect, and govern their citizens. The public's view of Plains Indian peoples as "lawless" was shaped by reports like those from Lewis and Clark, and these views often influenced policy-making.[3] Years after the Lewis and Clark Expedition, whites still believed that the Plains Indians were lawless nations. Even after the United States affirmed Indian nation sovereignty through the treaty-making process, most whites did not respect these Indian nations as legitimate sovereigns with sovereign rights, especially property and land rights.

Long before the establishment of the United States, the Louisiana Purchase, and the Lewis and Clark Expedition, Plains Indian nations like the Tsėhéstáno (Cheyenne Nation) had built themselves into powerful, stable, and proud nation-states. The Tsėhéstáno were building their nation over the course of nearly one thousand years and in that time developed as a sovereign Indigenous nation based on spiritual beliefs, principles, and responsibilities. Other Plains Indian nations created themselves under similar ideologies, and by the time whites arrived, most of these nations had already forged alliances with one another. The sacred alliances were secured by the unification of cultures, governments, and spiritual practices, not by loyalties, allegiances, or contracts. The sacred means of building alliances were developed under unwritten international laws and customs. Once united, federations like the Cheyenne, Lakota, and Arapaho alliance became strong military forces and were able to sustain and defend themselves within their shared territories.

Throughout the history of the United States, American Indian nations witnessed firsthand the diminishment and destruction of their sovereignty. Before their lands were colonized and they were removed to reservations, American Indian nations exercised absolute sovereignty and complete self-determination. Their vibrant cultures and spiritual practices were infused with these traditional governing structures, customs, and ways of living. While American Indian cultures and spiritual practices continue to survive, their governing structures have been vanquished or adapted to the modern way of living. Some traditional exercises of sovereignty remain embedded in ceremonial practices, language, and oral traditions. There are remnants of traditional American Indian concepts of sovereignty, and when we uncover these concepts, we find that they were much different from European concepts.

Before the establishment of reservations, nearly every Plains Indian nation, including the Lakota, Cheyenne, and Arapaho, depended on the great American bison for sustenance. Nearly every Plains Indian nation also organized under the band system, which fit the buffalo-hunting lifestyle. Typical precontact Plains Indian governments functioned as complex federations that united under principles of "geographical spirituality," which are ceremonial practices determined by the geography, land, environment, and flora and fauna of a particular area. In the land and environment of the Great Plains, the Sun Dance ceremony is an example of a geo-spiritual ceremonial practice. Other examples are the buffalo dances and the antelope hunting rituals. The nations of the Great Plains had numerous cultural and spiritual similarities, yet they all had differing origins. All nations had unique languages, sacred histories, and local geographic homelands. Most, if not all, Great Plains Indian nations also shared similar political and social characteristics. Indigenous nations in other geographical areas and during different eras did not necessarily follow the same band system as those located on the Great Plains, nor did they have the same ceremonial practices. This unique band system is what aided Plains Indian nations like the Cheyenne in nation building.

As I discussed in *A Sacred People*, the band system of the Great Plains Indian nations can be described as democratic federations or confederacies, yet no European type of government could compare. These band systems, like their spiritual practices, were adapted to fit the environment and thus those who lived in the system essentially became part of the environment. The bands then moved and functioned in synchrony with patterns of the seasons, the weather, the landscape, the waterways, and the life cycles of plant and animal life. In this system, several smaller, mobile units thrived and functioned as autonomous groups, but they were still part of a larger nation. The small bands were composed of extended families and were organized as small states. In this system, individual citizens had two citizenship identities: one was their local band and the other was their Indigenous nation. Band chiefs were primarily responsible for their respective bands and represented them in the larger national governments. Each band may have had unique customs, but all shared unifying national traditions, which were reinforced when reunited during functions like the Sun Dance ceremonies, intertribal peacemaking ceremonies, and, later, treaty-making ceremonies with the United States. The unified Indigenous nations were sovereign, but individual bands held a degree of sovereignty and autonomy.

DECOLONIZING SOVEREIGNTY

The mainstream concept of "sovereignty" is not the best term to use when discussing the type of sovereignty that American Indians exercised precontact and before colonization.[4] Vine Deloria Jr. (Standing Rock Sioux) explains the flaws in this concept but also defines sovereignty from an Indian perspective:

> I think that "sovereignty" was a European word that tried to express the nationhood of a people who could think with one mind. Since the king was the ruler, he was sovereign in the sense that he was supposed to represent what the people of his nation wanted. Indians had spread out the idea of governing to include all activities of life—thus, at times, medicine people would be influential and, at other times, warriors, or hunters, or scouts would be influential. Many tribes did not have "laws" or "religion," but a single belief system that was described as "our way of doing things." Sovereignty today, unfortunately, is conceived as a wholly political-legal concept.[5]

The term *sovereignty* as understood in mainstream society is an adaptation from a mid-fourteenth-century Anglo-French term, *sovereynete*, which means "pre-eminence," and it is primarily used to describe the authority of monarchs. Today sovereignty is defined as the supreme authority of a state; the independence of an entity; and the right to self-government. Throughout the history of the colonization of Native America, Europeans and Americans have relied on their concept of sovereignty to justify and legitimize the thievery of Indigenous peoples' lands.[6]

Another term that is widely used is *tribal sovereignty*. I believe *tribal sovereignty* is overused as the defining attribute of today's American Indian and Indigenous nations, and it does not adequately define the Indigenous view of sovereignty. American Indians need to begin raising and answering for themselves some critical questions: What is tribal sovereignty? Where does tribal sovereignty come from? How do Indian "tribes" exercise tribal sovereignty? Today the models of tribal sovereignty under which most tribes operate have deep roots in Western legal thought, since the laws and policies of the United States define tribal sovereignty. Treaties, precedent-setting US Supreme Court rulings, congressional acts, and executive orders shaped tribal sovereignty to what it is today.[7] This same tribal sovereignty has allowed Indian tribes to retain and regain some rights and even aided some in the economic growth and prosperity. Yet Indian tribes and tribal governments have remained politically unstable and in disarray, especially as they continue to fight to preserve and protect what little resources and rights they managed to retain.

Throughout history, tribal sovereignty has not been defined or determined by American Indian nations or peoples. Instead, it developed over the course of hundreds of years of conflict, and for some Indian nations these conflicts remain. Today most Indian tribes operate as quasi-sovereign democracies, similar to corporations or small municipalities. But because tribal sovereignty is determined and maintained by mainstream paradigms of law, governance, and self-determination, these tribal governments operate within the limitations set by others. Indian tribes and tribal governments then are not sovereign entities by mainstream definition but "somewhat sovereigns" that function within the limitations of a sovereign colonial system.

In a modern context, Western legal thought as a foundation of tribal sovereignty may be one reason why Indian tribes continue to struggle as peoples. Tribal sovereignty is arguably another instrument that serves the colonial agenda because it is a product of colonization.[8] Western legal thought, when reexamined from Indigenous perspectives, is foreign and at times alien and inhumane; it has been especially hostile toward Indigenous peoples and their rights. So-called tribal sovereignty must be decolonized or at least reevaluated from an Indigenous perspective.

Precontact American Indian and Indigenous concepts of sovereignty are rooted in traditional teachings of the unseen powers of the sacred. David Wilkins (Lumbee) and Heidi Kiiwetinepinesiik Stark (Anishinaabekwe) provide a definition of tribal sovereignty that is based on principles found in Indigenous cultural and spiritual dimensions, independence, and inherent powers and rights:

> Tribal sovereignty is the intangible and dynamic cultural force inherent in a given indigenous community, empowering that body toward the sustenance and enhancement of political, economic, and cultural integrity. It undergirds the way tribal governments relate to their own citizens, to non-Indian residents, to local governments, to the state government, to the federal government, to the corporate world, and to the global community.[9]

Wilkins and Stark's deconstructed definition speaks to the American Indian experience and the current situation of Indian nations. Deconstructing and redefining tribal sovereignty is proving to be a much more challenging task than expected, but the movement is on the rise.[10]

A challenge in redefining tribal sovereignty is that no single definition fits every American Indian or Indigenous nation. In the end, there may not be a single term or concept. Robert Porter (Seneca) asserts that Indigenous peoples must reject the notion that there is a universal definition of sovereignty; then they can re-create and exercise new models of "Indigenous Nation Sovereignty."[11] There is no one definition of sovereignty because each Indigenous nation has to develop it based on its people's unique principles, as Porter states:

> There are, within the United States, over six hundred recognized and unrecognized Indigenous sovereigns. They vary in every conceivable manner. By virtue of population, culture, geography, and the nuances of history, no two Indigenous peoples are

PART I: MA'HEÓNĖSTÓNESTÔTSE: SACRED COVENANTS

the same. It serves little purpose, other than to encourage mistake, to take the position that, with respect to defining Indigenous nation sovereignty, "one size fits all."[12]

Porter asserts, however, that Indigenous Nation Sovereignty depends on an Indigenous people's possession of three factors: *belief* in their own sovereignty, *ability* to carry out their belief in sovereignty, and the internal and external *recognition* of their belief in sovereignty.[13] In my exploration of the foundations of Indigenous Nation Sovereignty from a Cheyenne perspective, I redefine the meaning and significance of sovereignty relying on traditional Cheyenne epistemology.

SACRED SOVEREIGNTY

The form of Indigenous Nation Sovereignty that the Tséhéstáno (Cheyenne Nation) exercised is better defined as "sacred sovereignty." In fact, all Indigenous nations embodied and exercised sacred sovereignty because it is divine and relies on the people's ability to uphold the sacred teachings found in spiritual beliefs. Sacred sovereignty is based on each nation's unique spiritual principles. Following Porter's model of Indigenous Nation Sovereignty, sacred sovereignty depends on the people's *belief* in their unique spiritual ways, their *ability* to practice these spiritual ways, and their *recognition* of these spiritual ways as legitimate. Other nations also *recognize* the sanctity of these spiritual ways, especially when making peace and creating alliances. Sacred sovereignty is strengthened and reinforced through ceremonial practices, sacred histories, and the use of language.[14] Sacred sovereignty is threatened when the people no longer believe in their spiritual practices, do not have the ability to practice them, or no longer recognize their spiritual ways as legitimate.

Although there is no direct translation for the English word *sovereignty* in the Cheyenne language, the word ma'xenėheto'stôtse means "high authority." Ma'xenėheto'stôtse is exercised when political, community, or spiritual leaders address matters in government, peacemaking, and primarily during ceremonial practices. Basically, when leaders are confronted with a decision, they first determine who or what organization has the "high authority" at the specific place, time, and situation. Individuals typically have to earn the rights to authority, but they are also responsible for protecting these rights. Furthermore, they are responsible for their decisions and their outcomes. Leaders establish their legitimacy as the authorities through rites of passage or when they are formally initiated into a society. From that time, their creditability as leaders rests in their diligence, character, intelligence, and wisdom. A better translation for ma'xenėheto'stôtse is "the person or institution that is best suited for guiding us as we complete a ceremony or make a decision."

Individual authority, however, was not valued in the traditional Cheyenne governing system. Instead the Tséhéstáno relied on balance and hévese'onematsestôtse (brotherhood) to share responsibilities and authority among several

MA'HEÓNOHÉSTANOVE: A SACRED NATION

leaders and institutions. The Tsėhéstáno comprised ten bands, and four band chiefs led each band, making a total or forty band chiefs. These chiefs elected four principal chiefs to manage affairs for the entire Tsėhéstáno, thus creating the Council of Forty-four Chiefs, or the Véhoo'o. At the band level, the four band chiefs shared ma'xenėheto'stôtse over their specific band, but sometimes one would be assigned to lead and decide on a certain issue at a certain time. This same practice of shared ma'xenėheto'stôtse was employed for the four principal chiefs of the entire Cheyenne Nation. The traditional government of the Cheyenne Nation was also made up of four highly organized warrior societies, the Nótâxeo'o. Each warrior society elected a number of headmen—four was

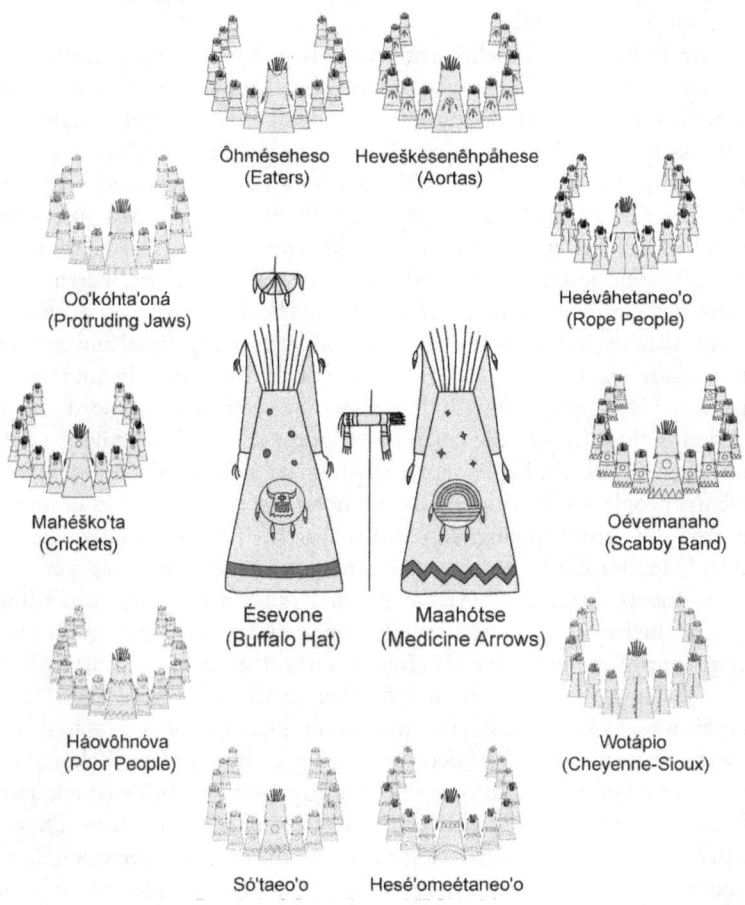

The ten band camp circle of the Cheyenne Nation

the common number—who also shared ma'xenéheto'stôtse under the principles of balance and hévese'onematsestôtse.

The Véhoo'o and the Nótâxeo'o also shared ma'xenéheto'stôtse among each other following the principle of hévese'onematsestôtse. Power and authority shifted among the chiefs, which prevented political instability. The Véhoo'o and the Nótâxeo'o held one another responsible for any poor decisions and their outcomes. The Véhoo'o and the Nótâxeo'o were established long ago and their legacies are preserved in the sacred history, which sanctified their legitimacy. The credibility of both the Véhoo'o and the Nótâxeo'o depended on their organizational stability, reputation, membership, and governance. For example, if a warrior society lost credibility as an honorable institution, its authority to make decisions was diminished and they would likely not be selected for later tasks. They always had the chance to rebuild their reputations and reestablish themselves as credible.

The Tsêhéstáno had other institutions that shared ma'xenéheto'stôtse with the Véhoo'o and the Nótâxeo'o. These were the ceremonial institutions, and these entities included the spiritual leaders, ceremonial guilds, sacred bundle keepers, and the sacred bundles themselves. Depending on the situation, high authority on certain matters could be transferred to a ceremonial society, the Sacred Buffalo Hat Keeper, or the Keeper of the Medicine Arrows. Ceremonial and spiritual leaders and their institutions specialized in maintaining a sacred relationship with the unseen powers of the spiritual realm: nature, Mother Earth, and the universe. After all, these powers are perceived as being the "highest of all authorities" over all living beings, as the Cheyenne understood. Spiritual and ceremonial leaders ensure that the actions and decisions of all Cheyennes do not violate any of the sacred laws associated with their respective ceremony, bundle, or covenant. Considering these factors, the Cheyenne concept of sacred sovereignty could be better translated as "the highest authority to make a decision that best serves the Cheyenne people, while adhering to and honoring the sacred laws bestowed to them from the spiritual beings and Mother Earth." This definition of sacred sovereignty is applicable to other American Indian and Indigenous nations.

In the traditional Cheyenne national government and according to Cheyenne belief, there were several "high authorities" that governed the Cheyenne people. There were also higher authorities that could determine the fate of the Cheyenne people: nature, Mother Earth, and the universe. Since the Tsêhéstáno was a living being and was itself a high authority, it was also limited by the unseen spiritual powers, the higher authority. The Tsêhéstáno as a whole, with all of its institutions, thus had to maintain a spiritual relationship with these powers by ensuring that citizens followed the sacred laws. These laws originated from the teachings and practices of the covenant ceremonies, which I discuss in chapter 3. The Tsêhéstáno is definitively the one and only sacred sovereign for the Cheyenne people; no other entity could have authority over the

MA'HEÓNOHÉSTANOVE: A SACRED NATION

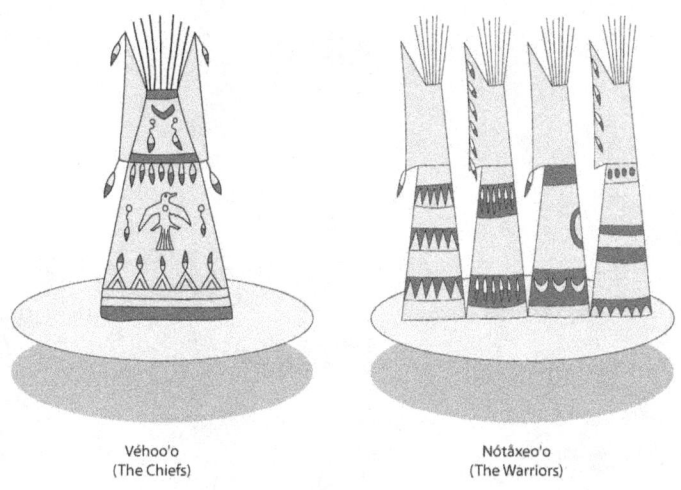

Véhoo'o
(The Chiefs)

Nótâxeo'o
(The Warriors)

The balance of power and authority between the Véhoo'o and Nótâxeo'o

Cheyenne people unless it was formally and ceremonially transferred or, in the case of colonization, taken through force.

The foundation of Cheyenne sovereignty is made from ancient and sacred promises, or covenants, and relies heavily on relationships, responsibility, and balance. Among the Cheyennes the teachings of these sacred promises are interpreted as sacred laws.[15] Sacred bundles represent these bodies of laws, which are then reinforced through kinship systems and ceremonial practices. Leaders and citizens of the Tsėhéstáno must be mindful of these covenants when making decisions in everyday life. For example, before leaders became leaders and earned rights to make decisions, they had to establish relationships with the unseen spiritual beings and Mother Earth through ceremonial practices. The leaders could then align their decisions with the spiritual powers. Before a leader made a difficult decision, he likely offered a prayer and conducted a ceremony using his devotional pipe. Through this ritual he created or re-created an ancient but extant sacred decision-making process that previous leaders had done to ensure that their decision best served the entire Tsėhéstáno. The decision and the decision-making process are sacred; and in the end, the leader's diligence and dedication to his pipe and pipe ceremony determined how wise and intelligent his decision was. Decisions could reinforce or diminish a leader's authority, legitimacy, and reliability. His decision, depending on how serious the matter was, also had the potential to strengthen or diminish the sanctity of his band or the sovereignty of the Tsėhéstáno.

The ancient covenants of the Tsėhéstáno were made centuries ago between humans and the spiritual powers. During the early days before the Cheyennes

PART I: MA'HEÓNĖSTÓNESTÔTSE: SACRED COVENANTS

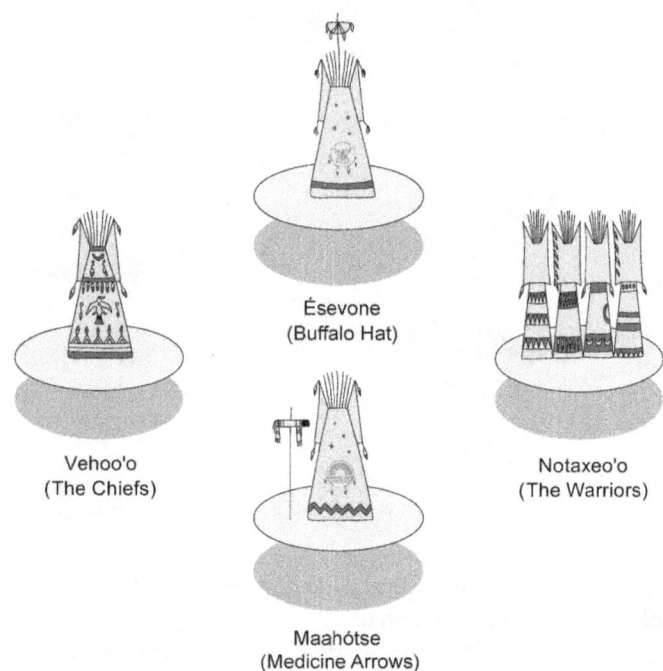

The balance of power and authority between the four sacred entities

had their sacred covenants, the Cheyenne Nation was still underdeveloped and the population of Cheyennes was small. Their social, geopolitical, and geo-spiritual presence was minimal on the Great Plains. Once the Cheyennes acquired their sacred covenants, however, they were able to create a unified and militarized nation with a presence that rivaled that of other larger Indigenous nations. At the center of this nation were two covenants of sacred sovereignty: the Ésevone (Buffalo Hat) and the Maahótse (Medicine Arrows). The Cheyenne believe that in order for the Tséhéstáno to remain in existence, they must continue to believe in the sanctity of these covenants, live by the associated covenant teachings, and conduct the covenant ceremonies. These Cheyenne "covenants of sovereignty" are understood as two sacred responsibilities: the first is to maintain a relationship with the spiritual powers, and the second is to maintain the relationships the Cheyennes have with other human beings, especially among Cheyennes themselves. These sacred relationships of responsibility also reinforced nationhood to foster nation-to-nation alliance building. Any diminishment of these covenants was a diminishment of sovereignty.

MA'HEÓNOHÉSTANOVE: A SACRED NATION

A SACRED NATION

Although there is no Cheyenne word that directly translates to "nationhood," this concept is understood as héstanovestôtse, which can be translated to mean "the life of the people" or "the living-nation." As I discussed in *A Sacred People*, the Cheyennes traditionally believed that their nation is a living being and that each individual Cheyenne is a child or grandchild to this living being. The health and well-being of the héstanovestôtse, the nation, depends entirely on the health and well-being of its children and grandchildren. Throughout the history of the Cheyenne Nation, the Cheyenne people survived and endured through much hardship from environmental catastrophes, famine, and internal conflict. Through each trial and tribulation, the Cheyenne people emerged and birthed new nations. This is the philosophy of Cheyenne nation building. The Cheyenne people, as citizens of their nation, belong to their present héstanovestôtse, and thus they make, sustain, and have the ability to remake the Tséhéstáno. The Cheyennes helped create and re-create their nation based on their experiences and the teachings from the spiritual powers. The living-nation in turn protects and provides for the people. This is the Cheyenne concept of nationhood and this is how the Cheyenne also viewed other Indigenous nations.

The Cheyennes never believed that they or their nation was above or better than other Indigenous nations. Although the Cheyennes belonged to a proud nation, they were not nationalists. Contrary to depictions in popular culture, which portray Indian tribes as being in constant competition with one another for resources before the arrival of whites, Indian nations like the Cheyennes valued peace over war. Competition and warfare on the Great Plains increased as whites moved west and as the bison populations declined. Nationhood as the Cheyennes traditionally understood it depended heavily and almost exclusively on the Cheyenne people's effort to maintain balance with themselves, other nations, and the spiritual powers. This spiritual sovereignty was sustained and strengthened when the Cheyenne people renewed and, in some views, healed their nation through ceremonial practices.

From the Cheyenne perspective, the Cheyenne Nation also has a spiritual presence, which is a sense of spiritual sovereignty that extends into every facet of the Cheyenne spiritual way of life. Spiritual sovereignty is the collective spirit of all Cheyenne citizens. It is the spiritual presence of the Cheyenne Nation, and it is sustained by spiritual relationships. This spiritual presence was extended to other Indigenous nations when the Cheyennes made alliances. In peacemaking, for example, the Cheyennes were able to establish long-lasting political and social alliances with other Indigenous nations by evoking spiritual sovereignty. They were thus able to create "spiritual alliances" with Indigenous nations following the traditions of the devotional peace pipe and the Sun Dance ceremonies. Conversely, the spiritual presence of the Cheyenne Nation clashed with others when they were at war.

PART I: MA'HEÓNĖSTÓNESTÔTSE: SACRED COVENANTS

The Cheyennes, like most Indigenous peoples, have spiritual loyalties to their nation. These spiritual loyalties, which are also part of spiritual sovereignty, are held with reverence because they strengthened relationships among the people, homelands, and ways of living. The Cheyennes, like most Indigenous peoples, viewed themselves as part of the much larger Earth. The Cheyennes also view their nation as a being that is both part of the Earth and a being of the universe.[16] A term that the Cheyennes used to describe this philosophy of their nation's presence on Earth and in the universe is ma'heónohéstanove, which translates to "sacred nation." The Cheyennes were citizens of their sacred nation, which meant they also had sacred rights and responsibilities to it. This is the traditional concept of loyalty and allegiance to the sacred Tsėhéstáno.

When the Cheyennes learned of the Christian Church's intention to convert Cheyennes, they were confronted with a serious matter. The Cheyennes believed that when other Cheyennes became Christian, they revoked their "spiritual citizenship" to the ma'heónohéstanove.[17] This meant that these converted Cheyennes parted from the spiritual power of the Tsėhéstáno and were no longer protected by the spiritual powers of the Ésevone (Buffalo Hat) and the Maahótse (Medicine Arrows). However, the Cheyennes believed that these Christian Cheyennes could be welcomed back into the ma'heónohéstanove, since they had voluntarily left and committed no crime. Other than being exiled for murder, this was the only known way a Cheyenne could lose his or her "spiritual citizenship" to the Tsėhéstáno. I should emphasize that the Christian Cheyennes were not ostracized, ridiculed, or exiled. For the most part, they were perceived as rebels or rascals who were "lost," whose family members tried to bring them back into the ma'heónohéstanove by any means necessary.[18] Today most Cheyennes do not necessarily carry the same beliefs as the pre-reservation Cheyennes.

The use of the term and concept of ma'heónohéstanove has significantly dissipated throughout years of assimilation and language loss. Despite the diminishment of the concept, ma'heónohéstanove remains omnipresent in traditional Cheyenne beliefs and ceremony. Sometimes it resurfaces in modern settings and forums that promote Cheyenne national unity and pride. For example, various boards, offices, and programs of the Northern Cheyenne Tribe have used the English theme "We are a Sacred People." At its core the term and concept of ma'heónohéstanove reinforces the sacred sovereignty of the Tsėhéstáno, which endures today. As a sacred nation, the Cheyenne Nation continues to reciprocate as long as the people continue to give back through prayer and offerings of food, water, tears, and blood. This is never more present than when the Cheyenne Nation unites for its annual Sun Dance ceremony.

EXERCISES OF SACRED SOVEREIGNTY

A nation's sovereignty is measured not by its successes in war but by its successes in peace. For the Cheyennes, the principle of héveseónematsestôtse (brotherhood) is vital in exercising sacred sovereignty, since it is the foundation of peacemaking and alliance building. Ceremonial practices, however—the source of nearly every aspect of Cheyenne sovereignty and nationhood—are the supreme exercises of sacred sovereignty. At the core of Cheyenne nationhood is the ability for individuals, families, bands, and a nation to make and keep promises.

1. Peacemaking

The roots of Cheyenne peacemaking can be traced to the time before the Tséhéstáno organized under the Véhoo'o (Council of Forty-four Chiefs) and the Nótâxeo'o (warrior societies). As I discussed in *A Sacred People*, the first two bands of Cheyennes, the Ohmésêhese (Eaters) and the Heveškêsenêhpâhese (Aortas), united when the two were engaged in an intense contest of the wheel game. In the story of "The Two Young Men," one fine-looking, finely dressed man arrived at the center of camp in the midst of an intense wheel game. He met another young man from another band who was also fine looking and nicely dressed. The two young men, representing their respective bands, at first argued over their outfits but later became friends and embarked on a quest into a waterfall. They both entered and an old woman fed them and taught them rituals and ceremonies about brotherhood and the sacred relationship of balance, which is fundamental to peacemaking. The two young men departed and returned to their respective bands with these teachings and stone jars, one containing buffalo meat and the other roasted corn. When the two young men returned to the camp circle, they organized and hosted a feast, which formally and ceremoniously unified the Ohmésêhese and the Heveškêsenêhpâhese. Both bands separated as independent entities but remained as part of one united nation. From then on, they frequently reunited for feasts and ceremonies.

The unification of these two bands is memorialized in Cheyenne oral tradition as the foundation of Cheyenne peacemaking. Although there are several versions of the story of "The Two Young Men," they all highlight the unification process. From the Cheyenne perspective, peacemaking was more than just a mutual agreement of friendship; it relied on the principle of hévese'onematsestôtse. Peacemaking was a sacred affair requiring each group to shed its individuality.

2. Alliance Building

From the Cheyenne perspective, alliances were spiritual as much as they were political and social. After the first two bands of the Cheyennes united, they expanded in size and territory. Eventually the Cheyennes comprised four bands and referred to themselves as the Né'ohma'ehétaneo'o (Sand Hill People).[19] Later the Cheyenne bands met another group of people, the Só'taeo'o. These people spoke the same language as the Cheyennes but had separate traditions, histories, and cultures. Over time the two subnations unified, politically and spiritually, relying on the sacred principle of hévese'onematsestôtse. This event is known as the Great Unification, and the peace was never broken. The unified camp circle was made up of the four bands of the Cheyennes, known as the Tsétsêhéstâhese, and one band of the Só'taeo'o. This is how the Tsėhéstáno was born.

The Tsėhéstáno grew and expanded their presence, and in time they united with other nations. The Cheyennes successfully made spiritual alliances with the Arapaho and the Oglala Lakota before treating with whites. A significant part of the traditional unification process was for the Cheyennes to transfer and share spiritual practices, which is why making spiritual alliances was the utmost sacred of tasks that required participation from the highest authorities of the Tsėhéstáno. The process of making alliances required years of planning, debate, and observation from the Véhoo'o, the Nótâxeo'o, and the keepers the Sacred Hat and the Medicine Arrows. This process was by no means simplistic or shallow, and neither was maintaining the peace that the Tsėhéstáno established with these other Indian nations. Today nothing compares to this form of peacemaking. It was truly a practice of sacred sovereignty. Building alliances represents the nation's ability to establish and maintain the promise of peace and unity with other nations.

3. Traditional and Cultural Practices

One of the purest acts of sovereignty for an Indian nation is to live in balance as its ancestors did in spirit and in fact. However simple and delicate, these acts require people to uphold the ways bestowed upon their ancestors from the sacred beings, which were handed down through the generations. The foundation of sacred sovereignty is in the life and vibrancy of ceremonial practices, especially annual events. The Tsėhéstáno had hundreds of ceremonies and rituals. Some were carried over from previous eras while others were central to the people's current world and ongoing way of living. These practices represent the life of a nation, as they also represent the continuing effort for the people to adhere to sacred laws and teachings. If the nation was healthy, then the ceremonies were alive and they renewed the lives of individuals, their families, and bands, and thus renewed the entire Cheyenne Nation.

Much of the indigenous way of living depended on how the people carried on traditions, which are based on spiritual principles. Traditions typically remain unchanged despite the changes in culture. Culture, on the other hand, is not necessarily founded in principles of spirituality, since cultures are allowed to change and adapt, especially with the introduction of new things like guns and horses. The Tsėhéstáno had to sustain itself as an Indigenous nation, while its people remained true to the nation's spiritual principles, especially when meeting and treating with other peoples. For example, the Cheyenne Nation would have difficulty in creating alliances with nations that did not respect Cheyenne beliefs or spiritual principles. This is why the Cheyennes openly shared spiritual practices when establishing alliances, assuming that their new allies would also share in kind. Traditional and cultural practices were the people's promises to the living nation and an acknowledgement of previous generations.

4. Food Sovereignty

The Cheyenne perspective of spiritual principles of balance requires that humans maintain a relationship with land, water, plants, and animals, since these are the sources of life. The Cheyenne maintain these relationships with these resources because they take from nature for food, shelter, medicines, and rituals. This spiritual balance is then a significant part of maintaining peaceful and healthy relationships with each other and with other peoples. The principles of "food sovereignty" are already embedded in Cheyenne spiritual and cultural ways and the Cheyenne concept of sacred sovereignty.[20] As is true for most Indigenous peoples, Cheyenne concepts of cultural, spiritual, and sacred sovereignty rely heavily on food sovereignty: how they gathered, prepared, and served their food.[21] Food and water are the life-giving elements that citizens must ingest to nourish and sustain their bodies and the growing bodies of their children.

Honoring this sacred relationship is the first and most significant purpose of Cheyenne ceremonies and the ceremonial cycle. In short, ceremonies and the ceremonial cycle are the foundation of Cheyenne sacred sovereignty because they honor food. The Cheyenne people, like all Indigenous peoples, held their food with high regard because of the understanding that it sustains all life. Much can be learned about a living-nation when examining how its citizens perceive food: from its harvest to its consumption; from oral traditions to eating etiquette; and from spiritual practices to cultural customs. The ceremonial realm of the Cheyenne incorporates elaborate instructions related to food and food preparation and provides teachings on how to live well. The instructions represent the people's promises to their food sources.

5. Storytelling and Ceremonies

Another exercise of sacred sovereignty was to reaffirm, through retelling of the sacred history and the reenactment of events, the traditional teachings that keep the nation alive and the people healthy. The major ceremonies represent reenactments of the old prophets, male and female, who endured challenges, pain, and suffering to bring about the ways of living that allowed for the Cheyennes to endure and thrive into the future. Storytelling and ceremonies also remind citizens of the traditional laws and principles of living as part of the Cheyenne Nation. Without the storytelling and ceremonies, the people would lose respect for the old prophets, forget their teachings and responsibilities, and eventually forget what it means to be part of the living-nation, the Tséhéstáno. Storytelling and ceremonies represent the oldest and sincerest acts of sovereignty because they represent the continuation of a way of living and allowed the people to experience what their people before them experienced. Storytelling and ceremonies are the formal means of keeping the promises and accepting the responsibilities and duties ordained by the spiritual beings that gave the Cheyennes life and a way of living.

6. Renewing Families

Another exercise of sacred sovereignty was to hold major ceremonies to promote community and unity—most important, to renew family ties and kinship relationships. Every family of the Cheyenne Nation was represented in every ceremony because each ceremony reiterated and reinforced the need to remain unified as a people. While not every family member participated in the major ceremonies, it was customary that at least one family member participate to bring blessings to the entire extended family. Without such inclusion, families could become isolated and become resentful toward other families or, worse yet, resentful toward the entire nation. The Cheyenne ceremonial system allowed for spiritual leaders to directly pass their knowledge to worthy individuals so the rituals, songs, and prayers remained intact. The ceremonies were created for all Cheyenne individuals and families; there was no exclusion. Every Cheyenne had national and band identities, but they also had ceremonial identities based on their and their family's participation. Family renewal allowed for individuals to make and keep their promises to their families.

7. Renewing the Nation

Before unification each subnation, the Tsétsêhéstâhese and the Só'taeo'o, had already developed sophisticated spiritual practices, but the unification revolutionized their cultures and governments into an advanced geopolitical, geo-spiritual living-nation. The revolution secured a stable Cheyenne spiritual way of living and ceremonial cycle that adhered to the supernatural demands to pay homage to the powers and elements that provided life. The ceremonial cycle belongs to the Tsêhéstáno, and part of the reason it survived for hundreds of years is that the Cheyenne people maintained its complex ceremonial cycle. The people kept their covenants and thus remained a sacred nation.

A significant part of the major ceremonies was to reenact the creation of the world (the Earth) and the universe. Through such ceremonial practices, the people reaffirmed their existence in the world and universe and their sacred sovereignty: that is their responsibility. They also renewed their identity and citizenship to their sacred nation, which only endures under the protection and guidance of the supreme power, the Great Medicine. The world and universe responded by providing for the Cheyenne Nation. The balance of the universe rested on the dedication of the Cheyennes to affirm the special relationship they have with the unseen powers of the spiritual world and supernatural beings. To do otherwise, the Cheyenne Nation would break its promises and cease to be a sacred nation.

CHAPTER 2

The Communal Ceremonies

The people were in hardship. The Sutaiu had a successor. He told them, "I'm going to send for animals which you people can eat." At the same time the Cheyennes had a successor, Matsioiv. He told them the same, that in due time there would be these animals: moose, deer, antelope, bears, birds and all the small animals for their food. "I am he," he said to the Sutaiu leaders, "descending from the foolish leader, Lime, from the Sutaiu." [Matsioiv said:] "I am Sweet Medicine, I will perform all from this generation for all generations to come." After they had finished, the two prophets, that night in the early morning, there were herds of buffalo and all animals and the birds of the air. At day there was great excitement, they chased and killed buffaloes; deer ran in every direction, and birds flew up. Then they stopped raising corn and began to live on these animals. So the herds of buffalo multiplied through out the world and the other animals likewise, and so did the birds of the air. They gathered and lived happily.

—Bull Thigh (Southern Cheyenne), Keeper of the Sacred Arrows[1]

Rituals and ceremonial practices teach discipline and dedication; they also spiritually unite people. The Cheyenne ceremonial practices and rituals shape people's behavior and align them with the Cheyenne spiritual way of thinking. These practices lay the foundation for everyday living, since a person's way of thinking determines his or her way of living and how he or she will treat others. The Cheyennes have always stressed that practitioners follow the "proper protocols" when conducting ceremonies and rituals: to conduct them exactly as they should be done and to leave them unchanged, without adaptations. Ceremonial practitioners are highly disciplined and dedicated to following the proper ritualistic protocols, preserving the sanctity of the ceremony or ritual. Such practices of discipline and dedication are the best examples of the Cheyenne concepts of "due diligence" and "due process," since ritual and ceremonial practices are all done in a highly sacred manner to prevent any harm

PART I: MA'HEÓNÉSTÓNESTÔTSE: SACRED COVENANTS

to any persons. The concepts of "sacred due diligence" and "sacred due process" are better suited for the Cheyenne experience.

One certainty remains consistent in the Cheyenne ceremonial realm: ceremonies and rituals must be done correctly every time. Structure and consistency ensure that the practitioners think, feel, behave, and experience the near-exact same thoughts, feelings, behaviors, and experiences that previous practitioners and original prophets did. A ceremony or ritual alone is not a singular significant act, but its participants, the onlookers, the plants and animals, weather conditions, and the time and place of the ceremony and ritual create an entire ethos. This ethos is the spirit of the living-nation, the sacred nation, the Tsėhéstáno.

Table 2.1. Traditional Cheyenne Dances and Dance Societies Identified in 1910

White Bull/Ice's List	American Horse's List	White Eagle's List
Bear Dance	Bear Dance	-
Bird Dance	Bird Dance	-
Black Bird Dance	Black Bird Dance	-
Buffalo Dance	Buffalo Dance	-
-	Contrary Dance	The Contrary Dancers
Green Corn Dance	Corn Dance	
Medicine Corn Dance	The Corn Dancers	
Coyote Dance	Coyote Dance	-
Crow Dance	-	The Crow Dancers
Foolish Dogs Dance	Foolish Dance	-
Grass Dance	-	The Grass Dancers
-	Ghost Dance	The Ghost Dancers
Fire Dance	Fire Dance	-
Squaw Dance	Squaw Dance	The Squaw Dancers
Sugar Dance	Round Dance	The Sugar Dancers
Tiger Dance	Tiger Ghost Dance	-
War Dance	War Dance	The War Dancers
Wolf Dance	Big Wolves Dance	-

During the time of the buffalo, the Cheyennes held numerous rituals and dances that honored animals and "enlisted spiritual forces" to aid in attaining meat and skins.[2] The dances ranged from social events to ceremonies performed by dance societies to full-fledged ceremonial dances that were sacred and vital to the Cheyenne spiritual way of living. American Horse, White Bull/Ice, and White Eagle identified several dances. Table 2.1 shows some of the oldest dances, some likely originated from the previous eras and others that disappeared when the Cheyenne lands were colonized and the Cheyenne people were forced onto reservations.³

The Nótâxeoʼo and Véhooʼo were also part of the ritualistic and social aspects of Cheyenne life. They were not exclusively political entities. White Bull/Ice identified the Bow String Society Dance as one of the social dances, while American Horse identified the Crazy Dog Dance and the Shield (Bull Society) Dance as well. White Eagle identified all of the warrior societies and the chiefs as part of his list of "dance societies," which further asserts their roles in the ongoing social life.⁴ White Eagle also identified an unknown Night Dancers society. American Horse and White Eagle both identified the Contrary Dance and Contrary Dancers as dance societies, but these societies and their dances could also be identified as warrior society dances and ceremonial dances. The same can be said for the Wolf Dance, the War Dancers, and the Ghost Dancers. American Horse identifies the two oldest dances as the Corn Dance and the Foolish Dance, which was also known as the Crazy Lodge. White Bull/Ice identified the Corn Dance as "the oldest of all dances" and the Buffalo Dance as the second oldest.⁵

Table 2.2. Other Dances Identified by White Bull/Ice in 1910

Dances from Other Nations	Animal Dances	Ritual and Ceremonial Dances
Arapaho Dance	Antelope Dance	Big Foolish Dance
Caddo Dance	Badger Dance	Kiss Dance
Wichita Dance	Claw Dance	Love Dance
Comanche Dance	Eagle Dance	Sacrifice Dance
Kiowa Dance	Horse Dance	Scalp Dance
Ponca Dance	Mink Dance	
Ree Dance	Rabbit Dance	
White Man Dance	Red Fox Dance	
	Snake Dance	
	Turkey Dance	
	Weasel Dance	

In Table 2.2, White Bull/Ice identifies other social and society dances as well as dances that the Cheyennes adopted from other nations, even whites. Some of these traditional dances were likely shared when the Cheyennes made peace agreements with the respective nation. Table 2.3 is a list of other dances identified by American Horse.

The Cheyennes also held berry dances to sacrifice and pay in advance for the nourishment they provided. All dances were an integral part of Cheyenne culture, as they facilitated celebrations, feasts, and social gatherings, thus creating a strong, healthy, and vibrant community.

PART I: MAʾHEÓNÈSTÓNESTÔTSE: SACRED COVENANTS

Table 2.3. Other Dances Identified by American Horse in 1910

Animal Dances	Ritual and Ceremonial Dances
Black Deer Dance	Give Away Dance
Deer Dance	Gourd Horn Dance
Elk Dance	Pipe Dance
Goose Dance	Telling Dance, Near Time As War Dance
Moose Dance	Willow Dance
	Wind Dance

Before living on the Great Plains and becoming hunters, the Cheyennes had spiritual practices that related to farming corn and fishing. They held onto these ways and continued to farm after they came to hunt buffalo, but the older spiritual ways from the previous worlds eventually declined, since they were no longer held in as high regard as the ceremonies of "the time of the buffalo."

Much of the old ceremonial practices related to corn planting had become outdated and therefore were abandoned. The Cheyennes did not, however, forbid any old practices or destroy old relics. Instead, old ways slowly faded naturally when replaced by new practices. For example, the "original corn" was a covenant from the old world and bestowed upon Hoʾehêvêsénóóʾe (Standing On The Ground), and it was incorporated into the Great Unification story presented later in the chapter. The Cheyennes kept the covenant bundle until it met its demise in the fires in the war with the whites in 1876 at the Dull Knife Battle in the Bighorns. The Cheyennes probably abandoned numerous other spiritual practices from the time of the corn, but they still maintained their identity by adding new spiritual beliefs. Eventually the new practices became most significant to sustaining a balanced spiritual way of living.

White Bull/Ice identified several dances that were not social dances but were likely part of traditional Cheyenne customs: (1) "The Contraries had a fire dance," which is also known as a "running dance" or "jumping dance." They performed this during the Crazy Lodge Ceremony; (2) "the Foxes" also had a "running dance," but they danced with a rattle and inside a lodge; (3) the "elk and deer bone dance" was also a "running dance," but known as a "shooting" dance; (4) the "fighting dance" existed and is related to the "Peace Dance"; (5) the "Leaving the camp dance" is also known as the "Following Dance" or the "All night dance"; (6) the "Peace dance" was done with a pipe and was a formality when asking "enemies four times for peace, if they rejected," then the Cheyennes could take up arms against them.[6] With the exception of the Contraries' and the Foxes' dances, these old dances, their significance, and their teachings have long disappeared. Other extinct ceremonies are the Painted Ceremony, the Horse Medicine Ceremony, the Ball Ceremony, and the Wolf Pup Ceremony.[7]

Historian George B. Grinnell explained several war dances, including the sweetheart dance, scalp dance, slippery dance, and the galloping buffalo-bull dance.⁸ The scalp dances were managed by a "Halfman-halfwoman" dance society called the Ŏttō ha nĭh' (Bare Legs). Members had both male and female names (e.g., Pipe and Pipe Woman). They served as matchmakers and "fine love talkers," which means they were equivalent to marriage counselors. The society was small and consisted of only five members, but they also took part in battle as medics and doctors, caring for the sick and wounded during battles. One of their primary duties in the community was to host and facilitate social dances so young men and women, who were of appropriate dating age, could court.

However rare, those who belonged to the he'emanehe (half-woman man) or hetanemane'e (half-man woman) gender were accepted as common citizens of the Cheyenne Nation. Wrapped Hair explained "Berdaches" existed in both the Só'taeo'o and Cheyenne peoples; that they were "that way from childhood"; "some dressed as men, some as women"; and that he personally knew of a "halfman-halfwoman" who "acts like a man, works like a man, but wears dresses," was about fifty-two years old, and "has acted that way for a long time, but not from childhood"; he also did not court girls, but was married once.⁹ The third and fourth genders were sometimes part of organized groups at traditional Cheyenne ceremonies. The Bare Legs society, for example—like other dance, ceremonial, and warrior societies—had its own system of organization and set standards for selecting worthy members. The society has long been disestablished, while the third and fourth genders remain among the Cheyennes and other Indian nations.

THE MEDICINE HUNTS

The major communal ceremonies from the time of the buffalo to the time of the horse were the medicine hunts: vó'kaehénooné (Antelope Singing) and vóhaenóhónestôtse (Surrounding Buffalo). These hunting rituals were practiced among numerous bands, as they did not require a unified camp of all bands. Ceremonial leaders resided and functioned at the band level. If a particular band had no "priest" to conduct a medicine hunt, then this band would likely join another band to participate. Each spiritual leader or priest of the communal ceremony possessed an associated covenant to conduct the ceremony. These covenants, or promises, had physical forms as vé'šeeseo'o (medicine bundles) or vonâhé'xá'e (talismans or relics). In spiritual forms these promises were known and remembered as a body of laws and principles.

The ceremonial calendar was in full effect during the nine months between the end of winter and its start the following year. Within the months of spring, summer, and fall, the Cheyennes fulfilled their promises to the unseen powers of the spiritual realm, the earth, and, most important, to each other as spiritual beings: human beings. The four major ceremonies did not follow exact calendar dates, but the people were resolute to hold each ceremony every year,

PART I: MA'HEÓNĚSTÓNESTÔTSE: SACRED COVENANTS

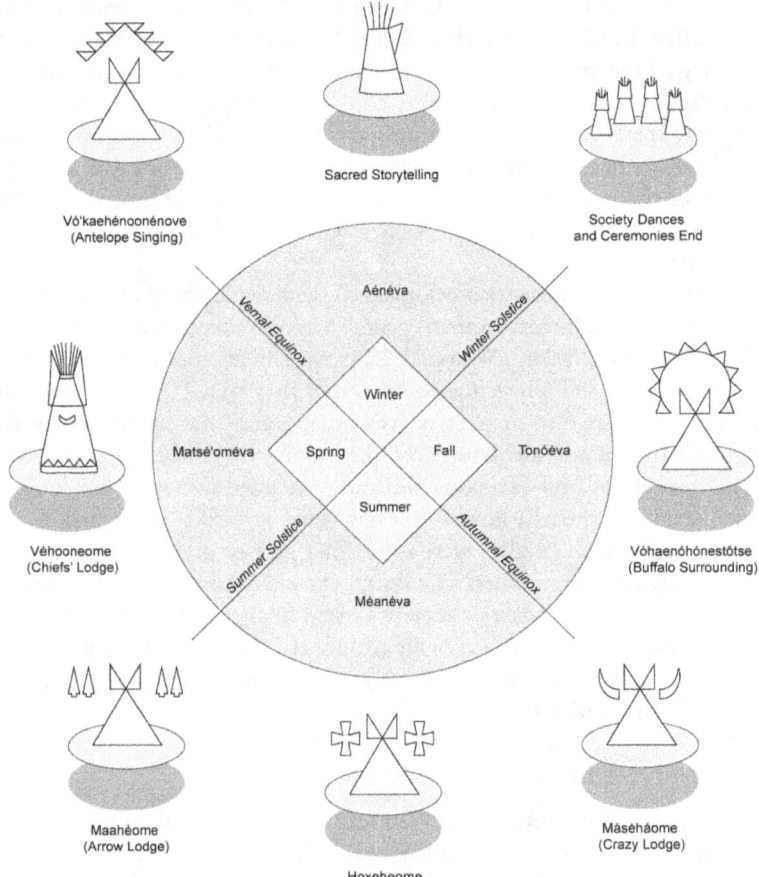

The ceremonial calendar of the United Cheyenne Nation

in sequential order, and dependent on the environment and nature. Before the imbalance of colonization and its drastic effects, ceremonies were easily scheduled based on each band's geographic location, population, and health, as well as the natural elements. The summer solstice marked the beginning of the ceremonial cycle and the renewal of the Cheyenne Nation.

When winter ended, the Cheyennes began the first major events on their ceremonial calendar, the communal hunts of deer, antelope, and buffalo.[10] In previous eras, the Cheyennes practiced medicine hunts, but these hunts were for capturing smaller game and birds.[11] The philosophy and spiritual beliefs associated with communal hunting rituals were the oldest of the hunting traditions and had origins reaching back to the time of the dog, when the Cheyennes planted corn and when they hunted in the forest of the land of the lakes. The

THE COMMUNAL CEREMONIES

Cheyennes carried this philosophy and associated spiritual beliefs to the Great Plains. Bull Thigh's account of Sweet Medicine tells of the significance of such powers.

> After the Cheyennes originated at the Black Hills, there was a big camp. On the outskirts was a small grass tipi. In it there was an old woman. She was just about starving. She went to dig, searching for roots to eat. While out doing this, she found a child. She grabbed him and picked him up. The child could barely see. He had a small little robe of a calf hide. She took him home. She got him in her lodge. After the child was warmed up she combed him and washed his face. "Grand child," she said to him, "I am about to starve and the people are about to starve." The boy was seated. He made a quiet little small noise. He looked towards the sky. There was a bunch of prairie birds [that] flew into the lodge right before the old woman. They were all dead. The old woman peeled the wings off and put the feathers into her parfleche. She cooked them for herself and for him.[12]

Bull Thigh's account is reminiscent of the old Cheyenne cultural and spiritual ways of living but reveals how the traditional philosophy of "animal calling" persisted. This philosophy remained as the guiding principle of the medicine hunts. Certain spiritual leaders had the power to "allure" or "charm" animals to come near, and these animals were said to offer themselves to the humans as sacrifices. The sacred human-animal relationship was preserved and reinforced through rituals: while humans relied on animals for subsistence, the animals consented to give their bodies and lives.

The Vó'kaehénooné (Antelope Singing or the Antelope Pit Ceremony) is the oldest practice of the Só'taa'e, but the Buffalo Ceremony followed the same principles and teachings and achieved the same goal in providing nutrition from the flesh of game animals. The communal hunt ceremonies were practiced among numerous bands that were camped at different locations and at different times. Unlike the other major ceremonies, which I describe later, the communal hunts did not require the unification of the entire nation. Before the arrival of the horse, each band could practice the communal hunt, under the guidance of the band's ceremonial leaders and societies.

The Antelope Singing Ceremony and the Buffalo Ceremony were fundamental to the Cheyenne spiritual way of life. The Buffalo Ceremony is remembered in the Tsétsêhéstâhese oral tradition as part of the legacy of Motsé'eóeve, while the Antelope Ceremony is remembered in the Só'taeo'o oral tradition as part of the creation of the Véhoo'o, or Chiefs Council. After the Great Unification, elements of the Buffalo and Antelope ceremonies converged. Later the ceremonies were adapted when the Cheyenne relied almost exclusively on the buffalo.[13] Badger recalled a converged origin story of the medicine buffalo hunt, which was retold by Standing In The Morning. The ceremony has Só'taeo'o roots.

PART I: MA'HEÓNĖSTÓNESTÔTSE: SACRED COVENANTS

The Medicine Buffalo Hunt, by Standing In The Morning

Among the band of Sutaiu there was a great chief. There was a big camp of Sutaiu, and many hostile people against them. The band of Sutaiu were told by the chief not to leave camp. Keeping close together they were nearly starving. The head chief said: "Do not meet any of the hostile people who want to fight us until they do something to us. We are not going to make any trouble first." In these days everyone obeyed the chief. The leader of a war-society came to see the chief about the starving people, saying that they must fight. But the chief said to him: "Wait, I will perform my trick to make the buffalo come right inside of the camp, instead of fighting the other Indians."

This chief one morning was dressing up, painted his face and body, and had a buffalo robe for a blanket. He started from the center of the circle toward the south. He held up his buffalo robe and made a motion four times to come in. He called the buffalo in four directions. When he had done that he told the people to look towards the east. They saw a yearling bull coming; the second time they saw a two year old bull; the third time a very old bull; the fourth time hundreds of buffalo running into the camp. The whole herd came into the circle. All the people came out with bows and arrows, and anything used in killing, and killed all the buffalo except four who ran out. The Chief said: "You should have spared at least five, but you have killed more than what is proper."

After a while the people were nearly in starvation. The chief did the trick again; he did it four times. This is the last telling.[14]

In modern oral tradition and in documented accounts, the communal buffalo and antelope medicine hunts have different elements but share commonalities. For example, both hunts feature an elaborate communal ceremony led by a single leader or covenant keeper. Both ceremonies also require the use of a relic and involve the participation of young, unmarried, virgin men and women. And finally, both demand that a sacrifice be made to the birds of prey.

One origin story of the communal hunt is preserved in the Cheyenne national history following the philosophies of the spear and hoop game: brotherhood, unity, sameness, and balance. This origin story has very similar attributes to the story of "The Two Young Men," which is evidence that the Cheyenne national history may have evolved but the principles and teachings have remained constant throughout time. The most common origin story of the communal buffalo hunt tells of two young men who follow the same path as in the story of "The Two Young Men" (see chapter 1). The two young men, in this case, are identified as Tsétsêhéstaestse prophet Motsé'eóeve (Sweet Medicine) and the Só'taeo'o prophet Ho'ehêvêsénóó'e (Standing On The Ground). As in the story of "The Two Young Men," Sweet Medicine and Standing On The Ground have a dispute over their dress, embark on a quest, and enter a cave where an old woman lives.[15]

The subsequent adaptations to the new story are subtle but still rely on the principle of hévese'onematsestôtse (brotherhood). After feeding the two prophets, Mâhtamâhááhe (Old Woman) taught them and then painted each of them red all over, each with a sun and a crescent moon in yellow. This was their new ceremonial "paint," which was also a symbol of unity and brotherhood. "This is how you will look from now on," she said. "Now look to the left." On a wall appeared a window and on the other side of the window there was a large valley and on it was a massive herd of buffalo. "Now look to your right," said the old woman. On the other wall appeared another window and through the window appeared another valley full of deer, elk, and antelope. "Now look behind you," said the old woman. On the wall behind them appeared another window and this time a large field of corn appeared. "Now look in front of you," and there appeared before them a group of warriors chasing wild horses. The warriors were painted as the two boys, in red with a yellow sun and crescent moon. The painted warriors caught the horses and rode fast toward another group of warriors on horseback. The two groups began fighting and counting coup on (striking) one another. "Do you see?" said Mâhtamâhááhe. "You will become brothers and your people will unite and fight together. You will be healthy because all of the animals will provide for you and your people."

Mâhtamâhááhe imparted to the boys spiritual teachings and gave them several gifts including sacred food: buffalo meat went to Motsé'eóeve and corn to Ho'ehêvêsénóó'e, both in stone dishes. Mâhtamâhááhe gave the boys a last gift, which was a flat, circular, red stone made from catlinite. She spoke to them, "This is a special stone, with special powers. It can make the animals gentle. You will need this when your people are starving and it becomes difficult to hunt game." She told them about the communal hunting ceremony. "When these animals are killed in the hunt, they are sacred. You cannot use arrows or spears when killing these animals in this way," she said and handed them a small pouch. "Take this tobacco and use it as an offering." The old woman hugged the two young men and they left her lodge inside the mountain and returned to their people. The red, circular dish is the central covenant in the communal ceremonial hunts.

VÓ'KAEHÉNOONÉ

The communal hunts were fundamental to Cheyenne nationhood and sovereignty, since the people depended on deer, antelope, and buffalo for sustenance. The hunts were therefore sacred and revered more as ceremonies rather than hunts. The objective was to "call" animals into a confined area where they could easily be hit with handheld weapons, but the entire affair was to be done ceremoniously and in balance with nature. The deer and antelope hunts required the Cheyennes to select grounds that were typically located between two creeks or drainages. The ceremonial society members constructed a crude pit, where the animals were killed, at the apex where the two streams joined. After years of mastering the practice, the people formalized the ritual by building a large pit with large stones and other wooden fixtures to corral and kill herds of pronghorn antelope in a community-organized hunt. The Vó'kaehénooné (Antelope Singing) became routine as the people frequently returned to ceremonial hunting grounds to refurbish and utilize the sites.

As the Cheyenne Nation grew in population and expanded its territory, the Vó'kaehénooné became a fully matured and formalized ceremony, lasting four days and managed by a group of men and women who belonged to an antelope society under the guidance of spiritual leaders.[16] This ceremonial society was disestablished long before the establishment of the reservations. Yet, the Vó'kaehénooné is likely the oldest tradition of the Só'taeo'o, who were already living on the Great Plains and accustomed to hunting animals before the Great Unification. The teachings of the ceremony originated from the oral tradition of Voestaehneva'e, the young woman who created the Véhoo'o. According to Só'taa'e oral tradition, Voestaehneva'e was also known as Naméhane (Big Sister).[17] While she was alone and starving with her younger brother, a spirit dog came to help and eventually empowered her with the medicine to "summon" animals and to kill them using her power to "stun" one and kill it when she looked at it. The more popular Só'taeo'o stories indicate that the first animal was a buffalo, while the Tsétsêhéstâhese stories identify this animal as a deer.[18]

Naméhane was credited with introducing the philosophy that humans could control the actions of big game and possibly even kill them without physical contact. The new philosophy, or "medicine," of Naméhane was revolutionary to the Só'taeo'o. Before the communal hunts, the Só'taeo'o relied on the athletic ability of hunters who ran and chased animals to kill them. In the winter, the common hunting method was for hunters to chase animals into deep snowdrifts and kill their immobilized prey.[19] The medicine of Naméhane and the winter hunting method led to the development of the formalized, communal medicine hunts of antelope, deer, and buffalo, which were corralled and killed in designated areas in the spring and summer months.[20] The ceremony reaffirmed the Só'taeo'o sacred laws of nature and the traditions of Naméhane, since some traditional Cheyennes believe that Mâhtamâhááhe and Naméhane were the same person.

The Vó'kaehénooné became a common practice across different bands because it reminded people of the older times. The medicine bundle that was associated with the Vó'kaehénooné originally held the feet of slain antelope from the very first medicine hunt. One of the last keepers of this covenant was named Ma'eomene (Red Lodge), but Vó'oménéhotoa'e (White Faced Bull) also held a bundle during the time of the horse. The first performance of the Vó'kaehénooné occurred one late winter at Little Antelope Creek and Big Antelope River, when game was scarce and the best medicine men were summoned to resolve this matter. The night before the ceremony the best medicine men were selected to sing "antelope songs" in a tepee all night and to bless two virgin young men who had not yet hunted. After a night of singing, the morning sunrise lit the top of the lodge. The medicine men saw antelope fur fall through the smoke hole of the tepee and believed it was from the heavens. The next day the young men were instructed to stand atop a ridge and "sweep" the antelope from afar toward the Antelope Lodge using "sacrifice flags."[21] The young men were to use a circular motion as if they were gently sweeping antelope fur toward their bodies. The first hunt was successful and became part of the Só'taeo'o tradition.

The Vó'kaehénooné took place around the start of the vernal equinox, when the prairie grasses were in full bloom, the antelope had not yet turned to eating sage, and the herds were not scattered.[22] The hunt signified the opening of the ceremonial cycle for the nation with the rebirth of the seasons of plenty, the spring and summer. The ceremony required participation from a much larger population of citizens and occurred once annually to mark and celebrate the spring and summer hunting seasons. Before the coming of white men, the pronghorn antelope populated the Great Plains in great numbers, probably more than the bison. The animals were known for their beauty and swiftness, and although antelope meat was not a delicacy like buffalo, their hides were of significant value and much smaller, making them easier and quicker to tan. There is no question why this animal became such an important figure in the cosmology and oral traditions of the Cheyennes and other Plains Indian nations.

The Vó'kaehénooné is documented as a ceremony that involves numerous rituals, a large ceremonial lodge, and a large pit.[23] Under the guidance of a ceremonial leader, two young women and two young men, all virgins, were selected as sacred persons for the ceremony.[24] The use of young people in the ceremony suggests that the ceremonial hunt represented rebirth and honored the youth and the future generations, following the Só'taeo'o tradition of Voestaehneva'e. The young people of the ceremony had to be of good health and well mannered; otherwise, the antelope would be thin and poor and difficult to catch. Spiritual leaders designed the hunt to channel a small herd of pronghorn antelope into a pit, which was dug about five feet deep, and shaped with vertical walls so no animal could escape. Preparers fenced the entrance and staked the area leading up to the pit in a V-shaped fence. The two young women were instructed to walk the path that the antelope were to follow into the pit. They were to look straight ahead at all times, for their actions were believed to influence those of the antelope. One ceremonial leader, Vó'oménéhotoa'e, used four special "antelope arrows" to call in the antelope. These arrows were used by the priest in an opening ceremony and then given to the four young people: the young women ran with these out toward the land, each in line with the V-shaped fence. The young men followed to catch them, signifying hunters catching antelope. Once the men caught the women, they took hold of their antelope arrows and continued forward while the women stopped and returned to the priest.

PART I: MA'HEÓNÈSTÓNESTÔTSE: SACRED COVENANTS

Grover Wolfvoice (Northern Cheyenne) recalled that instead of arrows, the medicine men of later times used "sacrificial flags," which were made of willows and feathers.[25] A group of the best hunters and fastest runners followed the same direction as the two young men. These hunters searched for the antelope in the prairie, then chased them into the pit. Specially made clubs, which were painted red, were placed at the entrance of the pit so the antelope ran over the very weapons by which they would meet their demise. The head priest or keeper of the Antelope Bundle performed elaborate and lengthy rituals after the hunting grounds were prepared for the kill. He painted himself like an antelope: "his mouth black, his back red, his belly, arms, legs, rump, and face white, and painted red streaks across his upper chest. On each temple, and running down his cheeks, he painted an antelope horn, black."[26] He sang four antelope songs four times each and, with an eagle feather, blessed the hunting grounds by walking the entire area, looking for imperfections and structural weaknesses. In the center of the pit, he placed the circular, red plate, which had been given from Mâhtamâhááhe. Meanwhile, all other citizens—men, women, and children—prepared for the hunt by lining up along the fence and beyond to eventually aid in containing the animals.

When the keeper made an offering by burning an herb on the red plate, all rituals were completed. He then called on the hunt. The hunters chased the animals from afar into the pit. Hunters, both men and women, strategically corralled the animals into the pit in unison and in a very calculated and cooperative manner. As the herd shifted, other hunters who were stationed along the route herded the animals toward the pit. Once the animals entered the pit, men and women took up the clubs and killed the trapped animals. No arrows or spears were used, since it violated the teachings from Mâhtamâhááhe and the projectiles could inadvertently kill other hunters involved in the hunt or those inside the trap. The antelope that escaped were tracked and killed, and sometimes other animals, like wolves, coyotes, foxes, and rabbits, were caught in the trap and met their demise. When the animals had all been killed, the people climbed out of the pit to wait for instruction. After the kill, the keeper prepared and smoked a ceremonial pipe and searched for a flat ceremonial stone, which was the talisman that, when activated, drew the animals to the location. Vó'oménéhotoa'e did not have such a stone but used a different form of medicine. Upon completion, the medicine men retrieved the antelope arrows or flags from participants.

Wooden Leg, one of several Cheyennes who favored antelope meat over buffalo, recalled his experience in the hunt as a young man:

> I have helped in the chasing of antelope bands over a cliff. In the Black Hills was one special place where we worked for our meat in that manner. The creek near by was called Antelope creek. The first time I went there an old man accompanied me. We located ourselves in hiding near the base of the cliff, with women and old people and children. Two young men rounded up a herd and drove them over for us. Many of them were killed or got broken legs. We clubbed to death the injured ones.[27]

After the kill, the head priest blessed the slain animals and afterward the people pulled them out of the pit, lined them up, and began to butcher the antelope. The first one was to be taken to the top of a hill where it was sacrificed to the sacred birds: eagles, crows, and magpies. The ceremony was redone no more than four times and thus produced enough to provide for all of the lodges in the band; as many as six hundred lodges could receive an animal, each family acquiring at least one antelope.[28] The entire body of the slain antelope was used, as the people wasted nothing. The hides were of particular value, because of their smaller size and soft tanning, and were made into dresses for young women or shirts for young men.

The Antelope Pit was not a big ceremony, but individual bands practiced it with the same efficiency and discipline without the presence of the entire nation. One interpretation of the ceremony is that it was done in honor of the sacred antelope and was a reenactment of the Great Race, in which the magpie won so humans could eat the buffalo and other four-legged animals. The Antelope bundle-keeper had to conduct the ceremony to the best of his knowledge; should he fail or an animal escape, then a family member would suffer the consequences by dying within a few years. Although those who could "call" the antelope did not hold any political status, citizens appreciated them, and other leaders held them in high esteem, respect, and honor. The Antelope bundle keeper did not have a formal seat at the Chiefs Council, but the lodge and spiritual leaders were granted the full support and cooperation of the Véhoo'o and warrior societies during the hunt. The Só'taeo'o bands continued to practice this method of killing antelope even after the nation acquired horses, but the practice eventually died out after the people were forced onto reservations.

VÓHAENÓHÓNESTÔTSE

While the Só'taeo'o primarily used the communal hunt to capture antelope, after the Great Unification, the Cheyenne Nation grew in numbers and the communal hunt spread to other bands. One band village or a union of bands would come together to surround and kill buffalo in a ceremonial hunt called vóhaenóhónestôtse, which means "surrounding buffalo."[29] The Cheyennes did not rely on hōtōw'ëanā'ŏ (buffalo jumps) but were aware of such ancient practices; instead, they hunted in accordance with traditional laws of balance and harmony.[30] The major difference is that the hunt did not require the construction of a large pit made of earth, stone, and wood. Rather, the entire band reconstructed its camp circle as an enclosure and built numerous wooden structures and placed them between the lodges, creating a large fence.

The origin of the Buffalo Ceremony comes from the Tsétsêhéstâhese culture and is part of the legacy of the prophet Motsé'eóeve.[31] The Buffalo Ceremony was a reenactment of the powers of Motsé'eóeve and, unlike the Antelope Pit Ceremony, took place near the autumnal equinox when the buffalo began to return in thick herds.³² Upon the Great Unification, the Buffalo Ceremony adopted elements from the Antelope Pit Ceremony, in particular the use of the flat, circular pipestone.³³ The Buffalo Ceremony became extinct with the decline of the American Bison in the late 1800s, due to overkilling from white, hide hunters. One can only imagine the time on the Great Plains when the buffalo herds were so vast that they could actually be "called" into a Cheyenne camp circle to be killed. Elements of the ceremony are preserved in the Cheyenne national history, and the origin of the Buffalo Ceremony serves as a reminder of the Cheyenne world during the time of the dog and the time of the buffalo, or before the coming of the horse.³⁴

Sweet Medicine's Buffalo Songs, by Wolf Chief

A great many years after he was gone, when the people were in starvation, they were moving in every direction that they might slay any game they might live on. While moving he [Sweet Medicine] came to a trail that led up to the camp. He found two boys on his way, eating sticky pears. He came to them and said to them: "What are you people eating?" They could not reply, they showed him the pears. He told the boys to go home and ask the old men to harangue the people and tell them to put up a big lodge right in the center of the camp; that the wonderful man had come back who had disappeared in that lodge years and years ago.

And when that lodge was put up about sun down, he went there with a skin of buffalo head with him and placed it back of the lodge for the night for his performance. There were many people that came to the center to listen to him sing beautiful [songs] that they had never heard in all their lives, songs of buffalo, songs of herds of buffalos, songs of buffalo to men, and songs of men how to be happy. After midnight the people all at once dropped asleep. And just before sunrise the people woke up, and saw the buffalos, herds of buffalos in the center so thick they could not move. And that was his first trick he performed for that clan. And that's the end.³⁵

Sweet Medicine's Buffalo Songs, by White Buffalo

They cooked hides for days and ate them. They started off on another trip. There were two boys way behind. They saw two puffballs. They ran and ate them. Pretty soon they saw somebody way behind coming up. When they saw the man coming, they sat down. When the man came up to them he said: "What are you boys doing?" They said, "We are eating these puffballs because everybody is nearly starved."

"I'm here now. You will have everything to eat." He [Matsīyōv, or Sweet Medicine] told them to get buffalo chips and pile them up together. He had something in his hand which he laid down on the ground. He was all painted. He had a robe around his waist. "You shall have all things to eat," he told them. After they gathered the buffalo chips, he took off his robe and covered the chips. When he took it off the chips had turned to mince meat. The boys ate them. After they had finished eating, he told them to take the rest back for the people to eat. After the boys went back to the camp, they gave the meat to the people. He had told the boys to tell the people he was coming back.

The boys were naked and greasy. The people asked them why they were greasy. They had the meat in their hand. They told them they had got the meat from him (Matsīyōv). The boys told the old man to tell the people to fix up a good place in the center of the camp for him to sit down; and that the buffalo were coming back. They had two big tipis. They put them together where he was going to sit. They raised the tipi up from the ground. Everybody was poor and skinny. They saw him coming. He was all dressed up and painted. Everybody was crying when he was coming up. Everything was faced up in the tipi. So he went in; sat down.

He had something in his hand. He told the people he was going to sing four days and four nights; that they would learn something; that they should be happy. After the four nights they shall see something. Everything shall be easy for you, not so hard. "I know that you people are nearly starved, but you shall be happy and have a lot of food to eat." That night he sang songs, and they joined. He told them, "I know you are all nearly starved, but you shall have good strength." After he had sung four nights, the next morning they saw the buffalo all over the plain right near where they were. After he sang four times, the buffalo went in every direction through the camp. And the people were all happy.[36]

Sweet Medicine Calls the Buffalo, by White Buffalo

There was a great big snowfall. People were starving. Animals froze to death. They could never have [meat] any more. When summer came, there was no fruit, no berries. All that they had to eat was grass and weeds from all the rivers and lakes. They ate grass like cattle. He was following them up all the time; all that time Matsīyōv had the secret bundles. There were six young boys that came to Matsīyōv. They were naked and nearly starved. They asked him: "What's that under your arm? If it is so wonderful, why not save us from starving?" He covered his secret bundle with his blanket. Matsīyōv asked one of them to get buffalo-chips and bring it to him. They brought the buffalo chips. Matsīyōv covered them with his blanket. He uncovered the chips. They had turned into buffalo meat all chopped up. He gave it to the starving boys. Then he told them: "Go to camp; tell the people I am coming."

They started off to the tribe. They told the people to form in a circle of the two tribes and put one large tipi in the center of the circle. When they had fixed the lodge, he sat down on a high hill so the people would see that he was coming. He told the people that six men should meet him on the hill. When they got to him he was seated with bundles in front of him. A large buffalo chip was on top of the bundle. The men were crying, they wanted to be pitied; they wanted the people to be saved from starvation. He asked the six men for one to come forward to him. And one of the six came forward to the place, here he told the man to tell all the people to go to the center of that lodge to hear the songs that he was going to sing. For four days and nights they fasted. After he sat down in the back of the lodge, he told a man to go after a woman so he (Matsīyōv) could get something he had left. This woman was called "Little Yellow Calf." She came out of her lodge. Before she came out [of] the big lodge, she said: "If there's no objection, I have something the matter with me." Matsīyōv said: "What's the matter with you?" She said she was having her menses. He told her to pass on; he was not going to use her. He sent another woman called "Holy Ear of Corn." He told her: "You go out to this spring. It's going to be foggy before you get there. There's going to be somebody [who will] speak to you before you get there."

As the woman got there, they opened the doors for her to come in. She went into the spring. After a while it was closed. That night she did not return. Matsīyōv began to sing for the people, asking the blessing to be given to these starving people. He told the people: "Put up the lodges as close as you can in the circle; and all the people must have clubs, stones, or spears, anything that will kill." All that night the buffalo came out of the spring. They appeared in the center of the camp until it was nearly overcrowded. They began to hear the noise of buffalo. The second [night] more noises; the third [night] more; the fourth night, it was overcrowded in the center of the ring. And then he told the people to kill the buffalos in the center of the ring. All were killed. None escaped. There was great rejoicing. That woman [Holy Ear of Corn] never came out. She disappeared. She drove all the buffalo out. She became corn. Right in the center where Matsīyōv was singing appeared five kernels of corn: red, blue, yellow, black, white. After this was done for these starving people, there was another great gathering to meet the Great Spirit.[37]

Old She Bear tells the origin of the Buffalo Ceremony as part of the Cheyenne-Lakota unification, which is likely an adapted history since other storytellers do not include the Lakota.

Sweet Medicine Calls the Buffalo, by Old She Bear

He kept on journeying. He sat down, smoked, dressed up, painted; he had his robe turned inside out. There were two boys hunting birds. They were using arrows, showing. The people were playing the hoop and ball game. The people saw him way off. They thought he was a buffalo. The Indians were nearly starved. Everybody was poor. The boys were coming close. They were naked, poor, dirty, and skinny. Pretty soon Matsīyōv spoke up and told the boys to come to him. The boys were afraid of him because he had the buffalo robe on. He told them not to be afraid. The boys came on, each pushing each other forward. He told them to come have a feast. He told them his name. He had dry meat so they had a feast. After they finished eating, he gave them some fat and meat and told them to go back and tell the people to eat this meat.

There were two games being played. He told one boy to go to one, the other to the other; and to tell the people they got meat from him and point to him,

Matsīyōv, and to say that he brought the buffalo back. These boys told one old man to tell the people that Matsīyōv was there and that he wanted to see the two chiefs. Everybody was happy, got out, walked around, when they heard the buffalo were coming back. The chiefs came to him: "Don't you know me? I'm Matsīyōv." They said they didn't know him. After he had talked to the chiefs, he told them to look down and they saw the buffalos coming. He told the chiefs to [go] back and tell the people the buffalos were coming, and to get ready. He told them to get a lodge and put it in the center of the camp. After they put the lodge up, he came down to see it. After the lodge was put up and he was coming down, he told the chiefs and told another man to tell the people to see what was going on. When he was coming down, he wore a robe representing a buffalo. They thought it was buffalo coming down. Everybody cried.

That medicine man (Matsīyōv) went around the entire camp. Everybody watched him. He came into the lodge which was put up in the center of the camp. All the chiefs and headmen were in that lodge. He went in around the right side inside. They had a place for him. They had sagebrush and five buffalo chips for him to sit on. He had turned into a buffalo when he ran around the camp. As soon as he sat down he turned into a man again. He talked to the people in the lodge. He told them all the instructions that he had received from his grandfather in the rock. He told them he had brought the buffalo back to the people, and they should live a happy life. After he finished talking, he sang the medicine songs. He told them to listen. He showed them so they could do what he had done, and live to an old age at the time of their death. And they (everybody) would resurrect seven times. That same night he sang the songs, and taught them the Sun Dance and all other medicine dances. They heard the buffalos; there all over the plains and around the camps.[38]

The Cheyennes preserved memories of starvation and suffering in the Sweet Medicine legacy, proving that they should never be so careless and wasteful in killing the very animals that provided life-giving nourishment and a material economy. Sweet Medicine's role in saving the people from starvation is emotional. The ceremony relies on the power of youth, male and female, and employs the powers of the round ceremonial plate made of pipestone. Stands In Timber describes the ceremony, which appears as a fragmented history of a ceremony that went extinct with the decline of the American Bison.

The Buffalo Lodge, by John Stands In Timber

The Cheyennes also had a red stone plate five inches in diameter. I have not seen this plate but they have described it. It is flat and about an inch thick, nice and smooth. The stone is used for ceremonies by appointed priests, and it was wrapped with buffalo hair. The hair is loose and covers both sides. Then they have a small sack of skin, which it fits in. The main purpose of this was for use in a religious ceremony to make the buffalo come. The story is told that this special sacred tepee is set up to last four days, because of a long ceremony.

There is singing inside and designs made on the ground, and some performances made in that tepee. The last day before daylight the priests or members of this lodge looked for a young girl who had good character and was not married, and they used this girl to sit inside and the stone was put in front of her, and a coal of fire taken from the fire in the middle of the tepee, and this charcoal is put on the red pipe plate. And they have certain kinds of medicine and used it for scent, burning it and causing it to smell good in the tepee.

    Before daylight they send out one young man. The tepee faces east, and the man goes out looking around until he comes to a place where he may see buffalo. Then he marks the place and goes back. He makes his report to the priests and points out the direction where the buffalo are grazing. They face the girl in that direction, and place a buffalo cowhide covering her, and the priests and young men with bows and arrows go out to the buffalo. When they approach the herd, the priests sit down and do some performance also by smoothing the ground and smoking the pipe. And they point to the buffalo by finger, each one to the animal with that pipe, and laid it down. And then men with bows and arrows start off toward the buffalo, some on each side, and they come to the buffalo, which never noticed them, or heard nothing, and looked like they were tame.

    And they walked up close to the buffalo, and the right distance—if they gone too close the arrow does not get speed enough to go through the buffalo's body. So they came to shoot them, and when the arrows struck, the buffalo jumped here and there and looked like they were blind, looking like they heard something and looking around, and another arrow hit them. And they came right up close to them and they bunched up and ran into each other, showing that they must be blind. And they killed all the buffalo.

    Then there is like a contest. All the young men run in as fast as they can and open up the buffalo and reach inside to get a piece of fat called sweetbreads, and start running back as fast as they could to go to the tepee. The fastest runner jumps back in that tepee and pushes that in to the front of the girl and lays it on the red plate. Then the buffalo are skinned, and everybody has a share of the meat.[39]

Stands In Timber explained how the warrior societies participated in the ceremony by dressing in their finest clothes and set up stations around the village. When the first young man brings the first piece of meat, the warriors parade into the circle and surround the lodge. Then the chiefs "do the singing and they have a dance, dancing in one place and not moving." The chiefs then select the bravest men, in increments of four, to honor them and assign them with the task to protect the village. Afterward, the ceremonial and warrior societies hold a special dance, hold giveaway ceremonies, and host feasts. The Buffalo Ceremony remains a part of Cheyenne national history and survives, as fragments of the four-day ritual are evident in the modern Arrow Worship and Sun Dance ceremonies.

CHAPTER 3

The Covenant Ceremonies

The Tsis-tsistas people have danced the great medicine dance for a long, long time, longer than anyone can remember or even imagine. The dance represents the making of this universe and was conceived and taught to the people by the Creator, Maheo, and his helper, Great Roaring Thunder. It portrays the making of the sun, moon, and stars; of rain, wind, and snow; of Grandmother Earth and the blue sky above her; of the mountains and rivers; of all living things, big and small. The dance is performed especially in times of starvation, distress, and widespread death. This, our most sacred ceremony, was brought to us by the Sutai medicine man Horns Standing Up, under the guidance of the Creator himself.

—Josie Limpy (Northern Cheyenne), Keeper of the Sacred Hat[1]

The covenant ceremonies of the Cheyenne Nation are large events that continue to this day among both the Northern and Southern Cheyenne nations. The ceremonies invite entire families and communities to camp at a given area. Among the Northern Cheyenne, members of my family, myself, and family friends and relatives continue to participate in our sacred Sun Dance ceremony. For this chapter I provide a basic review of the three major covenant ceremonies: the Arrow Renewal, the Sun Dance, and the long-extinct Animal Dance. Since I belong to two ceremonial guilds, I am cognizant of our traditional rules and customs of privacy and secrecy. As I mentioned in the Introduction, I am very careful not to reveal anything that would be considered a violation of our people's and nation's rights to privacy. The purpose of this chapter is to highlight the significance of sacred sovereignty and how the Cheyenne Nation exercised, retained, and sustained its "high authority" over the land as a sacred nation of Mother Earth. More important, this chapter explains the fundamentals of Indigenousness and emphasizes how and why Indigenous nations like the Cheyenne were so adamant in protecting their ways of life and their traditional homelands.

PART I: MA'HEÓNÈSTÓNESTÔTSE: SACRED COVENANTS

The covenant ceremonies each have sacred origins, but the ceremonies were adapted and refined over the course of hundreds and possibly thousands of years. For example, when animal hides became scarce and the Cheyennes began using cloth, they incorporated cloth into their ceremony. They also incorporated the use of rifles, horses, and metal implements for cooking. Nonetheless, the sanctity of the ceremonies remained and the Cheyennes preserved nearly every detail and passed it down to the next generations. The covenant ceremonies are ancient, and when I say ancient, I mean that these ceremonies are truly evidence that those who founded them were highly intelligent, wise, and very disciplined.

Of the three covenant ceremonies I discuss in this chapter, only two have survived the ravages of colonization and forced assimilation. The Cheyennes continue to practice these covenant ceremonies, even though the majority of the people do not necessarily follow traditional ways. There is also a large population of Christian Cheyennes who have never been to or would never go to a covenant ceremony, even though they may be fluent in the Cheyenne language and may even participate in social and traditional dances. Conversely, there is a population of Cheyennes who participate in the covenant ceremonies and, unlike fluent Cheyenne speakers or older generations, may not have the full understanding of what the purpose and significance of these ceremonies embody. This is why custom demands that practitioners of these ceremonies truly and sincerely dedicate and discipline themselves over the course of their lifetime. This is not an easy task to accomplish, especially as the vices of modern and mainstream life and technology dominate our cultures.

Regardless of the social situation of the Cheyenne communities, families, and individuals who participate in the covenant ceremonies, they renew the sacred nation by participating in these ceremonies. Families are also reunited and community ties are reestablished and strengthened at these unified camps. The covenant ceremonies invite all citizens of the sacred nation to offer prayers and sacrifices for whatever purpose and need. Each participant who enters into a covenant ceremony does so for his or her own spiritual purposes, but they also represent the healing and reunification of the living Cheyenne Nation.

My goal is also to explain how the major covenant ceremonies created and sustained the Cheyenne Nation, and I do this by highlighting the elements that reinforce my thesis. If readers wish to learn more about the Arrow Renewal or the Sun Dance, it must be done with respect and at the discretion of the sacred protectors who bear the knowledge, rights, and wisdom, not necessarily the sacred scholars. The Maahéome, for example, is a vibrant and extant ceremony among modern Cheyennes, in particular the Southern Cheyenne Nation of Oklahoma. With great care and respect for the traditions of my people, I have limited examination of this portion and rely heavily on previously published accounts.[2]

THE COVENANTS

The three major covenant ceremonies from the time of the buffalo to the time of the horse were the Maahéome (Arrow Lodge), the Hoxéheome (Medicine Lodge or Sun Dance), and the Måsėháome (Crazy Lodge). Each of these major events occurred only once a year, and each had an accompanying bundle, a véstomoó'hanestôtse (covenant or promise), a set of laws, and a lead person designated as a bundle keeper.³ Such keepers were selected based on the purity of their character, and once selected they could not deny their appointment. It was customary for them to exhibit reluctance and identify someone who was more worthy, and if he did not, others would criticize him for being too arrogant.⁴

The major covenant ceremonies of the Cheyenne Nation were national events, and most originated from the time of the dog and of the buffalo. These ceremonies can be described as the celebrations, reiterations, and reminders of each of their associated covenants. A more appropriate term for these celebrations or ceremonies is "lodges," which is telling of the physical structures that were built to shelter participants during a particular ceremony.⁵ This is not to say that only a certain group of people exclusively participated in one ceremony, but that there were specialists who managed the affairs of the lodge as high priests. Each lodge had its own structure and hierarchy: its own leaders, as well as its own leadership standards, duties, and responsibilities. One lodge that follows this tradition is the Véhooneome (Chiefs' Lodge), which is better known as the Chiefs' Renewal Ceremony. I highlight the Véhooneome in Chapter 6 in *A Sacred People*. The Véhooneome did not necessarily follow the ceremonial calendar determined by nature, as it was prescheduled every ten years, but it easily fit within the annual ceremonial calendar upon unification.

The Cheyenne government underwent significant changes during times of ceremonial activities. Like with the Véhooneome, the entire nation gathered and typically all ten bands met at a designated place in a large camp to participate in the covenant ceremonies. During these annual camp meetings, the Cheyenne Nation became a complete nation-state with a fully functioning military force, residing in a centralized location, within a much larger geopolitical homeland. Daily camp functions continued regularly, but the Nótâxeo'o (warrior societies) were complete in numbers, thus maximizing the "police" force. The Véhoo'o designated one warrior society to patrol the entire camp and then held councils with ceremonial leaders to organize and plan whichever ceremony was slated. The nation was a force to be reckoned with, as it held the ability to efficiently manage both internal and external affairs, with all citizens and ceremonial societies present.

Ceremonial or spiritual leaders of the covenant ceremonies were not necessarily warrior leaders or chiefs, although there was nothing preventing a person, man or woman, from engaging in both. It was customary, however, that ceremonial leaders dedicate their lives to one profession, since the demands and responsibilities among Cheyenne priests were equivalent to those of "medicine men" or "medicine women" of other American Indian and Indigenous cultures.

The unique ceremonial system of the Cheyennes ensured the survival of traditional and spiritual ways through a number of precautions. The first is that ceremonial leaders were required to be sincerely devoted to their profession. Any persons who strayed from their responsibilities would lose the respect of their people and thus lose any following, thus diminishing the nation's sovereignty. The second is that spiritual leaders acquired their knowledge over long periods of time: some take forty years, which is equivalent to likely half a lifetime, to learn their roles. Others took four years to learn and master a ritual, while some took four months or four days to learn a lesser ritual, ceremony, or song.[6] Traditionally, age and time dedicated to learning were deemed by far the most important features of good spiritual leaders, second only to reputation. Traditionally, the most trusted and knowledgeable spiritual leaders were aged forty and above. Today, however, the standards have shifted to value reputation over age.

The third element that ensured the survival of the Cheyenne ceremonial way of life is that spiritual teachings were handed down directly from instructor to apprentice. While some individuals may gain new spiritual insight or become knowledgeable about different spiritual concepts and ideas, to practice and perform ceremonies and rites a person (man or woman) had to be given the teachings and rights from a higher authority. A ceremonial leader (man or woman) may have four, eight, sixteen, or as many as sixty-four apprentices, as well as the knowledge of one or more—as many as forty—songs, rituals, rights, ceremonies, and spiritual practices. In short, the Cheyenne ceremonial realm is far-reaching and the knowledge vast, and rarely was the ceremonial knowledge funneled to just one person or family.

There were numerous covenant ceremonial societies, which were organized in a way similar to that of the warrior societies. Each society was unique, but all featured leaders who oversaw their own apprentices. Throughout the course of the existence of the Cheyenne Nation, there could have been as many as ten covenant ceremonial societies for each major ceremony.[7] The nation comprised a significant number of members who ranked from apprentices to spiritual leaders to priests. The societies and members kept the major ceremonies alive and vibrant.

The fourth and final attribute of cultural survival is that the Cheyenne ceremonial calendar and teachings were deeply intertwined with the Cheyenne homeland, language, and sacred history. The Cheyenne ceremonial leaders were great in number, creating a spiritually healthy Cheyenne Nation. During the great covenant ceremonies, the social and political balance shifted to accommodate the needs of the life-renewing and life-sustaining services. In comparison to the political organization of the Cheyenne Nation, which involved only two entities (the warriors and the chiefs), the ceremonial organization included the keepers of each covenant. The ceremonial organization lasted for the entire course of the gathering: four to five days before and after the ceremony as well as during the ceremony itself, for a total of nearly two weeks. Most important, the balance of power shifted to include the ceremonial leaders and the ceremonial societies. Power and authority shifted in favor of whichever covenant ceremony was conducted. As the calendar progressed, each lodge eventually held power for the duration of their particular ceremony but relinquished authority upon its completion and closure. The Cheyenne tradition of sharing power was also entrenched in prayer and sacrifice, which are core principles to Cheyenne sovereignty, law, and nationhood.

MAAHÉOME

Water was considered the most significant element to life, and for every ceremony the nation gathered in a beautiful place next to a major river, creek, or pond. Here they could also access the necessary plants and animals to fulfill their promises in ceremony. The first major ceremony on the calendar was the Maahéome (Arrow Lodge), which took place during the summer solstice. The ceremony completely renewed or healed the living-nation and required the presence of all Cheyenne families. It was considered to be the most sacred lodge. Wesley Whiteman stated: "That's the highest power in our religion, I'm sometimes afraid of it."[8] During the best decades of the Cheyenne Nation, in particular the early time of the buffalo, the Maahéome was not conducted every year because there was no need. The nation, its citizens, and the supernatural world were in harmony. Sometimes the ceremony was conducted at a later time in the year if the spiritual leaders believed that there was an imbalance within the nation or if a Cheyenne killed a fellow Cheyenne. During the time of the horse, imbalances became more common and the Maahéome became an annual event for the Cheyenne Nation.[9] The lodge was essential to the mental and spiritual health of the nation and no other major ceremony could be conducted until after its completion.

The Maahéome originated with the Tsétsêhéstaestse prophet Motsé'eóeve, as he is credited with bringing the covenant. The following is from the Sweet Medicine epic.

The Arrows of Sweet Medicine

After Motsé'eóeve created the four original warrior societies, he traveled deep into the Black Hills alone and came to a sacred mountain.[10] He lived alone at this mountain for four years and called it Nóvávóse.[11] He returned to his people with numerous teachings but left the people again after he married the daughter of a chief. Together he and his wife went on a holy pilgrimage back into the wilderness, and they seemed to be drawn to the supernatural power of the Black Hills. They eventually found their way to the sacred mountain where

PART I: MA'HEÓNÈSTÓNESTÔTSE: SACRED COVENANTS

Motsé'eóeve stayed before. They climbed to the summit where the young man found an entrance into the mountain. He entered and found that the inside was the same shape and appearance as a large tepee. Numerous people dressed in ceremonial garb sat inside and seemed to be holding a sacred meeting. Each represented a specific spiritual way or religion, and when Motsé'eóeve entered, one rose and said: "Come in, young man, we have been waiting. You are now more mature and older than when you left us. You are a husband now and therefore ready to make the decisions for your people."

Another rose and asked Motsé'eóeve after he sat: "Which one of us do you like? Which one of us do you want to be like?" Motsé'eóeve carefully looked around at all of the different people and took his time to pick one. Once he did, all of the beings began to grumble in discontent. The spiritual being asked: "Why did you pick that person?"

Motsé'eóeve responded: "Because he is good looking."

The being stated: "You picked the wrong one for the wrong reasons. Now you and your people will become like him and live short lives. You may be beautiful but only for a short time." The spiritual people began to talk to Motsé'eóeve about life and all of the things in the world that keep life going. They told him of the daily movement of the sun and monthly movement of the moon, and the slow movements of the stars and Milky Way and how all of these things worked together to keep life going. They told him of the waters of the earth, the power of thunderstorms, rain, frost, and ice. They told him of the sacred plants, animals, and medicines in and on the earth, the balance of the supernatural and natural, and how humans fit into the universe. They also taught him of the things that disrupt and destroy the beautiful things in life. They warned of the imbalance and especially the destructive potential of humans. One stated, "Humans can be beautiful and compassionate, but they can also be ugly and cruel. It is for them to decide."

Another being entered into the lodge as the spirits taught Motsé'eóeve. This new being was also a spirit, but he was not good-looking; he was red-faced and sickly looking. His eyes were sore and bloodshot, his nose bled, and his hair was matted. He had pain when he walked and wore ratty clothes. Motsé'eóeve could see suffering and despair in his face. One of the spirits said, "Look at him, his name is Háomóhtâhévêhanéhe (Sickness). He is your new friend and he will be with you always now. Do not underestimate or forget about him. Remember what we have told you."

The spirits presented Motsé'eóeve with two bundles, each containing four arrows. One set of arrows was made of hawk feathers; the other set was made of eagle feathers.[12] "Choose one," one spirit said. Motsé'eóeve chose the one made of eagle feathers and the spirits were glad. "This time, you have chosen wisely." They then instructed the young man how to use the arrows in hunting and war, but more important, they told him the four sacred laws of humanity. "Follow these laws and your people will become sacred and will live a long time: your people must not lie to one another, they must not cheat or steal from one another, they must not marry their own relatives, and most important, they must not kill each other." The spirits' final teachings were on how to conduct a peace-making ceremony and how to conduct the Maahéome, the renewal ceremony. Motsé'eóeve left the lodge after four days, and he and his wife returned to their people after completing their four-year trip. When he returned, he called in the chiefs and spiritual leaders to tell them his story and the teachings of the Maahótse (Medicine Arrows).

The Maahótse are considered the "Supreme Court of the Cheyenne Nation" and are the authority in approving anything and everything concerning matters that may affect the path of the living-nation.[13] Bull Thigh provides an account.

The Sacred Arrows, by Bull Thigh

Motsé'eóeve told the people: "Hereafter now you shall make arrows. Arrows shall be composed of skins of foxes with stone heads to kill the animals with. Then I am going to kill the highest birds. They shall come of which I shall make use of their feathers. These arrows shall be made only four. The feathers of the eagle must be put on them; one end with a stone-lance for your people to save you from starvation."

After they made these four arrows they put them in a bundle of deerskin and kept them from that time throughout all generations. But they were not to use these. They could make other arrows to imitate them and use these. That's the origin of the Arrows. When we fix the Sacred Arrows, every one in the tribe must be there in the camp circle for four days. When these are fixed up the whole bands of medicine and war societies, man and child are there. Women cannot come near. The medicine societies sing for these arrows.[14]

THE ARROW LODGE

The Maahéome encompassed a group of ceremonial leaders, practitioners, and keepers who were all part of the Arrow Lodge, which is like belonging to a religious caste or priesthood. The Maahótse were the medicine bundles and covenants that accompanied the ceremony. The wood shafts represented the people; the feathers represented the spirit world; the sharp, flint tips represented incorruption, health, and eternity; and the fur cover that held the arrows represented Ma'xema'heōe (Great Medicine).[15] The Maahótse were the soul of the nation: if they prospered, then so did the people; if they were desecrated, then the people suffered. The Maahéome was the formal renewal or cleansing of the Maahótse, likewise the renewal and cleansing of the people. Like all major ceremonies of the Cheyennes, the Maahéome was a four-day ceremony that required much preparation and organization.

During the ceremony the spiritual leaders and pledgers prepared offerings provided by the people by tying them on a pole in front of an offerings lodge. This lodge belonged to the pledger and was erected by his wife and family. Then a number of good men, with good reputations, were selected to construct a larger lodge using two tepee covers. Once erected, the spiritual leaders, the arrow keepers, and the pledger could enter the new Arrow Lodge. Inside, the practitioners conducted numerous rituals involving singing, smoking, blessing, and ceremonial painting.

The pledger was painted and prepared to formally enter the Maahéome. The Maahótse bundle was unwrapped and each arrow was to be remade in a very tedious but methodical manner. The eagle feathers were cleaned, but only "a man who has lived in accordance with Cheyenne ideas is appointed to undertake the great task. He must be healthy, clean, good tempered, kind, generous, wise, and brave, never guilty of a dishonorable act."[16] Part of the ceremony represented the reunification and blessing of every Cheyenne family in the nation. A willow stick represented each family, except for those families that produced a murderer. Traditionally the family sticks numbered no more than 445. One by one, a priest prayed and blessed each stick with sweet grass and other incense. The arrows were placed on a forked pole and exposed to the sun. They were then placed in the Maahéome, which was opened for every male to enter and observe. Boys from the camp came to make offerings and receive the blessings from the entire ceremony. Meanwhile, women and young girls remained inside their lodges to wait for the renewal to be completed. Near the conclusion of the Maahéome, the Sweet Medicine chief sang four sacred songs, retold the original prophecies, and used his spiritual wisdom to foretell future events significant to the future of the entire nation.

The Maahéome was a Tsétsèhéstâhese ceremony, and since they were patrilineal, the significance of the ceremony demanded the discipline and dedication of the men.[17] Women were not allowed to be directly involved in the Maahéome, but this did not mean that women were of lesser value, since the ceremony also depended on their presence and contributions. The ceremony emphasized the male character, but it was less about manhood and more about reunifying, renewing, and cleansing the nation. According to the oral traditions of Motsé'eóeve, the men were the ones who became corrupt, not the women, and therefore men held a degree of power and control in the direction of cultural and political affairs of the nation; they were responsible for finding and maintaining internal balance. In accordance with the oral traditions of Motsé'eóeve, men were inevitably held responsible for changing their ways for the sake of the nation. Furthermore, Cheyenne men especially had the duty of upholding and enforcing the four sacred laws of Maahótse in fairness and for justice. The Maahéome is the reaffirmation of the sacred history and restoration of the philosophy that brought peace and balance to the people long ago, in the time of Motsé'eóeve.

Each practitioner of the Maahéome had to be of good conduct, good health, and sound mind and spirit. Traditional Cheyennes assert that the arrows "have great powers. They contain rules by which men ought to live."[18] Males were required to exercise a high degree of "warrior discipline," which is physical, mental, and spiritual discipline, as they fasted to gain an understanding of the universe by contemplating their own deaths.[19] Through prayer and meditation, a young warrior could imagine his lifeless body, lying on the prairie after the excitement of war and in the calm after battle. In ceremony, with no water or food passing through his body, he was as close to death as possible without dying. Upon completion of the ceremony, the men abandoned their egos, which may have been fraught with fear, anxiety, jealousy, pettiness, and impatience. By the time he matured and was old enough to marry and father children, the warrior made for a fine warrior citizen, an elder, and even a chief. Not all men were required to endure the ceremony, but all were expected to know and follow the laws of the Maahótse.

MAAHÓTSE TSÉÁ'ENÖVÂHTSE

The Maahéome included numerous leaders; the highest was the Maahótse Tséá'enövâhtse (Arrow Keeper) and below him were four assistant keepers.[20] The original Tséá'enövâhtse (Keeper) was selected based on his character, and whenever necessary (when he became too old or no longer wished to be in such a position), the Council Chiefs and the spiritual leaders met to choose a new Tséá'enövâhtse. Baldwin Twins, keeper from 1936 to 1956, instructed on the selection process:

> Now you must select a good man; one who is good-natured and of good character in every way. He will be the man to take charge of the Arrows. He will be the man to take the pipe in his hands. This you must remember: in his daily prayers, beginning at daylight, he will smoke four times. In his prayers he must not forget to pray for the people, for their food, and for all the game, that the animals may be plentiful.[21]

The role of the Tséá'enövâhtse was first and foremost ceremonial as he was the caretaker for the Maahótse, responsible for the Maahéome, and keeper of all associated oral traditions and philosophies including prophecies. He, like all leaders, was required to have certain qualities and virtues and follow strict principles: "He must understand all sacred chants and all rituals pertaining to the Medicine-Arrow ceremony. Not only this, but he must be of extraordinary good character, a natural leader, and counselor of the whole Cheyenne tribe, but not necessarily a chief."[22] Before the time of the horse, the keeper's role as ceremonial leader was not limited because sometimes he would be consulted on political affairs, even though he had no political standing. In later times, especially with the arrival of whites, the Véhoo'o often consulted the Arrow Keeper to reach a resolution or decision on diplomatic matters, and this made the role of the Arrow Keeper unique.

The Maahótse Tséá'enövâhtse was also responsible for the moral character of every citizen and the sanctity of the entire Cheyenne Nation. He was a model of the ideal male personality, and practitioners of the Arrow Lodge became "arrow men" who earned sacred responsibilities but were also bound by sacred laws. As a follower of the Maahótse Tséá'enövâhtse, a Maahétaneve (arrow man) was a spiritual leader in his own right and became a worthy candidate to be the Arrow Keeper.[23] The Maahótse represented the sacred laws of the Cheyenne people, and if a Cheyenne murdered a Cheyenne, the Maahótse were renewed, thus restoring balance. The Tséá'enövâhtse, as enforcer of the sacred law, was a man of considerable integrity and honor. Stands In Timber asserted: "When things with the Arrows went wrong, they say that is why so many of our young boys committed suicide, four or five of them, or were in wrecks and were killed."[24] A Tséá'enövâhtse with poor character could lead to internal strife. Conversely, the rewards of a noble Arrow Keeper could reciprocate goodness and righteousness for the Cheyenne Nation. His ultimate purpose was to restore balance, however difficult to achieve.

Under the Maahótse Tséá'enövâhtse were the assistants, and these leaders were the ceremonial men of the nation who could take the place of the Tséá'enövâhtse if necessary. Their duties were primarily ceremonial, as they were the only other men who could handle the Medicine Arrows. During the Maahéome, these four assistants were the ones who changed the eagle feathers, buffalo sinew, buffalo blood, and buffalo glue on the four sacred arrows.[25] The position of these assistants was equally demanding and required as much discipline as that of the Tséá'enövâhtse, and they had to be prepared to answer the Arrow Keeper or serve whenever called upon. The four-assistant model is common in most traditional Cheyenne governing structures.

HOXÉHEOME

The Hoxéheome (Medicine Lodge or Sun Dance) is another covenant ceremony that is vibrant and ongoing among the Cheyennes, both the Northern and Southern nations. Wooden Leg explained: "The bodily torture incident to the full standard Great Medicine dance—what the white people call the sun dance—was the most severe test of hardihood, so upon as the highest form of self scourging."[26] The Northern Cheyenne practice the Hoxéheome in accordance with the Só'taeo'o teachings and the sacred laws of the Ésevone (Buffalo Hat). Numerous family members, close friends, fellow society members, and I are active participants in the Hoxéheome. As such, I have limited discussion of this covenant ceremony to prevent unwarranted exposure of these ways. With great care, humility, and respect to the teachings, laws, and customs of my people, I provide this description of this ceremony to reveal how it made the Cheyenne Nation a vibrant and prosperous living-nation. Once again I rely heavily on previously published material, as there is a substantial amount of literature on this covenant ceremony.[27]

The Hoxéheome followed the Maahéome during the later part of the summer, particularly when full-scale buffalo hunts took place. Like the Maahéome, the Hoxéheome was not held every year during the primacy of the nation, the time of the buffalo. Wooden Leg explained:

THE COVENANT CEREMONIES

Bull Thigh, Keeper of Sacred Arrow, in Native Dress with Feather Headdress and Lance Outside Log House, 1910. National Anthropological Archives, Smithsonian Museum Support Center, Suitland, Maryland.

PART I: MA'HEÓNĖSTÓNESTÔTSE: SACRED COVENANTS

Our tribal Great Medicine dance was a ceremony of one, two or three days, the period depending upon immediate conditions. In times before mine the full period had been four days, but in my time three days was the maximum. It was not held at any regular time. Once every two or three years was the usual custom. It would be held, though, in successive years if the tribe was having misfortune or if enough special devotees wanted to under go the trials. The summer season was the special time. The prime purpose was to ask the Great Medicine's favorable attention to the tribe as a whole, not to any particular persons. The prayers were for good grass, new colts in the horse herds, plenty of berries and roots, many children, success in hunting game and in repelling enemies.[28]

During the time of the horse, the Maahéome and Hoxéheome were held consecutively and in the same camp. The philosophy of the Hoxéheome promoted healthy lifestyles of humans and the growth of plant life, and it honored animal life, especially buffalo.[29] The purpose of this lodge was to renew the earth, while practitioners advanced personal medicine and promoted unity and healing. Although the ceremonial and warrior societies organized the ceremony, the whole nation—every man, woman, and child—was involved.[30] The Ésevone is the bundle covenant of the Hoxéheome, which came from the Só'taeo'o prophet named Tomôsévêséhe (Erect Horns).[31] Tomôsévêséhe, who was the successor to Lime, is remembered as the apprentice who became a great medicine man. The origin story of Standing Horns was told by Tall Bull and involves the Só'taeo'o prophet Lime.

Standing Horns, Part I, by Tall Bull

First night: The Sutaiu and the Cheyenne crossed the Mississippi and went east. Lime gave instructions to his brothers and sisters-in-law: "I am going on a long journey. I'll be gone for four days. Then I will be back on the fourth day with my successor. When that day comes you must put up a big lodge in the center." On the fourth day, he came back with Standing Horns. He took him to the center lodge. Where Standing Horns came from nobody knows. The people were starving. There were only Lime and Standing Horns in the lodge. The rest of the people were outside listening. Towards morning when they went out, when they looked about, the air of the world was gone. In a little while the people saw buffalo every place. There was great joy. They killed them all. The next night Lime and Standing Horns were singing again. The people came to hear the songs. They sing the same songs today. Standing Horns sang. Standing Horns came from the buffalo. He had horns. In the morning there were herds of buffalo in every direction. They chased them and killed them. They moved from there, went westward [until] they arrived to the Black Hills.

The people were starving. While they were camped in a circle, towards the opening there was a high elevation of cliffs. There was a spring there. One day he walked to it. He went straight in that spring. As people glanced he came out with a wooden pan filled with buffalo meat; it was all cut fine. He brought it to the people. The people at once came to where he was. He gave them the pieces of meat. As the meat gave out, he shook the bowl and the meat would always multiply. The people were satisfied. Standing Horns went into the spring again and brought up corn to the people. He did that to save the people from starvation. They moved away from the Black Hills southeast; they went near the Mississippi. There they raised corn. They came back westwards to hunt the buffalo in the spring after they had planted corn. They expected to return when the corn was ripe. The Rees came and stole a lot of the corn and went away with it. That is why people think the Rees were the first people to raise corn; but they stole it from the Cheyenne. The Cheyenne went back for their corn. Nearly half of the patches had been taken away.

Second night: Many years afterwards Lime disappeared. He went back to the place he was supposed to have come from. Standing Horns took his place after that to save the people from sickness and starvation. By this time Standing Horns took the lead in all beliefs. It was he that started all the medicine societies which study all kinds of herbs, seeds, berries, and mix medicines. He started all the different songs of the societies. Lime told him before he departed: "I leave these people to you; take good care of them; direct and guide them from harm. If you do not follow my instructions, you shall be judged, and return to your former home." Many years afterwards they were moving towards the west. They came to the Black Hills and lived there for a great many years. When Standing Horns performed his instructions and ceremonies for them, he went on his own responsibility. He disregarded Lime's instructions. He used his own judgment. One day while on a big hill to fast, a great big snowstorm came at him and he disappeared. Four days after he disappeared, the storm of snow cleared away. The people were out in search of him. While searching, they saw a group of buffalo. They seemed to have gathered together. The people came to the group. They found Standing Horns in the center in the midst of the buffalo. He had just come back to life. There was no snow where he was found although the snow [was] three feet high all over the earth. The buffalo melted the snow for him by their warm breath so that he would return to life again. So he came back to the tribe.

Third night: When he came back he told the people: "Early in the spring you will have to raise corn once more. During that summer Lime is going to come back. I will go home with him." They went to the Black Hills again. The very same place where he got the corn. When at this place, Standing Horns got two young girls from the tribe. He taught them to be his successors. After he picked them out, he went with them to the spring. When near there he left these girls sitting there. He went by himself to the spring. He went in. The whole tribe came to see him. He came out with corn and gave it to the girls. When they received the corn, they rose and turned back into the circle. The next morning the camp moved away; they went east of the Black Hills and made a camp at what is now Fast Creek (Running Creek). There they raised corn. They used pointed [sticks] to plant with. They were there one entire season. They moved about [until] the corn was ripe.[32]

Tomôsévêséhe is credited with bringing numerous teachings to the Só'taeo'o; he was their culture hero and had the same spiritual character and powers as Motsé'eóeve of the Tsétsêhéstâhese. The best origin story of Tomôsévêséhe and the Hoxéheome was told by former Sacred Hat Keeper Josie Limpy

PART I: MA'HEÓNÈSTÓNESTÔTSE: SACRED COVENANTS

(Northern Cheyenne), who was a Só'taeo'o medicine woman and my mother's great-auntie. Most narratives of the Sun Dance were collected from men, probably because the ceremony has been perceived as a strictly male-centered ceremony. The Hoxéheome, however, is the symbolic manifestation and continuation of "women's medicine."[33] Josie Limpy's narrative is by far the most poetic and fitting, because she best highlights the Só'taeo'o principle of "woman's power of perpetuation," which is a traditional philosophy of the continuation of the Cheyenne people, the Cheyenne spiritual way of life, and the living-nation. Limpy tells the story as part of the Cheyenne national history. In the story, the young medicine man is Ho'ehêvêsénóóhe (Standing On The Ground) and the chief's wife is named Ésevona'e (Buffalo Woman).

The Great Medicine Dance, by Josie Limpy

Long ago, when the earth and the people dwelling upon it were young, our tribe was starving. The earth itself was starving, for no rain was falling. Plants, trees wilted. Many rivers dried up. The animals were dying of hunger and thirst.

The Cheyenne had nothing to eat except some old, dried corn and their dogs, which used to carry their packs in those days before we had horses. There were not many dogs remaining, and very little corn. So the people left their old hunting grounds, left the land which had nourished them for generations, and started off in search of food. They went north, where the drought was less severe, but found little game and no buffalo at all.

One evening they came to a stream in which water still flowed. The leaders and old chiefs sat down beside this stream and sadly watched the thin, weary people pitching their tipis. Then it came to the chiefs, as in a vision, what ought to be done. They ordered all the men to go to the women, each man to the woman he felt most attracted to, and beg her to give him something to eat. The men did as they had been directed, and each chose the woman who was to feed him.

Among the warriors was a young medicine man. He went up to a beautiful woman who happened to be the wife of the head chief. She set a bowl of dog soup before him and waited for him to finish eating. Then he said: "I have chosen you from among all women to help me save our people. I want you to go north with me, as the medicine spirits have commanded. Take your dog teams and bring supplies for a long journey—now, right away!"

Though she was the chief's wife, the woman did what the medicine man had asked. She was ready to travel in no time, and the two left unobserved in the dark of night. Two days and one night they traveled without stopping, urging on the dogs who carried the travois with the tipi poles and hides and other things needed for survival.

At last they rested. The man told the woman to put up the lodge and to prepare two beds of soft, fragrant sage for them to sleep on. He said: "Make the tipi face the rising sun." He also told her that Maheo, the Creator, had sent him a vision revealing that the two of them must go north and bring back the great medicine lodge, Maheo's symbol of the universe, and with it a scared ceremony which they would teach to the Cheyenne. "In my vision," he said, "Maheo promised that if the people accept and perform his holy ritual, the rains will fall again and the earth rejoice, the plants will bring forth green leaves and fruit, and the buffalo will return."

And so they traveled, the woman every evening pitching the tipi facing east and preparing the beds of sage on opposite sides of the tipi, the man sleeping on his bed, the woman on hers. One night she said: "How is this? You made me run away with you, but you never approach me as man approaches woman. Why did you make me go with you, then?"

He answered: "We must abstain from embracing until we enter the great mountain of the north and receive the sacred medicine dance. After we emerge from the mountain, I shall embrace you in a renewal-of-all-life ceremony by which people will continue to be born, generation after generation, through the woman-power of perpetuation."

As they came to a vast, dark forest from whose center rose a cloud-wreathed mountain reaching far into the sky. Beyond the mountain they saw a lake of unending waters. They came to a large rock at the foot of the mountain, rolled the rock aside, and discovered an entrance. They went inside the mountain and, closing the opening behind them, found themselves in the mountain's great medicine lodge, which was wonderful to behold. Today the medicine tipi which the Cheyenne put up for their sun dances at Bear Butte is an imitation of that scared mountain lodge.

The young man and the woman heard voices coming out of the mountaintop—the voices of Maheo the Creator and his helper Great Roaring Thunder. Instructing them in the holy ways to perform the sacred ceremony, Maheo spoke for four days. When they had learned all there was to know about the dance, the Creator said:

> Now you will leave and teach the people what I have taught you. And if they perform the ceremonies in the right way, they will be favored for generations to come. The sun, the moon, the stars will move again in harmony. Roaring Thunder will bring soothing rain and winds. Corn and chokecherries will ripen again. Wild turnips and healing herbs will grow once more. All the animals will emerge from behind this mountain, herds of buffalo and antelope among them, and follow you back to your village and your people. Take this sacred hat, *issiwun*, and wear it whenever you perform the sun dance. With *issiwun* you will control the animals—the buffalo, the antelope, the elk, the deer—who give themselves to the people for food. The Tsis-tsistas shall never be hungry again, but live in plenty. Put on this sacred buffalo hat as you leave, and Grandmother Earth will smile upon you forever.

And so the young medicine man of the Sutai and the good-looking woman left the mountain through the secret passage. As they rolled the rock aside and emerged, buffalo without numbers streamed out of the mountain behind them, and the earth brought forth green shoots. Herbs and plants sprouted under a gentle rain, and the earth was like new, glistening in freshness. Thus the man and woman walked sacredly, clad in buffalo robes painted red, and the medicine man wore his horned cap. Their dogs walked before them, dragging their travois poles, while behind them flowed a thundering herd of buffalo, and after these came all manner of animals, male and female, big and small.

At the day's end the man and the woman put up their tipi and lay down on their beds of sage to rest, and all the animals settled down to rest also. And at some time during this journey back to their village, the man and the woman did lovingly what was necessary to ensure renewals and continuation of life through woman-power. Each morning during their travels, the man sang the sacred songs which the voice of Maheo had taught him.

At last one evening they arrived near the stream where the people were still camped, awaiting their return. The medicine man and the woman did not go into the village at once, but spent the night outside. In the morning the medicine man put on *issiwun* and entered the camp, accompanied by the woman. He told the people of all that had passed, told them that he had brought them the knowledge of the great medicine lodge and the great sacred dance, the songs and ceremonies that went with it, and above all, *issiwun*, the sacred buffalo hat which had the power to control the wandering of the animals. He told the people that if they performed the sacred sun dance, they would have plenty of buffalo to eat and would never suffer hunger again.

The people put up the medicine lodge according to the young man's instructions, painted their bodies in a sacred manner, and sang the right songs. The children made clay figures of buffalo, antelopes, and elk and brought them into the lodge as a symbol of life's renewal. Since then, whenever the little figures are placed inside the Medicine lodge during the dance, some of those animals will come near to gaze upon the sacred tipi, and some of their animal power will linger on. In the same way, our old friends, the Sioux people, fasten the figures of a man and a bison, both cut from buffalo hide, to their sacred sun dance pole. Then an eagle will come in and circle above the dancers to bless them.

Thus the Tsis-tsistas people performed the great medicine ceremony for the first time, and all was well again. And the people named the young medicine man Horns Standing Up, because the sacred hat has two horns on each side.[34]

When the people saw Hoʻehêvêsénóóhe, they called him Tomôsévêséhe (Erect Horns) and the name remained as part of Cheyenne national history.[35] The mountain is identified as Black Mountain and is shaped like a large buffalo drinking out of the lake. Nonómaʻe (Roaring Thunder) is known as the chief of the wind, clouds, rain, hail, and the beautiful rainbow. During their visit, Ésevonaʻe was also taught various women's ceremonies, including the girl's puberty ceremony and the wedding ceremony. Hoʻehêvêsénóóhe was taught the four sacred laws of nature: (1) kill animals or pick plants for survival and ceremonial practices, (2) kill or harvest no more than needed, (3) when killing an animal or taking a plant, do so in prayer, with respect, and not for fun or entertainment, and (4) sacrifice your bodies and pay homage to nature every year in the Hoxéheome. If the Cheyennes followed these instructions, they would remain healthy and never know suffering anymore. After returning and performing the first Sun Dance, Tomôsévêséhe and Ésevonaʻe had a sacred child.

The Hoxéheome represented the cyclical nature of life, procreation, and earthly renewal, while the Ésevone represented the sanctity of the four sacred laws of nature. The Ésevone (Sacred Buffalo Hat) and its teachings embodied the knowledge, teachings, and spiritual energy of the Sun Dance, which is also known as New Life Giving Lodge. The Cheyennes remember the sickness of the earth and famine but also know their role in maintaining balance through ceremony. This lodge is the epitome of Cheyenne sovereignty and nationhood.

After the Great Unification, the origin story of the Ésevone and the Hoxéheome was adapted to include the Tsétsêhéstâhese in a version of Old Woman's Spring. In the unified version, the Tsétsêhéstaestse prophet Motséeóeve and the Só'taa'e prophet Tomôsévêséhe discovered one day, while the people were playing a wheel and spear game, that they were dressed and painted alike. The two prophets questioned each other and found themselves telling the same story of the origin of their attire. Together they went behind a waterfall to a holy mountain to find answers to their questions. They entered the holy mountain together.[36] Inside the mountain, the old woman, also known only as Ke'éehe (Grandmother), fed them two sacred foods: corn and buffalo. She had given the boys the same clothing and paint much earlier, and this was her plan for them to find their way back to her lodge. The two young men knew nothing of buffalo but were instructed to follow a number of spiritual teachings. Ke'éehe gave Tomôsévêséhe the Ésevone and told the two boys to return to their people, to hunt the buffalo, and to honor them in the Hoxéheome. This version is another example of the unification of two oral traditions, philosophies, and spiritual practices.

ÉSEVONE TSÉÁ'ENÖVÂHTSE

Ésevone had been passed down for numerous generations and survived the destructive wars with the whites. Like the Arrow Keeper, the Ésevone Tséá'enövâhtse (Sacred Buffalo Hat Keeper) was selected based on his character and discipline as a spiritual leader. Sacred laws ordained by Tomôsévêséhe required the Ésevone Tséá'enövâhtse to be of good stature and live a healthy lifestyle. His wife was the only one who could carry the bundle on her back when moving it to different places.[37] Unlike the Maahótse, however, the Ésevone was traditionally the responsibility of the keeper's entire family, which is why good families were chosen to be caretakers of the bundle.

The Tséá'enövâhtse lived a life of solitude and prayer and made daily sacrifices for the well-being of the Cheyenne people. He rarely made public appearances but did not draw attention to himself when he was out and about. In the words of Stands In Timber: "The Keeper was supposed to be good-natured and honest and not get mad too easily."[38] Like the Arrow Keeper's position, the Hat Keeper's position was spiritually demanding, but his responsibilities also extended into the political realm since the Véhoo'o could call upon the keeper for advice. Stands In Timber continued: "The Keeper used to pray all the time, as if he were talking to somebody. He was talking to the spirit; it was right there, they claim. It was supposed to be this that kept the tribe clean, away from bad things."[39]

THE MEDICINE LODGE

The Hoxéheome honored life in its entirety, paying homage, in particular, to the female form and the importance of the feminine in nature.[40] The ceremony honored life and reproduction of all living things, especially the survival of the Cheyenne people.[41] Women are an important part of the Hoxéheome since they are required to be directly involved and even participate in the fasting and challenges of endurance along with men. One man and one woman pledge, or sponsor, the four-day ceremony. The custom was that the two pledgers should be a long-time married and healthy couple, as explained by a Southern Cheyenne woman: "One day when we were alone he pledged a Sacrifice Offering. This ceremony is a sacred ritual that is regarded as a prayer to the spirits for strength and health. When he made the pledge this included me, for the rule requires that a wife must be included."[42]

Sometimes as many as four sets of pledgers would sponsor the ceremony together. The entire ceremony involved numerous rituals; here I provide a brief description.[43] Experienced ceremonial leaders, who have already completed their "Sun Dance vows," organized the ceremony along with the warrior societies and the chiefs. The entire process reawakened the Cheyenne spirit of strength and endurance through deliberate and controlled infliction of pain and suffering. The ceremony was a trial of physical, mental, emotional, and spiritual power for individuals and for the nation as a whole. Other participants, primarily young men, requested assistance from their personal spiritual leader, typically an older family member who belonged to a ceremonial society or guild.[44] Each participant was instructed and mentored in the ways of good conduct and sacrifice, for he or she would eventually earn the same position as a "painter" upon completion of his or her vows.

Once the people came together in the big camp and all the dancers were ready, the spiritual leaders selected experienced priests who helped facilitate the ceremony. They, along with the pledger, ceremonially smoked and performed rituals to formally begin the big ceremony. They erected the "lone tepee," which represented the sacred mountain of the Só'taa'eo'o, Black Mountain. Inside, spiritual leaders and the Tséá'enövâhtse prepared for the upcoming Hoxéheome. One warrior was selected to hunt and kill a jackrabbit with a stick so that its skin could be used for the ceremony. This animal represented the very ancient time when the Cheyennes primarily ate rabbits in the first world. Different animal skins and parts of birds and animals (sinew, eagle feathers, deer and buffalo hides) were examined and prepared for the ceremony. The main item was the buffalo skull, which was filled with grass.

The pledgers were instructed on the teachings of the Só'taa'e prophet and his wife; they were to take on the spirits of these people to ensure the survival of the nation. Meanwhile, individuals were with their families and instructors, making preparations to enter the big lodge. Individuals were preparing their eagle bone whistles and other paraphernalia and regalia, while their instructors prepared earth powdered paints. The dancers' families, especially their wives, were equally responsible during the ceremony, since they prepared the food, managed the camp, and exchanged gifts. During this ceremony, the entire camp was filled with much happiness and sharing.[45]

The ceremonial leaders constructed the big lodge. The first task was to find and erect the center pole, which was a two-pronged fork. A priest rebuilt the "thunder's nest," which comprised offerings from the people, tied together, and placed in the center pole between the two prongs. The chiefs were responsible for the center pole, while other societies were assigned to construct rafters and side posts. Upon completion of the lodge, the high priests blessed it with offerings and prayers to begin the big ceremony. The dance portion encompassed numerous smaller ceremonies and rituals associated with giving and sacrifice. Instructors followed the wishes from the primary spiritual leaders but also maintained their roles as the principal sponsors and representatives of their disciples and respective ceremonial societies.

Individual dancers danced in one place, supported and guided by their instructors, who were stationed behind them. The priests then built an altar made of fresh sod, arched sticks, and branches from plants, which represented the new earth. The dancers continued almost nonstop for four days without food or water. At different intervals, the dancing stopped and the lodge closed so the singers and dancers could rest and they could be washed and repainted. The entire affair was public, as onlookers (men, women, children, elders) could view their family members and fellow tribesmen in unity. The Hoxéheome uplifted the spirit of the entire nation as the dancers and priests renewed the earth. As it concluded, pledgers, priests, painters, and dancers also closed with rituals, feasts, and gift-giving ceremonies to celebrate the newly created earth.

After the Great Unification, several elements were added to the Hoxéheome that were of Tsétsêhéstâhese and related to the Maahótse. These elements dealt with war with enemy nations. Warriors would voluntarily undergo self-torture through piercing their chests with two skewers above each breast. These were then tied to the center pole from which the dancer would tear loose after a day and night of dancing. Sometimes a dancer would attach skewers to his back and drag buffalo skulls about the lodge until the flesh broke loose.[46] Such practices became popular forms of self-sacrifice and made for strong and daring warriors against enemy nations and invading whites in later years. Five scalps of enemy nations (Crow, Ute, Shoshoni, Pawnee, and Blackfeet) were also added and placed into the Ésevone and became part of Hoxéheome.⁴⁷ Although the ceremony served a function of war, it was primarily one of earthly renewal and national unity.⁴⁸

MÅSĖHÁOME

The fourth major ceremony was the Måsėháome (Crazy Lodge), also known as the Animal Lodge, Buffalo Lodge, or Crazy/Foolish Dance.⁴⁹ My great-grandmother, Hattie Killsback, was a medicine woman who participated in the last Måsėháome of the Northern Cheyenne. As before, I approach telling of the Måsėháome with great humility and sincerity, especially since the covenant ceremony has long vanished as an annual practice. According to Cheyenne oral tradition, the Animal Lodge was established when the Tsétsêhéstâhese transitioned from being primarily corn planters to relying on dogs to travel. The origin of this ceremony began long before the Great Unification, when either the Tsétsêhéstâhese or the Só'taeo'o came to the Great Plains from the land of the lakes and knew little of hunting big game, especially buffalo. The origin of the Måsėháome is part of the Cheyenne history, and versions of the origin story have already been published.⁵⁰

The story begins, like most origin stories, with the people living in poor conditions. They were starving and the leaders asked for the two fastest runners to travel into the wilderness to search for food. The runners ran in opposite directions, and after four days they returned to report that there was nothing out there. The leaders did this two more times, and on the fourth time two prominent leaders sent their own sons. With heavy hearts, the leaders instructed that the boys not return until they find something to help their people. Unlike before, these two went together in one direction, north. One was named Hawk Feather and the other, Little Bird.⁵¹ They traveled to a large lake and experienced something great. Wrapped Hair told his version as a Só'taeo'o story.

Everybody Was Starving, by Wrapped Hair

Several young men were looking for buffalo. None were to be found. They all returned empty handed. Then two young men started out again. They were out for 2 days and went to a river. They sat on the riverbank. One was afraid to cross and one wanted to cross. The one who wanted to go across said he would lead the way and the other to follow. Finally, he started to wade, the afraid one held back all the time and when the leader was across he [the scared one] was in the middle of the river. The one in the middle of the river claimed that some beast of the alligator type had got him fast and [he] wanted his friend to come back and shake hands for the last time. While shaking hands, they saw a man dressed in a wolf's hide in the middle of the creek with a knife in his hand. This fellow jumped into the river when he saw what was the matter. He dove in the water and cut the beast's head off. He was glad and called him grandchild. He was glad to have the chance to kill this beast as it had been his intention for some time to kill this beast. This fellow pulled the beast out on the land and cut him in several pieces. He doctored the fellow that was bit and asked the two young fellows where they were going. They told the man that everybody was starving and they were hunting for buffalo. The old man after hearing this told them to go to a certain hill, remove a flat rock and to go in and see their grandmother. And ask her to let you have the dogs. The old man also told them to notify their grandmother that he had killed the beast he had been so anxious to dispatch for some time.

When the young men got the dogs, they took them to the old man. The old man packed the beast on them and in this way took the beast to where he lived. After this, the old woman had a daughter that had red hair, and told her to go with these boys and to take pity on the people over there that were starving. [She said] that there would be a bunch of buffalo to follow her that night which they could kill the next morning, and that this girl must own these buffalo; they had come out of the same hill in which she lived; and that her father had told her not to be sorry for her pets even if they were killed the next day, and that if they did they [the animals] would disappear. The next day when everyone was chasing the buffalo someone had wounded a calf, and it ran by the place she was staying, and she saw it dripping with blood from its nose and mouth and from its wound. She forgot what her father told her, and made the remark "my poor calf, poor thing." And by saying that she had broken her word, the buffalo all disappeared.[52]

The Mȧsėháome is a reenactment of this story. The old man was named Coyote Man, and he performed a healing ceremony, which is part of the Mȧsėháome. After a day, the boy was miraculously healed. Soon all was well and they ate a fine meal, courtesy of the slain animal, which is remembered as a giant water snake or dragon. When the two young men entered the cave and met the daughter, Coyote Man asked which one was to marry her. The older of the two boys recommended that his younger friend marry the beautiful woman, upholding the Cheyenne principle of brotherhood. The young woman was Heovėstaée (Yellow Top-to-Head Woman) and is credited with bringing this ceremony to the nation, among other teachings.[53] The four sacred laws associated with the Mȧsėháome are (1) uphold the principle of hévesėonematsestôtse (brotherhood); (2) honor the animals that provide nourishment for humans; (3) do not cry for animals because they are sacred and to do so will cause them to leave; and (4) hold the Mȧsėháome to frequently reinforce these laws.

In the Só'taeo'o oral tradition, the older of the two young men in the story is identified as the culture hero Lime, while the younger is identified as Ho'ehêvêsénóóhe (Standing On The Ground) before he became Tomôsévêséhe (Erect Horns). After the Great Unification the Mȧsėháome remained intact as a reenactment of the story and to reinforce the sacred teachings from Heovėstaée, Coyote Man, and the grandmother, Ke'éehe. The origin story however, changed

PART I: MA'HEÓNÈSTÓNESTÔTSE: SACRED COVENANTS

and adapted to fit the oral traditions of both the Tsétsêhéstâhese and the Só'taeo'o by identifying the two culture heroes, Motsé'eóeve and Tomôsévêséhe respectively, as the two young men who brought the ceremony.[54]

The Mâsêháome has also been identified as Tsétsêhéstâhese in origin, since Schlesier asserted that this lodge comprised the oldest philosophies of the Cheyenne culture, dating back as far as 500 BC, and is reminiscent of when the people lived as mound builders in the first world, "the very ancient time."[55] But similar elements of the Antelope Pit and Voestaehneva'e also reveal that the Mâsêháome is actually of Só'taa'e origin. What is known for certain is that no other ceremony of this kind ever existed among other nations on the Great Plains, and the converged oral tradition spiritually united the Só'taeo'o and the Tsétsêhéstâhese.

The laws associated with the Mâsêháome related to balance in nature, the supernatural, and action. The old ways of this lodge were kept under strict guard as the keepers belonged first and foremost to certain families, with the men and women of the family retaining high statuses as priests and priestesses. Ceremonial teachings were inherited primarily through the female members of the family, but the men were the primary facilitators of the actual ceremony, as dictated by the tradition of Heovéstá'e'e. The lodge had no formally elected leaders, and members came directly from families and those who married into the ceremonial societies. Principal leaders of the Mâsêháome did not have political authority in any other matters. The responsibilities of priests were limited to the ceremony and individual doctoring. But as with all major ceremonies, the leaders of the Mâsêháome held the highest of ceremonial authority for the two weeks of ceremony: four days to prepare, four days to perform, and four days to close the ceremony.

The covenant bundle of the Mâsêháome contained the horns from a hermaphrodite buffalo, said to be one of the first to have come into existence.[56] Spiritual leaders of this lodge followed sacred laws that honored the delicate balance between man and nature, life and death.[57] During the Mâsêháome several inactive ceremonial societies came alive to organize and execute the ritual. The ceremonial societies included the Hohnóhka or Contrary Society, the Grey Wolf Lodge, and the Grass Buffalo. Female members made up the Young Wolf Society, the first women's society of the nation. Each consisted of practitioners, male and female, who were responsible for the proper practice of the entire ceremony and whose status rose at no other time. The Mâsêháome itself had several purposes, including reenacting the creation of the world and all of the life-giving plants and animals, especially honoring the deer, buffalo, and wolves. Another function was to maintain balance, as participants acted "crazy," doing things in the opposite, and thus reminding citizens of proper behavior and the importance of respecting the unfavorable human traits through humor.[58] This ceremony was unique from others in that men and women societies shared central roles.

Two primary leaders directed the lodge; the first was a male who represented a red wolf called Ma'heónehó'nehe (Sacred Wolf) and the second was a female who represented a white wolf called Eveveseevehó'nehe (Horned Wolf).[59] Both positions were significant to the lodge, which valued life in balance, male and female, and the perpetuation of existence through procreation. Despite limitations in political leadership, the male spiritual leader of the lodge, likely the Sacred Wolf, commanded respect and was often feared in the community, even though he could never hold a seat at the Chiefs' Council. His responsibility was for the ceremony and he was never to involve himself in political affairs. During ceremony, however, he became the prime ceremonial adviser and organizer until completion of the Måséháome. When finished, the person in the position of the Sacred Wolf reverted to his medicinal and spiritual duties until the following year. No ceremonial leader was to ever maintain supremacy for all eternity. Ceremonial responsibilities, as with political, were shared among worthy individuals to maintain balance.

Before the arrival of horses, the Måséháome was traditionally held every two years, alternating with the Maahéome, after the summer solstice and always after the Hoxéheome. The ceremonial ground was at the center of the camp and featured a double tepee lodge and several other lodges. The ceremony itself included numerous rituals and dances. The sick and elderly were invited to receive medical attention and spiritual blessings, since the participants, who were already medicine people, gained higher spiritual powers during the ceremony. Ceremonial leaders doctored sick patients, but the primary purpose of the ceremony was to provide healing and restore balance to the entire nation and its citizens, while honoring the supernatural: from the smallest to the largest plants and animals. Ceremonial food consisted of dog meat (ceremonial flesh), corn and chokecherries (plants from above ground), turnips and root teas (plants from underground), and red currents and raspberries (plants found on the ground).[60] The first meat used was that of the slain méhne, a giant water serpent or dragon, but the Cheyennes adopted dog flesh (sometimes wolf, coyote, bobcat, or porcupine) as a sacrament with this ceremony because of the close spiritual relationship between humans and domesticated dogs.[61] The Måséháome was a very accurate reenactment of the story of the two young men who met Coyote Man, which held central principles of the Cheyenne worldview.

The most popular events were the displays of theater, athleticism, and remarkable feats of physical strength.[62] Under the direction of the Wolf priests and the women's Young Wolf Society, all participants reenacted the story of the nation. All participants dressed and painted themselves ceremonially.[63] Women and young girls dressed in grass hats and attire. Belle Highwalking (Northern Cheyenne) witnessed part of the four-day ceremony, the Buffalo Dance:

> The Buffalo Dance Tipi was set up in the middle of the camp circle, and four special tipis were placed in different parts of the circle. Men were painted to look like

PART I: MA'HEÓNĖSTÓNESTÔTSE: SACRED COVENANTS

Buffalo Dancers—Annual Dance—Cheyenne. Nov. 16, 1927, Edward S. Curtis, 1868–1952, National Anthropological Archives, Smithsonian Museum Support Center, Suitland, Maryland.

animals, such as the deer, buffalo, and magpie. I can't remember all the animals but I do remember those. Each different animal was painted according to the animal's color so that deer were painted yellow. Those imitating buffalo had buffalo hides over their heads and were painted red and looked like gods. Many little girls followed after them and were supposed to be the buffalo calves.[64]

Warriors wore hats of buffalo fur with horns or the skins of wolves so as to emulate the animals, and some participants dressed up as deer and elk with antlers, some real and some made of branches. The Hohnóhka participated and appeared in awkward paints and "backwards" clothing, meaning they wore clothes inside out, upside down, backward, or sometimes with their top and bottom garments reversed. These sacred clowns represented everything that was backwards, while they displayed their acrobatic talents by jumping high into the air and flipping onto the ground. They did this several times while holding small bows and arrows, which they tried to shoot in reverse. Other participants dressed as coyotes, foxes, mountain lions, bears, otters, and antelope joined and retreated in an organized ceremonial fashion. Their purpose was to first make a ceremonial trek around the grounds and enter into the center where they would be hunted and symbolically killed. The entire affair was a manifestation of all life on the plains, and they all danced and moved around in response and reaction to the sacred women. Once an animal was hit, the participant spit blood from his or her mouth and symbolically died.

One of the dances included the boiling of dog soup, which was held in a hide and in later days in a large kettle. The Hohnóhka used their hands to retrieve pieces of meat, without injury, and gave it to onlookers as sacrament. Belle Highwalking witnessed:

> When the ceremony started, someone pounded on a drum and the dancers scattered around and acted scared. They hid way off, some of them under small sage bushes with no shade. After the drum stopped, the dancers came back and lay in the shade with their feet up on the tipi and their heads on the ground. When they finished this, they went into the tipi and finished what was to be done in there. Then they came out and danced outside while someone inside sang for them. The dancers danced around the pot in which the dog was cooking, and then they lifted the arms of the person putting on the ceremony. They did this four times, after which they stirred the boiling dog soup with their bare arms. In this ceremony a special plant was picked and used. The people watching the ceremony wore white sheets and sat in the four directions. They placed something on the ground in front of them that they could throw at the dancers if they got scared. Everyone wanted a piece of dog meat which is believed to bring good luck. A feast is had of this meat, and then the dancers race to the creek to bathe and cleanse themselves. This is how the medicine ceremony was held. Both men and women who wanted to be cured of their fear of lightning danced in this ceremony. [According to Cheyenne custom, a person who fears lightning will likely be struck by it. Those who do not overcome their fear of lightning are likely to become Contraries.] The Contraries do everything the opposite of what is natural. They say that what is good is bad and what is bad is good.[65]

PART I: MA'HEÓNÈSTÓNESTÔTSE: SACRED COVENANTS

The Måséháome became nearly extinct during the early reservation era, but it survived as a sister ceremony to the Sun Dance until the last Måséháome in the 1950s. The old Só'taeo'o were aware of the looming colonial forces that targeted their ceremonial ways, and their awareness is present in their oral tradition. As with the apocalyptic prophecies of the Tsétsêhéstaestse culture hero Motsé'eóeve, the Só'taeo'o culture hero Tomôsévêséhe (Erect Horns) foretold the coming of the white man and his destructive ways. Tall Bull completed the story of the prophet who brought the Måséháome, among other powerful and wondrous things.

Standing Horns, Part II, by Tall Bull

Fourth night: Many years after, Standing Horns went away. People expected him to return, but he disappeared forever. Just before he disappeared he foretold to his people what was going to happen in the far future. "The day will come when a man will be seen. He will be hairy all over. He shall be called White Man. These buffalo you see around will live with you as long as the sun endures. But this person will wipe them out. Then there will be an animal from the south with a long mane, long tail, four legs, two eyes, for your use, and the dogs will die. You can use this [new] animal to carry you on its back; you can travel as far as you can see. And when these shall come in due time, then will be the time when your ways, these instructions I have given you, shall be gone and wiped away from you by the white man. He will come from the east to drive all the animals away to the west." Then he was gone.[66]

CHAPTER 4

Ma'heónetanohtôtse: The Sacred Way of Thinking

To "make medicine" is to engage upon a special period of fasting, thanksgiving, prayer and self denial, even of self torture. The procedure is entirely a devotional exercise. The purpose is to subdue the passion of the flesh and to improve the spiritual self. The bodily abstinence and the mental concentration upon lofty thoughts cleanses both the body and the soul and puts them into or keeps them in health. Then the individual mind gets closer toward conformity with the mind of the Great Medicine above us.

—Wooden Leg (Northern Cheyenne), headman of the Elk Horn Society[1]

The major covenant ceremonies reaffirm the sacred sovereignty of the Cheyenne Nation by reinvigorating spirituality and the responsibilities to maintain balance with nature, the cosmos, and among fellow humans. Not every citizen desired or sought to participate in a covenant ceremony, nor belong to a ceremonial guild, but all citizens benefited, either directly or indirectly, from the ceremonial institutions and practices. In the time of the buffalo, not one lodge or ceremonial event was of greater significance than others, as all were essential to the continuance of the sacred nation. The ceremonial organization shows that the Cheyenne people were not obsessed with power and authority, but they trusted leaders and one another to accomplish sacred tasks. Citizens and their families, one way or another, worked in harmony to ensure the perpetuation of a unique and sacred Cheyenne way of living; this is the definition of sacred citizenship.

Even with the introduction of the horse, the Cheyennes continued to maintain their old traditions and even added new ones. The most notable was the Horse Worship Ceremony, which honored the horse as a sacred animal. Even though the Spanish-bred mustangs originated from the brutes that ravaged the Indigenous peoples of the south, they became part of the spiritual realm of the Cheyenne Nation.[2] The Horse Worship, however, never became routine in the

PART I: MA'HEÓNÈSTÓNESTÔTSE: SACRED COVENANTS

Cheyenne culture to the extent it did in the Lakota culture. Nonetheless, it is evidence of the adaptive and inclusive nature of Cheyenne spirituality and citizens; they follow a body of laws, or principles. These principles allowed for the inclusion and unification of spiritual practices from other nations but also allowed for the abandonment of others.

With the end of the corn-planting ways, so declined the ceremonial practices related to farming. This does not mean that the loss of such ways was tragic or done in despair; it reveals that the nation was able to adapt itself in relation to the environment. The ceremonial organizational structure of the nation did not completely abandon some of these ancient ways either. The new "buffalo culture" of the Cheyenne Nation was able to retain old covenants, oral traditions, and spiritual beliefs that may not have necessarily been appropriate for the Great Plains. These adaptive and inclusive mechanisms would secure the survival of the Cheyenne Nation until the reservation era, when such mechanisms and the ceremonial practices were targeted for destruction.

In the spiritual realm, the ceremonial leaders had the burden of carrying the old ways and philosophies in their generation. They did not, however, have the duty to ensure that the next generation learned and lived by these ancient teachings, because this responsibility belonged to the parents, other family members, and individual ceremonial instructors. This system was directly challenged when the US government adopted assimilation policies and strategically broke down the Cheyenne family and inevitably the ceremonial structures. Traditionally, not all citizens were destined to become ceremonial leaders, but individual involvement in ceremony created a culture that inevitably saved ceremonial practices from assimilation policies. Even if the top ceremonial leaders were killed or forced to assimilate or resign, the Cheyenne traditions would have continued because the apprentices, aided by the oral tradition, would have remained. As history has proven, those who completed any of the major ceremonies or any number of smaller ones kept the ways alive. Part of the ceremonial process was for an individual to test and improve himself or herself mentally, physically, emotionally, and, above all, spiritually. This practice continued, especially when the US government imposed bans on the larger communal and covenant ceremonies. These "ceremonial tests" were fundamental to traditional Cheyenne National citizenship.

Through ceremonial practices, individuals gain an understanding of their significance as members of a family, men and women in the community, citizens within the sacred nation, humans on earth, and spiritual beings of the universe. In short, they learn how to be a sacred citizen of the sacred nation. The citizen is the building block of a sacred nation; with strong citizens, the nation is strong, and without, the nation would collapse. I have identified ten major principles of spirituality that Cheyennes were to discover upon completion of their sacrifice in ceremony. These principles also reflect the covenants that the nation upholds to remain in balance with the supernatural powers. There are numerous other spiritual teachings in the Cheyenne spiritual way of life, so these principles reflect only the major traditions and those that can be openly discussed. I have been careful not to reveal those teachings that should remain private, as I am also a citizen and am dedicated to the protection and preservation of the traditional Cheyenne way of life.

These spiritual ways are difficult to express in any language and easier to understand within the cultural context of the indigenous reality of the Cheyenne worldview. The principles I provide in this chapter are rooted in what is known as the ma'heónetanohtôtse (sacred way of thinking) or the Tséhéema'heónetanohtôtse (Cheyenne sacred way of thinking).[3] This way of thinking allowed for the previous leaders and prophets to bring the nation out of hardship, for example, by traversing the different worlds, or to improve the life of the people by attaining spiritual knowledge and wisdom. Within the cultural and spiritual reality, the presence of these principles is accepted, assumed, and respected, yet rarely spoken of in intellectual or academic contexts.

THE TEN PRINCIPLES OF THE TSÉHÉEMA'HEÓNETANOHTÔTSE

1. Hardship, pain, and suffering are unavoidable to any person, regardless of his or her status, possessions, physique, mental capabilities, age, experience, and place in society.

As humans, we are all part of the earth and the universe, and therefore we are subject to its laws of happiness, joy, and health, as well as pain and suffering. These laws are not to be internally ignored or suppressed by individuals; they are also not to be left unchecked or unhealed. A nation is defined by how its citizens cope with collective pain and suffering; a citizen is defined by how he or she responds and reacts to his or her own pain and suffering. The spirituality of the Cheyenne way guides people to seek out the appropriate corrective measures to life's challenges. The Cheyenne way is not the solution but one of many instruction manuals to repairing the human soul. Spiritual leaders are not healers but are coaches and teachers to help one improve his or her life.

2. Healing requires attention from the healer, the patient, the patient's family, and the supernatural powers.

Wooden Leg recalled one class of spiritual leaders who practiced a formal form of medicine: "[Red Bear] was a wise medicine man for sick people. Many of our doctors in the old times made wonderful cures."[4] Red Bear cured temporary blindness using ritual with general physical treatments. Spiritual leaders may have had expertise in only one area of healing, but some would gain proficiency in several. Although medicine men and spiritual leaders can heal most injuries, they cannot heal them all. They sometimes need the help and sacrifice of others and rely on the supernatural powers to obtain their blessings. There are four categories of ailments or areas of pain that spiritual leaders can target in a person: physical, emotional, mental, and spiritual. Each area can affect the other, which is why healing has to be holistic. After suffering physical hardship, a person must choose to heal to improve himself or herself from the remaining emotional, mental, and/or spiritual suffering. Nobody else can make this choice. A patient must consult with an elder, a spiritual leader, or someone else who is able to help ease the pain. But inevitably a patient must endure the healing process to improve his or her life and restore balance. This conscious decision should become a daily goal to improve one's life.

3. Suffering can either destroy or strengthen a person's life.

If a person cannot face his or her pain, then the suffering will continue to slowly destroy that person's will to live. Soon the person will become unpleasant to be around, as his or her life will be dominated by anxiety, drama, anger, and sadness. Should a person endure the hardships of suffering, he or she will likely gain the spiritual strength and knowledge to become a higher being of earth and, more important, a trusted spiritual adviser in the community. The person becomes "sacred" because he or she was able to survive and endure the challenges of life. Other Cheyennes see these people as worthy and legitimate possessors of wisdom and often talk about such people using phrases like, "she lived a hard life" or "he has seen hardship." But this spiritual enlightenment is not a goal for citizens to reach, and it often happens without choice and as a result of unforeseen circumstances of despair and depression. Most who endure this natural process of spiritual enlightenment become practicing spiritual leaders in their own right, with their own medicine, and maintain authority and responsibility among their own families. Other community members, who may seek them out for assistance when enduring similar challenges of pain and suffering, recognize them for their veracity and humility. If such a spiritually enlightened person is also involved in the ceremonial realm and participates in any of the big ceremonies, then he or she may earn a reputation as a medicine man or woman. That person is respected, feared, and held in the highest regard as a keeper of sacred knowledge and wisdom.[5] This life is not for just any person and requires much discipline, integrity, and responsibility.

4. Sacrifice in ceremony can strengthen a person's life.

The ceremonial practices provide a controlled and ritualistic forum for citizens to deliberately place themselves into situations of physical, emotional, mental, and spiritual discomfort and pain. These environments allow for practitioners to overcome their fears and insecurities, similar to the natural or unforeseen incidents of life discussed previously. A citizen can reach a degree of spiritual enlightenment through ceremony. The spiritual teachings embedded in the ceremonial practices allow for citizens to gain the strength and wisdom necessary to endure any future unforeseen and unexpected hardship, pain, and suffering. Upon completion of the ceremony they become physically strong, able to endure hunger, injury, and sickness; emotionally resilient, able to securely endure loss of loved ones; mentally proficient, able to remain clear-minded and reasonable when making tough decisions; and spiritually competent, observant of the unseen powers of the universe, possessing internal patience and presence of heart and mind. The ceremonial path to enlightenment facilitates growth and increases the odds of physical, emotional, mental, and spiritual maturation. Merely completing ceremony does not guarantee a practitioner's growth. This is why Cheyenne law allows for all citizens who are of blood to participate in ceremonies and demands that each participant complete a set number of sacrifices, thus increasing the chances that a person can gain a higher state of being.

5. Death is unavoidable; it must be embraced as a part of life.

Traditional Cheyennes were not obsessed with death, but they were also not infatuated with the illusions created by want and desire. All living things eventually meet their demise, whether an insect, a fern in the forest, or an animal on the prairie. Humans are also bound by this fact of life and therefore they should not try to avoid or defeat the inevitable; doing so would only create imbalance or internal discomfort. By accepting and embracing death through prayer and grief, humans also acknowledge the beauty and miracle of life and that they live it to the fullest, even amidst its challenges. Like living things, nonliving and abstract things will also meet their demise, whether a tool or object, the feeling of joy, or the feeling of misery. Spiritual leaders are keenly aware of the life and death of the unseen elements in the world and universe in their practices. They cannot create such things, but they help them come into existence; they cannot kill such things, only help them diminish. Just because a person embraces death and has no fear, it does not mean that the person is suicidal or selfish. Suicide is not an act of embracing death; it is perceived as the denial of life. Embracing death enriches life because it makes a person selfless and releases a person's petty burdens, allowing him or her to be grateful for the Cheyenne essence of life.

6. Unkind and inhumane acts will reciprocate in spirit and in fact.

The world and universe are controlled not by human power but by the unseen spiritual forces of nature and energy. These forces and energy will be transferred on destined paths; nothing can stop them from moving between living beings and lifeless objects or between one another and vice versa. Should a person generate negativity from within his or her own pain and suffering and release it into his or her locality, then the people and objects in proximity can become

PART I: MA'HEÓNĖSTÓNESTÔTSE: SACRED COVENANTS

negatively charged and thus create a cycle of discomfort or imbalance. If a spiritual leader should unwillingly or purposefully release negative energy into the universe, whether directed at a person, family, or the nation, then sooner or later the negative energy will return to his or her lodge, inflicting the same pain or curse on the person, members of his or her immediate family, or his or her descendants in the next generation or two. Citizens who commit violent acts and abuse their own spouses, families, and community have already endured the pain and suffering introduced earlier by an elder family member or ancestor. All citizens are bound by this karma, but those who are of spiritual rank and status (i.e., those who completed the big ceremonies) and who are unkind or inhumane have the potential to contaminate the lives of larger populations of people and future generations. The difficult task is to strive for balance.

7. Thoughts are just as important and powerful as are words and actions.

A person has control of only his or her own thoughts, words, and actions, not those of others. As children we learn from adults to control our actions by following directions. As we mature, we learn to guide our actions for personal purposes but also learn to cooperate to achieve unity for collective success. Our actions can become sacred when we participate in ceremonies, but they can also cause imbalance. A person is responsible for his or her own actions, and the people can force a person to be held accountable for his or her disapproving acts. As with action, we learn to talk and are also taught to control our words by learning the proper pronunciation of words, but most importantly the etiquette of speech. As we mature into adults, we gain the necessary knowledge of when and where to talk, how and with whom to converse, and what to say. These words can be sacred with prayer and in ceremony. As with action, a person is responsible for his or her own words. A person must be careful of what is said, how and with whom he or she converses, and when and where to speak. The people (families and the community) can hold a person responsible and accountable for telling lies, speaking out of place, or speaking disrespectfully or with anger and hostility. Should a person become a liar or an unpleasant person to be around, then he or she could lose status and respect or be labeled unreasonable and simply be ignored.

As with action and words, we are all taught to think in a particular manner by parents, grandparents, and other members of the community through language, storytelling, and other forms of teaching. Children learn how culture heroes thought as a story unfolds and young adults learn how elders think by following directions. Neither the family unit nor the people of the nation, however, can govern the thoughts of individuals. An individual may not necessarily control every thought that crosses his or her mind, but he or she must determine for himself or herself which thoughts to pursue and which to ignore. This is a choice. This consciousness is a fundamental element to the "sacred way of thinking." Citizens must become conscious of their thoughts, good and bad, and build a relationship with thinking that promotes the transfer of positive energy. A spiritual leader endeavors to align his or her actions and words with his or her thoughts to remain in harmony. Some of the most spiritual people have little to no need of action, words, or thoughts, especially those who have reached the summits of spiritual enlightenment. Laura Rockroads (Northern Cheyenne) explains the power of thought:

> I believe in that sacred way of thinking, I like it that way because my father and mother liked it that way, and the way I was brought up, and I don't make fun of anything, I don't pretend to know it all (look over everything). And (my parents) never talked (as if they were better), like my mother didn't think herself above other people, she didn't make curses and like ourselves here, for instance, I don't believe in that when someone, when I don't like that person, when someone becomes angry at me I don't even think about it.[6]

8. Food is sacred.

From harvest to consumption, food animals and plants should be handled with the utmost respect and honor. Without food the body would slowly deteriorate and die within three weeks. The Cheyenne people center their ceremonial practices on honoring the food animals and plants the earth provides. Hunting animals and gathering and harvesting plants are all done in prayer as sacred actions. I have heard several Cheyennes tell how our ancestors had challenges finding the right plants to eat in the ancient time; sometimes they would choose the wrong plant and get sick and sometimes die. This is why the people began to talk to plants before harvesting. A person could find out a lot about a new plant before consuming it, and years after, it became custom to talk and thank the plants for providing. The relationships between large game and humans were also ancient and extended back to the Great Race (see chapter 1 in *A Sacred People*). Afterward, the buffalo, elk, deer, and antelope remained bitter and would kill humans to protect themselves. Even during the time of the horse, buffalo and ungulates were known to gore or trample hunters to death.[7] Bears were common predators as well, especially when young women were picking berries along creeks and rivers. Animals and humans shared the same world that is governed by the unseen powers of nature, and preparing meals and feasts are all done ceremoniously. Preparers of meals become priests in the sacred act of cooking and serving food.

9. Water is life.

Water is used in every ceremony and is honored as a gift from the universe. The Cheyennes are careful not to pollute their local streams and moved camp often for sanitary purposes; conscious of the human presence, they believed that the ground, water, and air could become unclean with their prolonged presence in one area.[8] Water nurtures the plants used for food, medicine, and ceremony.

PART I: MA'HEÓNĖSTÓNESTÔTSE: SACRED COVENANTS

Water provides for the animals that the people rely on for subsistence, as well as the sacred dogs and horses that the people rely upon for survival and transportation. Water quenches thirst and brings clarity and peace of mind. Water is used for cleanliness and represents the spirit of health. Without water the human body would die in four days, and this is why water is such a sacred element to the Cheyennes. Wooden Leg described his experience in ceremony without water: "Fitful slumbers, prayers, smoking, efforts at meditation, these alternated in my quiet activities. I was hungry and thirsty, especially thirsty. My body was hot. My heart was heavy. My ears constantly listening, listening, to every faint whisper of Nature."[9] In the sweat lodge, water released the "spiritual curative forces" held within heated stones; this "vivifying and purifying" aura among the steam is soaked into human flesh, driving out sickness, evil spirits, and polluted thought.[10]

10. The physical world is predetermined by the spiritual world.

Just as the universe was created out of the unknown and unseen elements found in nothingness, everything in the world is created from nothingness. These unknown and unseen elements comprise the building blocks for the future world as well as the particles from previous worlds that have long been destroyed. They also comprise the charge of energy transferred from previous peoples, beings, or objects. Further, they have the potential to be charged by surrounding peoples, beings, or objects. Until the arrival of white men, these elements followed a steady cycle of transference without much change. But with increase in human population, urban sprawl, and the dramatic changes to the environment, these elements have become more unpredictable and destructive. These unseen elements create the physical world, its beings, and other objects and allow for the present to come into existence, even if the present is chaotic. These unseen elements can also create the movements, situations, and in some cases actions, depending on their positive or negative charge.

The spiritual world is understood by these unknown and unseen powers. Sometimes the elements are associated with the sense of smell, as citizens often smell the stench of a person's bad medicine, or smell the stench of sickness or the presence of an alien force or power. The burning of cedar or other herbs cleanses the air and recharges the elements. Spiritual leaders endeavored to study the natural flow of the unknown and unseen elements that can only be described as air or essence. Spiritual leaders can feel these unknown and unseen elements, but they cannot control them. Meditation, patience, observation, and prayer allow for spiritual leaders to "breathe" in these elements to predict future events or find meaning in present events. Spiritual leaders also practice the art of breathing during ceremonies of sacrifice to perfect their craft in understanding the spiritual world in relation to the physical. Wooden Leg recalls: "I have heard many old Cheyennes say that a long time ago the Great Medicine used to come down to the earth to talk with people. They said He had camped and visited and

MA'HEÓNETANOHTÔTSE: THE SACRED WAY OF THINKING

smoked with the old-time Cheyennes. Lots of time I have heard them talk about Him given to our people the Black Hills and all of the gold there."[11]

CONCLUSION

Over the course of hundreds of years, the Cheyennes developed and refined sophisticated spiritual beliefs and principles, which allowed them to manage the spiritual health of their citizens and the nation as a whole. These were the building blocks for Cheyenne nationhood. These building blocks did not change much after the arrival of horses, but they would nearly be destroyed with the arrival of whites and white ways. The Cheyenne spiritual principles and ceremonial practices were the foundation of all forms and exertions of ma'xenéheto'stôtse, the Cheyenne concept of sovereignty, because the entire existence of the Cheyenne Nation depended on sustaining and protecting the spiritual relationship they had and have with the earth and nature. The Cheyennes had to continue the ceremonial cycle to uphold the covenants, which represented the foundation of Cheyenne laws, customs, and ways of living. Without the major ceremonies, the Cheyennes would break their promises to the earth and nature, which would eventually destroy the sacred relationship of balance and which the Cheyenne people relied on for prosperity and happiness. The oral traditions reminded them of the hardships of starvation and disorder before the great prophets brought change. With the ceremonies, the people had the spiritual entitlements and autonomy to organize, hunt, feast, celebrate, live, and prosper as the spiritual powers intended. Without the ceremonies, the Cheyennes would cease to thrive, cease to reproduce, and eventually cease to exist.

Much of what I have discussed in this chapter has remained a part of the traditional Cheyenne ceremonial world, but a lot has been lost throughout the years as Cheyennes assimilated. The ceremonial realm that I shared is a fragment of what was known at the time of the dog and the time of the buffalo. Today the colonized Cheyenne world is a place not much different from that of American society, where science is the dominant means of explaining life and where Christian stories and ideologies abound. Most Old Testament teachings contradict Cheyenne beliefs and spiritual practices, especially foundational concepts like brotherhood (compare the story of Cain and Abel) and the sacred relationship with animals (compare Adam's role in the Garden of Eden). And although New Testament stories promote a gentler and more peaceful body of teachings, the Cheyennes, like most Indigenous peoples, were not met with gentle treatment and peaceful intent from whites. It seems there will always be a mismatch in beliefs, but this does not mean we cannot live together and work to build and rebuild spiritually healthy societies. Regardless of beliefs and differences, the Cheyennes continue to rebuild their society, and looking back into time and history has been a favored practice. As modern Cheyennes begin to spiritually reawaken and decolonize their views of traditional Cheyenne spiritual practices, and oral traditions, I believe they will be more inclined to rely on the old spiritual ways. Nothing fits a Cheyenne like Cheyenne spirituality.

As I conclude this chapter, I will reiterate that I have omitted a lot of information for protection and out of respect for our traditional ways. I am conscious that the Cheyenne living-nation has endured so many challenges and suffered so much loss that it remains a miracle that the remaining pieces of the old world survived. Unfortunately, simply reading and studying the rituals and principles described in this chapter cannot lead a person to gain a complete understanding of the Cheyenne ceremonial realm and concept of spirituality. Nor can such study generate worthy spiritual leaders. Those of us who wish to decolonize need a good place to start, and what better place than the origins of a nation and its sovereignty.

PART II

Noónêho'emanestôtse: Traditional Law

The concept of law for the Cheyennes is like religion in that it could not easily be separated from their way of living. The Cheyenne concept of law is intertwined with the Cheyenne cultural and spiritual ways of living and is viewed as a set of guiding principles for proper and balanced living with one another and Mother Earth rather than as a set of rules to obey. The Cheyennes also had concepts of formal laws, or ho'emanestôtse, which were decrees from the Véhoo'o, or the keepers of the sacred covenants. The highest laws, however, were a set of sacred instructions from the highest spiritual powers.

The Cheyenne concept of ho'emanestôtse in general does not equate to the mainstream Western worldview, which associates "law" with a system of rules created by legislators, enforced by officers, and interpreted by attorneys and judges. In the history of the West, political and religious leaders could make or break laws, manipulate legal systems, and, in some cases, rise "above the law." Throughout Western civilization numerous people and groups gained power to reinterpret the law to their liking, as is the case with tyrannical monarchies and corrupt states. Laws could be made to control a select few while privileging the elite. Laws were also used to oppress and destroy entire communities, like with apartheid and segregation. Nonetheless, Western systems of law were primarily designed to control and regulate the behavior of citizens and others. These systems relied on the people's belief and trust in the creation, rule, and enforcement of laws, all of which were controlled by humans. And historically, this system was controlled exclusively by white men.

In the Cheyenne legal system the creation, rule, and enforcement of law traditionally rested in the people's customs, ceremonial practices, and oral traditions. When legal decisions are made, Cheyennes apply the sacred way of thinking but also rely on the principles of discipline and dedication they learned when conducting rituals and ceremonies. They approach law as they approach ceremonies, in that every action must be well thought out and done in "sacred due diligence" and by following the proper protocols of "sacred due process." The Cheyenne belief and legal system was spiritually based; people did not make laws, but they had the responsibility to uphold and enforce them. This was their promise or covenant to the sacred nation and each other.

The Cheyenne system of formal law traditionally rested in the sanctity of the four sacred entities: Véhoo'o, Nótâxeo'o, the Medicine Arrows, and the Sacred Buffalo Hat. The Véhoo'o, or Council of Forty-four Chiefs, were a judicial body for civil and criminal affairs. They made critical decisions as the judiciary, but they always interpreted the law in accordance with the spiritual teachings of the Medicine Arrow and Sacred Buffalo Hat covenants. Never were their decisions or decrees to be self-serving or beneficial to individuals or a select few. Most if not all of the traditional laws were traced directly to the teachings and ceremonies of the Medicine Arrow and the Sacred Buffalo Hat covenants. The Nótâxeo'o traditionally served as both protectors and police to carry out punishments and assist the Véhoo'o, but they did not have any power as judges. Altogether the four entities contributed to the legal system to serve and protect the citizens of the Cheyenne Nation and the sacred nation itself. Although people were part of the legal system in fact, they did not have control of it. Inevitably, the unseen spiritual forces have the ultimate power to rule and enforce laws.

As with most Indigenous peoples, the Cheyennes lived by an inseparable set of sacred principles. These principles, or codes of proper behavior, are also understood as traditions or traditional ways, which are the foundation of Cheyenne traditional law. The Cheyenne concept of noónêho'emanestôtse literally means "old law," but it encapsulates traditional law and customary law. The concept of old laws is nearly equivalent to the concept of the old ways. These old ways of living are valued as the original and most traditional ways of doing things. Basically, the old ways are "the way it was always done," or the custom. In this section I highlight some of these traditional laws, customs, and old ways of doing things.

CHAPTER 5

Tséhéstanove naa Nevo'êstanémaneo'o: The Cheyenne Way and Kinship

I have brought you many things, sent by the gods for your use. You live the way I have taught you, and follow the laws. You must not forget them, for they have given you strength and the ability to support yourselves and your families.

—Motsé'eóeve[1]

Tséhéstanove is defined as the Cheyenne spiritual way of life. This concept is much deeper than Tséhéseamanēō'o, which is the Cheyenne cultural way of life. The term Tséhéstanove can be translated to mean "the ways of the Cheyenne families that belong to the living, sacred Cheyenne Nation, which is an omnipresent being of the Earth that rests under power of the universe." It is the set of spiritual rules that help the Cheyenne people and their families remain in spiritual balance and thus keep the Cheyenne Nation alive and healthy.

The Tséhéstanove and noónêho'emanestôtse (traditional law) are deeply intertwined with the Tséhéseamanēō'o, which makes any discussion of traditional laws quite challenging. In some families, traditional laws may not necessarily be "laws" as we know them, since they are also habits, beliefs, and part of everyday practices. Conversely, the origins of some traditional laws can be directly traced to actual incidents and memorialized in family and community stories, thus making them customs, not laws. Some traditional laws were not based on traditions or customs but were created and sustained by the body of knowledge embedded in sacred histories (legends), ceremonies, and the Cheyenne language itself. These traditional laws are culturally and spiritually based; they are ceremonial and ritualistic and are the responsibility of all families of the Tséhéstáno (Cheyenne Nation).

Throughout the development and building of the Tséhéstáno, the Cheyennes acquired new ways of "doing things" and also acquired new traditions, thus creating new laws. The Cheyenne people and families then had to change, adapt, or completely abandon archaic and outdated noónêho'emanestôtse. The traditional laws that managed to survive the tests of time are perceived as the purist forms of the old ways, primarily because they helped build and sustain the nation. Today's Cheyenne families are fortunate that some of the old laws remained as part of the collective memory of the Cheyenne spiritual way of living.

Traditional laws are believed to have originated from the experiences of sacred people and their interactions with the unseen powers of the universe. The unseen spiritual forces of power are ever-present, according to the Cheyenne worldview, and these forces continue to have a role in controlling all human behavior. This is why the Cheyenne system of law and ceremonial cycle were practically one system.

The stability of the Tsėhéstáno depended on the sanctity of the Tsėhéstanove, which depended entirely on Cheyenne families to sustain cultural practices, ceremonies, oral traditions, language, and spiritual devotion. The Tsėhéstanove and the Cheyenne way of law were most apparent through the exercises of cultural practices, social dances, and ceremonies, but rules and laws did not burden every facet of Cheyenne life. Instead, community and social events were joyous celebrations that reaffirmed and instilled the values that promoted healthy relationships among citizens and across families. The ceremonies, dances, and celebrations were then the prime grounds for people to demonstrate their knowledge of the "old ways" and the "old laws."

The highest laws, the four sacred laws of humanity and four sacred laws of nature, did not dictate that families live solemn and restrained lives. Much of traditional Cheyenne life was the opposite: full of freedom, humor, joy, and happiness. The traditional Cheyenne family structure facilitated and fostered happiness, and it is in the Cheyenne kinship system where we find the starting place for learning the traditional laws of Cheyenne life. In fact, one defining characteristic of Cheyenne sovereignty and self-determination rested in the stability and strength of the Cheyenne family structure.

CHEYENNE KINSHIP

Numerous non-Cheyenne, white scholars have researched and recorded the interworking of Cheyenne kinship, but none were born into a Cheyenne family or grew up in a Cheyenne household and community.[2] Many of the texts from anthropological studies do not fairly portray Cheyenne kinship relationships and tend to focus more on incest taboos rather than kinship responsibilities and the extended family structure. It is important to reconstruct the traditional family system, since it was directly assaulted with the federal assimilation policies, which forced children into boarding schools, severing kinship ties and destroying traditional kinship roles and responsibilities. Parents were also forced to adopt mainstream Anglo American concepts of family, which do not necessarily value grandparents, aunts and uncles, cousins, and other relatives as do the Cheyennes. These relatives were as responsible as parents in making a complete and healthy Cheyenne family. The assault on the Cheyenne kinship system was a direct assault on the Cheyenne spiritual way of life of the living-nation: the Tséhéstanove.

Today the Cheyenne language is still the foundation of the traditional Cheyenne kinship system. This system is defined by the principles of heške'estovestôtse (motherhood) and héhe'estovestôtse (fatherhood), which emphasize the importance of parenthood. As modern Cheyennes begin to rebuild our nation and revive lost Cheyenne customs and laws, we must also sincerely reconstruct our traditional kinship system. Current and future generations can learn a lot from the basic principles of Cheyenne kinship. But as I mentioned before, traditional knowledge must be protected. Therefore, I have limited my discussion on Cheyenne kinship and Cheyenne laws by adhering to the teachings of the Tséhéstanove that were bestowed upon me from older, wiser Cheyennes.

My siblings and I cannot definitively say that we grew up in a traditional household, since our family was also influenced by assimilation and mainstream culture. Nonetheless, we grew up as most did on the Northern Cheyenne Indian reservation, with siblings and in the presence of numerous extended family members: aunts, uncles, grandparents, cousins, and in-laws. We mimicked the behaviors of our older Cheyenne relatives, nearly all of whom were bilingual and grew up in small reservation houses with their parents and grandparents. These were the last havens for traditional kinship relationships. Much of traditional Cheyenne kinship relationships, responsibilities, and roles survived in reservation households, which is a testament to the strength of Tséhéstanove. By far, the most important principle of Cheyenne kinship is love, méhósánestôtse. Everything is to be done out of sincere love. A traditional Cheyenne family may have strict rules and customs, but if a family does not uphold the rules or practice the customs with love, then their meanings and values are lost. A Cheyenne child must grow up in an environment of love to gain a positive view of what it means to be part of a family, village, band, and nation.

THE IMMEDIATE FAMILY

In the traditional Cheyenne kinship system, several relationships emerge as fundamental. These kinships are initially found in language but are primarily displayed in relationships. That is to say, kinship terms are the basis for creating and sustaining these relationships. When children learn the language, they also learn kinship terms while experiencing the kinship relationship. First and foremost, the term for "family," nevo'êstanémaneo'o, is one that is unifying in itself. The term can also be translated to mean "my people," and it can and has been used when a person references his or her community, band, or nation. Table 5.1 lists basic Cheyenne kinship terms using the modern Cheyenne alphabet according to Leman's Cheyenne Dictionary (2002) as well as Black Wolf's 1913 list and Mack Haag's 1930 list.[3]

Table 5.1. Basic Cheyenne Kinship Terms

English	Black Wolf (1913)	Haag (1930)	Leman (2002)
My mother	-	náckuEe	náhko'éehe
Mother!	náx'kue	-	náhko'e
My father	-	níhoEē	ného'éehe
Father!	nihue	-	ného'e
My grandmother	níske'e	niškeEE	néške'éehe
Grandma	-	-	ke'ééhe
My grandfather	námśim	námEšim	namêšéme
Grandpa	-	-	mémééhe
My sibling (also my cousin)	-	-	navéséso
My younger sibling	nésima	násima	násemáhe
My older brother	na'nï	náEniα	na'neha
My older sister	-	nαmEhán	namêhäne
My brother (female speaker)	-	-	nâhtatáneme
My sister (male speaker)	naxa ehim	-	naaxaa'éhéme
The one who is my younger sibling	tsi'ivasimitu	-	tséhevásemeto
The one who is my older brother	tsi'i'nihiu	-	tséhe'néheto
The one who is my older sister	-	-	tséhemêhéto

The Cheyenne kinship system starts with the child, since the child is considered a new human, with a free and uninfluenced mind and spirit. Cheyenne tradition has always held children with ma'heónevetôtse (godliness/sacredness) because they are pure. The first person of a child's influence is the mother; her behavior and virtue will influence her unborn child's character. A child's perceptions, behaviors, and worldviews are shaped while still in the womb. The Cheyennes were conscious of prenatal development, as evidenced by the fact that expecting women underwent numerous ceremonies throughout their pregnancy. They frequently met and stayed with their female relatives to visit, talk, and laugh about all matters of motherhood. All the while, the child developed its mind, body, and spirit, listening to the mother, feeling her emotions, and

Oivit (Scabby) or Baldwin Twins, His Wife Amitsehei, and their Daughter Nakai. June 28, 1908, De Lancey W. Gill, National Anthropological Archives, Smithsonian Museum Support Center, Suitland, Maryland.

experiencing her actions. Mothers frequently sang family songs, or made up their own, so the child became familiar with her voice and the melodies. Once the child was born, he or she was inseparable from the mother. The mother-child relationship is the most sacred and strongest in the Cheyenne kinship system and the best example of the Cheyenne principle of ma'heónevetôtse.

The second person that influences a child is the father. The child begins to recognize the father as it grows and soon they establish a strong relationship of méhósánestôtse (love). The father is the protector and disciplinarian, making the father-child relationship a foundation for the child's development of good behavior. Both the mother and father are the first and primary teachers of a child's morals and values. The child learns most of his or her morals and values from the actions of the parents, secondary to their spoken teachings and lectures. Traditional Cheyennes today still say, "If you want to know how a person really is, take a look at their children." The parental relationship is the foundation of all other relationships, especially in the family unit.

The third person influencing a child's growth and development in the Cheyenne kinship system is the grandmother (both maternal and paternal). Since infants and toddlers spend most of their time with the mother, and the mother spends most of her time with her mother, a child will acquire an early and strong relationship with grandmothers. Grandmothers embody the Cheyenne principle of Éškemane (Grandmother Earth), the ultimate giver of life. Grandmothers possess the knowledge and wisdom of childrearing and are always willing to help and advise their daughters in motherhood, especially first-time mothers. Throughout a child's life, the grandmother-child relationship is strong. Grandmothers learned and experienced the same teachings and lessons in childrearing from their mothers, as part of the continuum of the Cheyenne culture and tradition.

The fourth relationship of significance is the grandfather (both maternal and paternal). The grandfathers, as with grandmothers, have knowledge and wisdom of childrearing and also impart lessons of parenting to their daughters and sons. Grandfathers are the ultimate examples of Cheyenne héhe'estovestôtse (fatherhood): they taught the fathers how to be fathers. Children, especially those first born, may see their grandparents as another set of parents, only more experienced, wiser, and a bit more childlike and playful. The grandparent-child relationship is the foundation for relationships in the community involving elder and ceremonial and ritualistic leaders. Stands In Timber (Northern Cheyenne) states: "Another thing, they never mocked old people. I have heard the mixed-bloods do that, in English. Sweet Medicine told them never to mock an old woman or an old man."[4] Older Cheyenne children learn how to treat elders from the oral tradition, which reaffirms principles of respect and sincerity.

The fifth group of relationships that are crucially important to the traditional kinship system are those with siblings. The principle of ka'ëškónevestôtse (childhood) is paramount for all children in the community. A child develops deep and strong relationships with siblings and cousins, which is the foundation for the child's social development and eventual acceptance into a dance, social, ceremonial, or warrior society. The sibling and cousin relationships are also the foundation of any future friendships (which can and do lead to induction into guilds) and relationships with members of the opposite sex, which also lead to romantic relationships and marriage. As dictated by the Cheyenne Way, all cousins, even distant ones, are viewed and treated as siblings.

Cheyenne children, especially siblings and cousins, also played the roles of their parents, often making their own camps and assigning kinship roles: parents, grandparents, and children. This play was practice for living the Cheyenne cultural way of life. Once children matured into adulthood, the play stopped and they were bound by a new set of kinship rules.[5] First and foremost, siblings of the opposite sex (including cousins) could not talk to one another, except through their friends. The rule was to prevent any appearance of incest. The incest law of the Medicine Arrows was one of the four sacred laws, which is why adult siblings and cousins could not even communicate as they did when they were children.[6] Another rule related to the incest law is that a young man cannot interfere with his sister's relationships, even through marriage; otherwise, it would appear that they had an incestuous relationship.[7] These rules were likely strictly enforced for families that belonged to the covenant ceremonial societies, since these families were held to higher standards and under constant scrutiny from other families. Preventing the appearance of incest is one method to avoid criticism altogether. Today's traditional families and older Cheyennes continue to practice this custom.

THE EXTENDED FAMILY

Paternal uncles and maternal aunties are as responsible to their nephews and nieces as fathers and mothers are to their sons and daughters. The words náhko'éehe (my mother) and náhko'e (mother) are used when addressing "my maternal aunt" and "aunt," respectively. The formal term or phrase for a maternal aunt is tséheškamóonéto, which literally means "the one who is my maternal aunt." The words ného'éehe (my father) and ného'e (father) are also used when addressing "my paternal uncle" and "uncle," respectively. The formal term or phrase for paternal uncle is tséhéhamóonéto: "the one who is my paternal uncle." The relationships are the foundation to Cheyenne kinship and the survival of the traditional family system. Table 5.2 lists the Cheyenne kinship terms of the extended family.

Under the principle of héhe'estovestôtse (fatherhood), paternal uncles, especially unmarried uncles, take on the role of second fathers in a child's life. A tséhéhamóonéto (paternal uncle) is expected to accept the responsibilities of guardian, teacher, adviser, and disciplinarian. This relationship is very important, since a child under these conditions learns that he or she belongs to the much larger family on the father's side. Involved paternal uncles specifically protect and mentor boys through childhood and into manhood. Boys learn the acceptable behaviors of manhood from those closest to them.

Under heške'estovestôtse (motherhood), maternal aunts, especially unmarried ones, take on the role of second mothers to children. A tséheškamóonéto (maternal aunt) is expected to accept the responsibilities of mothers, with all of the rights and privileges of a caregiver. The auntie-child relationship begins while the child is still an infant and toddler, since the mother spends much time with her sisters and cousins. Like paternal uncles, maternal aunties provide consistency in customs, rules, teachings, and discipline when confronting unacceptable behavior. If a child falters in behavior, he or she is scolded and reproached by parents, grandparents, and aunts and uncles, and thus the child learns right and wrong from the extended family. If on the other hand only one or both parents discipline a child, there is still a chance for the child to seek a second opinion on behavior. In this case, which is not part of the Cheyenne kinship system, the child may be told by an outsider that his or her behavior is acceptable, compromising the parent-child relationship. Abuse, ridicule, and condescending acts were never part of Cheyenne teachings.

Despite the seemingly simple patterns in kinship terminology, the Cheyenne kinship system became more complex when dealing with paternal aunts, maternal uncles, and non-blood aunts and uncles. Children may refer to

Table 5.2. Cheyenne Kinship Terms for the Extended Family

English	Black Wolf (1913)	Haag (1930)	Leman (2002)
My paternal uncle (father's brother)	-	-	ného'éehe-
My father	-	-	ného'éehe
Father!	nihue	-	ného'e
The one who is my paternal uncle	-	-	tséhéhamóonéto
My paternal aunt (father's sister)	-	naháue	nâháa'e
Mother!	nax'kue	-	náhko'e
My mother		-	náhko'éehe
The one who is my paternal aunt	-	-	tséhehaehéto
My maternal aunt (mother's sister)	-	-	náhko'éehe
My mother	-	náckuEe	náhko'éehe
Mother!	náx'kue	-	náhko'e
The one who is my maternal aunt	-	-	tséheškamóonéto
My maternal uncle (mother's brother)	-	-	nâxäne
My father	-	-	ného'éehe
The one who is my father	tsi-iśítu	-	tséhéhéto
The one who is my maternal uncle	-	-	tséhešêhéto
My father's sister's husband	tsi'iśítu	-	tséhéhéto
The one who is my father	-	-	tséhéhéto
My father's brother's wife (same as my maternal aunt)	tsi'iś-kumōn nihtu		tséheškamóonéto
My mother's sister's husband	-	-	-
My father	-	-	ného'éehe
Father!	nihue	-	ného'e
My mother's brother's wife (same as my paternal aunt)	tsi-hihahitu		tséhehaehéto

maternal uncles as both tséhéhéto (the one who is my father), andného'éehe (my father). Formally, when talking about them specifically, children refer to maternal uncles as nâxäne (my maternal uncle) and thus avoid confusion for listeners. The role of the nâxäne is more in line with mainstream notions of an uncle, in that they do not necessarily have the same roles and responsibilities as a paternal uncle who is also the child's "father." The same system applies for the paternal aunt, nâháa'e. Children may refer to their father's sister as náhko'éehe (my mother), náhko'e (mother), or tséheškamóonéto (the one who is my paternal aunt), but the formal term nâháa'e literally means "paternal aunt." This relationship, like that of nâxäne, does not necessarily have the same responsibilities as those of a mother, birth or otherwise.

The Cheyenne kinship system sometimes adapted to circumstance. For example, Cheyenne custom dictates that the siblings of parents are equivalent to parents, but this is not the case in every instance. Non-blood-related uncles, like a father's sister's husband, were not always endeared with the same term, roles, and responsibilities as a német'e, "father." Such uncles are viewed as a distant tséhéhéto, a maternal uncle. According to Black Wolf, non-blood-related aunties, like a father's brother's wife, were viewed as tséheškamóonéto (maternal auntie) but were not necessarily bestowed with the honor, roles, and responsibilities of being "mothers." Leman assumes the same about distant aunties, like a mother's brother's wife; she is identified as a maternal aunt, but not viewed as a mother.

That said, at times distant relatives or non-blood-related people could become formal "mothers" and "fathers," taking on the role of a maternal auntie or paternal uncle. For example, it was common for a father's childhood best friend to remain a part of his life into adulthood, especially if they established a lasting "buddy" relationship based on the principle of hévese'onematsestôtse (brotherhood). As a lifelong "buddy" this man was no stranger to his friend's family and could easily fill the role and responsibilities of a father, especially if the birth father should happen to meet an unexpected and unfortunate death. This relationship also exists among two women who share a lifelong "sisterly" relationship, although they merely refer to one another as "big sister" or "little sister."

THE NUCLEAR FAMILY

The typical Cheyenne nuclear family was like all typical human families, comprising both parents and their children. As tradition dictated, rarely did the Cheyennes have more than two children. The tepee was the vee'e (lodge)—the traditional home of the Cheyenne family—and was considered the sacred place of living. The vee'e was the family's home and the child's sanctuary. Cheyenne custom dictated that families follow proper etiquette, which included kinship rules, while in their homes. The lodge doors always faced east to welcome the rising sun; this was a universal practice even though the Cheyennes were both patrilineal and matrilineal. Parents who followed the Tsétsêhéstâhese tradition, the patriarchal tradition, placed their beds on the south side of the lodge.[8] Coyote (Northern Cheyenne) described the Tsétsêhéstâhese tradition: "The head of a family, man and wife, occupy the south side of the tipi. All tipis face the rising sun. The west side is the place of honor; that is where the firstborn is placed to sleep."[9] According to Tsétsêhéstâhese tradition younger children occupied the north side, and when appropriate, sons occupied the west side, while daughters occupied the north.

Families that followed the Só'taeo'o tradition, the matriarchal tradition, placed the beds of the mother and father on the north side.[10] The Só'taeo'o, like the Tsétsêhéstâhese, also placed the firstborn on the west side, the place of honor. Daughters, however, had priority over sons to sleep in this place. Meanwhile, sons typically occupied the south side, if they had sisters. In short, the Só'taeo'o home was situated counterclockwise: starting at the east door, with parents to the north, then the firstborn or daughters to the west, ending with sons and younger siblings to the south. The Tsétsêhéstâhese home was situated clockwise: starting at the east door, parents to the south, sons or the firstborn to the west, ending with daughters and younger siblings to the north. The origins of such customs are unknown, but they made homes that honored parents and children. The home was considered a sacred place and children retained the same customs, either Tsétsêhéstâhese or Só'taeo'o, when they started families of their own.

Table 5.3. Cheyenne Kinship Terms for the Nuclear Family

English	Black Wolf (1913)	Haag (1930)	Leman (2002)
My wife	naxtsi'im	-	nâhtse'eme
My husband	naiyam	-	naéhame
My daughter	naxtan	ma'tónna	nâhtona
My son	nāa	nāaEhaE	nae'ha
My nephew	natśíñotu	natsínotα	natsénota
My niece	-	naEhámme	na'häme
Friend!	hōwi	-	hóovéhe
Youngest daughter!	-	-	ma'ko'sá'e
Youngest son!	-	-	ma'kö'se

According to the practices of the Tséhéstanove, adult family members referred to children and spouses by their names. Cheyennes primarily use the fundamental kinship terms nâhtse'eme (my wife), naéhame (my husband), nâhtona (my daughter), and nae'ha (my son) when talking about them to others and in prayer. But parents and spouses never directly addressed them using these terms. In Table 5.3 I list the kinship terms of the nuclear family from an adult's perspective—parent, aunt, or uncle—using the modern Cheyenne alphabet. I also list the terms recorded from Black Wolf in 1913 and Mack Haag in 1930.

The term that is used for a man when addressing his close friend is hóovéhe. This term is used for good friends whom the children may also perceive as an uncle. The terms ma'kö'se and ma'ko'sá'e are very common kinship terms for firstborns and the youngest siblings. These terms are equivalent to names and can be carried into adulthood. Ma'kö'se is also the name of a culture hero from the oral tradition who, among other feats, is credited with defeating a number of monsters.

THE IN-LAWS

In chapter 7 I highlight the Cheyenne marriage ceremony, but it is important to discuss the kinship rules of the in-laws. These parental in-law relationships are very sensitive. Parents-in-law in particular had responsibilities as forthcoming grandparents. They had the duty to teach and advise their family members in following norms and customs as well as upholding traditional laws of the Cheyenne Nation. They were the backbone of the entire family.

When a couple marries, both the man and the woman acquire a new set of kinship terms along with their new families. More important, they acquire new kinship relationships and rules. The new kinship terms, relationships, and rules are built on the foundations of the kinship system of the nuclear family, which is why it was important for suitors to select good spouses—ones that came from good families. Table 5.4 lists the new and old terms and relationships that a husband and wife acquire after marriage. Spouses of either gender use the term néške'éehe (my grandmother) to mean "my mother-in-law" (maternal and paternal). The term for my namêšéme (my grandfather) is the same as for "my father-in-law" (maternal and paternal). Mothers-in-law refer to their sons-in-law as néxahe, grandchild. Fathers-in-law also use this term for their daughters-in-law. The roles and relationships of each person are also carried from the immediate family to newly acquired kin.

Once two people are married, both sides of the family become part of each other's lives. Families celebrate together, hold rituals and ceremonies together, and share experiences and stories.[11] Traditionally, they retained unity with ease under the principle of love, but they also lived by the Tsėhéstanove, which provided a framework to avert conflict.

Humor played a significant role in the traditional Cheyenne kinship system and in-law relationships. The use of humor started in the home as birth mothers and fathers frequently teased and jested with their children. Humor created and reinforced happy and secure homes. Outside of the home, nephews and uncles joked as fathers did with their sons. Nieces and aunties teased as their mothers did with their daughters. Male relatives, however, were particularly bound from using profanity in the presence of their female relatives. Even before a couple married, their relationships to the brothers-in-law and sisters-in-law already formed around common senses of humor.

Table 5.4. Cheyenne Kinship Terms for In-laws

English	Black Wolf (1913)	Haag (1930)	Leman (2002)
My mother-in-law	níske'e	niškeEE	néške'éehe
My father-in-law	námśim	námEšim	namêšéme
Brother-in-law (female speaker)	-	nitαmma	nétame
Brother-in-law (male to male)	-	-	né'tóve
Brother-in-law!	-	-	máéšééhe
Sister-in-law (female speaker)	-	-	násée'e
Sister-in-law (male speaker)	-	nitαmma	nétame
My sister-in-law	-	-	na-axaa'éhéme
My son-in-law/ grandchild	nixa	níxα	néxahe
My daughter-in-law/ grandchild	nixa	níxα	néxahe
My son his wife	nāa hist tsi-imu	-	nae'ha he-stse'emo
My daughter her spouse	naxtan hiyam	-	nâhtona heéháme

Joking was common between same-sex sisters-in-law and brothers-in-law, and somewhat constrained between in-laws of the opposite sex.[12] While male relatives could not jest with female relatives, it was almost demanded that female relatives tease male relatives to the point of humiliation. These kinship rules of the Tsėhéstanove were also created years ago to promote good relationships, prevent incest, and avoid even the appearance of incest:

1. A brother-in-law can say anything to a brother-in-law.
2. A sister-in-law can say anything to a sister-in-law.
3. A brother-in-law must not use profanity to a sister-in-law; the reverse is the same.
4. A mother-in-law must not talk to a son-in-law; the reverse is the same.
5. A father-in-law can't talk to the daughter-in-law; the reverse is the same.[13]

Following the rules of kinship, Wrapped Hair (Só'taeo'o) provided some of the following teasing rules of the Tsėhéstanove in 1931:

1. An uncle must not use profanity to his niece; the reverse is the same.

2. An aunt can say anything to a niece; the reverse is the same.
3. An aunt must not use profanity to a nephew; the reverse is the same.
4. Brothers and sisters are not supposed to talk [to each other]; this takes effect as soon as they grow up.[14]

Grandparents were the best jokers and at any time could tease to embarrassment. Mack Haag (Southern Cheyenne) explained: "Grandfather and grandmother are privileged to jest obscenely with their grandchildren."[15] The grandparental sense of humor was also present in the relationships between parents-in-law and their children-in-law. Wolf Chief (Ôhméseheso) also discussed the basic kinship rules of the Cheyenne in-laws in 1931:

> A man can't talk to his mother-in-law. In case of sickness or emergency, he can go near but must not talk. But a father-in-law can talk to his daughter-in-law. If the daughter-in-law was away, the mother-in-law might talk to the son-in-law, but not look at him. If the mother-in-law wanted to say something to the son-in-law, she would give him a horse or something that the whole tribe would know about. This might be done at a dance. But the permission for her to talk to him would be for this time only. The same regulations apply to the son-in-law.[16]

In the 1950s in Montana, Stands In Timber discussed how the kinship system changed due to the poor living conditions on the reservation:

> And he [Sweet Medicine] said in order to keep trouble from your wife's people [family] and your own, don't talk to your mother-in-law or father-in-law. That meant both man and woman. That's where the trouble begins. I have noticed the daughters-in-law and sisters-in-law start quarreling over little things. Anyone in an Indian village can tell you that. But now they talk to each other. I used to notice the son-in-law's camp, if he camped with his wife's parents was quite a ways away, so they would not see each other. They acted ashamed; they would not come near. But since 1920 they even live in the same room with their mother-in-law. And some of them talk to them, and they still make fun—they make a remark about being ashamed and then they come near. They may have to get in the same car and go together. But I never talked to mine. I am still ashamed of myself.[17]

I believe Stands In Timber's final statement may have been mistranslated or misinterpreted. He may have meant to say, "I am still in my heart, upholding the custom," but used a shortcut in the English language, which has proven to be disastrous to his intended meaning.

Generally speaking, traditional Cheyennes assume that other Cheyenne people carry the same relationships within their families; that they have mothers, fathers, aunts, uncles, grandparents, and cousins. The assumption of sameness and similarity is positive for a healthy nation and for sustaining a healthy society, especially when children begin to rely on the kinship system when making friends and establishing relationships with the opposite sex.

PART II: NOÓNÊHO'EMANESTÔTSE: TRADITIONAL LAW

THE CHEYENNE NATION OF FAMILIES

Table 5.5 presents a list of terms that are significant to a child's understanding of self and his or her position on the Earth and among the Tséhéstáno. I list the terms that were collected by Haag in 1930 and the terms using the modern Cheyenne alphabet. These words are also kinship terms for a Cheyenne person's sense of belonging to the Cheyenne Nation. The term mâhta'sóoma is equivalent to a person's soul or spirit. The term vo'êstane can be translated to literally mean "surface of the Earth dwelling beings." Xamaevo'êstane means "ordinary person," which refers to all people who are indigenous to Native America. The séo'ôtse should not be confused with a lifeless corpse; instead it is the spirit of a dead person who recently passed away. These concepts are fundamental to the Cheyenne kinship system because the family system extends beyond the nuclear family into the entire Cheyenne Nation.

Table 5.5. Cheyenne Kinship Terms for Citizenship

English	Mack Haag (1930)	Leman (2002)
Shadow (ego)	ma'taEsómma	mâhta'sóoma
Person (human)	wóEstan	vo'êstane
People (human family)	wóEstániyoEU	vo'êstaneo'o
Indigenous Person	xamaí wóEstan	xamaevo'êstane
Ghost (soul without a body)	síyoEutse	séo'ôtse

Citizenship to the Tséhéstáno was not based on an individual's rights and privileges; it was based on his or her duties and responsibilities. A citizen was part of a much larger kinship system than that of the nuclear, immediate, and extended family. It was a system that emphasized a family's roles and responsibilities to the band and nation. A family was part of the economic, ceremonial, cultural, and/or military life of the band, and therefore, citizens also had to contribute to the band-kinship system. Based on this system, individual Cheyennes had three identities: their family, the family's band, and the Cheyenne Nation.

The Tséhéstáno comprised ten bands, and each had slightly different customs and laws. Each held a degree of political, social, and religious independence, much similar to modern townships. They all, however, had similar kinship systems because all families were to follow the sacred laws of the Medicine Arrows and the Sacred Buffalo Hat. All the ten bands also shared a sacred history, the major covenant ceremonies, a unified governing system, and a philosophy of living, the Tséhéstanove. Individual bands also had unique band stories, rituals, and ceremonial practices. At the band level, citizens participated in band cultures while remaining true to the Tséhéstanove. Citizens and their families were part of an extended band-kinship system, which required all members of the band to behave as proper and valuable citizens.

The stories in the Cheyenne national history provided the foundations of the Cheyenne band-kinship system. In each story were embedded teachings of band-kinship roles and responsibilities, acceptable and unacceptable behaviors, and proper etiquette toward immediate and distant family members. Stories also showed how Cheyennes treated strangers, non-family members, and non-Cheyennes. The stories alone, however, were not enough to sustain the Tséhéstanove. Children had to practice the values and teachings, especially the behavior of culture heroes and other Cheyennes who demonstrated good behavior and Cheyenne values. While the household was the place where children learned acceptable and unacceptable behaviors, the band was the community where children practiced their manners. This is how the Cheyenne band-kinship system kept the living-nation strong and vibrant.

Within the nuclear and immediate Cheyenne family, siblings played and acted out stories from the Cheyenne national history. This story-play essentially prepared children for adulthood, parenthood, manhood, and womanhood, thus laying the foundation for their living as Cheyennes. Children also interacted with other families and played with other children in their respective bands. In the camp circle, children easily re-created the same story-play in the house. Children assigned each other the roles of culture heroes, spiritual leaders, families, and animals from these stories. Boys played hunting and war, while the girls sang and held victory dances.[18]

Since nearly every story of the Cheyenne Nation's history had roles for every age and gender, the children's play became training for everyday living. Cheyenne children learned how to establish healthy relationships and how to navigate and manage different personalities, even those of unfavorable traits and characteristics like those of petty tyrants. Young men, in particular, enacted one of the core principles that sustained the Cheyenne Nation: héveseónematsestôtse (brotherhood). It was not enough that the grandparents and parents told the heroic and unifying stories of Vóetsénaé (White Clay), Tomôsévêséhe (Erect Horns), and Motséeóeve (Sweet Medicine); the children had to truly become them. Young women also took on the roles of sacred women: Ésevonaé (Buffalo Woman), Heovéstaée (Yellow Top-to-Head Woman), Naméhane (Big Sister), and even Keéehe (Grandmother), since the Cheyennes did not view old women as inferior to young women.

The band-kinship system adapted when bands adopted and intermarried with larger groups of people from other Indian nations. In some cases, as with a band's intermarriage of the Lakota people, a large enough number of families could adopt or marry members of another nation so that the kinship system slightly changed. In addition, some of the Cheyenne bands may have had notable differences from the outset, as with the matrilineal Sóʾtaeoʾo band; their customs eventually became widely accepted and practiced. Nonetheless, none of the changes from intermarriage or adoption were significant enough to compromise the Tséhéstanove and the traditional kinship system.

PART II: NOÓNÊHO'EMANESTÔTSE: TRADITIONAL LAW

Traditionally, a person's Cheyenne identity depended almost entirely on his or her upbringing in a Cheyenne family and band, which is why kinship was so critical to Cheyenne nation building. In chapter 7 I describe Cheyenne personhood and identity in detail. Basically, a person could be Cheyenne in only one of three ways: if he or she was born from and grew up in a Cheyenne family and band; he or she was adopted as a child into a Cheyenne family and band; or if a woman was married to a Cheyenne man and moved into her husband's camp and band. Then and only then did the kinship rules apply. Citizens of the Tséhéstáno had to be a member of one of the 444 original families, as dictated by the law of the Sacred Arrows, and individuals who were adopted or intermarried were not always subject to or protected by Cheyenne laws. Therefore, they were not citizens.

The sanctity and future of the Cheyenne Nation depended on its ability to produce and reproduce a body of citizens that upheld the Tséhéstanove: it had to produce and reproduce true Cheyenne individuals and families, people who would be loyal and faithful to the Tséhéstanove. Citizenship required more than a person's proclaimed loyalty to the Tséhéstáno; they had to live and practice loyalty every day. A nation could not be sovereign if it did not have a vibrant set of family values to create and strengthen the nation's families. As today's Cheyennes—the Northern Cheyennes of Montana and the Southern Cheyennes of Oklahoma—seek to reclaim their identities and rebuild their families and communities, a reevaluation of the traditional kinship system will provide some insight into their endeavors. As Indigenous nations rebuild and reclaim nationhood and assert sovereignty, they may only need to look at their traditional kinship systems to find guidance.

CHAPTER 6

Tsėhéstanove naa Ho'emanestôtse: The Cheyenne Way and Law

If anyone in our immediate tribe should speak evil of us, or gossip about us, we were never in any case to antagonize the party or parties by quarrelling or fighting.

—Slow Bull (Southern Cheyenne), age sixty, 1931[1]

In this chapter I discuss the structures and systems of law as they relate to the internal sovereignty of the Tsėhéstáno. In the modern context, sovereignty to Indigenous nations of the United States refers to rights of self-determination and self-governance. Sovereignty is also defined according to classic European international law as "the power of a particular nation to exercise governmental authority over a particular territory."[2] By this definition, a nation has the "absolute and inviolate power" to manage its own affairs—specifically, its internal affairs.[3] A nation does this by passing and enforcing laws that affirm the privileges and protect the rights of its individual citizens. From an American Indian perspective, leaders retained and exercised the power to pass laws and enforced them, but not out of the necessity to affirm privileges or to prioritize individual above collective rights. Rather, the purpose of regulating internal affairs was to protect the sanctity of the Indigenous nation itself and to preserve balance and promote peace and unity among citizens. This was done by prioritizing the responsibilities of individuals to their families, bands, and the sacred nation.

The fundamental difference between Indigenous and Western concepts of sovereignty and law is that Indigenous societies affirmed and assigned *responsibilities*, while Western societies affirmed and assigned *privileges* and *rights*. Onondaga peacemaker Oren Lyons emphasized: "Sovereignty, as I heard the word, is responsibility. I think that the United States would have been much better off if, instead of making a Bill of Rights, it made a bill of responsibilities, because that is what is lacking in this country today and in the world at large."[4]

Western law depends on the written word of men and women found in statutes and cases. Throughout the history of the Western world, the wealthy have dominated, manipulated, and changed lawmaking. The Western world has also used laws to oppress one group of people while advancing another. Numerous American laws were developed in order to oppress American Indian peoples.[5] The creation of such a system would not have occurred through American Indian and Indigenous concepts of sovereignty.

Indigenous nations managed their internal affairs on three primary levels. The lowest was at the individual and family level; an Indigenous nation really had no authority to meddle in people's business. Individuals and families were bound by custom, tradition, and ceremonial practices and thus managed their own affairs within. When a person committed a crime against the nation, crimes against the sacred covenants, higher power structures located in the middle of the hierarchy enforced laws and made judgments in the interest of preserving and protecting the health and quality of the people's lives and livelihoods. At the highest level, internal sovereignty was governed by the unseen powers of the spiritual realm, which no human or human structure controlled. These laws were more or less respected and revered as universal laws.

Cheyenne law originates from the spiritual powers, spiritual events, and nature, like Éškemane (Mother Earth) and Ma'xema'hēö'e (Great Medicine). Because Cheyenne law was intertwined with the spiritual world, the body of Cheyenne laws could not be easily manipulated, nor could laws be made to benefit an elite few or used to privilege one group while persecuting another. The guiding principles of the Cheyenne body of laws and legal system were also spiritual doctrines that affected individual citizens in a deep, personal manner and united customs and laws with the human spirit. Neither the elite nor the wealthy could dictate the development and rule of Cheyenne law. Because of these fundamental differences I refer to the entire body of laws of the Tséhéstáno as simply ho'emanestôtse (law). This body of laws remained an integral part of the culture, oral traditions, ceremonial practices, and worldview of the Cheyenne people, and any diversion would yield devastating results to the entire nation.

HO'EMANESTÔTSE

In this exploration of ho'emanestôtse, I try my best to provide the Cheyenne perspective by highlighting the origins and purposes of some laws. I also emphasize how certain laws were assigned as responsibilities for various people or systems. I divided the body of laws into different categories according to these people or systems. Before colonization, the Tséhéstanove comprised codes of conduct that applied to all citizens without exception, even those who may have had only one Cheyenne parent or who lived as a citizen among the people. Not one teaching that a child learned became arbitrary in their adulthood, because every lesson is part of the Cheyenne way of learning the Cheyenne way of life. Adoptees or captives from other nations were expected to learn and follow the ho'emanestôtse, but not required to know all of them since they were "new." Furthermore, some laws may have been applied only to children because they were expected to falter. Other laws may have applied exclusively to particular spiritual leaders, ceremonial societies, or warrior guilds, because some adults were held to higher standards demanded by their positions.

In accordance with the Tsêhéstanove, every ho'emanestôtse holds a place in a space or continuum of rules that guide every man, woman, and child. Each space that can be perceived is an invisible bubble that makes up the entire system of the ho'emanestôtse, which encompasses the entire living-sacred Cheyenne Nation. The nation, which is represented by the outermost bubble, is rooted to the Earth by a pole, and this pole reaches to the highest frontiers of the universe. Figure 6.1 is a representation of the Tsêhéstanove and ho'emanestôtse. At the base of the bubble, which extends below the surface of the Earth, are the ho'emanestôtse that apply to all of the beings of the Earth, the "natural laws" of Mother Earth. Where the bubble meets the surface are the laws that build the foundation of the Tsêhéseamanëö'o and Tsêhéstanove, which are taught through stories and ceremonies: they are cultural laws, traditional laws, ritual laws, and spiritual laws. Each layer inside the bubble comprises a set of laws and authority figures that have the power to enforce those laws. As we climb out of each layer through physical, mental, emotional, and spiritual maturation, we develop and improve our bodies, spirits, and minds. Most important, we learn at each level new and higher laws.

The highest layer of the bubble comprises the strict laws for spiritual leaders, the Véhoo'o, and the Tséá'enövâhtse (keepers). When we remove ourselves completely out of the bubble, we enter the highest level of laws, the sacred universal laws, which apply to all beings that exist in time and space. This level has only one authority, the Great Medicine. The universal laws control all humans and living things, like the sacred birds and spirits that live in the sky and the spiritual beings that control the weather. The universal laws extend past the moon, the sun, and the stars; they regulate everything in the universe. This highest level also holds the laws that rule and govern the Cheyenne Nation as a living organism of the planet Earth; these are the laws of the universe but are connected to the cultural, traditional, ritual, and spiritual laws. The bubble represents the stability and health of the Tsêhéstáno.

The Cheyenne kinship system was the foundation of Cheyenne law. It created a society in which citizens shared the same concepts of family and therefore shared the same concepts of law. For the most part, all Cheyenne citizens learned the basic concepts of responsibilities toward the family, band, and nation. Each person and family experienced the Cheyenne system of law at the family level, unless they were adopted; therefore, each person and family was expected to uphold and protect this system. I have identified four major classes, or levels, of Cheyenne law; the most basic were cultural norms and taboos, or cultural laws.

PART II: NOÓNÊHO'EMANESTÔTSE: TRADITIONAL LAW

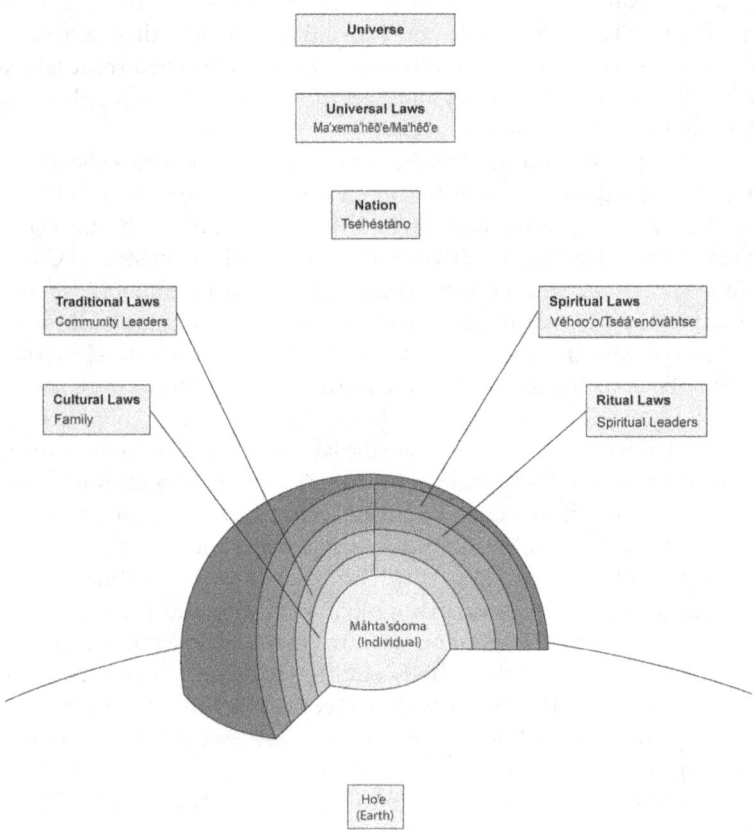

Traditional laws and the responsible authority figures

CULTURAL LAWS

Cultural laws were traditionally taught beginning at a young age and continued through puberty and into adulthood. Parents and grandparents were the primary teachers of cultural laws, and much of the schooling occurred in the household, among immediate family members. Most of these ho'emanestôtse were not gender specific and they typically applied to all Cheyenne children who lived in households of a Cheyenne village, even those who were of mixed blood or adopted from other nations. Stands In Timber (Northern Cheyenne) explains some of these laws:

Then, stealing: they must not take anything by force from another Cheyenne, or steal it. And never to brag: if you do, hard things may come upon you. And do not be ashamed of yourself. Your face, limbs, body are natural—no one can change them, do not be ashamed of them. Never say anything against anybody, even your leaders in the soldier bands, or your chiefs. If you say bad things about them, you will have trouble. And to disregard your parents or brothers and sisters, that's a bad thing.[6]

Mack Haag (Southern Cheyenne) also explained some cultural laws:

The old people say the young people eat too much spicy food and attribute this to it: coffee is forbidden for a pregnant woman. They are not supposed to look at a dead person, if they do, the baby will be subject to nightmares. A woman expecting a child is not allowed to stare at owls, if they do the child will have a bad habit of staring at people. Girls are not allowed to urinate on the same spot twice, if so twins will result. The same with boys. But defecating twice on the same spot is ok. If a girl eats the rough end of a [buffalo] tongue, she will do fine quillwork. If a boy eats the last, small rib [of a buffalo] he will be a fast runner. As a child is being born, when the woman attending the child announces the child is out, a man hits a dog making it howl. The idea, that the child will not in the future be frightened by unexpected noises. A woman is not allowed to eat persimmons when pregnant, it will make the child shriveled and hard to bear. If a woman looks at a dead person, if the child sleeps during, it will not entirely close its eyes. If 2 girls urinate on the same spot, the 1st will have twins, if they face each other both will have twins.[7]

Cultural laws were typically associated with taboos and other norms that were simple for Cheyennes to understand but at times difficult for outsiders to grasp, primarily because the Cheyenne way of life was simultaneously taught and reinforced. Nonetheless, the cultural laws all followed a simple formula of cause and effect, with either positive or negative outcomes. The first formula for this class of laws is as follows: If action A, then action B. For example, if you tell stories at the wrong time of the day, you will become hunchbacked. Laws in this class can be developed as warnings or taboos. Another formula would be: If you do not do action A, then action B will certainly happen. An example of such a cultural law has already been mentioned: if you do not wake up before the sun, you will certainly become a lazy person. A third formula would be: Do not do action A; otherwise, B will happen. There are always values and teachings associated with every rule, but sometimes the values are not shared with outsiders. Traditional Cheyennes do not think that Cheyenne values matter to outsiders, which is why elders do not necessarily tell people from non-Cheyenne backgrounds the cultural laws or the associated values. It is best that these laws and values are learned while a person is still young.

The people who held the authority to teach cultural laws—parents, aunts and uncles, grandparents, and older siblings—also held the authority to enforce them. The procedures to enforcing these laws required no formal due process. Violations of cultural laws tended to lead to a certain punishment from one of many prosecutors, who would advise with compassion, would lecture, or would sometimes ask for compensation through chores or restrictions of privileges, like curfews. This custom continues today. Violations of cultural laws never lead to physical punishment, but to certain scorn. Violations and punishments are discussed in private; usually the teacher schools the learner about what he or she did wrong and why his or her actions resulted in an evident reaction. Most, if not all, cultural laws advocated for proper living and promoted the appropriate etiquette of being a Cheyenne person. Through Western eyes, cultural laws may be compared to "old wives' tales" or merely as superstition that holds no real value as laws. These ho'emanestôtse, however, are valued as part of the complete way of living as a Cheyenne and, more important, lay a foundation for future teaching and learning of higher levels of laws.[8] Some of the common cultural laws (action A), with their outcomes (action B), are as follows:

1. Do not speak when another is speaking, especially an elder; it is disrespectful.
2. Do not argue or fight with your relatives; you will always lose.
3. Do not play with water; you will become sick.
4. Do not whistle at night; you may awaken a spirit.
5. Do not tell lies when playing with others; they will not like you.
6. Do not play with others who tell lies; they will tell lies about you.
7. Comb your hair and fix it nice before going out into public; others will judge your family.
8. Clean your body with cold water in the morning, even in the winter; you will be warm and happy all day.
9. Properly dispose of your loose hair, fingernail, and toenail clippings; a person can curse you if they get hold of a piece of you.
10. Always leave some food when you eat; you will not become greedy.
11. Do not play with, in, or near dust devils; they are spirits and may take your soul.
12. Do not cry unless you mean it; otherwise, you will be faced with a true reason to mourn.
13. Do not eat greasy food outside after dark; a spirit may wipe your face and twist it.
14. Do not disturb the house of an animal, bird, or ant; they can harm you in return.
15. Do not cry for animals; they are sacred.

Numerous other cultural laws exist to teach a child to become a good citizen. Some cultural laws are taught into adulthood because learning to belong and function in the Cheyenne society never ends. Some examples of higher-level cultural laws, etiquette for adulthood in the household, are as follows:

16. Treat dogs with respect; they have always protected the people, especially children.
17. Young men and women should always do what they are told; otherwise, they will be unable to marry.
18. Do not sweep out the house after dark; you may sweep away someone's spirit.
19. Always pay attention to infants; otherwise, they will return to the spirit world.
20. When traveling and you see a hawk, continue; you are on the right path.
21. When traveling and you come across a snake, you are on the wrong path; return home and start again.
22. When you see a falling star at night, you are thinking correctly.
23. When you hear an owl at night, do not look for it; it is looking to curse.
24. When you see an owl, something bad will happen; prepare yourself.
25. When you see a magpie, you will eat some good meat soon.
26. When you see a coyote, be careful; someone wants you to fail.
27. When you see a fox, listen carefully; something is trying to advise you.
28. When you see an eagle soaring, someone is praying for you; acknowledge it.
29. When you see an eagle sitting, someone is patiently waiting for you.
30. If a bird flies into your house, then you are careless and must change your ways.
31. If your tepee blows open or falls over, your household is not kept in good spirits and those who live there are unhappy.
32. Always eat slowly; otherwise, you will become greedy and unhappy.
33. Prepare food with happiness and thankfulness, or do not prepare it at all; otherwise, your food will taste bad and those who eat it will feel as you did when you prepared it.

Cultural laws assigned small responsibilities but also prepared maturing citizens to follow and practice the higher order of laws, which reach into ceremonial practices and positions of leadership. Cultural laws were practiced throughout a person's lifetime, well into old age, and then taught to younger generations. New cultural laws were also taught at various junctures or changes in a citizen's life, like during puberty ceremonies, marriage, joining a society, enduring a covenant ceremony, and parenthood. Sometimes a person or family adopted cultural laws that applied only to their family or to an individual; for example, those families or individuals who kept a covenant bundle, a ceremonial pipe, or medicinal knowledge. Some cultural laws required stricter rules of conduct and resulted in harsher punishment; they can become traditional laws, a higher class of laws.

TRADITIONAL LAWS

Traditional laws are the most commonly practiced and widely known in the community and are applied to all citizens of the nation. The traditional laws were typically practiced and enforced in social settings, dances, feasts, and among the general public; elder family members and community leaders taught and held the authority to enforce them or at least inform family members of an individual's mishaps. No formal punishments were performed because the community, as a whole, enforced the laws by public sanctions against undesired or unwarranted acts that violated tradition. Typical punishments resulted in unavoidable public humiliation, shunning, and, in severe cases, the loss of status, rights, or privileges. Elders, parents, close friends, and leaders were merely responsible for informing the families or individuals of their wrongdoing. It was up to the individual and his or her family to generate their own means of reconciliation and restitution.

Most traditional laws follow the same formulas as cultural laws but typically place more emphasis on protecting against the consequence (action B). This was because action B resulted in public shame from the entire community and could be imposed on entire families, not just the individuals who violated the law. Traditions are very important, subjecting nonviolators to potentially long-lasting criticism. Some common traditional laws are as follows:

1. Do not joke or tease with another's spouse; it will lead to conflict.
2. Do not talk to your friend's spouse (who is of opposite sex); it will lead to conflict.
3. Do not touch another person's head or hair; it means you want to change their behavior.
4. Do not touch an elder's back; it means you want to harm him or her.
5. Do not hold another person's belongings in public; it means you desire others' property.
6. Do not speak in public unless you have earned the right; you may cause the audience to become angry, uncomfortable, or irritated.
7. No man should hunt alone; he will most assuredly cause conflict.
8. Never leave your child, infant or toddler, alone in public; you will be accused of being an unfit parent.

TSÉHÉSTANOVE NAA HO'EMANESTÔTSE: THE CHEYENNE WAY AND LAW

9. Never ask for pity from a person; you will earn a reputation for being pitiful.
10. Never ask to borrow an item unless you plan to return it promptly; a person will likely give it to you and ask for something in return later.
11. Never ask for the return of a gift; it will cause conflict.
12. Never refuse food or a gift; it is a sign of being selfish and that you are in a perpetual state of dissatisfaction.
13. Do not argue in public; you will be labeled an angry person.
14. Do not talk to certain people or compel them to talk to you. If you talk to criminals, liars, or troublemakers, you will be associated with these personalities.
15. Do not attend certain events. If you attend an event that is not necessarily for you, you may be ridiculed or burdened with responsibilities that are not yours.
16. Do not show off or brag; otherwise, people will not respect your accomplishments and lose respect for you.
17. Do not cry or show sadness in public, unless the time calls for it. This especially holds firm for ceremonial people, who may lose respect as spiritual leaders and people on whom others can rely in times of need.
18. Never judge another or point out their mistakes; you are not better than that person.
19. Do not talk bad about people or criticize the pain of others; else their problems will soon be yours or your family's.
20. Do not complain about trivial problems; you may make them much bigger.
21. Never quarrel or fight with your own people.
22. Never show anger or frustration.
23. Never show jealousy or greed.
24. Do not ridicule or humiliate your own people.
25. Do not imitate or make fun of someone who is hurt, crippled, or disabled; you will be injured as they are.

Traditional laws were also preventive to ensure that proper procedures were done when holding public events and services. The formula for these laws was simply to do action A. In the development of these ho'emanestôtse, the meanings became lost, probably because the teachings were obvious or violations were rare and the resulting outcome (action B) rarely came to fruition.

PART II: NOÓNÊHO'EMANESTÔTSE: TRADITIONAL LAW

For such laws there is no real explanation for doing action A, as it is accepted simply as tradition and known as "the way it has always been done." Slow Bull (Southern Cheyenne) described a fundamental law of the Cheyenne way of living: "If anyone in our immediate tribe should speak evil of us, or gossip about us, we were never in any case to antagonize the party or parties by quarrelling or fighting."[9] Some examples of similar laws are as follows:

26. Always do your best in public; it is a reflection of how you live your life.
27. Always keep your word to others; it is a reflection of how you value your life.
28. Women should not show off in public.
29. A man should not approach a woman in public, unless he wants to marry her.
30. Do not speak unless called upon.
31. Always feed visitors.
32. Always show respect and courtesy to visitors.
33. Humor and teasing are a part of life; do not be easily offended.
34. Pray before holding a meeting or hosting a feast.
35. Elders must eat first, then families with children, then the warriors, and lastly the chiefs.
36. When someone accomplishes something, they should host a giveaway.
37. Mourn the death of someone for only one year.
38. Walk patiently in public; do not rush.
39. Children are sacred; do not abuse them.
40. Women are sacred; do not abuse them.
41. The elderly are sacred; do not abuse them.
42. "If a man has a 'gift,' he must not commercialize it, a man died for doing so."[10]

Coyote (Northern Cheyenne) explained Cheyenne traditional law in reference to visitors:

> If a person visited the head of the family, he was greeted very heartily and invited to occupy the seat of honor on the west side, whether or not he was a stranger. If the visiting person happens to be a member of the tribe and not a stranger, the first thing the head of the family asks [is] if he has lunch. If not, the man of the family orders his wife to prepare the food for [the] visitor. On the other hand, if the visitor be a stranger or of another band or tribe, the host gives him a pipe smoke before asking as to the purpose of the visit. After having the smoke, the host now asks the visitor his purpose of entering the tipi. The host further states the purpose then he has given the pipe

smoke as a symbol of welcome and the stranger may proceed with what ever object matter he has in mind. At this point the visitor explains his purpose of his visit.[11]

Traditional laws prevented internal disputes, feuds, and the proliferation of unwanted drama. They were also the rules of proper etiquette and the ultimate source of Cheyenne manners, especially in formal matters. There were numerous other traditional laws that transcended into the higher classes of the Tsėhéstanove; some applied exclusively to people who had more responsibilities, like leaders and spiritual practitioners. The purpose of these higher traditional laws was to sustain national and band unity and to promote cooperation to the citizenry. While the majority of traditional laws became ingrained in the minds of citizens merely by the act thereof, some were very formal and were rarely used. As is the nature of humans, conflict was inevitable and the Cheyennes had a sophisticated system of justice to resolve conflicts, make judgments, and enforce punishments for serious crimes like murder. Ho'emanestôtse that directly addressed more serious challenges transcended traditions and were typically based on the ancient spiritual teachings found in ceremonies and rituals.

RITUAL LAWS

Ritual laws were established through patterns of ritual, which can be verified through the practice of ceremonies and were accepted as legitimate, official legal practices. This body of ho'emanestôtse was part of a system governed by formal rituals conducted by ceremonial or warrior societies. Those who interpreted the laws relied on their experience and knowledge of rituals associated with the law; specifically those aimed at achieving one goal: marriage, adoption, naming, puberty, or childbirth. Not all rituals of one type were exactly the same, as each may follow dissimilar processes and may be conducted by different, yet qualified, leaders. For example, a marriage ritual from one band may be different from that of another band, yet the leaders conducting the ceremonies may be of equal stature. Regardless of the differences in ritual, the end results (e.g., an adoption) were more important. When disruptions occurred (e.g., divorce, orphanhood, infidelity), they had potential to disrupt an entire family. Sometimes spiritual leaders and the chiefs were then called to intervene and use their expertise to come to fair and just resolutions in the matter. But the primary leaders for ritual laws were those who were part of the ceremonial or warrior societies. Slow Bull described how his father's role as a practitioner of traditional ceremonies gave him authority over others in teaching Cheyenne values of living. He was sixty years old at the time, in 1931:

> My father's name was Lame Bear, [he] was a medicine man, a member of several sacred ritualistic orders, and was regarded an authority upon these matters. His opinion on matter[s] of his character were without dispute. He was looked upon as a man of strong personality. He died at the age of 86. He was still hardy until about a month before his death. My mother died when she was about 60 years old. It was through my

PART II: NOÓNÊHO'EMANESTÔTSE: TRADITIONAL LAW

father's training and teaching that I became acquainted with the traditions and customs of our people and it was largely due to the fact that I became a member of these sacred orders in later years. I have also found that his teachings upon good behavior and respect of others has been valuable to me. My father's teachings and his talks to me and to other brothers of mine are still fresh in my memory.[12]

Before the establishment of reservations, ritual laws applied to all people who were of Cheyenne blood and lived among the people, because all citizens underwent a number of rituals from birth to death. Ritual laws did not necessarily apply directly to captives unless they also underwent appropriate adoption and marriage ceremonies; once done, they were recognized as Cheyenne citizens and required to adhere to the laws. I discuss traditional Cheyenne citizenship rules and captivity in more detail in this chapter.

If a person was Cheyenne and lived with another nation, then Cheyenne ritual laws did not necessarily apply to that person unless he or she moved back. If this person violated a law while with another nation, then he or she was not held responsible because that person was not considered Cheyenne. Conversely, if a person from another nation was adopted into the nation as a child and grew up in the Cheyenne culture, then he or she had a responsibility to the Tsėhéstanove. A woman who was captured as an adult and later married into the nation (Cheyennes never captured and adopted adult males) was also treated as a Cheyenne, but she had more freedom from Cheyenne laws than a child adoptee because she did not grow up among the Cheyennes. In other words, if a non-Cheyenne child was adopted into the nation and grew up as a Cheyenne and violated a ritual law, this person would face the same punishment as if a Cheyenne committed the same violation because they were both raised as citizens. By comparison, adult captives or those who married into the nation were likely ignorant of the Tsėhéstanove, and sometimes their ignorance benefited them. Their lack of knowledge, along with the lower expectations from the community, would factor into their punishment if they violated a law.

The remedies and processes for interpreting ritual laws were embedded within an associated ceremony, and the primary interpreters of these laws were family members who were initiated into guilds of social, ceremonial, and warrior societies. Families had a major part in cases involving violation of ritual laws. In the event that a ritual law was violated, the associated ceremony (including its origins, teachings, and purposes) was the starting point of evaluating a case. Typically a qualified person acted as a judge or peacemaker, or a qualified judicial body interpreted the violations of ritual laws. These folks were almost always the band chiefs or high-ranking ceremonial leaders. In the end they sought fair solutions, resolutions, or conclusions to the problem. When violation B occurs, the judge, peacemaker, or body must reevaluate ritual A (including associated oral traditions and previous cases) to reach resolution C. Not all ritual laws follow this method because an associated ceremony was not always present with all possible unforeseeable violations. In such cases the judge, peacemaker, or body reevaluated numerous A scenarios (previous, similar cases) and agreed upon one or more C resolutions. The goal was to achieve some balance where all parties reached an agreement and prevented any further dispute and animosity. Sometimes a band chief was part of the judiciary at this level, but not always.

NAMING CEREMONIES

The first and most basic ceremony in a Cheyenne's life was a naming or name-giving ceremony, which usually took place when a child began to talk and walk. Until a child was formally named, he or she was called by a nickname, typically a name given by a parent. These childhood names often remained as the child's primary name, even after ritually receiving a name, and they remained with a person into adulthood. A person's formally given Cheyenne name is his or her identity by which the entire nation will know him or her. While childhood names represent a child's membership to his or her family, the formal name is an emblem of band membership and national citizenship. Although traditionally there were other identifying factors of kinship and social status, a person's name told all other citizens that this person belonged to a legitimate Cheyenne family, a band, and the nation. As stated by Wooden Leg: "It was the common custom to pass down names to junior relatives," thus preserving consistency in families.[13] It was common for young men and women to formally acquire second and third formal names as rewards for accomplishing something great. Named individuals were then publicly recognized by others for their deeds and thereby gained other privileges and responsibilities, however small or large. Most important, a person who was ritually named was subject to the ho'emanestôtse of the nation. If the community did not recognize a person as a citizen, then he or she likely did not have the same rights and privileges. The naming ceremony or formal naming of a person addressed two fundamental principles in Cheyenne law: (1) Is the perpetrator a Cheyenne? (2) Is the victim Cheyenne? Once these fundamental questions were answered then the judge, peacemaker, or body easily determined a proper path to finding resolutions.

ADOPTION CEREMONIES

Another ritual of significance was the adoption ceremony, which allowed children to become part of a Cheyenne family. The ceremony was traditionally used for finding homes for orphans, which were typically adopted by extended family members: aunts and uncles or grandparents (no particular order of preference). Couples who had previously lost a child because of sickness or another unfortunate act were generally the first in line to adopt. Sometimes, if an orphan had no extended family and there were no foster parents, a chief adopted the child into his household and family. The orphaned child grew up as part of the new family, following the oral traditions of Sweet Medicine, Youngest, Red Buck, Red Hair, and

Blood Bachelor—all of whom were also orphans—thus providing the child with the infrastructure for a healthy living environment, which fostered proper psychological growth and a healthy upbringing.[14] Once a child became part of a family, the entire family was responsible for that child's behavior as well as the child's schooling in the Cheyenne way. Another common custom of adoption was for parents to ceremonially "give" one of their children to grandparents so they would not become lonely and could pass on the old ways, wisdom, and knowledge directly to the next generation.[15] This form of adoption ritual was done within the family.

Before the reservations, the Cheyennes frequently captured children from other nations and Cheyenne families adopted them. This form of adoption did not necessarily have a formal ritual, since the act of war was sanctioned through the Medicine Arrows covenant (I highlight war customs in chapter 12).[16] In the rare cases of non-Cheyenne, noncaptive adoptions (e.g., if a child was from another friendly nation and not a captive of war), the adoption ritual was performed in private among the family. The ritual required a renaming of the adoptee, typically the name of a long deceased member of the family. Afterward the newly adopted Cheyenne was recognized as a part of the family and part of the band. The new adoptee, however, did not acquire all rights and responsibilities of a citizen until the child became an adult or if he or she were initiated into a social, ceremonial, or war society.

The family was responsible for teaching their new relative the rights and responsibilities of Cheyenne citizenship, and inevitably the adoptee was responsible for knowing the Cheyenne ways when they matured into adulthood. Should the new citizen ever commit a crime, he or she faced the same consequences as did a born Cheyenne. Nobody could argue otherwise. When a non-Cheyenne adopted child matured into an adult and married a Cheyenne spouse, their children were considered Cheyenne and belonged to their parents' band.[17] Wooden Leg's (Northern Cheyenne) uncle was captured from a Crow village as a child. After a number of years of his living with the Cheyenne, the people "recognized" him: "He knew he was born a Crow, but he never showed any desire to leave us for returning to them."[18] The man married a Cheyenne woman and had children and grandchildren who were all considered full Cheyenne. All family members, despite their Crow blood, even the Crow-born man, were responsible for adhering to the Tsėhéstanove. Sometimes captives tried to escape but if they could not, "they ordinarily became reconciled to their lot and were as proud of their adopted tribe as if they had been born into it."[19]

Before reservations, the Cheyenne people rarely questioned the identity of their own. Citizenship and identity were always assumed because Cheyenne people rarely married outside of the nation, and few outsiders married in. Those who married in conformed to the Cheyenne way and if they did not want to, they could leave and rejoin their people. Even with a small population, in comparison to that of much larger Plains Indian nations, the Cheyennes were able to sustain autonomy and familial lineages. Intertribal intermarrying primarily occurred with allied nations like the Arapaho and the several bands of the Lakota. But even in such cases, Cheyenne ritual laws could have only extended within the boundaries of the nation. For example, a Cheyenne who married an Arapaho and moved to live with his or her spouse as an Arapaho essentially withdrew citizenship from the Cheyenne Nation. The people expected him or her to attain citizenship of the Arapaho Nation, according to Arapaho custom. If, however, an enemy tribe captured a Cheyenne child, then this child was removed from its family and household without choice and the child's citizenship would not be revoked. If the Cheyenne family regained their child then the child could easily be restored as a citizen.

EAR-PIERCING CEREMONY

Another rite related to ritual law was the ear-piercing ceremony, which children of both genders underwent in public. The ceremony represents the time when children are old enough to talk and communicate at a higher level of learning, around the ages of three to six. Piercing the ears signifies that children have begun to consciously listen and obey their parents. Pierced ears are a symbol of discipline in a child's development and learning, but they also reveal to the public their presence in the community. Traditionally, others were permitted to ask the children for help and may even discipline them for misbehaving. Elders

Aquqavenuts (Crossed Feathers) with Wife and Daughter. June 1908, De Lancey W. Gill, National Anthropological Archives, Smithsonian Museum Support Center, Suitland, Maryland NA.

may taunt: Be brave, be honest, be virtuous, be industrious, be generous, do not quarrel! If you do not do these things, people will talk about you in the camp; they will not respect you; you will be shamed. If you listen to this advice you will grow up to be a good man or woman, and you will amount to something."[20]

A child with pierced ears belongs to the nation as a citizen, but more importantly as one who serves the community. Piercing ears affirms competence, consciousness, the ability to listen, and resistance to pain. A child should not cry when the ceremonial leader pierces his or her ears, but they typically do. The philosophy behind ear piercing is connected with future obstacles of enduring puberty and the challenges in life including joining a society, participating in the big ceremonies, marriage, and parenthood. Cheyennes could also identify Indians from other tribes by their style of ear piercing.[21] The ear-piercing ceremony was a safeguard but answered three fundamental principles for the spiritual leaders and the judiciary when they evaluated a case of a person who violated a law: (1) Is the perpetrator competent? (2) Does the perpetrator understand what he or she did? (3) Does the perpetrator choose to obey or ignore the Cheyenne way of living? More likely than not, the affirmative to these questions were assumed without much debate when a child had pierced ears.

PUBERTY RITUALS

The high traditional and ritual laws associated with puberty, adulthood, and parenthood were exclusively for specific genders at certain ages. Men did not take part in the puberty rituals of womanhood and women did not necessarily take part in those of manhood. Nonetheless, the puberty rituals served several purposes. One was to prepare young men and women to become functioning members of the Cheyenne society—that is, functioning citizens of the Cheyenne Nation.

He'eévestôtse (Womanhood), Part I

One of the old rituals that came from the ancient time was the young woman's puberty ceremony. The "menstrual lodge" was done to formally bring young girls into he'eévestôtse (womanhood) once they underwent their first menses.[22] The event lasted four days and was primarily a private family affair, organized by older female members of the family, particularly those on the mother's side. A young girl was ceremonially bathed in cold water, purified with white sage, and then painted the sacred color, red, before she was schooled on the rules of he'eévestôtse. Her conduct and behavior as a woman were cloaked in responsibility and duty, since women were the backbone of the nation, the mothers, teachers, and caretakers of the family. She was taught to be a good woman and was in training to be a mother and matriarch of her future family. Her initiation to womanhood also came with restrictions.

As preserved in the oral tradition and in practice, women held a sacred place in Cheyenne culture; women were influential in creating numerous rituals and ceremonies (see chapters 2 and 3), and young women were credited for creating the Council of Forty-Four Chiefs (see *A Sacred People*). The Cheyennes, however, were not completely absent of holding women to a different set of standards than men, especially in ceremony. The differing standards are evidence that Cheyenne society recognized the differences between the two genders without devaluing one as inferior or valuing one as superior. For example, the Cheyennes had customs that restricted women from participating in ceremonies during menstruation. The roots of such restrictions lay in traditional Cheyenne views of the sacredness of procreation. Yet without a knowledge of such roots, traditional laws can be viewed as misogynistic. Take, for example, the rules described by Wrapped Hair (Só'taeo'o): "Cheyenne and Só'taeo'o are strict about menstruation. They [the woman] can't eat with anyone else or go anywhere. They are supposed to have a little tent by themselves."[23] Also recall the story of "Sweet Medicine Calls the Buffalo," by White Buffalo, in chapter 2, when Sweet Medicine replaced the ceremonial woman with one who was not "on her moon."

Traditional views toward menstruation are often misunderstood by outsiders and viewed as archaic and patriarchal, but traditional gender restrictions served a higher purpose, even though the Cheyennes were not free from occasional incidents of chauvinism and toxic masculinity. Traditional laws served as the basis for nation-building, law and justice, and the sustenance of a way of life that fit seamlessly with the Cheyenne people. I am careful to not sanitize or fabricate the traditional Cheyenne views of women in this discussion. I do, however, believe that, as earlier asserted, it is a worthy pursuit to uncover Cheyenne perspectives instead of relying on the colonial lens when studying traditional customs and laws. Without a doubt, mistakes were made in previous studies conducted by whites, but the traditional system remained and was never completely compromised until the full-scale efforts of forced assimilation. I will reemphasize that a major goal of this book is to provide a Cheyenne perspective of themselves. And if some of these traditional and ritual laws and customs should one day become prioritized values above others, the Cheyennes can rely on the ancient mechanisms to adapt their culture and converge it with others. This is how the Cheyennes kept their nation alive over the course of its entire existence.

After discussing matters related to menstruation and ceremony with elder and ceremonial women, and referring back to former Sacred Hat Keeper Josie Limpy's story about the Great Medicine Dance (see chapter 3), I offer a rare, but necessary, Cheyenne perspective. First, among the Cheyenne, both the Tsétsêhéstâhese and Só'taeo'o, it was universally believed that "woman's power of procreation" was a sacred force because it is the ultimate source of all life on earth. Woman's power is a physical, mental, emotional, and spiritual force that is largely unknown to men. Every woman has "woman's power," whether she fully understands her power or not. It is a very personal and private force that only other women talk about, yet it only reveals part of itself to the family in physical form on certain occasions. One is during menstruation; other times are during pregnancy, motherhood, and menopause. Men do not endure these events, so they are not expected to learn about them as women do. But men are expected to respect a woman's power, since all humans have mothers and grandmothers, and they likely have sisters. There is a strong likelihood that a man will eventually have a wife and daughters as well, so basic knowledge and respect for the unknown often reveals itself in traditional and ritual laws.

Collectively, the Cheyennes traditionally believe that a woman's power as a force of energy could inadvertently disempower a man's medicine (spiritual energy), especially if a woman came into contact with his spiritually charged devices, such as his eagle feathers, pipe, spear, or shield. For these reasons the Cheyennes adopted numerous laws and customs with respect and reverence to woman's power. Menstruating women, for example, were not allowed to speak to certain family members, especially adult males.

Other laws that revere women's power of procreation are linked to the women's puberty ceremony. Michelson's unknown Southern Cheyenne informant explained some of these ritual laws:

> During menses Cheyenne woman formerly ate alone. Buffalo meat would be cooked on an open fire, not in a soup, so that a [menstruating woman] might eat a part of the meat not cooked in a soup. Otherwise, no matter how far off she was, the meat would be tainted and a man eating it would become pimply. Under no circumstances is a [menstruating woman] permitted to enter a tipi where a sick person is, the sick would be worse.[24]

Mack Haag (Southern Cheyenne) also explains ritual laws related to menstruation:

> When a woman or girl menstruates she is not allowed to enter a tipi where a medicine bag is under any circumstances. Even after her time is over. She enters 4 different tipis before she is allowed to enter the tipi where a medicine bag is. Sun-Dance priests and some others who are the ones to keep the women out. The others (besides the Sun-Dance priests) are taught by dreams only.[25]

Both men and women were responsible for maintaining ritual laws and customs, even if they may not have participated in a woman's "coming of age" or puberty ceremony. Women, however, were particularly responsible for protecting others against "woman's power" because they and no one else knew their bodies. The Cheyennes believed that "woman's power," like most forces of energy, had a positive-negative duality that had to be kept in balance. Such tasks were the responsibility of other women, either those in an individual's kinship system or those who shared membership in the ceremonial or social societies.

The hoʼemanestôtse associated with the women's puberty ceremony also centered on adolescent behaviors in courting, marriage, and childrearing. During courtship, they were to not be so easily convinced by young suitors to engage in sexual acts. Young women were not to run off with boyfriends; they had to be models of virtue and heʼeévestôtse.[26] The primary enforcer of the rituals associated with women's puberty was the grandmother, who was always a ceremonial leader and authority. Until a young woman was married, no other person was of higher authority, as Wooden Leg (Northern Cheyenne) described:

> An old woman was an important part of every household organization. This was the custom among all of the plains Indians, especially in families where girls were growing up. This old woman saw that each occupant of the lodge used only his or her own proper bed or place of waking repose. She compelled each to keep his or her personal belongings beside or at the head of the owner's assigned space. She was at the same time the household policeman, the night watchman and the drudge. Ordinarily her badge of office was a club. She was conceded the authority to use this club in enforcing the rules of the lodge.[27]

Wrapped Hair described this club as a "stone war club, fixed in rawhide, a women's weapon alone, not used by men."[28]

After puberty, a young woman earned the rites of passage and was allowed to own her first "paints" for ceremony, along with the rights to use sweet grass, cedar, and white sage in blessing. Her family members gave her a robe, decorated with beads and shells, which she tied with a finely decorated belt to signify her maturity and virtue. She should always keep clean and comb her hair nice, and always wear nice clothing to show her beauty. She could now join a woman's society and, during her menses, attend their lodge away from the household and in the comfort of older and wiser friends. Violations of her newly found womanhood could result in the loss of such rights and respect.

Hetanévestôtse (Manhood), Part I

The puberty ceremonies, by their practice and nature, reinforced that women were the first teachers of both girls and boys, which is why Cheyenne mothers were especially important to the survival of the Cheyenne way. Boys first learned the laws of Cheyenne hetanévestôtse (manhood), as explained by Red Eagle (Southern Cheyenne), from their mothers:

> My mother was a very good woman. She taught me how to grow up a good man. She told me never to tell lies, to be always sympathetic towards people who were "crazy"; never to make fun of them, nor to laugh at them, but always to treat them in a kind and considerate manner. I had to treat the crippled and the wounded and people born disfigured in any way in the same manner. If I broke any of these injunctions, my mother told me that I would never go to heaven.[29]

When a boy reached the age of puberty, typically identified by his change in voice, his father and uncles took him into a sweat lodge to begin his spiritual development as a man and the teachings of hetanévestôtse. They recounted to him at length the responsibilities of being a good man, provider, protector, and warrior. Boys belonged to their mothers until they reached puberty; then they became part of their mother's group or band, so the camp no longer perceived them as children.[30] Male relatives were responsible for teaching growing boys the proper conduct of courtship, marriage, and héhe'estovestôtse (fatherhood).

In time, the young man would join a warrior society and engage in intertribal warfare, so his reputation and appearances should exemplify his personality. A good appearance signified a good personality, care, and confidence, but looks were not the only defining factor in a young man's maturity. His character was paramount. The only thing that would prevent him from joining a society would be if he accidently or intentionally killed another Cheyenne, but if he had a poor character, warrior societies may not recruit him.[31] Violations of his newly found manhood could result in the loss of these rights and respect. Unlike for the roles and responsibilities of young women, when a young man matured into adulthood, his schooling in the ways of courtship and marriage was a bit more intensive. Cheyenne custom dictated that young men take the initiative when courting, which is why it was important for young men to learn how to court properly and to follow the proper etiquette to win a prospective bride. The Cheyenne traditionally placed a lot of responsibility on women and appear to demand an unfair amount from them during their menses. However, as I highlight in the next chapter, the institutions of courtship and marriage demanded a lot from young men. In particular, young men had to be courageous without being overambitious and they had to demonstrate financial stability and physical strength while remaining humble, among other challenges of the young heart. The purpose for such demands was to create and re-create a healthy nation.

CHAPTER 7

Tsėhéstanove naa Néé'éve:
The Cheyenne Way and Marriage

When all is ready, they will ask an old woman—not a man—connected with ceremonial customs, such as the Sun Dance, to get consent of the girl's parents.

—Coyote (Northern Cheyenne) [1]

The Tsėhéstáno, through the Tsėhéstanove and the Tsėhéseamanēö'o, provided several outlets for the social lives of young adults. There were numerous opportunities for young people to get together and mingle to facilitate the creation of healthy relationships. At various festivals, feasts, and dances, young folks could engage in formalized courtship. Partnered and group dancing allowed for formal social interactions with members of the opposite sex. Young men especially enjoyed these dances, as they facilitated courtship with a young woman if he was too shy to approach. Wooden Leg (Northern Cheyenne) described this trend:

> It was entirely a social affair for young people, not a ceremonial or war dance. In the midst of the open area within our camp circle the women and girls cleared off and leveled a broad surface of ground. The young men brought a tall pole and set it up at the center of the dancing ground. Charcoal Bear, the medicine chief, brought the buffalo skin that regularly hung from the top of the sacred tepee. He tied it to the top end of our long pole before we raised it. We built a big bonfire. The drums and the Cheyenne dance songs enlivened the assemblage. It seemed that peace and happiness was prevailing all over the world, that nowhere was any man planning to lift his hand against his fellow man.[2]

Participants attended these dances dressed in their finest clothing and regalia, and they always went in groups with friends and relatives. The events were filled with joy and glee as few married adults attended such social dances. The he'emanehe (half-woman man) facilitated the social dances and were willing to serve as formal matchmakers.

COURTSHIP

The traditional marriage ceremonies and customs originated from the story of Ho'ehêvêsénóóhe (Standing On The Ground) and the chief's wife, Ésevona'e (Buffalo Woman). The marriage ceremony fortified a body of ho'emanestôtse associated with courting, domestic relations, and parenthood. Courtship was considered a ritual on its own, since young men learned the trials and tribulations of rejection, dating, romance, and the art of love. This was considered to be an important part of the Cheyenne way and hetanévestôtse (manhood).

Hetanévestôtse (Manhood), Part II

Young men often courted young women over long periods of time, and the culture of courtship was not clouded with bashfulness where there was a genuine pursuit of love and companionship. Sometimes a man would travel for miles to a neighboring camp to meet and mingle with a young woman he may have met previously.[3] "Talking to women" was the custom that facilitated proper courtship between a young woman and her suitor, but adults knew that courtship could potentially turn to unacceptable practices of premarital sexual relations. "Cheyenne custom did not tolerate this; fathers and husbands were very strict, and Cheyenne women and girls were famous among the Plains tribes for their virtue," asserted George Bent (Southern Cheyenne).[4]

In courtship a man should not be overanxious, jealous, or bitter. A young man should yield if a young woman refused his advances.[5] Young men had to demonstrate discipline following traditional values of hetanévestôtse. As a man he should not brag or fight with his fellow tribesmen. He should hunt to support his mother and sisters and always be around good friends, those who would boast for him and join him on hunting trips.[6] He should begin to remember his dreams and talk to spiritual leaders to find their meanings; this will help guide him in his life. As a maturing young man, he must also take care of his own appearance by keeping his face clear of unwanted hair around the chin and cheeks, since bushy faces and eyebrows were associated with immoral men and murderers.[7] His hair should be braided nicely and he should always be clean and present to the community the beauty of his manhood. A man should not have too many children, not more than three, and try to have children not one after another, but separated by seven or ten years. This would allow him to adequately care for and concentrate on raising a quality family. He should refrain from having multiple lovers and only have one wife, but Cheyenne custom did allow polygamy. These were some basic, pre-reservation customs.

Stands In Timber (Northern Cheyenne) recalled that the Cheyennes used to live in a time when they did not have the formal marriage ceremony, which occurred in a time before the Véhoo'o and Nótâxeo'o. The population was low and they had to increase their numbers, which led to early marriages; inevitably, this practice has since changed. Stands In Timber explained:

> The story I was going to mention was that one time they were killing each other, and one time they made a rule—it was announced that all young men and all young girls were to be married and have children, and that way their people would be increased. And that rule was changed by Sweet Medicine. When the chiefs made laws when they were about thirty years old they were old—that was about the age when a young Cheyenne was married. If he was married too young he was criticized by the people. Sweet Medicine himself had said, the time is coming when you are not going to wait for the period of your age when you are with a woman. There will be young kids, young children, be married to each other not old enough to be married, not old enough to be a man.[8]

The Sweet Medicine tradition reemphasizes that the Cheyennes were to be mindful of their marriage practices, since they could potentially revert to old practices if they failed to uphold his teachings.[9] White Eagle (Southern Cheyenne) discussed the changing customs during the early reservation period in 1910: "Boys usually marry now from age 16 to 17, long ago they had to be over 20. The same applied to girls."[10] Before that, the Cheyennes were not pressured by mainstream culture, assimilation policies, or Christian dogma. Pre-reservation marriage standards were dictated by custom and rooted in sacred teachings of procreation, which made marriage a lifelong commitment to child-rearing. There was no dating, so marriage was a sacred and serious custom. Once a couple engaged in consensual sexual activity, they were considered married and belonged to one another.[11] A formal marriage ceremony typically followed.

The proper courting etiquette of traditional Cheyennes occurred while suitors were in the late teens and early twenties. A courageous young man approached a young woman while she was picking berries, fetching water, tanning hides, or doing other daily chores. Some women considered night courtship unromantic and unacceptable, but the practice occurred regularly at large social dances and gatherings. A bachelor openly expressed his feelings and was unafraid of rejection, even though the likelihood of rejection was greater than success if he sought an eligible and virtuous bachelorette. This encouraged the young man to further his pursuit with more creativity and imagination in later encounters; it also showed the self-discipline and self-respect of a virtuous Cheyenne woman. If, however, a young man went too far and attempted to violate a young woman's virtue, the consequences were shameful, as told by Mack Haag: "If a man is caught trying to get in the tent of his girl, the mother will attend to this. He is hog-tied, stripped of clothes, even breechcloth, and placed outside. In the morning women will come and have a laugh over it."[12]

The Cheyennes had a formal courtship process that was not considered a taboo, as Wolf Chief (Ôhméseheso) explained: "Courting girl at her home, the young pair wrapped in a blanket, or elsewhere they don't need a blanket. If a young man visits a girl with a blanket, his intentions are known. If he doesn't he is presumed only to be visiting."[13] "Blanket courtship" was the common courtship custom, where a suitor may wait for a young woman near her parents'

PART II: NOÓNÊHO'EMANESTÔTSE: TRADITIONAL LAW

Young Man and Wife, 1893. James Mooney, 1861–1921, National Anthropological Archives, Smithsonian Museum Support Center, Suitland, Maryland (NAA INV 06115700, OPPS NEG 323).

lodge to cloak her with a blanket or a fine elk or deer robe. A young man "talked to," or "courted," a young woman while he wrapped her in a fancy decorative blanket or robe. The blanket courtship was a formal means for establishing a relationship for marriage. Sometimes numerous young men, who were serious about marrying the same girl, lined up and waited for their chance to "talk" with her.[14]

A young suitor may consult with elder male relatives, even a medicine man to use "love medicine," which could be given with a flute or the tail of a white-tailed deer.[15] He may give a ring or a bracelet made of elk antler or buffalo horn. He may also give her some sweet chewing gum made from tree sap or a gift of wildflowers gathered from the hillside. The young warrior may also bring her food or a present. There was a fine line in seeking help from medicine men, since it was sometimes perceived as witchcraft and some suitors could be labeled cowards if they relied exclusively on medicine to win a woman.[16] Young men proved themselves in hunting and in battle, and those who relied on medicine to get women were perceived as unworthy suitors. Nonetheless, after months of courting, a young suitor may win the consent of a girl for marriage. A girl's formal consent to marriage was the most common way a young couple were wed, as explained by Wolf Chief (Ôhméseheso):

> The marriage customs of the Cheyenne and Sutaio were the same. There were three ways of getting a woman.
>
> 1st — to win the consent of the girl
>
> 2nd — to trade for the girl, giving horses, etc. The bridegroom's mother giving beaded goods, meals once in a while before the marriage to wish good will of the girl's parents
>
> 3rd — when young men were out scouting, if a member has a sister at home that another wants, the latter will treat the former man as brother-in-law, takes care of his horse, does his cooking for him, etc. Then the girl and her mother will be told if the brother has agreed. Then the man can have her.[17]

Both the second and third methods relied heavily on the participation and blessing of both families, suggesting that the Cheyennes had arranged marriages. Each method relied on the Cheyenne principles of brotherhood and kinship responsibility.

In arranged marriages, the two families had long conversations about their relatives to find out if they were related by blood or through a previous marriage of relatives. Parents typically knew their relatives for generations and could easily identify blood relations with the utmost certainty. If either party found out that they were blood relatives, then the other was informed and the courtship stopped immediately. No longer did the two mingle. If no such blood relation existed, then the conversations about one another continued, as parents knew the obvious intentions of their children. Relation by marriage was not forbidden but often raised questions for both families because it sometimes *appeared* to be a violation of the incest law. Both sets of parents had to consent to a marriage, but custom dictated that the young man talk directly with the girl's father, thus exhibiting his courage and discipline in formal affairs. After consent, the young man's family gave a generous dowry for a man's daughter; horses were the most valued gifts. If the father did not consent, if he thought the suitor was unworthy, he returned all gifts within a day. The young suitor then gave up his pursuit and sought another.[18]

Young men were encouraged to choose women of virtue and to be bold but sincere in their courtship. More important, they were to accept rejection with humility if a girl turned them down. A young man who did not yield gracefully to a girl's rejection brought shame to his family. Wrapped Hair described how parents, especially mothers, protected their daughters' virtue:

> Sometimes, not often, a young man will hang around and crawl in when all are asleep. If the girl don't want him, they will try to beat him there, and when he gets away, the girl's mother (or father sometimes) will go over to the young man's mother's camp and tear everything up. The young man's mother can not get angry at this.

He'eévestôtse (Womanhood), Part II

Mothers, aunts, and grandmothers were particularly strict in protecting their daughters' virtue, as Mack Haag explained: "If she catches a boy copulating with her daughter, she will use a butcher knife on him, so she would with regard to granddaughters and her niece."[19] The fear of violence was enough to prevent young men from violating the rules of courtship, and most suitors followed the sacred teachings that reinforced the sacredness of women.

Young women were also taught to be true representatives of Cheyenne he'eévestôtse (womanhood) in such matters and to embody all virtues and sacredness of femininity. Young women wore chastity belts that had both practical and symbolic meanings to preserve their virtue. Young women could neither criticize how other people looked nor ridicule others if they were poor. Beauty of personality and heart was just as important as physical beauty. At the proper ages, both males and females were bluntly advised on sexual norms and taboos by their older relatives. The direct and frank conversations served a great service to avert misinformation and perversion of the nature of human sexuality. Sex was not discussed in shame or embarrassment, as elder relatives imparted practical knowledge when the time was appropriate. A Southern Cheyenne woman advised her niece:

> You must remember that when a man touches your breasts and vulva he considers that you belong to him. And in the event that he does not care to marry you he will not hide what he has done to you, and you will be considered immoral. And you will not have a chance to marry into a good family. In short, you will not be purchased, which is surely the ambition of all young women. What I mean by marrying into a good family is that the young man's people are not liars, thieves, or lazy, nor have they committed any offensive crime. If you allow the young man to take advantage of you willingly he will make jokes and sing songs with words about you. The people will know and we will be embarrassed and ashamed, especially since you have been brought up and taught in a good way.[20]

Young women were encouraged to avoid families of poor character. This was a social mechanism that created a culture in which every family strived to protect their image and reputation. Belle Highwalking (Northern Cheyenne) also described the challenges that women experienced:

> I don't brag about being rich and owning good things because I remember what a hard life I had when I was young. But when I chose my husband, I must have used my head. I never talked to many boys although some married men who were women-crazy wanted to date me. I always knew they were married so I didn't talk to them. I answered them but I never hated [*sic*; dated] them. If I had talked to them, I would have lost my respect. Since I had no mother, I was poor and it was my father who lectured me. He told me to stay single for a long time because it was hard when you had children. "But you won't get left out. When you get married, there will be a purpose in your life," he said. I listened to him and never sassed him back when he lectured. He told me, "Never sass back no matter what people say, whether you like it or not." The reason why I decided to get married was to take care of my grandmother.[21]

A young woman was encouraged to marry a good man, one who was caring and loving, who would treat her and their future children with love and respect. Despite the human tendencies to pursue exclusively out of desire and passion, suitors were encouraged to practice proper courting rituals and did not "steal" girls in the heat of passion. Eloping was considered a violation of the marriage rituals but not the courtship rules. Elopement carried no formal punishment but was an insult to the girl's father or, in the absence of her father, her brothers. It was an act of stealing, a shameful act, a violation of sacred law, but a violation that could be forgiven if the elopement was mutual and developed into a marriage. The relatives of the girl typically retaliated in cases of elopement by shaming the young man's family. An elder female relative may use her club or knife on the young man to inflict or threaten injury, but not to kill. Young women had the final say in whom they married, but if a girl eloped with her beau as a willing accomplice, they were devoted to winning the hearts of their relatives, as Wooden Leg (Northern Cheyenne) explained:

> They went together to the lodge of the young man's brother or sister or to a place where dwelt elder relatives of his. The next morning two intruders were discovered there, a young man and his young wife. The discovery was announced, all parties interested were informed. Not often was the information displeasing. Ordinarily all concerned were contented and manifested their contentment in the usual exchange of gifts.[22]

In successful cases of elopement, newly wedded elopers lived with the young man's band, among his family and relatives, and it was sometimes considered poor judgment even after reconciliation. The formal marriage ceremony was the best path for two young lovers, which is why it typically followed an elopement.

MARRIAGE

The formal marriage ceremony called for much celebration.[23] The Cheyennes perceived marriage not as the unification of two individuals but as the unification of two families. Each family had important roles in the formal wedding customs, which often differed from band to band. Weddings were organized much like arranged marriages, where the suitor sought the hand of a girl by formally asking permission from the girl's father. If a father accepted the proposal from a worthy suitor, he formally consented to the suitor's family by accepting a dowry. This was done if the father knew that his daughter and the suitor were already an item. If he did not know, the father asked his daughter about the relationship. This was her chance to refuse, and if she did, the gifts were returned. Sometimes fathers made such decisions if their daughters were growing too old to live with their parents and were old enough to start a family of their own. Most women consented in their first marriage; few consented to be second wives and typically refused to wed a married man. Coyote (Northern Cheyenne) explained a process in which a suitor's male relative formally asked a family member to help him with his marriage. It begins with a pipe ceremony:

> [When a] young man of their immediate family should be mated in marriage to a certain maiden and all have approved of the proposed marriage, by the purchase of the girl. He therefore asks for aid to go in this purchase such as horses, blankets and dried goods. The [elder relative] replies, yes, if agreeable, and at once acts by giving a horse for the visitor to take back to where he came from. And if otherwise, he gives nothing. Now the [elder relative] will follow the latter [the young man] to where the marriage is to take place. When all is ready, they [the young man and the elder relative] will ask an old woman—not a man—connected with ceremonial customs, such as the Sun Dance, to get consent of the girl's parents. She [the old woman] cannot be refused because of her ceremonial affiliation. It is considered a bad omen to refuse an old woman. She brings back the report that she has gained the consent of the parents. The parents before consenting must gain the consent of the girl's brother if she has any. It is considered bad form to ask a woman's consent to this marriage (that is, the girl nor her women-relatives may be asked).
>
> The next move for the young man's folks is to bring horses. Bringing the horses is done by women. Men do not participate in this performance. Then it is up to the girl's folks to decide where they will take these horses. Then they (the girl's folk) call in men to select their horses one by one. If a girl has a brother, he is the one to direct [who] should select a horse first. He very rarely has the first selection. When all the horses have been selected by the girl's men folks, these men folks in turn must give their own horses to the groom's men folks. The girl's women folk will take the horses to the groom's men folk; approaching the home of the groom.
>
> The women will take the girl and the groom's women folk to go meet, [with] the horses and bride. At that point there are 2 ways of welcoming her: a blanket may be spread on the ground and the bride sits on, and the groom's women folk take each a corner and carry her to the tipi of her future husband; or a stout woman will carry her on her back and another will keep her legs and feet up. This last has gone out of use. Now she is in the tipi of her future husband, sits on the west side. Then the groom's women folk come in one by one to hug her and show their personal affection for their new relative. Then the women folks bring in their robes, trinkets, bracelets, and dress her up in full regalia, braid her hair, paint her face. In the meanwhile the bride's people are making great preparations in the way of erecting a tipi for the couple and prepare food to feed the groom's folks. This done, word is sent that all is ready. The bride goes

back with all her gifts to be divided among her women folks. After the division of the property, then the girl is personally instructed by her folks to call her husband. And nobody is to be with them. The groom arrives at his new home. Then an announcer cries out to the groom's folks inviting them to a big feast at the groom's home. Then the bride's folks give away moccasins to the groom's people. In return for the personal property the girl's women folk give away tipis [to the] man's women folk. In this case the tipi put up for the groom and contents is given away. Then the girl's folks will put up another tipi for them to live in thereafter.[24]

In all marriages both families had some responsibilities for preparing a formal ceremony. Sometimes the matchmaker or ceremonial priestess was the primary organizer of the event; they prepared the bride by conducting numerous small rituals: combing hair, preparing food, dressing, and much advising on the conduct of marriage.[25] It was common for the female relatives from both families to facilitate the wedding. A Southern Cheyenne woman described her wedding ceremony, which was an arranged marriage:

> My people saddled one of the horses on which I rode over to my future husband's people, leading the four other horses. My future husband's women folk met me near their camps and I dismounted. They carried me on the blanket the rest of the way, and let me down at the entrance of my future husband's tipi. I walked in and sat beside him. This young man was no sweetheart of mine; he was a stranger to me: he never had come to see me when I was still single. I wondered if I would learn to love him in the future. After some little time the women brought in many shawls, dresses, rings, bracelets, leggings, and moccasins. They then had me change clothes. They braided my hair and painted my face with red dots on my cheeks. When I was completely arrayed in my marriage clothes I was told to return to my people. My husband's women folk carried the balance of my clothing to my tipi. In the meantime my mother and aunt had prepared a large feast. Towards evening my own tipi was erected. The crier called in a loud voice inviting all my husband's relatives, naming my husband as the host. My husband came over with his male relatives. While there they told jokes, and some related their war exploits; still others narrated funny things that had happened to them in the earlier days.[26]

After the Southern Cheyenne woman was married a year, she had her first child and professed the sanctity of their arranged marriage: "It was at this time that I began really to love my husband. He always treated me with respect and kindness. We had eight children before he died."[27] It is impossible to determine the success rate of arranged marriages, but what is known is that they did exist among the Cheyennes.

Cheyenne marriages truly celebrated the sincerity and dedication in the union of man and woman. The wedding ceremony was symbolic of the sacred union between man and woman, reflective of the union of the Só'taeo'o culture hero Tomôsévêséhe and his wife, Ésevona'e. White Eagle (Southern Cheyenne) also described the marriage ceremony and the power that a would-be wife had in stopping an arranged marriage:

PART II: NOÓNÊHO'EMANESTÔTSE: TRADITIONAL LAW

Man and Woman inside Tipi, 1893. James Mooney, 1861–1921, National Anthropological Archives, Smithsonian Museum Support Center, Suitland, Maryland (NAA INV 06079500, 1).

When a young man wanted to marry, he got his brothers and relatives together. If they approved his choice, they got horses, etc., together to buy the girl for him. These presents are taken before the girl's father's tipi. He calls all the girl's brothers or nearest relatives to decide whether they should give the girl to this young man or not. If they agreed to do so, all pick out what they want from the property [that] has been brought there of the young man's relatives. [The] same day or next they bring about the same amount of property to the young man's people, the girl with this. The girl's people put up 2 or 3 tipis for them to live in. These are near her father's place. There she is married. If the girl has sisters, they go to her lodge and are married to the young man. If the girl's relatives didn't agree [to the marriage from the beginning], then the young man's people go to the girl's father and ask what he wants to be added, e.g., a special horse, etc. Then that is brought and ceremony continues.

It sometimes (though rarely) [happens] that brothers and relations wanted the girl to marry a young man she never met; so as to get his property. Then if she was in love with some other young man, she would let him know by another girl and they would elope. Then the property would be returned to the fellow that got left. Then the successful fellow would give presents and receive them as above.[28]

When a wife became part of her husband's family, the mother-in-law introduced her to all of the family members and proclaimed: "We brought my daughter-in-law home. Do not speak harsh to her or ever scold her. Treat her well and take good care of her, I beg of you and also your children."[29] Because of the spiritual unions of marriage, very few couples divorced. The men were instructed directly on their responsibilities as husbands, fathers, and men, as told by an unknown Southern Cheyenne man:

After marriage of young couples, [the] father of male person is one that lays down the law to his son. He tells his son never to find fault or purposely start a quarrel with his wife, or to beat her up on slight provocation. It is silly and unmanly to abuse your wife for your own grievance and fancy. The first thing you will know, your wife will be leaving you, and you will follow her and plead with her to come home. In the event she returns with you, you will be hugging and kissing her. She in return will slap you and pound upon you. You will laugh and make a fool of yourself. Now if you have a child, and your wife leaves you because you have hurt her feelings, she takes the child with her, by no means interfere with the child or your personal belongings. If you take the child it is an evident sign that you do not desire to permanently separate from her. People will learn of your unmanly act, and in every tipi, there will be jokes and laughter about your conduct. Be patient and be honest, if you have a very good reason to separate from your wife. Do so with great care so that nothing will cause you to go back to her, even your own child. When the child grows up he will come back to you.[30]

The unknown informant's advice is obviously fraught with statements that would be unfathomable by today's standards. For example, the man's advice that his son not "beat" his wife "on slight provocation" insinuates that beatings were not only common but accepted among traditional Cheyennes.

PART II: NOÓNÊHO'EMANESTÔTSE: TRADITIONAL LAW

After discussing this and other statements with Cheyenne elders and spiritual leaders, both women and men, and reevaluating archival and published sources, I can provide a commentary about spousal abuse with confidence. The Cheyennes did not condone spousal abuse, although, as with any society, it happened. Sometimes the male relatives of an abused wife would retaliate, inflicting injury or even death upon her abuser (see Wooden Leg's story about Dirty Moccasins and Tall White Man in chapter 8). What is known for certain is that the Cheyennes believed that divorce and separation were acceptable. Socially, the Cheyennes viewed spousal abuse against a Cheyenne woman as in direct violation of the Tsėhéstanove, and it was considered cowardly and shameful.

The marriage ceremony was a public ritual, so all other citizens respected and honored the union as if the marriage were their own. If a husband belonged to a warrior society, that society helped by offering gifts and horses, constructing a lodge, and participating in the celebration; but the marriage was largely a family affair.[31] Outsiders were welcomed to eat and bring gifts to the new household, which was represented by a new, unpainted lodge already filled with gifts. The two families met and exchanged gifts and then ate. The newlyweds may have spent the rest of the night talking to one another, while the family members sang and danced. Once married, the pair became an independent family unit, no longer supported by their parents, even though parent-child and other kinship relationships persisted for life. Marriage came with a new body of laws: wives do not talk to male in-laws; husbands do not talk to female in-laws; brothers-in-law must always tease one another; sisters-in-law must help each other in raising children.[32] Conversations took place between intermediaries to preserve the Tsėhéstanove. Newlyweds and their families gladly adapted their behavior to ensure that the couple could live happy lives together in love, to eventually raise their children to carry on their way of living. The old-fashioned "Cheyenne love" was tender, sweet, and truly sincere. Cheyenne marriages and love lasted into old age, grandparenthood, and even after death. It was common for a child to grow up with four grandparents, which is testimony of the success of the old-time marriages.

POLYGAMY

Although a fundamental law was that Cheyennes could not marry their own relatives, they had no laws that prevented plural marriages in which a man married sisters. Polygamy was an uncommon custom, but according to Old She Bear (Northern Cheyenne) and others, if a man married an eldest daughter, he could marry a younger one as well.[33] Wolf Chief (Northern Cheyenne) also states: "If a man married a girl who had a sister, when she became mature he could marry her, but [he] could not marry more than one sister of his wife."[34] White Eagle (Southern Cheyenne) also attested: "If a man marries a woman who has a younger sister, he marries them too."³⁵ Wrapped Hair (Só'taeo'o) asserted that this was a practice adopted from the matrilineal Só'taeo'o: "The Sutaio had a custom, when a young man married a girl, if she had younger sisters, when they grew up, he married them too."³⁶ The rule only applied, however, if (1) the younger sister-in-law was unmarried and (2) she and the family consented. Wooden Leg (Northern Cheyenne) explained how polygamy worked:

> Plural wives were kept by many of the old Cheyennes. The one family lodge sheltered the entire combined family. Commonly the two or more wives were born sisters. This condition checked or prevented the jealous quarreling likely to occur were they from different families. Two wives ordinarily was the limit. But in my time I knew of two different men who each had three wives living with them. In each of these instances the three wives were sisters.³⁷

The Cheyennes were both matrilineal and patrilineal, and polygamy sometimes complicated traditional customs and beliefs because it created the appearance of incest. Families encouraged their children to marry people from other bands and families to completely bypass any questionable unions, which is why plural marriages were rare. In such cases of polygamy, however, the custom was typically reserved for men of stature, mostly Véhoo'o or those who could provide for a much larger household.³⁸

There are very few cases in Cheyenne history where the polygamous marriage involved two unrelated women. A first wife who did not consent to a polygamous marriage simply left in divorce, but if she stayed and had children, then she would retain her status as the first wife. Sometimes a man would take care of the wife of a dead brother, but never if his brother was still alive, for it would be considered incest. This was considered a marriage even if the relationship was not sexual. Sometimes a family arranged for an unmarried woman to wed a married man. This custom was rare and done purely for the sake of companionship. There are other scenarios that may lead to a polygamous household, like if a married man formally offered a dowry to a young woman's father and she was not yet married, but this often led to divorce of the first marriage. The Tsėhéstanove advocated for love and partnership, which is why the majority, if not all, polygamous marriages comprised one man and two born sisters. As discussed later, a girl's refusal to a plural marriage had to be upheld and her wishes respected to prevent internal conflict and violence. Men who sought plural marriages risked divorce.

In the 1930s, Wooden Leg was named a US judge in the Court of Indian Offenses to enforce a law that prohibited plural marriages on the early Northern Cheyenne Reservation. During this time, two wives typically lived in different households, while the husband took care of both. Wooden Leg had two wives himself but severed the marriage with his second wife, who was his first wife's sister and who had no children. He expressed no loss or injury of his manhood and was "glad" that his second wife remarried to "a good husband."³⁹ Wooden

Leg's experience is proof that the custom of polygamy was not centered on sex or status; it was about family and companionship.

DIVORCE CUSTOMS

Before the reservations, married men were sometimes gone for days on hunts or for war adventures, so married women were especially careful and did not want to appear unfaithful to their marriage. Married women were careful to be seen in public alone and often kept company with female relatives or members of their women's society. In the case of a woman who decided to divorce and marry another man, however, she did so without public scrutiny or any public penalty, but she was careful not to make divorce a habit. Divorces were never to involve any violence, as each party was to maintain a high degree of civility; nonetheless, Cheyennes were human and occasionally had conflict in divorce.

Several scholars have discussed the rare practice of divorce at a public dance.[40] This practice was uncommon, foreign in origin, and adapted from the social dances of the Omaha people when they gave away horses. In the Omaha custom, a man at a public dance may have announced that he wanted to give away a horse and threw a drumstick into the air. Whoever retrieved the stick became the owner of the horse. With divorce, a man who no longer wanted to be with his wife used the method, along with some theatrics, to symbolize his separation from his wife by throwing a drumstick into the air, thus proclaiming his liberation. Although some incidents of this type of divorce occurred, the practice was not the custom for the Cheyennes and was accepted as a public stunt for quarrelling couples. The recorded accounts reveal the divorce ritual to be an incidental act and not a formal ceremony; not institutionalized by the spiritual powers, nor rooted in the old traditions, nor done in accordance with the sacred laws.

Grinnell's account of the public divorce is described as a breakup ritual full of humor and teasing. Meanwhile, Llewellyn and Hoebel described the event when the warriors were engaged in heavy drinking of whiskey, so gathering an accurate precontact analysis of the ritual is impossible because alcohol obviously had a role in the events.[41] Marriage was viewed as one of the most sacred acts because children were to have both parents, and divorce was perceived as a breakdown of a family unit and the potential destruction of the souls of children. Since marriages were unions of families, divorces represented the breaking of this union, which is why divorce was a traumatic event for numerous folks, not just the divorcees. Traditionally there was not one formal method of divorce, as it was uncommon before the increase in warfare with whites. The wars with whites led to a decline in populations and an increase in male aggression. As in all societies, divorce was bound to occur, but the success of Cheyenne marriages far outweighed the failures. Ultimately, assimilation and the reservation system proved to be the most destructive forces against the family unit.

Cheyenne husbands were protective of their wives, and if a man assaulted a woman in her husband's absence, the husband retaliated by killing the offender's best horses or destroying his property.[42] A Cheyenne man could not (and cannot) kill the assailant but was afforded the right to inflict any physical punishment upon him that he saw fit. In such rare cases, the public did not criticize the husband for his actions because they sympathized with the family. The assailant could do little to prevent a certain beating from a husband, but Mack Haag described one method to resolve the matter:

> If it is known that the vengeful man is going to shoot the horses, the guilty man's folks go to a witch-doctor or sun-dance priest; and this doctor or priest fills a pipe with tobacco and takes it for him to smoke. Very rarely is this pipe refused. When it is smoked it means the injured husband has forgiven. The matter is at once dropped. The doctor or priest does not get paid.[43]

The ceremonial pipe for such violations was used in a ceremonial peacemaking process. The assailant was rarely exiled; most certainly he was shamed and ridiculed by other Cheyennes.

According to Cheyenne custom, an unfaithful woman was evidence of a failed marriage because unfaithfulness always led to divorce. Unlike a man who assaulted another man's wife, which was explicitly unacceptable, a man who "stole" another man's wife was an unfortunate but accepted part of life. Wooden Leg explains: "An unfaithful wife did not incur any public penalty, according to the laws of the Cheyennes and the Sioux."[44] Sometimes a betrayed husband would violate traditional customs and inflict harm upon his unfaithful wife, but his acts were viewed as unacceptable and he was branded as cowardly and unmanly. The general assumption was that a betrayed man was not a good husband and his wife had the right to divorce and leave him for another husband. The best thing for such a case was for a man to smoke his pipe and consent to the loss by accepting gifts and reconciliation from the Véhoo'o or a spiritual leader.[45] Iron Teeth Woman (Northern Cheyenne) explained:

> Our men sometimes stole each other's wives. According to our old-time ways, married couples were allowed to break their union at any time either of them might want to do so. Each of them might then take another mate at once. Among us, when any man took another man's wife, the victor got the woman on a horse with him and they rode about the camp. Young people followed them and sang lively songs. In one case of this kind, when I was yet a young girl, the losing husband came with his friends, all bringing their bows and arrows. The old men came and made them go away. The young people went on with their gaiety.[46]

A wronged husband understood that he lost his wife and this reflected upon his character as a husband, not necessarily as a man, as Wooden Leg explained: "Ordinarily, though, the loss of his wife's affection was looked upon as a joke on the husband, and he kept quiet about it or pretended that he did not bewail the loss."⁴⁷ A wronged husband sometimes sought to inflict injury to his wife's new beau, as Coyote described: "When a man's wife is unfaithful, the husband usually resorts to 2 things. One is, he cuts the braid of the accused man's hair; the other, he demands ponies to settle the affair. I thought my friend would do one or the other to me. When a man loses his hair that way, it is thought as disgrace."⁴⁸ The Cheyennes were neither savages nor fundamentalist, but their traditional laws and rituals provided a structure that fit their society and built their nation, however difficult and challenging.

Adultery was rare among the Cheyennes as with most Plains Indians because of the high standard and respect placed upon women. Adultery was considered divorce, and it was common that the two absconders married and therefore the woman was not to be punished or ridiculed. Rarely did a woman have an affair and keep her husband; she almost always left in divorce. Members of the Véhoo'o were held to the highest standards of restraint, and if a member's wife divorced him, he was to refrain from any retaliation. The idiom Oeškeso mâxhéxaesto nevenôtse he'póeo'o (When a dog urinates on your lodge, just take your pipe and smoke it) speaks directly to such unfortunate incidents of infidelity.⁴⁹ Citizens followed the behavior of the Véhoo'o, and if a woman left a man he was to behave "chiefly" and accept the situation with patience and humility. If a man stole another man's wife, six patterns of action followed:

1. There is the basic and ideal norm—according to which the husband made no move, but waited for the emissary, usually a tribal chief, to come from the aggressor bearing the pipe and, (a) bringing horses or other goods acceptable to a man, or, (b) asking the husband what he desired in way of settlement. Smoking the pipe meant acceptance; the matter was closed, and the status of the woman in question changed.
2. When the aggressor failed to carry out his legal duty, the wronged husband occasionally sent a chief with a statement of his demands.
3. The aggrieved might take his pick of the herd of the aggressor, or be blocked by him or a relative. Or,
4. The husband shot horses of the aggressor.
5. Rarely, the husband was so angered as to kill (or try to) the absconder without any attempt at legal settlement. This must be regarded as illegal.
6. The husband could demand the return of his wife.⁵⁰

With such a small population and in such close living conditions, the people were conscious of the delicate balance of their shared society. Any act of dishonesty or promiscuity could lead to family feuds and unhappiness, which is why strict rules of restraint were adamantly taught and protected in the household at early ages. Furthermore, any Cheyenne person could potentially become a relative through marriage, so a high degree of modesty was sustained for all members, for this possibility was more likely to occur than not. This also worked as a preventive measure against promiscuity. The same respect was granted to captives of non-Cheyennes, as they often became adopted.

A wronged husband was known to cut his wife's hair or braids, but any physical harm beyond that went against the Cheyenne way. The archaic and grotesque practice of nose cutting that some white scholars highlight as a common custom was merely a scare tactic used as social pressure to prevent infidelity; there are no known or recorded incidents of the practice among the Cheyenne.[51] The Cheyennes view the act of nose cutting as evil, wicked, and cowardly, originating from a villain known as "Nasty," as preserved in a story told by Wolf Chief (Northern Cheyenne). The story also highlights the challenges of courtship and the power of the pipe.

Plover Wings

There was a big camp of lodges where a young woman resided. One night, a man came to court her. He caught her with his blanket. The young woman told the young man, whom she liked, to come at a certain time to her lodge and visit. The young man said, "all right." After the people were asleep at night, the young woman went off with the man, but he walked ahead. She did not know she left with a different man. Later, when the man she liked arrived, she was already gone. She disappeared. The next night, another young man went to court another young woman. He caught her with his blanket as before. She told him to come for her after everyone was asleep. Later that night, she walked out of her lodge, and a man caught her. He ran off with her. In due time, she realized it was the wrong man. When the true fellow came to her lodge, she was gone.

The big chief had a beautiful daughter and everyone wanted her. Young men courted her. When she came out of her lodge, a young man caught her with his blanket. He stood with her and talked to her. She told him to come see her after everyone was sound asleep. "All right," he said. In due time, she met him but was the wrong one as before. She left with him as he walked ahead. The earth was his ear (he could hear everything). When they stopped, she saw him. His robe was decorated with porcupine quills of different colors. She followed him in the morning, she looked at him, she saw him, he looked ugly and nasty. He took her into the forest where a lodge stood. They went in. There were numerous young women in the lodge; [they] sat in the lodge. Their noses were all cut off, and also their ears were cut off. The man went out. When he did, one of the young women told the new girl, "You mustn't refuse to do anything for him, he cuts off noses." He quickly came back in and asked a question: "What did you say?" The young woman said, "We just talked to her." The man had a power: the earth was his ear. He told the new girl, "You go out and fix the guide pole of the tipi." She went out to the rear of the lodge. A young man stood there, it was he, Plover Wings, the man she liked. He must have followed them. She told Plover Wings about the man:

"he tortures us and tells us to get him water." Plover Wings said, "If he tells you to bring water to him, you must do it for him." Plover Wings told the girl that he would enter the lodge after she gave the man water. He told her to throw it in his face. "Then I will go in," said Plover Wings. When she brought water to the torturer, he didn't drink it for a long while. He teased the girl, "surely Plover Wings, he must be at hand, he will come in due time." Then the torturer knocked her nose off. After the torturer did this, the girl threw the water in his face. Then Plover Wings came into the lodge.

The torturer said, "Plover Wings, you should smoke with me." Plover Wings agreed and sat in the back of the lodge. Nasty filled a pipe for Plover Wings, talked to him, and handed Plover Wings the pipe. Nasty said, "I too, my comrade, wish to smoke." Plover Wings lit the pipe and slowly drew in the smoke and blew it out. He sat smoking. He puffed it out. Nasty repeated, "I too, my comrade, wish to smoke." Plover Wings then filled the pipe. "Smoke," he said to Nasty. Nasty smoked but after he puffed it out, it was his last breath. He died.

Plover Wings told all of the young women, "You can all go out now, take your bedding and belongings out, you can return to your supposed husbands. First bring me rocks, then cut me some willows. I will make a sweat lodge." He made a sweat lodge and they all went in. He conducted a ceremony and they all steamed themselves. When they were finished, they all came out and were healed; their noses and ears returned to normal. He told them, "Take this fire and burn the lodge." The young women burned the lodge with the dead body of Nasty still inside. As the lodge burned, his body melted and different shapes and beads scattered about. Plover Wings ordered, "Do not take any of these, if you do he will be resurrected." Plover Wings and the chief's daughter went homewards, while the young women went in different directions, scattered towards their own home. So be it.[52]

As I emphasized earlier, the Cheyenne body of laws was deeply intertwined with the Cheyenne worldview. Seemingly meaningless stories held sacred teachings that prepared children for citizenship in the Cheyenne Nation. When they courted, married, and eventually had children, they continued to build and rebuild the sacred nation. This is how the Cheyennes remained true to their sacred promises to the earth and the unseen spiritual powers.

CHAPTER 8

Ma'hëö'o Hesto'emanestôtse: Sacred Laws

All night through, he taught the people what the spirits inside the holy mountain had taught him. These teachings established the way of the Tsistsistas, the true Cheyenne nation. Toward morning Sweet Medicine sang four sacred songs. After each song he smoked the pipe, and its holy breath ascended through the smoke hole up into the sky, up to the great mystery. For many nights to come, Sweet Medicine instructed the people in the sacred laws. He lived among the Cheyenne for a long time and made them into a proud tribe respected throughout the Plains.

—Unknown[1]

This chapter explores the highest of Cheyenne law, which is better understood as ma'hëö'o hesto'emanestôtse, the laws of the Sacred Medicine or the sacred laws. The Cheyennes believe that only a select few gain the knowledge and wisdom to interpret ma'hëö'o hesto'emanestôtse; typically interpreters rise to positions of sacred leadership as chiefs or spiritual leaders. Humans have limitations according to the Tsêhéstanove and we have limited knowledge and wisdom compared to the beings of the spiritual world. The flaws of humanity limit all of humankind, and therefore humankind is also bound by the unseen powers of the spiritual world. Humans can interpret or practice law from their known world, but they can only observe and respect the laws outside of humanity. By comparison, humans have a degree of dominion or jurisdiction over each other but do not have control of anything higher. Humans cannot challenge, manipulate, or change the laws of the higher powers.

According to the Tsêhéstanove and ma'hëö'o hesto'emanestôtse, humans do not have dominion over animals and nature but must maintain balance as demanded by the sacred covenants. Highly spiritual people, however, have the potential to gain the knowledge and expertise to interpret the spiritual laws of nature, which are closely associated with ceremony, medicinal practices, doctoring, and healing. On the other hand, certain leaders can gain expertise as sacred leaders and therefore can gain the knowledge and expertise to interpret the laws associated with internal affairs, like civil and criminal disputes. Within the Tséhéstáno, these leaders become practitioners of law and their interpretations assist them in making decisions, resolving conflicts, moving camp, organizing hunts, and declaring war or securing peace.

The ma'hëö'o hesto'emanestôtse was never intended to function as a bureaucracy to regulate people's rights and privileges; it served to bring balance and harmony. This is why only the best and brightest leaders were selected to be Véhoo'o, who were chosen to interpret Cheyenne law. The system functioned with some room for contradiction or debate, but outside cultural influences from colonization posed unforeseen challenges that eventually led to the breakdown of the entire system. The rules a child learned directly related to laws that he or she would follow later in life in ceremonies and into adulthood. Sometimes the origin or meaning of rituals or ceremonies was told through story and was not revealed until much later, when a person uncovered such knowledge on his or her own terms. A sure way to destroy the system was to destroy the culture and outlaw the religion. Nevertheless, the Cheyenne sacred laws have survived the tests of time.

The ma'hëö'o hesto'emanestôtse secured stability and unity, as nearly every law served to sustain or strengthen the nation. Before colonization, there could be no laws that promoted the destruction or deterioration of the Cheyenne spiritual way of life (for example, laws that prohibited the speaking of the Cheyenne language), and none could have been developed because the spiritual ways were too strong to be compromised. Changes to the ma'hëö'o hesto'emanestôtse were nearly impossible, since dramatic changes would lead to the eventual decline of the Cheyenne Nation. Smaller, subtle changes occurred periodically but were achieved in relation to changes in culture. The best example of such a change would be the introduction of horses and guns. Both were products of trade and ritual but also came to possess animate and spiritual significance. With a new set of laws, the owners of horses and guns were also burdened with new responsibilities that fit with traditional Cheyenne beliefs of the Tséhéstanove.

Llewellyn and Hoebel's *The Cheyenne Way* is a comprehensive study of traditional Cheyenne legal ways including elements of the ma'hëö'o hesto'emanestôtse. Unfortunately, the study was conducted through a mainstream, ethnocentric perspective and comprises numerous flaws that traditional Cheyennes, past and current, criticize and sometimes ridicule for its unfair treatment and misrepresentation of Cheyenne people and culture.[2] *The Cheyenne Way* is a close evaluation of case law or customary law, which required the interpretation of events by legal scholars. Throughout this chapter, I provide evaluations of select cases in *The Cheyenne Way*. However brief, my assessment of Cheyenne law is not limited to case law and it is not limited by a Western paradigm. My assessment of Cheyenne law highlights ma'hëö'o hesto'emanestôtse as the Cheyennes traditionally viewed and practiced it as a part of their way of life, and how they sustained a relationship with traditional laws to build their nation and strengthen sovereignty.

SPIRITUAL LAWS

Spiritual laws are the most sacred and oldest body of rules that were established by the spiritual powers and given to humans. Cheyennes were instructed to adhere to these ma'hëö'o hesto'emanestôtse by prophets and the Great Medicine; violations could result in the destruction of the Cheyenne people and way of life. The laws are viewed as promises or covenants, connected to the creation of life and other elements of the way of living that built the Cheyenne Nation. The Véhoo'o held authority in interpreting and handing down judgments and punishments, but the Tséá'enövâhtse (keepers) and the covenants, as animate spirits, held the highest power. Crimes against the nation were perceived as crimes against the covenants, their sacred teachings, and the sanctity of the covenant ceremonies. Crimes were viewed as a violation of the sacred promises. The Véhoo'o were responsible for protecting these ways by keeping the peace. Violators of spiritual laws were likely to be exiled or sentenced to a "spiritual death" through the denial of rights to participate and be represented in certain ceremonies and events. Most cases had one formula (if crime A then punishment B), but sometimes it was not as simple because some crimes allowed for mitigation, which traditionally led to fair and just punishments depending on the situation.

While some crimes were punished on the spot (e.g., the punishment for illegal hunting was to confiscate property, kill a violator's horse, or whip the violator), others may have required much thought and discussion after interpreting events and questioning involved parties before finding the best possible punishments or restitutions. Sometimes two cases of the same nature would result in different outcomes because the primary purpose of spiritual laws was the restoration of balance and unity rather than punishment and the continuation or the creation of feuds and dysfunction. Most, if not all, types of these cases had no formal ceremony, but the pipe ceremony was the universal ritual for resolving conflicts of such caliber.

THE PIPE AND PEACEMAKING

Tsetoenomósanéo'o, "offering the pipe," is a peacemaking procedure that has spiritual origins and is employed on several occasions in international affairs and communal spiritual practices, as well as for individual discipline and peacemaking in internal disputes. Only certain individuals could carry a pipe with a bowl made of red stone called catlinite; and there were different types of pipes: some were "medicine pipes" that were strictly for ceremonial use, while others were "devotional" and were used exclusively for solemn occasions like internal peacemaking.[3] The peacemaker, nanomónéhe, and his "devotional pipe" were universal symbols of respect and civility with spiritual powers, and any disrespect or violation of any promise or associated ceremony could be punishable by death through spiritual powers or forces.[4] A person charged with a crime could bid to prove his innocence by offering the pipe, present his case, and help resolve the matter. But if he was wrong or could not prove his innocence, then he would be labeled a liar.

The nanomónéhe held a high degree of responsibility and authority when "offering the pipe," but a person's character determined the value and sincerity of the offering. All pipe carriers are required to adhere to the strict principles of ována'xaetanohtôtse (peace), hetómestôtse (truth), and xanoveostôtse (righteousness). If a person was known to be dishonest or of poor stature, then few people would smoke with him, and even fewer would expect him to be righteous. Conversely, if a person was of high stature, a ceremonial person, or a chief, then using his pipe was considered a high honor and demanded smokers to speak the truth. Any violations from a pipe carrier reciprocated as karma. While all citizens respected the pipe, all pipe carriers had to have "earned" their pipe or at least exhibit worthiness of "devotional or ceremonial smoking."[5]

Voestaehneva'e, the young woman who created the Véhoo'o, brought the pipe, and the first oath she imparted on the first chiefs was a pledge to be honest and care for the entire nation.[6] Véhoo'o often used their pipes when making decisions but also brandished their pipes as the primary nanomónéhe in disputes. They embodied righteousness and could use their pipes to compel a person to tell the truth. When seeking a resolution to a dispute between two parties, the Véhoo'o or a single chief would act as an intermediary and offer the pipe, with gifts and horses, to the person who came out on the losing end of a dispute (such as a man whose wife left with another man).[7] Once a resolution was made, then the dispute could no longer be carried any further. Each party respected the outcome even if they did not like it, and they agreed to the wishes of the Véhoo'o. Nearly every adult Cheyenne man, but not all women, possessed a medicine pipe and was therefore schooled on the demands of carrying such a sacred item.[8]

Ideally, the Cheyenne were to live together in unity and harmony, but as with all humans, disputes arose and some were bound to escalate into full-blown conflict. Although rare, from time to time quarrels called for intervention and the first respondents were the Nótâxeo'o. Wooden Leg described:

> Fighting between Cheyennes, either men or women, was forbidden by the tribal laws. In case of a fight some chief near at hand would call out: "Warriors, separate these fighters and whip them." The warrior policemen then on duty would respond to the call. A band of them would give such punishment as seemed to them fitting. If the fighters renewed their strife they might have punishment added, might have their tepees torn down, their horses killed, property damage done to them in some other way, any suitable and sufficient punishment—except, no policeman warrior nor anyone else lawfully could kill a Cheyenne.[9]

While Véhoo'o were peacekeepers, Nótâxeo'o were enforcers and they were willing to do anything to stop a Cheyenne from killing another, especially when stopping fights. Victims of physical harm were typically paid material items to settle disputes. The Véhoo'o, as nanomónéhe, facilitated the exchange and reconciliation process. Every citizen was subject to adhering to offerings from the pipe, regardless of his or her blood or adopted or captive status. On the plains, the pipe was universally recognized as a sacred item and the act of ritual smoking was respected as a common ceremony.[10]

Smoking, both socially or ceremonially, was considered a privilege and perceived as connecting oneself to the spiritual world, especially the Mother Earth. The pipe is offered to the four cardinal directions to affirm the smoker's presence on Earth; the smoker asks compassion for allowing him or her to live in delicate balance and gives thanks for all of the blessings and gifts of life.[11] Smoking was reserved for adult men, as Penney emphasized: "Only the older men smoked. Young men were forbidden to smoke, for they must be strong and able to run fast for long distances, in the hunt and to fight the enemy. Of course, no woman or child was permitted to smoke."[12]

Smoking privileges, however, can be easily revoked should they violate any of the sacred laws decreed by the spiritual powers. Smoking unites humans with the tobacco, as the essence of the plant is released when it burns and humans breathe the life-giving powers from Mother Earth. The red pipestone bowl symbolizes the flesh and blood of humans who sacrificed their bodies long ago so that the people could survive into the next worlds, and the wooden stem represents the backbone of the entire nation.[13] When the smoke is inhaled and released into the air, the smoker's prayers and thoughts travel from the heart, out into the air, and eventually to the heavens where Ma'xema'hēō'e listens, feels, and answers the pleas of humankind. This connection is valued so dearly to the Cheyenne that if a person committed intratribal murder, then the privilege to smoke out of the red pipestone would be forever revoked and under no circumstances could it ever be restored.

In 1910 A. E. Somers (Southern Cheyenne) told an origin story of the pipe and smoke, highlighting the significance of the ceremonial pipe but also including Christian teachings, likely resulting from assimilation policies during the early reservation era:

Story of Pipe and Smoke, told by A. E. Somers

In due time, before anybody could know about the pipe, there was a great hill somewhere in this world where there were all the tribes of Indians came together at the bottom of this great hill. They spoke but one language, upon this hill, there were four signs of smoke [that] came down each side of the hill. It was so wonderful, no one could dare say a word, as they noticed four places of smoke to them. Someone upon this hill said, "It shall live with you throughout the ages to come upon the earth; [it] shall make the people live in wise and peace of good will to men." It was the gift as to renew the spirits of hills, plains, forests and the animals that live therein with us. After four days when this happened, the people were very anxious to go upon the hill and see if there is anything left there for them. When the smoke was disappeared, cleared away, from the mountain, there were thousands of more people going up the hill, like [an] ants lodge, and behold, there was some strange signs, [that] were left there as the people to witness. The pipe was found and it was still burning [with] smoke to it. It was said, "whoever smoke this pipe, it shall be [to] rest and live in peace, between earth and heaven shall be glad to laugh as to make us happy in the universe, as the children of the one father, "in heaven." The pipe of peace shall make you free from evil one, that will lead you in to horrible. As it was the gift of holy one to all men alike.[14]

Despite the Christian dogma in Somers's story, the teachings, values, and philosophy of the pipe and pipe rituals remain central to Cheyenne concepts of peacemaking and conflict resolution.

MEDICINE ARROW LAW

Probably the most studied ma'hëö'o hesto'emanestôtse of the Cheyennes is their sacred decree against intratribal murder.[15] The murder law upheld the sanctity of the principles, teachings, and values from the covenant of the Maahótse (Medicine Arrows). The repercussions of such a violation disrupted all facets of the Cheyenne world because murder was considered to be the worst thing a Cheyenne could do to his or her own people. When a Cheyenne man killed another Cheyenne man, it was the ultimate violation against the sacred principle of hévese'onematsestôtse (brotherhood), and it was viewed as murder among brothers even if the two men involved were unrelated. Although the sacred murder law applied to both men and women equally, the law was institutionalized and reinforced to preserve peace and harmony among men because of the conflicts that arose between them; recall the story of Sweet Medicine's creation of the warrior societies in *A Sacred People*. Men were the primary perpetrators of murder, so the law and its associated traditional teachings centered on prevention among males.

Murder forced the nation into spiritual imbalance, and the Maahéome (Arrow Lodge) was the only ceremony that could restore balance.[16] The ceremony was required for every instance of murder, even in cases of accidental deaths or involuntary homicide. In murder cases, the Véhoo'o held exclusive jurisdiction, as Wooden Leg attested:

> The killing of any Cheyenne was the most serious offense against our tribal laws. The punishment was prompt. A council of the big chiefs and the warrior chiefs was called at once. The case was inquired into. If guilt was evident, the offender began without delay the payment of his penalty. Sometimes action was taken without the council

being assembled, the situation being so clear that unanimity of feeling was expressed either for or against the person charged with the crime. The defendant was not permitted to be present at the trial council. When the decision was rendered he was notified at his lodge by the warrior policemen. If found guilty they proceeded at once to put into effect the regular fixed and standard punishment.[17]

The goal was to reach a thoughtful but swift resolution to prevent more conflict and instability. Sometimes witnesses and relatives of both parties were called in to share their side of the story. Under no circumstances was an accused murderer allowed into the lodge or to take part in the proceeding, a rule that placed a heavy burden on the Cheyenne people to trust in their traditional justice system. Such a practice, when compared to modern systems of justice, is in clear violation of individual rights to a fair trial. But traditionally, the Cheyenne system was strong enough, and its leaders disciplined enough, to function this way. Should modern Cheyennes choose to reinstate some form of their historic and traditional justice system, they must evaluate the current people's trust in the justice system to the fullest extent and re-create an effective system from there.

In cases where the Véhoo'o decided that no murder was committed, they sent out the criers to announce the decision and the accused was free to leave. If the Véhoo'o decided that the killing was accidental and the accused was held responsible, then they facilitated a peacemaking ceremony in which the responsible person was compelled to give generous gifts and horses and promptly make amends to the bereaved family. The ceremonial men would then renew the Maahótse. If the Medicine Arrow covenant was in a different band, "runners" were sent to notify the Arrow Keeper of the incident. Accidental killings were especially difficult for the family of the victim. The Maahéome and peacemaking ceremonies, if done with integrity and in sincerity as dictated by custom and the spiritual, prevented future conflicts resulting from the accidental killing.

The accused, after being found innocent, also had a difficult time after the accidental death, since he was held responsible and understood the seriousness of his mistake: "It was customary for him to show in some such way his sadness of heart because of the occurrence."[18] Sometimes the person fell into depression and punished himself emotionally and spiritually. Those who were responsible for accidental killings were not ostracized or banished. They did not lose any status or privileges, ceremony or social, but they always displayed sadness to show the people their sorrow in apologetic gentleness thereafter. Sometimes this was enough for the community to bear after losing one member. The ma'hëö'o hesto'emanestôtse was profoundly emotional and understood by everyone as one of the most sacred teachings blessed upon the people.

Wooden Leg recalled such an incident in which two young brothers were trying to kill a wolf in its den. While one was pulling a wolf out with a stick, the other was preparing to shoot the animal, but the brush from the stick diverted the rifle. One brother killed another. The survivor was in shock and weeping, but he managed to put his brother on his horse and return home. People flocked around and some accused the boy of murdering his own brother out of anger. He cried that it was an accident and explained what happened. A group of on-duty Nótâxeo'o took the boy and returned to the wolf's den where the young man re-created the incident. The Nótâxeo'o were convinced that the killing was entirely accidental, and the boy was released without punishment.[19] Although this case was intrafamilial, the same rules applied in accidental killings between nonrelatives.[20]

One case of accidental near-murder occurred when the wife of Wolf Medicine nearly poisoned the entire Elk Warriors society. She mistakenly used a mixture of poisonous powder, probably arsenic, which she bought from a white trader and thought to be baking powder. She prepared bread for a feast. All of the men became sick and nearly died. They had to induce vomiting to save themselves. Nobody was killed, and Wolf Medicine's wife was neither accused nor punished for attempted murder. She was so distressed with sorrow and guilt, however, that she nearly succumbed to depression until the people consoled her and brought her back into the community.[21] Although nobody died, if one or more had, the Véhoo'o would have likely ruled the death or deaths as accidental. Guided by their principles of compassion and forgiveness, they would not have been so quick to label the accused as a murderer, because of such an understandable mistake.

Murder was heinous and if a person willingly killed another and was found guilty, then he or she was completely removed from the nation and no longer considered Cheyenne. Most known incidents involved only men, but the law applied to women as well. A person who was "thrown away" because of the crime of murder became "nothing" and was spiritually removed from the Medicine Arrows, as Wooden Leg stated: "The chief spiritual guide or medicine man of the tribe withdrew the sacred protection, so the outlawed one was altogether out of touch with the Great Medicine."[22] Physical exile was not enough; the murderer had to also be spiritually exiled because a murderer's sickening aura could potentially spread and infect others in the nation. Murderers were not harmed in public, but if they protested their removal, they were likely whipped by the warriors and physically taken away from the people. They had to leave at once, and if they did not the warriors killed their horses and destroyed their property. The warriors took the murderer's pipe and smashed it, if the murderer did not do so on his own. If a murderer cooperated and voluntarily left, then he or she was allowed to pack up his or her property and leave. Anything the murderer left behind was destroyed by fire because it was tainted with the person's sickness.

Before the time of the horse, in particular during the time of the dog, the warriors escorted the murderers across four ridges and four rivers to leave them there. Murderers were considered enemies and any Cheyenne could kill them without penalty if they intruded.[23] In the old times, violent and irrational murderers were left for dead while the camp moved away. John Sun Bear (Northern Cheyenne), who was born in the early 1840s, described this old custom as well as its change:

> My father told me that among the Cheyennes a long time ago any person who killed a fellow member of the tribe was starved to death. He was put upon a hilltop, where all could see him, and he was guarded to keep him there. If necessary, he was tied, to make him stay. Sometimes, one of such imprisoned murderers would beg for somebody to kill him, but it was not allowable to do so. The law was that he must starve to death. In my time, our law was that a murderer was banished for four years. He then was allowed to come back and live with the tribe. It was considered not right to harm him when he came back, but always after that he had no associates except his own relatives.[24]

During the time of the buffalo and the time of the horse, the four-year banishment became the common practice because of the smaller world created by the horse. Wandering exiles could attract enemies and threaten the main village, so they were allowed to camp within a few miles of the rest of the people. The warriors prevented murderers from entering the circle. Murderers truly became "nothing." Sometimes the Véhoo'o ordered that a murderer should not live in a tepee and had to find other means for shelter. He or she was always willing to follow the rules in hopes of returning to the nation after the four-year banishment.

The murderer's spouse, extended family, and children typically went with him or her into exile, and if other family members joined him then they also were ridiculed or considered outcasts. This was common for murderers who were once men of status. Members of the band of outlaws were not allowed to hunt with others, nor were they allowed to involve themselves in spiritual practices. The murderer and his men folk were revoked of their warrior society membership and status, and any war deeds of the outlaws were not considered worthy of recognition from others.[25] If the murderer had children after committing the crime, especially during exile, then his children could be tainted with his poison and likely ridiculed.[26] The shame of murder did not, however, apply to his children born before the crime.[27] The murderer label and punishments were never intended to transfer to his other family members or namesakes, even though ostracism was sometimes transferred, which is why his name was forgotten. After four years, the murderer could come back into the protection of the nation but never regained full status as a citizen. Nobody abused him, but people may give him gifts of pity, not out of friendship. Any cup, bowl, knife, or eating utensil he used belonging to others was destroyed by fire. Any blanket or robe he sat on or touched was tainted and either given to him or burned after use.[28] If he came to a feast he brought his own utensils and ate alone. If he was to smoke, he did so out of the old deer or antelope bone pipes. No woman

PART II: NOÓNÊHO'EMANESTÔTSE: TRADITIONAL LAW

wanted to marry him and no society wanted his service, as all people avoided him.[29] However cruel and unusual, this form of punishment worked for the old Cheyennes.

Although the murder law was strictly enforced on all blood Cheyennes, the ma'hëö'o hesto'emanestôtse also applied to non-Cheyenne adoptees who were children when they were adopted. The law protected these non-Cheyenne Indians who were adopted as children because they were raised in a Cheyenne band, had kinship relationships, and were recognized as citizens of the Cheyenne Nation. If a Cheyenne killed them, or if they killed a Cheyenne, then it was a violation of the spiritual law because they were held to know the oral traditions and ceremonial practices and beliefs of the Maahótse.

The law did not necessarily apply to outsiders who married into the nation, because they were non-Cheyenne adult Indians who did not necessarily have the same training, knowledge, and loyalty to the Maahótse, the Maahéome, and the oral traditions, customs, and values. One non-Cheyenne, Eagle Bird, accidentally shot himself (suicide is viewed as tragic and painful as murder) and when the Véhoo'o deliberated on renewing the Maahótse, Stump Horn asserted that Eagle Bird was an "alien" and that there was no need.[30] The historian Grinnell also asserts that the law protected non-Cheyennes without discrimination, and he provides two cases.[31] The first case involved an Arapaho, Nahktowun, who lived among the Cheyennes but killed Walking Coyote, a Ponca who had a Cheyenne wife and family. Nahktowun was exiled. In a second case Gentle Horse, a Cheyenne, killed his brother-in-law, who was a Sioux man who had half Cheyenne children. Gentle Horse was also exiled and punished accordingly. Llewellyn and Hoebel concur with Grinnell.[32] While some cases applied Cheyenne law, others did not.

The Véhoo'o as a judicial body were the ultimate deciders of whether the murder law applied because there were exceptions. For example, if a non-Cheyenne Indian spouse had half-Cheyenne children, and the spouse lived in a Cheyenne band, then it was assumed that he or she was recognized as a band member and citizen and therefore the spiritual law applied. This rule changed if a non-Cheyenne Indian spouse was committing crimes against Cheyennes. Wooden Leg highlighted one such case:

> An Ogallala Sioux man had one of our women as his wife. They lived with our people. The couple had much domestic trouble. It was said the husband grossly abused his wife. The matter came to a climax as our Cheyennes were camped on the Giving Medal river. I was a baby or a small child, and my knowledge of it comes only from hearsay stories. But in later times I knew the people involved.
>
> The maltreated wife had two brothers, Dirty Moccasins and Tall White Man—not the present old man Tall White Man, but another Cheyenne dead many years ago. These two brothers decided to end the continual humiliation of their sister. They got their bows and arrows and went man-hunting. Each of them sent an arrow through

the body of the offending Sioux and put out the lights of his life. They were not banished. Besides their having the natural sympathy of the people, the dead man was a Sioux, not a Cheyenne. Nevertheless, ever after that, Dirty Moccasins smoked only a deer bone pipe and Tall White Man used always a little stone one. For many years I saw him as a scrawny and feeble old man smoking the tiny short-stemmed pipe.[33]

Although the two killers were not banished, they inflicted punishment upon themselves for killing their brother-in-law. Such cases were rare but tested the murder law and the integrity of the Véhoo'o as they sought the most reasonable and spiritual solutions.

Before the time of the horse, intratribal murder was almost nonexistent in the Cheyenne world. The spiritual laws and Tsėhéstanove were quite successful in preventing homicide in the nation. During a forty-four-year period (from 1835 to 1879) the nation suffered only sixteen murders: an average of one murder every thirty-three months. This statistic is reflective of the life of peace so valued and enjoyed by Cheyenne citizens, even amidst the invasion of whites and the introduction of alcohol.

MEDICINE HAT LAW

The spiritual laws associated with the Ésevone (Buffalo Hat) and the Hoxéheome (Medicine Lodge) centered on maintaining balance with nature, Mother Earth, and protecting and preserving her life-giving forces. The first body of Medicine Hat Laws focused on hunting practices. For example, the Véhoo'o often decreed that a person who violated hunting laws should "put up a Sun Dance" as the payment for reinstatement of rights and privileges, as was the case for Sticks Everything Under His Belt.[34] The four Cheyenne sacred laws of nature are spiritual laws, but there were also other ma'hëö'o hesto'emanestôtse specifically aimed at preventing conflict or imbalance. No Cheyenne could hunt alone, or without the consent of the assigned warrior society, or among the assigned warrior society if he was not a member. Violators were ridiculed for acting more important than everyone else. Their selfish acts were interpreted as voluntary and were viewed as if they had temporarily revoked their own citizenship for personal gain.[35]

Communal hunts of buffalo herds were organized to prevent casualties, but more important to hunt animals respectfully, resourcefully, and honorably following the strict principles of spirituality. Deviants could stampede the herds through a village or scatter the animals miles away from ideal hunting areas.[36] Violators also desecrated any associated ceremonies, like the Antelope Calling or Buffalo Surrounding. Uninvited hunters were perceived as ill mannered and subject to ridicule or even violence. In one case, Feathered Wolf, an Elk warrior, decided on his own to hunt with the assigned Crazy Dogs. The Crazy Dogs ignored him after the kill and even after Feathered Wolf invited the men to his lodge for a tobacco-smoking meeting to trade for some meat. The warriors wanted nothing to do with him. His wife punished him for his foolish actions by giving him the strongest tobacco, which induced vomiting after it was smoked.[37] Following the principles of womanhood and exerting woman power, she punished him for his insolence.

Younger men especially loved the thrill of the hunt, but the on-duty warriors were quick to punish overanxious hunters by killing their horses, breaking weapons, and even whipping and beating the violators. Even chiefs were subject to the spiritual law, as witnessed by Wooden Leg:

> Old Bear, a big chief, got four or five other Cheyennes to slip out with him for a premature raid upon the herd we had located for our Elk warrior adventure. Little Wolf, at the time a little warrior chief, took with him a band of Elks and followed the lawbreakers. Little Wolf opened the attack upon them by sending an arrow that killed Old Bear's horse. The Elk band pony-whipped all of the Old Bear group, including the big chief himself, and made them go back and stay in camp.[38]

Disobedient hunters could gain immunity from punishment if they immediately stopped and confessed. Noncitizens were also subject to the Cheyenne spiritual laws of hunting, and they often faced the same brutal punishments regardless of their non-Cheyenne status. Wooden Leg explained:

> We always were friendly with the Sioux, about the same as if they were Cheyennes, but these were out of place at this particular time, and they knew it. Little Wolf led a party of his Elks in whipping them away. Two or three of the uninvited guests had blood running from head cuts made by the heavy handles of the pony whips. The Sioux—the plains Indians generally—had laws and customs similar to ours, so it was considered they had incurred our penalty. Often a disobedient Cheyenne or an intruding hunter might gain immunity from a whipping by prompt confession of guilt and by voluntary yielding of horses to be killed or of their property to be destroyed.[39]

THE RIGHTS OF WOMEN

The spiritual laws that protected womanhood were reinforced in the Cheyenne culture through ceremonial practices and the oral tradition. As highlighted in previous chapters, the Cheyenne Nation built itself and its culture with the contributions of women leaders and prophets. The kinship system and the roles and responsibilities of women in Cheyenne society and ceremonial practices reinforced their significance to the survival of Cheyenne sovereignty and nationhood. These factors created a social system that protected women and women's rights almost exclusively through prevention; that is the prevention of physical and sexual violence, the prevention of sexual abuse, and the prevention of exploitation. The Cheyennes, however, were also human, and there were times when the traditional system was challenged. As I examined the murder law and justice in the previous section, I examine here the laws and punishments that protected the rights of women.

One of the biggest challenges to the spiritual laws of the Ésevone and the Hoxéheome arose when protecting the virtue of Cheyenne women, especially young women. The spiritual laws of the Ésevone and the Hoxéheome also serve to prevent incest, and one such law combines the incest law of the Medicine Arrows and the protective Medicine Hat law against sexual violence and abuse. Sexual abuse of children was unfathomable; there are no stories or reports of any such crimes. Incest was virtually nonexistent in oral tradition, but there is one story, which I examine here. The crime of incest among the Cheyenne exists when an older male has sexual relations with a young woman who is also his relative. The crime is perceived as disgusting, immoral, and a complete violation of the Tsėhéstanove. Theoretically, incest warranted the death penalty. Although there are no recorded or known reports of such a punishment, the story of "Buffalo Bones" speaks to such a case. The Cheyennes likely preserved this one story to serve as the only necessary preventive measure.

"Buffalo Bones" reveals the law, crime, and punishment of incest, and it has survived through the ages. In 1970, Belle Highwalking (Northern Cheyenne) told a similar story, and in 1975 Laura Rockroads (Northern Cheyenne) told the story as "The Man Who Turned into Buffalo Bones."[40] In the following pages are two never-before-published accounts; first is Black's (Southern Cheyenne) story, which he told in 1932.

The Buffalo Bones, by Black

A man, his wife and two daughters left the main big camp, so that they could camp alone to a far off distant place. The man hunted the buffalo and after some length of time, "I am going to die and my bones will turn into buffalo bones. After I am dead, when you wrap me up, do not forget to put lots of pounded buffalo meat with my body and do not cover my body with dirt, but lay me on a raft suspended by four large poles above earth, and at the end of the fourth day, come and see. There you shall see a pile of buffalo bones on the ground," said he. "After another fourth day, ease your eyes to the rising sun. There you will see a man sitting on top of that hill yonder. His face and body will be painted with black charcoal and his hair will hang over his face. My oldest daughter shall carry water to him to quench to his thirst. Henceforth, she shall be his wife," said he. Upon the death of the man, his right arm stuck up so stiff that it could not be bent, so the wife suggested to cut it off at the shoulder. The arm then began to go down a trifle. Then the wife said that will do, so they wrapped him just as he had instructed and suspended his body on the poles. At the end of the fourth day, they went and looked. There they saw the buffalo bones piled on the ground just as he had said, and upon another fourth day, the wife looked toward the rising sun, and saw a man sitting on the top of a hill. She therefore called her oldest daughter to carry water to him to quench his thirst. The daughter immediately made haste to carry the water and to meet her future husband, just as her father had said. She saw that his face and body were all painted with black charcoal and hair hanging

PART II: NOÓNÊHO'EMANESTÔTSE: TRADITIONAL LAW

over his face. They then walked to their new tipi which the mother had made and erected. The young woman became pregnant. The man hunted and provide[d] food for the family. One day he slept during the daytime, his wife raised his hair from his face and she found that the man had a sear on his right temple, just like her father had. "Mother, come and see," said she. Upon close examination she [the mother] found that the man was her original husband. So she went and got her stone mallet and a piece of sharp pronged deer horn, applied it to his right ear and drove it through his skull. Thus the length of the legend is ended.[41]

In 1931, Mrs. High Walker (Southern Cheyenne) told a version of the same story, proving the significance of the law. Here I present the never-before-published and untitled legend, which includes an appearance of the Cheyenne trickster named White Man.

Buffalo Bones, by Mrs. High Walker

Once there was a man, his wife and daughter living in a tipi. This man told his family that he would die someday and that his bones would turn into buffalo bones. He knew the day he was going to die, so again he told his family there would be a man come in sight, singing. His wish was to have his daughter, "go after a bucket of water, and then this man would have pity on her." And this man [the father] died. He had his arm up in the air. After the man died a white man came along and saw this dead man with his arm in the air, and White Man said to him, "the man is dead, I might as well cut his arm off." After White Man said that the dead man's arm came to his side. Well, they took this dead man to have him [placed] in the tree. "After 5 days come back and see my grave," is what the dead man's wishes were. After the 5th day his wife went up to see his grave. When she got there all she saw was buffalo bones in the tree where he had been hung. After she returned to her camp the next day, a person came along singing. The mother told the daughter to do her father's last wishes to get a pail of water. After she got the water and gave this man a drink of water, and he lived with her for four days, she recognized him as her own dad. She recognized him by the scar on his face. After she recognized her dad, she went out and told her mother, "I believe this is my dad for he has a scar on his face." And the mother picked up an elk horn and ax, and the mother stuck the elk horn and pinned him through his ear to the ground—told him, "You'll be tired here lying like buffalo bones." After she did it the daughter and mother moved back to the main camp. They left him there to turn into buffalo bones again if he wanted to.[42]

However unreal and unlikely, the story implies that the crime of incest was unforgivable and called for swift action because of the long-lasting pain and suffering it caused to victims. Theoretically, if such a crime were committed, older female relatives would carry out the death sentence by driving a long sharp stick or pounding a tepee stake, a thin bone, or horn knife into the ear of the perpetrator while he slept. The body would be carried away from camp and thrown into a ditch in the middle of night for the wolves to devour. The executers would work in complete secrecy to protect the honor and dignity of their family, which suggests that this form of execution was also unacceptable according to the murder law.[43] Nonetheless, there are no recorded incidents of such an execution, probably because the punishment was as rare as the crime.

The violent method paralyzed the man, as he slowly died an agonizing death and was likely still alive when his body was "thrown away," according to Cheyenne tradition. The execution left little traceable evidence as to the cause of death, and the entire affair could have passed as an accident. If we were to take the story as doctrine, incest and sexual abuse were two crimes that warranted a justifiable death penalty. If the death penalty of this nature existed, it was not institutionalized or sanctioned, yet the story has survived the tests of time and assimilation. The story itself is evidence that the Cheyennes traditionally had a law to protect against incest, even if it was only a preventative measure.

According to the spiritual law, victims of incestuous sexual violence or assault who killed their assailants or abusers would likely not be charged with the crime of murder. For example, Comes In Sight stabbed and killed her father, Bear Rope.[44] The Véhoo'o held no sympathy for Bear Rope, the abuser, releasing Comes In Sight. On the other hand, the Véhoo'o and their wives sympathized with victims of rape under the principles of ševátamehestôtse (compassion) and vonanomótåhtsestôtse (forgiveness). There are very few accounts of cases such as Comes In Sight's.

The body of spiritual laws that protected women's rights were associated with the Ésevone and the Hoxéheome. These laws were not institutionalized because it was widely assumed that all citizens of the Cheyenne Nation, who had family, band, and national identities, knew these rights. According to Cheyenne traditional law, women had the right to protect against kidnapping, rape, and assault and both men and women had the duty to defend this right. The Cheyennes viewed rape as a heinous crime, since all Cheyennes viewed themselves as part of a larger "family," as part of a band and a nation. Even captives from other Indian nations were treated with respect and were not to be harmed physically or sexually. As I discuss in chapter 11, captives were adopted into Cheyenne families and were viewed as potential grandmothers, mothers, sisters, and wives; so to violate a captive was viewed as violating a relative. As with violations of the murder law, the violations of the "laws of womanhood" were rare. Nonetheless, between 1835 and 1879 there were four incidents in which individuals violated or attempted to violate these sacred laws; an average of once every eleven years.

The first and most well-known incident was when Holy Hat Woman (wife of the keeper of the Ésevone) created a symbolic lodge for Little Sea Shell to seek asylum from Buffalo Hump's immoral attempt to facilitate her kidnap and rape.[45] A summary of the incident follows:

PART II: NOÓNÊHO'EMANESTÔTSE: TRADITIONAL LAW

Crooked Nose Woman informed Llewellyn and Hoebel about Little Sea Shell. Buffalo Hump wanted to marry her, but she hated him and refused him. Buffalo Hump was married to Red Leaf, the elder sister of Little Sea Shell. Buffalo Hump wanted to kidnap Little Sea Shell with the help of his relatives. They planned to do this while they were moving camp, during which the wife of the Medicine Hat Keeper, Holy Hat Woman (the formal name for this position), carried Ésevone on her back. Buffalo Hump and his gang of cousins then came to kidnap Little Sea Shell. She ran to the Holy Hat Woman for protection. The Holy Hat Woman put her arms out and formed a symbolic lodge to protect Little Sea Shell. Crooked Nose Woman was present and helped protect the girl by using a spear. The men threatened to take Crooked Nose Woman instead, but they could not. The Holy Hat Woman warned Buffalo Hump not to touch her, but he tried to grab the girl anyway. The Holy Hat Woman pulled a stick from the Ésevone bundle and stuck it in the ground and held it with both hands while holding the girl in her arms. Buffalo Hump finally retreated. Little Sea Shell's father, Strong Eyes, and her uncle, Red Eagle, threatened to kill Buffalo Hump but did not harm him. Red Leaf divorced Buffalo Hump shortly after.[46]

The incident is the most telling of the spiritual laws associated with the Ésevone and the Hoxéheome and the strength of the Cheyenne way. Llewellyn and Hoebel admitted that they "could never get a full explanation" of how the Holy Hat Woman used the stick. Had they known the philosophies and oral traditions of the Cheyenne way, they would have understood. The Holy Hat Woman initially created a symbolic tepee—which housed the Ésevone—to protect the girl. When that failed, she used a stick to symbolically create the center pole of the ceremonial Hoxéheome, the great Medicine Lodge. To prevent the kidnapping and any further violence, the Holy Hat Woman harnessed woman's power, which was founded in the spiritual power of the Sacred Hat, the teachings of Buffalo Hat Woman, and the principles of the covenant ceremony, the Hoxéheome. With her strength and under the spiritual laws she stopped Buffalo Hump and cursed him, or he ultimately cursed himself for his crime.

Violence against women, especially kidnap attempts, often led to retaliation from the victim's male relatives. The case of Dirty Moccasins and Tall White Man reveals that the ultimate goals of such retaliations were to bring the criminals to justice by inflicting severe physical punishments or killing the perpetrators. Here is where the "laws of womanhood" and the murder law meet to raise serious questions about how the Cheyennes were able to sustain a peaceful society. In the end, the Cheyenne Nation was able to sustain itself balancing laws, customs, and traditional practices of justice.

In their book *The Cheyenne Way*, Llewellyn and Hoebel examined four incidents of intratribal kidnapping or attempted kidnapping (I have already discussed one involving Little Sea Shell). While Llewellyn and Hoebel define these incidents as "cases," I do not because they do not fit the standards in Cheyenne traditional law. In fact, Llewellyn and Hoebel made the mistake of including these in their study of Cheyenne law and jurisprudence because these incidents were uncommon and not part of the traditional Cheyenne cultural and spiritual ways of life. Llewellyn and Hoebel further blunder by classifying these incidents as "practices" of Cheyenne "marriage and sex," when the acts had nothing to do with either. Simply put, they were crimes or criminal ventures of the unworthy. The fact that Llewellyn and Hoebel included these incidents in their study raises concerns about their purposes, methods, and goals: why did they choose to highlight four anomalous incidents of intratribal kidnapping, which occurred over the course of forty-four years? Why did they assume that the Cheyennes accepted intratribal kidnapping as part of their marriage and sexual practices? If we were to evaluate the scholarship of Llewellyn and Hoebel by today's legal and ethical standards, it would be considered completely biased, distasteful, and without regard to Cheyenne human rights. It must be deconstructed.

Llewellyn and Hoebel claim that on four different occasions groups of men attempted to kidnap young women, and the authors assume this group of men planned to sexually assault her.[47] From their view, Cheyenne society was a savage one in which gangs of men ran amok. If evaluated from a Cheyenne perspective, relying on traditional Cheyenne concepts of law and justice, we find that this view does not fairly represent the traditional Cheyenne culture. The Cheyennes never condoned intratribal kidnapping. If, however, a "kidnapping" of a woman were to occur, the assumption was that a man wanted to elope with his sweetheart and "stole" her from her parents. This "stealing" does not embody the same meanings as assumed by Llewellyn and Hoebel, who emphasize that the men wanted to commit the crime of rape. As discussed earlier, eloping was socially acceptable, even though it was culturally frowned upon. Intratribal kidnapping for the purpose of sexual assault was socially and culturally unacceptable, and criminal. In fact, there are numerous stories in the oral tradition that speak against the act, most of which take place in an uncivilized time that existed in a previous world, long before the Cheyennes acquired the sacred laws and teachings from Sweet Medicine (see the story of Plover Wings in Chapter 7, and chapter 8 in *A Sacred People*). But even this era did not produce the society that Llewellyn and Hoebel assumed the Cheyenne lived in. When we deconstruct the colonial paradigm, we find instead that the incidents highlighted by Llewellyn and Hoebel are evidence of a successful Cheyenne system that upholds sacred laws of womanhood. The heroic acts of the Holy Hat Woman who saved Little Sea Shell and Crooked Nose Woman, for example, prove and reinforce the sanctity of the laws of womanhood.

According to Llewellyn and Hoebel, during the time of these attempted kidnappings, the Cheyenne people engaged in increasing military conflicts with whites and other Indians. In response, the Cheyenne culture, according to their theory, became more militaristic and therefore more male-dominated, thus leading to the creation of such violence against women. This theory, although plausible, is debunked from its outset for reasons already discussed and because such an imbalance would have not reverberated within the Cheyenne nation;

PART II: NOÓNÊHO'EMANESTÔTSE: TRADITIONAL LAW

it would have had consequences externally, in intertribal disputes and diplomacy.[48] In the end, Llewellyn and Hoebel also doubt their own analysis, which raises the question again of why they chose to highlight the incidents as part of the Cheyenne way in their studies.[49] Traditional Cheyennes agree with Hoebel's declaration of the "practice" to be "an anomaly in terms of Cheyenne ideals."[50] It is worthwhile to deconstruct the incidents that Llewellyn and Hoebel collected about the crimes, especially since their study represents the Cheyennes and their culture in the most negative and racist ways.

I must preface this analysis by asserting that such topics are very sensitive to discuss among most, if not all, human societies. Yet no society, culture, or group of people wants to be memorialized by a few atypical incidents of inhumanity or indecency in their history, nor do they wish to be stereotyped through one-sided studies conducted by outsiders. My effort here is not to fabricate or change history but to deconstruct the colonial lens from which history and historical events are viewed and interpreted. I provide a lesser-known Cheyenne perspective, relying on traditional concepts of law, sovereignty, and justice that have been previously discussed in this book as well as *A Sacred People*, along with the trusted teachings from traditional leaders, male and female, of the ceremonial guilds and societies, as well as elders and spiritual leaders who have dedicated their lives to the Cheyenne way.

Before we review the four incidents that occurred between the years 1835 and 1879, we need some context. Each follows a traceable pattern: (1) In each scenario the older man sought the companionship of a younger woman who despised and openly hated him. It was completely fair and legal, according to the Tsėhéstanove, for women to refuse to enter into a marriage, especially polygamous marriages. (2) In each incident, the man who wanted to kidnap the girl rallied the support of his male relatives, which Llewellyn and Hoebel identify as the man's warrior society. According to Cheyenne kinship rules, a man's brothers and fellow warrior society members are identified using the same terminology and kinship relationships. Although these men may be fellow society members, their collective act was likely unsanctioned by their warrior society because they were not formally petitioned (see chapter 9 and 11). Essentially these men were acting out of selfishness and without regard to any traditional Cheyenne laws. (3) In each incident, the family members of the victim quickly rallied to protect and/or rescue the young woman, implying that the incidents were completely out of the ordinary and unacceptable under any circumstance. (4) In each incident, the male family members of the victim quickly sought justice by vowing to inflict a punishment of physical violence against the unworthy suitor and his coconspirators. The kin of the victim even vowed to kill the criminals and break the sacred law that prohibited murder. This proves the severity of the situation, as few crimes yield a response of this magnitude. (5) Each incident resulted in a complete breakdown of family and community dynamics, causing immeasurable dysfunction, imbalance, and eventual retaliation, divorce, and resentment. This proves, as do the previous four patterns, the destructiveness of attempted intratribal kidnapping. Without a doubt the Cheyennes were aware of the destructiveness. (6) In the end, the young men who participated in the crimes on behalf of the unworthy leader were publicly shamed and ostracized, especially by the women in the band. Like murderers, their names became synonymous with their crime throughout the nation, thus further demonstrating the sanctity of traditional Cheyenne law.

With that background in place, I present the remaining three stories.

1. Black Wolf informed Llewellyn and Hoebel about Big Laughing Woman, who divorced her husband as a young girl. Her husband retaliated by kidnapping her. She was reportedly abused and assaulted by a group of unmarried men. She survived, never married again, and lived to be more than 100 years old. This seems to be the only instance where such a kidnapping was carried out. The unmarried men were assumed to be part of the husband's "society," which could have also referred to his relatives. It cannot be confirmed if the men were brought to justice. This is the only recorded incident of its kind.

2. Dog informed Llewellyn and Hoebel about One Eye's young wife, sister of Buffalo Woman. The young wife returned to a former lover, and One Eye tried to kidnap her with the help of other men, reportedly members of the man's society. Once again, however, it cannot be confirmed whether the men were instead One Eye's relatives. The mother told the brother, Red Bird, and he vowed to kill the group of men. Red Bird was able to charge the group of men and scatter them away. Red Bird rescued his sister before she was kidnapped and assaulted. She divorced One Eye and later married Corn Tassel.

3. Calf Woman informed Llewellyn and Hoebel about Carries the Arrows. He was an orphan who grew up and eventually married. He then wanted to marry his wife's sister, Stands Different Colors. She hated him, but her mother, Owl Woman, took her to Carries the Arrows. Stands Different Colors refused him. Carries the Arrows told Last Bull to kidnap her. She resisted but was caught by Last Bull. Tassel Woman and her husband, Blue Wing, made a plan to rescue the girl. Blue Wing went to the camp and was able to help Stands Different Colors escape with Tassel Woman. The girl returned to camp, where her blood brother and her father took up arms against Carries the Arrow and his relatives. At that point the warrior societies intervened and stopped the fight. The brother of the kidnapped girl ordered his older sister back as well, leaving Carries the Arrows alone. When they returned to camp, the brother and father cut up Carries the Arrows' lodge, destroyed his property, and eventually drove him from their camp. The people praised Blue Wing and Tassel Woman for informing the family about the kidnapping.

Llewellyn and Hoebel assert that the kidnapping attempts were an actual "practice" that was part of the Cheyenne culture, arguing that the "practice" would have disappeared if it were not for "the rise in power and effrontery of the military societies."[51] In reality there was no "practice." These four anomalous incidents that occurred over the course of forty-four years were never, ever accepted as custom or ritual. These violent acts went against Cheyenne ways and had more to do with the egos of unworthy and unmanly men who believed themselves better than they actually were, above Cheyenne spiritual laws, and who unfortunately held positions of power over younger, unschooled men.[52]

Selective and skewed studies like Llewellyn and Hoebel's do not give accurate depictions of Cheyenne traditions. Furthermore, the actions of a few corrupt men who went against tradition cannot taint the gracefulness of Cheyenne marriage customs. This is why it is vital to deconstruct and decolonize the historical lenses from which we view American Indian history and culture.

From a Cheyenne perspective, violence against women, especially sexual assault and rape, was considered a crime as heinous as murder. In fact, upon review of the Medicine Hat Laws and the Medicine Arrow Laws, the perceptions the Cheyenne people held toward kidnappers and rapists is the same as, if not more hostile than, their views toward murderers. For example, the family members of victims of kidnapping sought to inflict a punishment of death upon the criminals. It may be that the Cheyennes had developed a culture and society that protected women's rights but had not yet formalized and institutionalized the proper punishments. I believe that if such punishments ever materialized in traditional Cheyenne culture, without Western influence, the punishment would have been similar to that of the crime of murder: death by exile and starvation, permanent exile, or exile with the opportunity to return with a significant loss of rights. Someday modern Cheyennes may consider creating or re-creating similar punishments under a decolonized paradigm in formal courts of law. Until then, reintroducing preventative measures through story, ceremony, and cultural and spiritual rebirth can certainly be a starting point.

Part of the spiritual laws of the Tsėhéstanove was to return relationships between male and female to balance under the principles and teachings of the Medicine Hat. For example, a man may pledge to "renew" a woman who was divorced more than four times to wed her, while a younger pledger may do the same for a society girl who lost her status because she had premarital relations.[53] Probably the highest level of purification was done at the Hoxéheome, when a committed and longtime married couple pledged for the sake of the entire nation. The married couple essentially renewed their vows to each other, while they renewed the entire Cheyenne Nation.

The teachings of the Ésevone also function as a form of spiritual healing to address and rehabilitate traumas. When young women were traumatized through violence or when they endured spiritual, emotional, mental, and/or physical hardship, their family members brought them to a ceremonial leader to conduct healing ceremonies and rituals. The Cheyennes believed that sacred women, those who participated in the covenant ceremonies, held the sacred knowledge to heal broken and wounded spirits. This practice and others have since diminished, yet the Medicine Hat and its spiritual laws remain a part of the backbone of the sacred nation. The history of spiritual oppression has directly contributed to the increase in crimes and social dysfunction. There is a dire need to promote positive change; the Cheyennes may be on the path of a major spiritual movement relying on traditional philosophies.

UNIVERSAL LAWS

Universal laws are the highest but sometimes the most mysterious rules of the universe. None other than the great mysteries of the universe controls them, and some can be compared to modern laws of physics and science. The historian Michelson collected some of these ma'hëö'o hesto'emanestôtse in relation to ceremonial practices: "Singing Medicine Arrow songs lightly [carelessly] will bring supernatural punishment on the one so doing. If singing Sun Dance songs it wouldn't. If an individual walked across the camp circle, north or south, during the Medicine Arrow Ceremony, invariably sudden death soon after. [The unknown informant] cites case of 2 boys."[54]

Since humans cannot enforce these ma'hëö'o hesto'emanestôtse, they can merely come to understand them and interpret them, but only after years of observation and study. Phenomena that adhere to universal laws will always occur, and the only plausible human response is for people to come into balance with the mysteries of the universe. In doing so, they can become spiritual leaders who can interpret and sometimes predict events in the cosmos. Most universal laws are obvious and easily found in nature. The Cheyennes understand the spiritual world and universe through spheres, which cover a place or area and protect it and its contents from harm.[55] These spheres are their own dimension and are governed by their own unique measure of time (see illustration that follows). The first sphere is the måhta'sóoma, a person's soul, spirit, or "shade," which can be perceived also as a personal realm.[56] This is a person's individual perspective of the world and universe. Universal laws related to every individual's måhta'sóoma have already been discussed throughout this chapter; the laws promote health and protect against physical, mental, and spiritual harm. Violation of personal universal laws can lead to sickness, mental disease, depression, and even insanity or death. Mack Haag also explains some universal laws:

> The bad spirit of a person is the skeleton itself wherever it lays underneath the ground. The good spirit of a person goes to the other world. Also comes back and visits the people. Northwest is the location of the dead. The evil spirit causes paralysis, headache, etc. Therefore falls upon Indian doctors to suck the evil spirit out. They suck out a piece of skin, bone, hair. These are parts of the evil spirit's body. The good spirit is the one that guides the Indians to their place when dead. They see the old folks, buffalo, etc. The good spirit is called "Crow" because he is a messenger. Goes back and forth into the other world.[57]

Suicide was a violation of universal law because life is considered a gift from the spiritual powers. The Maahótse were renewed after such incidents because it was understood as a destructive misfortune that could potentially thrust the entire nation into dysfunction. The ma'hëö'o hesto'emanestôtse is one of the highest of these laws. The Cheyennes do not believe in a heaven or hell as in the Christian view. There is no division between sinners and adherents, nor is there a set place of eternity for each in the afterlife. The Cheyenne concept of afterlife is not as black and white. The Cheyenne believe in Séáno, which has no accurate literal translation but is known as the happy hunting grounds. When a Cheyenne dies, his or her spirit travels through the galaxy along the Seánemeo'o (Milky Way) and passes through time to return to a re-created, "spiritual" Earth. They arrive and reawaken in a different dimension (Séáno) in the beautiful homeland where they meet all of their relatives who had died before them, as well as other Cheyennes. Here they live eternally and hunt buffalo as they did on Earth.[58] If a Cheyenne commits suicide, however, the spirit falls away from the Seánemeo'o, during the sacred journey. It stays trapped at the "place of the hanging ones."[59] This is not "hell," per se, but a place where the soul remains with other unknown spirits to live in another unknown dimension. They are alone in a strange land, among strange people, without relatives and the rest of their people; such an afterlife is hell enough for traditional Cheyennes. The spirit can continue on its journey only when it is healed and when the family on earth is healed, which takes a generation or two. Sometimes the wounds never completely heal. Suicide was as rare as murder but became more common following colonization.[60] Restoration of balance and harmony becomes the ultimate goal when such tragedies occur.

The higher levels or jurisdictions of universal laws govern spheres that cover much larger areas.[61] All humans, plants, and animals live on the surface of the Earth in a place known as the Táxéto'vóóma, the "On-top-realm." This place can be physically described as the space between the Earth/ground and the tip of the tallest of trees, or as high as a human can climb up a mountain without dying from suffocation. In the Táxéto'vóóma is the Vóto'sóoma, which translates to "Human-realm" and is the human dimension and perception of the universe. Noávóóma (the realm of nature) is the dimension of animals, and Ma'táa'evóóma (the realm of the forest) is the dimension of all plants and trees. Naévóóma (the realm of the dead) is the dimension where spirits, typically those that were from "wicked people," did not leave Earth but "roam about restlessly trying to find an abode in the bodies of living people, and otherwise are bent on causing disease and mischief."[62] All four realms—Vóto'sóoma, Noávóóma, Ma'táa'evóóma, and Naévóóma—are located within the Táxéto'vóóma. Humans, plants, animals, and spirits can gain the ability to enter into each other's realm, but in doing so universal laws of that world bind them until they leave, and none can leave the safety of the Táxéto'vóóma. Humans often enter Naévóóma during ceremony, where they interact with dead relatives or other spirits. Humans benefit the most from Táxéto'vóóma, where they can easily witness the most basic

MA'HËÖ'O HESTO'EMANESTÔTSE: SACRED LAWS

The worldview of Tséhéstanove

of spiritual events in fact: when the leaves change color in the fall, when waters freeze in the winter, when flowers and the brush bloom in the spring, and when insects multiply and berries ripen in the summer. Animals shed their coats and antlers and grass grows, but they also die and decay, just as do humans and plants. Universal laws of this realm are easy to observe and children begin to appreciate these beautiful events, knowing that they will always occur.

Above the Táxéto'vóóma is another breathable, but dangerous, place known as the Sétóvóóma, "Middle-of-the-water-realm," which is the space between the breathable human world and the outer worlds where living beings suffocate. The Cheyenne perceive entering into outer space and on the verge of suffocation as they do entering the middle of a large body of water, where they would be on the verge of drowning. Humans and animals reach Sétóvóóma when they die from drowning and strangulation, and such deaths are both unholy and mysterious since the loss of air causes the death. Humans can witness universal events of Sétóvóóma, especially during the daytime when birds fly into this realm and return with ease. Birds such as eagles were especially revered as sacred beings for such spiritual abilities. Mountains, also revered as sacred, rise above the Sétóvóóma, but mountain plants cannot grow beyond the boundary and the mountaintops remain bare. Smoke rises from the Earth but cannot escape the Sétóvóóma because an invisible barrier protects everything underneath it. Thunderhead clouds can float in and above the barrier, and they often release their powers in the Táxėto'vóóma in the forms of wind, rain, snow, and lightning as gifts to the living plants and beings on Earth. The ho'emanestôtse from the Táxėto'vóóma are environmental laws, and challenging or violating the laws can lead to imbalance in nature and disruption in humanity.

Above the Sétóvóóma is the higher, mysterious space called the Otá'tavóóma, "Blue-sky-realm." The Otá'tavóóma is perceived to have mass like an immense body of water. The éše'he (sun), taa'eéše'he (moon), and vóóhéve (morning star, Venus) are located here where they move across the sky on easily identifiable time intervals. This realm houses another place: He'amo'omēē'e (Above-the-sky-realm) or He'ämahéstanove (Above-world), which is located at the far end of the Otá'tavóóma, past the taa'eéše'he, just behind the éše'he, but before the vóóhéve. The universal laws of this realm are witnessed daily as the sun rises in the morning and sets in the evening. The seasons change in accordance with universal laws in a deliberate order: from winter, to spring, to summer, to autumn, and back to winter. The moon renews itself every month, and the morning star departs and returns every eight years. The Ma'xema'hēö'e and Nonóma'e (Thunder) reside in the He'amo'omēē'e and the spirits of all dead beings eventually make a journey through He'ämahéstanove. The ma'hëö'o hesto'emanestôtse of the Otá'tavóóma are laws of science, and attempts to disrupt or challenge them not only would be futile but could lead to insanity.

Above the Otá'tavóóma is the highest and most enigmatic place, known as the Vono'omēē'e, which translates to "Lost-in-time-and-space-realm." This infinite and unknown realm is a perplexing mass of black darkness. Located on this mass of darkness are all of the stars in existence and the Seánemeo'o, the road to heaven (Milky Way). The universal laws in this realm can be witnessed when observers see the movement of the hotóhkeo'o (stars) and mano'otóhkeo'o (constellations) as they spin while anchored to the Hono'ke (North Star). Just as the known, measurable universal laws of time determined by the sun, moon, and seasons govern humans on Earth, the universe is governed by the comparatively unknown, immeasurable universal laws of time determined by the stars and universe. Every once in a great while, the night sky will alight with meteor showers or a single fallen star on this timescale. All of existence rests in the balance of the ma'hëö'o hesto'emanestôtse from this realm: they are laws of the universe. If one day the powers of the Vono'omēē'e decided that all of existence should end, there would be no stopping them.

While the laws of the above worlds required higher-level thinking to comprehend and appreciate, the universal laws of the underworld are quite simple. Ho'e is Earth, the ground that living beings walk upon. Below the Earth is a realm called A'ó'tonóóma, which is the "Into-the-ground-realm," where humans can fall into but still reemerge. The roots of all plants belong to the A'ó'tonóóma and follow a complex body of universal laws. Animals and insects that live underground also adhere to these laws, as well as those that burrow when searching for food or shelter. Failure to comply with these laws could lead to poor growth in vegetation. Wooden Leg explained: "All of our teachings and beliefs were that land was not made to be owned in separate pieces by persons and that the plowing up and destruction of vegetation placed by the Great Medicine and the planting of other vegetation according to the ideas of men was an interference with the plans of the Above."[63]

Below the A'ó'tonóóma is Átonoome, the "underworld." Átonoome is a deeper world that is unknown to most humans and living beings. Some animals find solitude in this place, but it is understood as the place where the first Cheyennes emerged before entering into the first world. Humans also had to honor and acknowledge the ma'hëö'o hesto'emanestôtse from this realm; otherwise they could suffer from severe earthquakes and floods. Nearly every Cheyenne adult was conscious of and versed in the universal laws of the Earth and underworld, and they were completely devoted to protecting the spiritual and physical connection between the land and Indians. None other than Wooden Leg expressed the most provocative rendition of the universal laws:

> Another thing the white people appear not to understand: The old Indian teaching was that it is wrong to tear loose from its place on the earth anything that may be growing there. It may be cut off, but it should not be uprooted. The trees and the grass have spirits. Whatever one of such growths may be destroyed by some good Indian, his act is done in sadness and with a prayer for forgiveness because of his necessities, the same as we were taught to do in killing animals for food or skins. We revere especially the places where our old camp circles used to be set up and where we had our old places of worship. There are many of such spots on our reservation. White people look at them and say: "These Indians are foolish. There is good land not plowed." But we like to see these places as they were in the old times. They help to keep in our hearts a remembrance of the virtues of the good Cheyennes dead and gone from us.[64]

CONCLUSION

As mentioned in the introduction to this chapter, I have provided in-depth evaluations of the Cheyenne concepts of law without relying on anthropological and legal paradigms of study. Ideally, the laws were to make for a peaceful and just society, and the Cheyenne before the time of the white man should be commended for sustaining their ways for the sake of posterity. Without a doubt, the people faced numerous challenges relating to crime, law, and order, but the legal and spiritual philosophies of my ancestors reveal a near-utopian world that rivaled Christian perceptions, old and modern, and that even the best societies would envy. Numerous leaders, spiritual and political, came into existence before the time of the white man; all were students and teachers of the old ways, proponents of the sacred laws, and devoted to a cause: Tséhéstanove. The Véhoo'o held fast to ancient principles, the warriors remained disciplined despite the few bad apples, and all the while the citizens, women and children, remained loyal and continued to trust a system created by the spiritual but managed by humans and subject to human error. The Maahótse and Ésevone were of great significance to the social and political organization of the Cheyenne Nation. Tséá'enövâhtse (keepers of the sacred bundles) were the ultimate protectors of the Tséhéstanove and they were unyielding in protecting the life made by previous generations. Stands In Timber (Northern Cheyenne) elaborated:

> Those Keepers were important. They claimed fifty years ago that the character and actions of the Hat and Arrow Keepers—how they acted and felt—set the way the whole tribe went. Everything was smooth if the Keeper lived quietly and prayed all the time and the people followed his instructions. If he did wrong, everything went wrong. If a member of the tribe drew the blood of another member, one of the chiefs had to renew the Sacred Arrows—nobody but a chief.[65]

The health of the sacred nation was strengthened because each citizen held the sacred laws with reverence, as the guiding principles to healthy and happy living. The purpose of law was to provide some control over the behavior of citizens, and for the Cheyenne, law was a part of life and could not be easily separated. The Cheyenne system worked. Although an individual person may become corrupt, this person could never corrupt the system. If someone tried to do so, he or she would inevitably lose citizenship. If one chose to break a law and go against the norm, then that person faced dire consequences by eventually becoming an outcast. This system would have failed if the culture and spiritual practices were also compromised, and if leaders acted without principle.

PART III

Néstaxeo'o: Allies

You will find the Arapahos first, next Sioux, next Pawnees, fourth you shall find your own people, the Cheyenne. And your name shall go over all the nations.

—Instructions to Motsé'eóeve[1]

Before the wars with Americans only a few Plains Indian nations had acquired horses and established ways of living with the horse. The Comanche Nation, for example, was one of the first Plains nations to acquire the Spanish-bred mustangs that came from the south. In the 1700s the horse significantly contributed to the military and geopolitical prowess of southern Plains nations in particular. During the same era and to the north, Plains Indian nations like the Hóheeheo'o (Assiniboine) acquired muskets from French traders to gain military advantages over foes. The first guns on the Great Plains were unrefined, difficult to load, and unpredictable when shooting, which is why some nations remained loyal to their bows and arrows even through the early wars with the Americans. Eventually larger nations like the Lakota in the north and Apache in the south gained access to both horses and guns through trade. Each "horse nation" has its own accounts of how these items came into their world, but each came to rely on horses and guns for survival. The history of these horse nations influenced the American perception of the west and created the "Wild West" culture that is still popular in today's history of the plains. Without a doubt, horses and guns were two foreign tools that proved to be innovative and beneficial for Indian nations in expansion and in intertribal wars and wars with Americans.

Before the Cheyennes had horses and guns, they were threatened by those nations that had mastered the art of horsemanship and developed horse economies, relying on the beasts of burdens for travel, war, and trade. Eventually, the Cheyennes acquired horses and guns and also adopted a horse economy and culture. More important, they built new relationships with other horse nations, which proved to be essential to the survival of the Cheyenne Nation. At its primacy, particularly during the era known to the Cheyennes as "time of the horse" (1680–1880), the ten bands of the Tsėhėstáno held a prominent military and geopolitical presence on the Great Plains. The Rocky Mountains to the west, the Arkansas River to the south, and the Missouri River to the northeast bordered their hunting grounds. Some bands were known to travel and camp as far north as present-day Canada, some as far east as the Mississippi River basin, and others as far south as the Red River in what is now northern Texas.

The heart of the Cheyenne homeland remained centered in the Black Hills, where the sacred mountain Nóvávóse is located. Before the arrival of the horse, the Tsėhėstáno already interacted with other nations, and when the horse arrived, the Cheyennes were able to travel over greater distances and explore larger tracts of land. The Cheyenne bands, however, were able to remain secluded within their own territory and encountered other nations only while hunting or moving camp. Some encounters led to conflict while others led to long-standing friendships. The Cree, for example, were one of the first allies, as I discussed in *A Sacred People*. The Lakota (Sioux) were also allies and this friendship never ended. The Hóheeheo'o (Assiniboine) were one of the nation's first enemies.

Early skirmishes between them and the Cheyennes eventually led to the creation of new intertribal relations or international policy regarding war. Nevertheless, the old policies of peace, manifested by the Great Unification between the Só'taeo'o and Tsétsêhéstâhese, became refined and instituted as an international peace policy between other Indian nations like the Lakota and Arapaho. These war policies and peacemaking practices laid a foundation for diplomacy, sovereignty, and nation building, which secured the survival of the Tséhéstáno.

In this section, I discuss the external sovereignty of the Cheyenne Nation, as achieved through two practices of international law: making peace and declaring war. Despite popular belief that precontact life on the Great Plains was lawless and fraught with intertribal warfare, nations like the Cheyennes sustained stable living conditions and spent the majority of their time enjoying a peaceful coexistence with other Plains Indian nations. War was seasonal and took place in the late summer. It was considered a sport for younger men who belonged to the Nótâxeo'o. The practices of this sport are evidenced particularly by the perfected art of war without killing in horse raiding, which quickly adapted into the art of counting coup. Peace, on the other hand, occupied the majority of the calendar year and the lives of Plains Indians. Peacemaking, unlike war, was considered an exertion of sacred sovereignty and primarily practiced by older, wiser leaders of the Véhoo'o.

Intertribal or inter-Indigenous-national conflicts did arise between enemy nations, but these conflicts were rather short-lived when compared to the time that each nation existed. Eventually, warring nations reached long-lasting peace agreements. These intertribal or inter-Indigenous national peace agreements can be viewed as international peace relations that were significant in nation building. The principles of inter-Indigenous national law eventually became the means that Plains Indian nations utilized when addressing the challenges posed by the Americans and their fledgling nation. This section aims to answer these questions: What is inter-Indigenous national law and what are its guiding principles? How did inter-Indigenous national law develop and how was it used in peacemaking and declaring war? But before we answer these questions, we must first answer a fundamental question: How did the Cheyennes perceive and interact with other Indians and Indigenous nations?

CHAPTER 9

Tsėhéstáno naa Xamaevoʼêstaneoʼo: The Cheyenne Nation and Indigenous Peoples

A first principle of Indian conduct was: Be generous to all Indians.

—Wooden Leg (Northern Cheyenne)[1]

Before the Cheyennes had horses, they traveled by foot and used dogs as beasts of burden. After the Great Unification, the Tsétsêhéstâhese and Sóʼtaeoʼo continued to camp separately, periodically uniting for ceremonial purposes. The two nations were strong allies and thus conscious of other Indians that likely posed the same threats as did the Hóheeheoʼo. Standing in the Morning, a Sóʼtaeoʼo, recalled that Vóetsénaʼe (Lime) spoke against meeting other Indians to the point of starvation:

> Among the band of Sutaiu there was a great chief. There was a big camp of Sutaiu, and many hostile people against them. The band of Sutaiu were told by the chief not to leave the camp. Keeping close together they were nearly starving. The head chief said, "Do not meet any of the hostile people who want to fight us until they do something to us. We are not going to make any trouble first." In those days, everyone obeyed the word of the chief.[2]

The Cheyennes called all Indigenous peoples of the known lands xamaevoʼêstaneoʼo, which means "ordinary, original people." Before the arrival of the horse, the Cheyennes were a small nation and did not trust other Indigenous nations. The Cheyennes, however, were familiar with and friendly to a few nations they interacted with around their homeland. Occasionally they found evidence of other Indigenous peoples, especially those who encroached onto traditional planting grounds to steal corn or those who used their antelope pits. Despite the threats of violence from other nations, the core of Cheyenne Nation etiquette was rooted in the principles and teachings of their two covenants: the Maahótse and the Ésevone.

Table 9.1. Indigenous Nations Identified in 1910

White Bull/Ice	American Horse	Grasshopper
Apache	-	Apache
Arapaho	Arapaho	Arapaho
Assiniboine	Assiniboine	-
Blackfeet	Blackfeet	Blackfeet
-	Bloody Bits	Bloods
Brulé	Brulé	Brulé
Burners	-	
Caddo	-	Caddo
Canoes	-	-
Chickasaw	Chickasaw	-
Choctaw	Choctaw	-
Comanche	Comanche	Comanche
Cree	Cree	Cree
-	Crow	Crow
Fish Eaters	Fish Eaters	-
Flatheads	-	Flathead
Grey Blankets	-	Gray Blankets
Kickapoo	Kickapoo	Kickapoo
Kiowa	-	Kiowa
-	Mexican Indians	Mexican Indians
Navajo	Navajo	-
Nez Perce	Nez Perce	Nez Perce
Osage	Osage	Osage
Otoe	Otoe	Otoe
Pawnee	Pawnee	Pawnee
Piegan	Piegan	Peigan
Ponca	Ponca	Ponca
Pueblo	Pueblo	Pueblo
Rabbit Blankets	Rabbit Blankets	-
Ree	Ree	-
Seminole	Seminole	-
Shoshoni	Shoshoni	Shoshone
Sioux	Sioux	Sioux
Ute	Ute	Utes
Wichita	Wichita	Wichita

TSÉHÉSTÁNO NAA XAMAEVO'ÊSTANEO'O: THE CHEYENNE NATION AND INDIGENOUS PEOPLES

The covenants laid the foundation for international Indigenous diplomacy. They provided the basis for the creation and development of exercises of external sovereignty, the elements of the Tséhéstanove that promoted peace and unity with other peoples. The Tséhéstanove became the apparatus for building alliances with all nations, even the Americans. The Cheyenne principles of ováná'xaetanohtôtse (peace) and hévese'onematsestôtse (brotherhood) manifested among the Cheyenne people as friendly conduct, as expressed by Wooden Leg: "Yet every Indian who might prosper in any way was expected to hold himself always willing to share and desirous of sharing his prosperity with his fellows, with all friendly people, even with avowed enemies if such should come peaceably and should be in want. A first principle of Indian conduct was: Be generous to all Indians."[3]

XAMAEVO'ÊSTANEO'O

Throughout the history of the Tséhéstáno, any one of the ten bands of the nation was bound to interact with other Indigenous nations. To assume otherwise misunderstands Indian history and culture. In 1910 White Bull/Ice (Northern Cheyenne) was familiar with some Indian nations when the United States was still only thirteen colonies. White Bull/Ice was about seventy years old when he provided a list of Indigenous nations and peoples that he knew. He identified the "Red Rocks," whom the Cheyennes had "known long, long ago," who were probably in existence when the Só'taeo'o still resided near Catlinite. American Horse stated that the Red Rocks were located at the mouth of the White River along the Missouri and that he met some Red Rocks people when he visited the Santee and Brulé Sioux. These people, according to White Bull/Ice, were originally located in Minnesota and were also called Pipers and Medicine Lodges; they mostly planted corn but also hunted buffalo, just like the Tsétsêhéstâhese and Só'taeo'o in previous eras. The fate of the Red Rocks people remains a mystery, but the Cheyennes believe them to be relatives among the Lakota.[4]

White Bull/Ice also stated that long ago the Cheyennes knew the Winnebago, who were called "Pipe Dancers," and the Kickapoo, who "used to be great medicine doctors." He stated that at one time the Cheyennes knew of and fought against the Sac and Fox for "a long time." He also identified the "Canoes," who lived near Salt Lake, and several Oklahoma peoples, including the North Ponca, Kaw, and Omaha, among others cross-listed in Table 9.1. He identified other unknown peoples like the "Turning Eyes" and "Bows and Arrows," who were "entirely uncivilized" and had no horses; the "Tonkawa" or "Human-Flesh-Eaters," who lived the furthest north and had no horses, he said lived in caves of ice and never had summers. In the northern plains up to Canada, White Bull/Ice identified the "Turn Bloods" (who are from Canada and related to Piegans), "Grey Blankets" (who lived with Piegans), and "Short Hairs" (who lived in west Canada). He also identified the Stockbridge, "Half-Civilized"

PART III : NÉSTAXEO'O: ALLIES

Kamxwiwiyaxtah (Wooden Leg). March 1913, De Lancey W. Gill, National Anthropological Archives, Smithsonian Museum Support Center, Suitland, Maryland (NAA INV 9172100, OPPS NEG 2).

(who were related to Stockbridges), and Hōhēēū, and the Snakes of California. White Bull/Ice identified the Saōtāhōn, who lived along the Mississippi River and fought with Custer at the Battle of the Little Bighorn. He also identified peoples to the east, like the Haudenosaunee (Iroquois), whom the Cheyennes called "Burners," who were "5 civilized tribes" located in New York. He also identified a people known as the "Red Jackets," who were from New York. The United States captured them as prisoners, split their ears, branded them, and relocated them near "the Cheyenne where Standing Rock Agency is now."[5]

TSÈHÉSTÁNO NAA XAMAEVO'ÊSTANEO'O: THE CHEYENNE NATION AND INDIGENOUS PEOPLES

American Horse, who was age sixty-three at the time of his interview, also identified numerous Indian nations and peoples he knew.[6] He mentioned peoples like the "Red People," "Boat Rowers" of Utah, "Fish Eaters" of southern Utah, and the "Rabbit-Blankets" (Paiutes). He also identified the "Bloody Bits" (Bloods) and the "Goose Warriors" (Peigan), who were part of the Blackfeet Nation or the Blackfoot Confederacy. American Horse also identified a band of Cheyennes that were "not our Cheyenne" who "lived near source of Missouri River."[7] This band was probably one of the northern bands of the Cheyennes.

Grasshopper, who was age fifty-three, identified a number of Indigenous nations, which are also listed in Table 9.1. Grasshopper stated that the Cheyennes first met the Arapahos, then the Sioux second, the Kiowa third, and the Comanches fourth.[8] Grasshopper identified unknown Indian peoples like the Sahaptin or Shipitan, who lived by the Shoshones, and the Sahée, who lived in central Canada and were likely a band of Chippewas. He also identified the "Bloods" and the "Northern Piegan" of the Blackfoot Confederacy.

The knowledge of numerous Indigenous nations is evidence that the ten bands of the Cheyenne Nation had a strong presence in precontact Native America. Table 9.1 is detailed but may be incomplete. Arguably, Grasshopper, American Horse, and White Bull/Ice may not have been knowledgeable of the Indian nations that other Cheyennes of other bands may have known. Furthermore, at the time and place of the collection of these data, numerous Indian nations were removed and settled in Oklahoma, where we can assume that the Southern Cheyenne people interacted and shared their history and culture with other Indian nations. Despite the circumstantial influences that likely affected the informants, the Cheyennes did preserve the presence and interaction with other Indian nations in their oral history through storytelling. The Indigenous peoples and nations commonly known to the Cheyenne people today are listed in Table 9.2.

INTER-INDIGENOUS NATIONAL PEACEMAKING

The Great Unification of the Tsétsêhéstâhese and Só'taeo'o served as the model for peacemaking and alliance building with other Indigenous nations. Since the Great Unification was part of the Cheyenne national history, every citizen was aware of the Cheyenne national policy and practice of unification. Any band

Table 9.2. Indigenous Nations Commonly Known to the Cheyennes could unify with other Indian nations under the principles of ovánaxaetanohtôtse (peace) and hévese'onematsestôtse (brotherhood), pending the approval of the Véhoo'o and keepers of the sacred covenants. Unfortunately, the Great Plains were under pressure from competing nations, and when the United States and Canada began to expand, all Indian nations began to vie for land and survival. White Bull/Ice describes how the Cheyenne Nation adapted to meet the challenges:

PART III : NÉSTAXEO'O: ALLIES

Table 9.2. Indigenous Nations Commonly Known to the Cheyennes

English	Cheyenne	Translation
Apache	Móhtséheonetaneo'o	"Occupied-Camp People"
Arapaho	Hetanevo'eo'o	"Man Cloud"
Atsina	Hestóetaneo'o	"Cedar People"
Assiniboine	Hóheeheo'o	"Wrapped People"
Bannock	Panâhke'eo'o	"Bannock People"
Blackfeet	Mo'ôhtávêhahtátaneo'o	"Black-footed People"
Cheyenne-Sioux	Tsêhésêho'óhomo'eo'o	"Cheyenne Sioux"
Cherokee	Sena'kaneo'o	"Cherokee People"
Chippewa	Sáhea'eo'o	"Little Fighter People"
Comanche	Šé'šenovotsétaneo'o	"Snake People"
Cree	Vóhkoohetaneo'o	"Rabbit People"
Crow	Óoetaneo'o	"Crow People"
Dakota	O'óhomo'eo'o	"Dakota"
Eskimo	Hesta'sévo'êstaneo'o	"Snow People"
Hopi	Xaehétaneo'o	"Weasel People"
Ice People	Ma'ométaneo'o	"Ice People"
Inuit	Nomá'nôhmévose	"Fish Eaters"
Flatheads	Kâhkoestséataneo'o	"Flat-headed People"
Gros Ventre	Pôhonóeneo'o	"Gros Ventre People"
Kiowa	Vétapâhaetó'eo'o	"Greasy-wood Ones"
Mandan	Tséhešé'émâheónese	"The Ones in Earth Houses"
Navajo	Póevónaneo'o	"Navajo"
Northern Arapaho	Váno'étaneo'o	"Sage People"
Nakota	Náhtovonaho	"Nakota"
Nez Perce	Otaesétaneo'o	"Pierced-nose People"
Oglala Lakota	Hotóhkêsono	"Little Stars"
Omaha	Onéhao'o	Omaha
Osage	Oo'kóhtâxétaneo'o	"Cut Hair People"
Paiute	Vóhkoohévoomaheo'o	"Rabbit-Robed People"
Pawnee	Ho'néhetaneo'o	"Wolf People"
Piegan	Péékáne	"Piegan"
Ponca	Onéhao'o	"Omaha"
Pueblo	Hotamó'keeho	"From Out West"
Ree/Arikara	Ononeo'o	"Taking-off with Teeth People"
Rocky Boy Cree	Ho'honáeka'êškóneho	"Rock-Children"
Shawnee	Savanaho	"Shawnee People"
Shoshoni	Sósone'eo'o	"Shoshoni"
Lakota (Sioux)	Ho'óhomo'eo'o	"Lakota"
Tonkawa	Mévavêheo'o	"Cannibals"
Ute	Mo'ôhtávêhetaneo'o	"Black men"
Wichita	Hevêsóhetaneo'o	"Tatooed People"

TSÉHÉSTÁNO NAA XAMAEVO'ÊSTANEO'O: THE CHEYENNE NATION AND INDIGENOUS PEOPLES

> A lot of other tribes began to appear in the world. The Sūtaiū had a medicine that would exterminate heaps of people. Mattsīŏ'iv: his medicine killed more of the other tribes than that of the Sūtaiū. By and by they (the Cheyennes and Sūtaiū) clanned together under that medicine and became the strongest tribe of the world. They began to war every place. This was long before the white people came to this country.[9]

As intertribal conflict increased, the Cheyenne oral tradition merged and intertribal relations were incorporated into the epic of Sweet Medicine. When the holy beings taught him the future of the Cheyenne Nation, before the Cheyennes had horses, the storytellers highlighted their confrontations with other Indian nations. White Eagle (Southern Cheyenne), who was a Dog Soldier, provides his account of Sweet Medicine.

Sweet Medicine, by White Eagle

Whenever they find some other tribe of Indians, they should capture them and take them for prisoners. After that the Indians went towards Big Horn [Mountains] and kept on going. Finally they saw a big camp of Crow Indians. They captured all the women. The men were all killed. They took all the property, horses, and everything. After that they got along pretty good. Then they went towards the South. Finally they found a large camp of Pawnees. They did the same as they had done to the Crows. The Cheyennes shall be the bravest in the Indian nations. Then they went towards Idaho. They killed one Shoshone. They went all over the west but could find no Indians so they had to come back. Then they went south towards Indian Territory. They wanted to capture all the Indians they could. They found the Kiowa and Comanches. They killed some and captured some. (You see that's the reason boys were born from captured woman). They found the Arikara and Ponca, also Missouri, Omaha. They captured them. They found the Utes (Moktu'uahAtAn). They captured them. The buffalo were thick all over the plains in the west. You shall have lots of horses, no matter [how] far you go the horses will take you. It shall be easy to kill buffalo. You shall eat the food now, you shall eat it not cooked well. You shall eat the buffalo (after you have killed one) standing up. [Meaning they will not have to hide as they did before in the earlier story by Standing in the Morning.][10]

There are some inconsistencies when examining which Indian nations the Cheyennes met and when they met them. For example, American Horse states that the Cheyennes met the Arapahos first, then the Cree at the same time.[11] Grasshopper states that the Cheyennes met the Arapahos, then the Kiowa, and then the Cree.[12] Despite the inconsistencies, what is of greater significance to the Cheyenne national history is whether the Cheyennes made peace agreements or formal unifications following the protocol set by the Great Unification.

Any formal unification had to undergo a peacemaking process: First, a formal unification agreement had to start at the band level, which typically began when a warrior society or group of hunters met another group of people. The time from the initial encounter to the time a person or society made a petition to the band chiefs could be years. Second, if the band chiefs and warrior societies decided to pursue a relationship with another Indian nation or band, their relationship did not include the entire Cheyenne Nation or other bands. Sometimes these band peace agreements centered on trade and did not develop into military alliances or ceremonial amalgamations.

After a number of years, the band chiefs may decide to pursue a stronger and longer-lasting peace agreement; they then brought a petition to the entire Council of Forty-four Chiefs (the third step). Peace agreements at this level were unifications and considered a serious matter since they were equivalent to the Great Unification of the Só'taeo'o and Tsétsêhéstâhese; all bands of the United Cheyenne Nation were bound by the agreement. Such an amalgamation or unification also meant that the citizens would share their culture, traditions, history, knowledge, and way of living. Each band was expected to intermarry to secure a future of the unification in perpetuity. A petition of unification at this level may not even reach the Véhoo'o until after several years. Indian nations friendly to the Cheyennes may secure peace agreements but may never unify.

At the third level, the Véhoo'o discussed the matter, sometimes over the course of years, at the annual and decennial Véhooneome (Chiefs' Lodge). The Véhoo'o, as the peacemakers, handled the matter with much care and thought, over ceremony and smoking the pipe. If the Véhoo'o rejected the petition of peace, they likely did so because the Indian nation was still seen as a threat or because the two nations were still at war. If, however, the Véhoo'o approved the unification, the other Indian nation established a peace agreement with the Cheyenne Nation. This was typical in peacemaking with once-enemy Indian nations, but the peace agreement was not a union, which is significantly different. Some Indian nations retained such partnerships with the Cheyennes in perpetuity without formally unifying. Conversely, some nations achieved formal unification by completing the fourth and final step of unification.

The fourth level of unification was the highest and required formal approval from the Tséá'enövâhtse (Keepers) of the two covenants: the Maahótse (Medicine Arrows) and the Ésevone (Buffalo Hat). As part of unification, which included the re-creation of a new, sacred relationship between the two nations, the Arrow Keeper and Hat Keeper performed rituals to formally acknowledge the amalgamation. The unification meant that the Cheyennes were to acquire new partners in all facets of living, including trade, hunting, war and peace, ceremony, and marriage and kinship. The unification was consecrated when the Cheyennes hosted a Hoxéheome (Medicine Lodge) ceremony, in which the ceremonial leaders, warriors, and families from the joining nation participated alongside the Cheyennes. This ceremony also served as a formal gift from one héstanovestôtse (living-nation), the Cheyenne Nation, to another héstanovestôtse, the other Indigenous living-nation. Indigenous nations that unified with the Cheyenne Nation frequently camped and participated in the Hoxéheome throughout their coexistence, as was expected of lifelong allies.

Vóhkoohétaneo'o (The Crees)

The Cheyennes did not unify with all allied nations, even though the opportunity was available depending on the circumstances of the two nations, their interactions, and historical relationships. After the Great Unification, for example, when the Cheyennes still farmed corn, they met the Crees, or Vóhkoohétaneo'o (Rabbit People), along the Missouri River.[13] Both the Cheyennes and the Crees planted corn at the time, and the Cheyennes and Crees intermingled and intermarried enough for the Cheyennes to adopt some customs, like their dances.[14] Grasshopper stated that some of the older Cheyennes recalled that the Crees and Cheyennes parted ways because the Crees were accused of stealing Cheyenne corn.[15] What is certain is that the two nations parted ways about the same time they started relying heavily on buffalo hunting. During this period the Só'taeo'o and Tsétsêhéstâhese unified and acquired the Ésevone covenant. Had the Crees and Cheyennes stayed together longer, they would have likely unified under the principles of peace and brotherhood and approved by the Cheyenne covenants of the Maahótse and the Ésevone. Nonetheless, the Crees are remembered in the United Cheyenne history as close allies, with a shared history dating back to a previous time in a previous world.

Hestóetaneo'o (The Arapaho)

One of the longest-lasting unifications was between the Cheyenne Nation and the Arapaho. The Arapaho consisted of five bands, and some spoke different languages: the first band was Northern Arapaho and consisted of two bands called the Ná'kasinĕ'na (Sage Brush Men) and Ba'achinĕna (Red Willow Men, Blood-Pudding Men, or Mother People); the second band was the Na'wunĕna or Nawathi'nĕna (Southern Arapaho); the third band was the Aä'ninĕna (White Clay People) or Hitu'nĕna (Begging Men), who were also known as the Gros Ventre; the fourth band was the Baä'sawunĕ'na (Wood Lodge Men); and the fifth band was the Ha'nahawnena or Aanu'hawa, which was absorbed by the other Northern Arapaho bands.[16] While the location and time of the first meeting of the Cheyennes and Arapahos remains unclear, we can assume that bands from each nation preserved their version of the Arapaho encounter. Goes in Lodge (Arapaho), the wife of Arapaho Chief Sharp Nose, and who lived during the 1800s, recalled:

> When I was young I heard the Old Ones tell how the Arapaho lived east of the Mississippi, and over time we migrated to the northwestern corner of Minnesota and

PART III : NÉSTAXEO'O: ALLIES

possibly into the eastern provinces of Canada. As we entered the West we remained close to our brothers, the Cheyennes, who share our identity of habitation. The Great Plains became our territory, as far west as the Rocky Mountains and east beyond the Missouri.[17]

The Tsétsêhéstâhese bands and the Só'taeo'o each had different accounts. Nonetheless, the Arapaho alliance eventually became an amalgamation like the Great Unification. Stands In Timber recalled: "The Cheyennes claim that they were here at the Black Hills, they and the Arapahos came from the west or north, the second ones allied. The Suhtai were first."[18] American Horse states that the Tsétsêhéstâhese met the Arapahos about the same time they met the Crees on the Missouri River, and like the Tsétsêhéstâhese and Crees the Arapahos still raised corn.[19] Grasshopper stated that the Arapahos and Cheyennes met before they hunted buffalo, when the two nations ate turnips and fruits.[20] Coyote was seventy-two years old when he told how the Tsétsêhéstâhese met the Arapaho:

> They came to a country heavily timbered with cedar. No'awús' is the name of the big mountain. "Bear Mountain" is what the white man probably call it. All this time the Cheyenne were at war with all tribes, no matter who. There were a few in a party out hunting and come on an Indian not a Cheyenne. He was alone. They asked him by signs who he was. He replied in signs, hitáni no^S e'yo^U (Blue Cloud Indians), used index finger of right hand on right side of nose, going up and down. He asked the Cheyenne what tribe they were. The Cheyenne spokesman using the sign language crossed, or cut, one index finger with index finger. They shook hands. That sealed the friendship between these tribes. There would be no more war between these two. The party of Cheyenne on their return repeated the incident to the chiefs. At that time there were no chiefs as today. At the time a man earned his chieftainship in battle or war. The chiefs said the children had shaken hands with the stranger, it was all right, from then on there would be no war with those people. This chief said if the Arapaho comes to my camp, he will not be molested and they have been together up to the present day.[21]

The Tsétsêhéstâhese, Só'taeo'o, Cree, and Arapaho all shared a common linguistic lineage as Algonquian-based language speakers, which is another possible reason why their peace agreements were easily reached. The Arapaho, unlike the Cree, also shared a sacred mountain with the Tsétsêhéstâhese, Nóávóse, where the Arapaho were given a sacred cedar medicine bundle.[22] The Arapaho are also credited with finding and using a certain black pipestone from the Rocky Mountains.[23] The Arapaho man in Coyote's story gathered cedar from the holy mountain Nóávóse, the same place that the Tsétsêhéstaestse prophet Motsé'eóeve received the Maahótse. The Tsétsêhéstâhese thus believed this Arapaho man to be a man of stature, probably a spiritual leader or chief, and they named him Hetanevö'e, which literally translates to "man-cloud" or "person from the clouds." As part of the peace agreement, the Arapaho gave the Tsétsêhéstâhese some of the sacred cedar and taught them of its ceremonial significance and spiritual powers. Afterward, the Tsétsêhéstâhese customarily named the Arapaho Hestóetaneo'o, which means "Cedar people." This first meeting led to the unification of a Tsétsêhéstâhese band with an Arapaho one that was sanctioned by the Maahótse covenant and preserved in United Cheyenne national and Tsétsêhéstâhese band histories. The exact band of the Arapaho is not known for certain, but we can assume it to be the Ba'achiněna (Red Willow Men), since they were part of the Northern Arapaho group and were close to Nóávóse.

When the Arapaho united with the Tsétsêhéstâhese, the alliance strengthened their cultural, political, and military presence as well as their guiding principles on the Great Plains. Coyote spoke of this alliance in an account that elevated the significance of the Arapaho unification equal with the Só'taeo'o, as an effort to reinforce the importance of the Arapahos to the Cheyennes:

> The Su'taiyo^U were in a band of their own, but they spoke practically the same language as the Cheyenne, but they were at war with them. They seemed to recognize that since the Arapaho had joined the Cheyenne, that they (the Su'taiyo^U) would be powerless to make war against the two tribes. They recognized the Cheyenne had the medicine arrows and that the Arapaho the sacred pouch (which contains the pipe, etc.). The Su'taiyo^U had the medicine cap. The medicine man of the Su'taiyo^U through a vision recognized that if the Su'taiyo^U were to survive they must be at peace with them. The Su'taiyo^U made friendship with the Cheyenne.[24]

The Só'taeo'o have a different story of unification but highlight the principles of ována'xaetanohtôtse (peace) and hévese'onematsestôtse (brotherhood). Their story goes like this: One day while hunting in the Black Hills, a group of Só'taeo'o noticed a boy hiding behind the rocks. The lead hunters told two younger men to follow that boy and they gave chase. Not long after, one of the hunters returned and reported that someone should return to camp to bring the chiefs to come see what they had found. Meanwhile, the hunters followed the young man to meet the other scout. When they went over a hill, they found a small village of people. The other Só'taa'e hunter was sitting next to some older men trying to communicate, and when the lead hunter arrived, he also tried to communicate. The people spoke a similar language but relied on sign language to talk. They were from the west, and were poor, as it seemed they suffered a great deal for some unknown reason. Some of the Só'taeo'o believed that these people were the survivors from a massacre in a war against an enemy nation, because they had very few warriors. Others believed that these people were once farmers who lived in the southern lands and suffered from a great famine or disease and had to abandon their old homeland to find a better life in the northlands. The Só'taeo'o talked with these people and came to have ševátamehestôtse (compassion) for these unfortunate people.

When the Véhoo'o arrived, they brought many gifts of food and clothing, and the old men of the new people received fine buffalo robes. The Véhoo'o invited the people to their camp and these new people accepted the invitation.

When they arrived to the Só'taeo'o camp, the people were generous and gave up their own possessions to these folks. The Véhoo'o sat with the leaders of the new people to smoke; one of the leaders told the Véhoo'o that his people had suffered a great deal but that they could not talk about what happened in the past and could only look to a brighter future. The Véhoo'o respected the man's wishes and were so pleased with their new friends that they hosted a Hoxéheome (Medicine Lodge) in their honor. The Véhoo'o told the people that this ceremony would help them strengthen their nation, as they would never again suffer from starvation and if they faced hardship, they would come out of it stronger and wiser. In the spirit of sharing, one of the leaders from the new people brought out a medicine bundle, which contained the people's sacred cedar. "This is our sacred plant that has kept us alive throughout our hardship," said the spiritual leader. "We will share with you this plant since we are now friends." The two nations were unified under a single Hoxéheome lodge, which was confirmed and blessed by the Ésevone. This is how the Arapaho band called the Ná'kasiněna (Sage Brush Men in the Arapaho language) became allies to the Só'taeo'o and how they came to practice their own version of the Hoxéheome.[25] The Só'taeo'o named these people Váno'étaneo'o (Sage People in the Só'taeo'o language).

The Hoxéheome established a spiritual place for the Arapaho in the United Cheyenne Nation and positioned the Arapaho people in the hearts and minds of all citizens of the Cheyenne Nation as relatives. The stories of the Cheyenne-Arapaho amalgamation are still preserved in the Cheyenne national history and thus ensure that the peaceful relationship was carried into later generations. Elements of Arapaho culture, traditions, and sacred histories converged with Cheyenne, especially after intermarriage. During the time of the dog, through the time of the buffalo and the time of the horse, the Arapaho Nation remained the closest allies to the Cheyennes, periodically reuniting to participate in ceremonies together to reinforce and reenact the amalgamation.[26] The conjoined ceremonies, however, declined during the wars with whites, as Wooden Leg recalled:

> The Cheyennes and the Arapahoes had their two Great Medicine ceremony dances together on one occasion when I was about twelve years old (1870). We were south of the mountains beyond the headwaters of Powder river. The two tribes camped as one, in one great camp circle, but all of the Cheyenne lodges were at one side of the camp and all of the Arapaho lodges at the opposite side. Each tribe had its Great Medicine lodge at its own side of the combined camp. I went back and forth looking on at both of them. The other people of both tribes did the same. I was not quite old enough during our free roaming days to take a part in the important tribal affairs. I merely looked, listened, kept quiet and thought about them. This double sacred dance of the Cheyennes and Arapahoes was for only one day. During that one day all of the participants and many other people took neither food nor water. After sunset they had a great feast.[27]

Stands In Timber expressed the consistency of the spiritual unification and how the Cheyennes and Arapahos preserved their ceremonial practices into the modern era:

> The Arapaho ceremony was always close to the Cheyenne one, and it still is. It is another that continues today. There are differences among all these ceremonies, even between the Northern and Southern Cheyenne ones because of the Suhtai influence. Between tribes many more things are done differently. But the central idea and spirit are the same, and many of the songs are shared from tribe to tribe. Some of them are like hit tunes; after you hear them you can't get them out of your head.[28]

The Northern Arapaho band, which included the subgroups Ná'kasiněna and Ba'achiněna, retained a sacred pipe covenant called the Seicha. Like the Só'taeo'o, who kept the Ésevone and used it for the Hoxéheome, the Arapaho also used their covenant for their Sun Dance. Goes in Lodge (Arapaho) described the key elements of the ceremony and its philosophy; both are strikingly similar to those of the Só'taeo'o:

> Twice a year, in the fall and the spring, the entire tribe would come together to hunt buffalo. The biggest, most exciting event of the year was the Sun Dance, which took place in the summer. What a wonderful sight it was. I enjoyed watching each band move in and find its position in the camp. While people were still coming to the location, the chiefs would stake out the gateway entrance. Once the entrance to the circle was established, all the people knew where to place their tepees. It was a thrill for me to help the men and women place the tepees in a circle with the openings facing the morning sun.
>
> West of the center of the circle, the men placed a large tepee that would house the Sacred Pipe. The Keeper of the Pipe occupied the tepee all during the meeting period. The Chiefs' Council met in that tepee. My husband and other chiefs spent most of their time there. Between the sacred tepee and the gateway of the circle was the sweat lodge of the older men's ceremonial age societies, called Nănăhăxwū.
>
> All of us looked forward to this annual summer meeting. It was the most sacred event in our lives. We believe all law and order for the tribe originated with the Sun Dance. It came about to help the people live a better life. Our Arapaho Sun Dance is much the same as that of other Plains Indians. Each ceremonial is meaningful. I took great pride in being one of the women who cooked for the men when they performed the ceremonies connected with bringing the poles down from the mountains. The women could watch but did not participate as the men erected the center pole; built the dance lodge, a shelter of poles set in a circle around the center pole; and placed the altar and the Sacred Bundle containing the Flat Pipe in their proper places.
>
> The early word for the Sun Dance was hăsăă, meaning "tanned hide or robe," perhaps because each dancer had a hide or robe lying in front of him. It is also called ha'sāyăt, which means "sacrifice." The dancers fast to prove their worthiness to have their prayers heard and answered by the Creator. The time of the Sun Dance was one of prayer renewal and the beginning of a new year.[29]

After the Cheyenne-Arapaho alliance, bands of Arapaho joined the Cheyennes on hunts and warfare and in other capacities connected to diplomacy and international relations, primarily acting as intermediaries for enemies seeking proposals of peace with the Cheyennes.[30] Because of their smaller population, the Arapaho benefited greatly from alliance with the larger Cheyenne Nation, especially during the time of the horse. The two never broke their peace with one another, even during and long after the wars with whites. The Arapahos were militarily, culturally, and spiritually allied to the Cheyennes, and during the time of the horse they perceived the Kiowa, Comanche, and Pawnee as shared enemies. Bass explained the Arapaho perception of the unification:

> Since long before the white man came, the Cheyenne and the Arapaho had followed much the same road. We had been joined together against common enemies and so had made war together; our religion, our stories, our ways of doing things in camp and on the hunt and the warpath were much alike. But the Cheyenne had outnumbered us for a long time. They had always been more war-like and proud than we were, and perhaps that is why there were more of them.[31]

The Cheyenne-Arapaho alliance became significant in law and punishment, since a Cheyenne who was exiled as a murderer could camp among the Arapaho and restart a new life and family.[32] The practice to join another allied nation was not prohibited; in fact, it was seen as a compassionate means for a sorrowful and regretful Cheyenne man to make the best of his situation: marry, make a new family, and belong to a new community. The life of a regretful and exiled Cheyenne was not completely over.

MO'ÉHNO'HA NAA ASEEHE: THE HORSE AND MOVING CAMP

The introduction of the horse signified the inevtiable end of the Buffalo Surrounding and Antelope Calling/Singing Ceremonies. The horse changed the Cheyenne way of life, as expressed by White Eagle when he stated that they would "eat standing up," in part three of his story of Sweet Medicine presented earlier. Mo'éhno'ha is the Cheyenne word for horse, which literally means "domesticated elk." The Cheyennes called the horse an elk because the first generation of Cheyenne horsemen perceived the horse as a relative to the elk. The horse must have also been perceived as a strange but sacred animal because the Cheyennes did not have any horses in the creation stories or previous worlds. Sweet Medicine, however, foretold the coming of the horse in his early prophecies.[33] Stands In Timber recited: "Another animal will come, with a shaggy tail almost touching the ground, and a mane, and round hoofs. This animal you can ride on its back. You see that blue vision way off in the hills. That animal will take you over there in a short time, but if you walked it would take a long time to get there."³⁴ Horses, like rifles and other metal implements, were items that the Cheyennes acquired and used for years without ever directly interacting with whites.

The Cheyennes of the north credit their allies, the Hestóetaneo'o (Arapaho), for bringing them horses through trade with unfriendly nations in the early 1700s.³⁵ When the northern bands of the Cheyenne Nation acquired horses, they engaged in trade and frequently visited the Mandan in their city located on the Upper Missouri River, in what is now North Dakota. The Cheyennes became trade partners with the Mandan, who also traded with Cheyenne enemies, the Ree and Assiniboine. The Mandan and Ree also established trade relations with English and French traders; the Cheyennes avoided both at all costs. Cheyennes viewed whites as disease-ridden, "hairy-bodied" brutes, according to the Sweet Medicine tradition.³⁶ The Cheyennes were relatively unknown to the first whites, but the Cheyennes knew about them and considered them strange and unnatural as evidenced by bizarre manufactured trade items.

The southern bands of the nation found horses much earlier and used ropes made from rawhide and the hair of buffalo to capture them from wild herds.³⁷ These southern bands were known as Heévâhetaneo'o (Rope-hair-people). Grasshopper states that the Cheyennes got horses from the Kiowa, while White Eagle believed that they got them from the Pawnees, who "were the first Indians to have horses, living in Nebraska."³⁸ When the Cheyennes first saw horses, they caught them and the animals became sacred, since they helped the people as the dog did in previous worlds. Some spiritual leaders eventually initiated a new ceremonial practice called "Horse Worship," which honored the sacred animals.³⁹ The horse improved mobility and revolutionized Cheyenne society, as Tallbull reflected on the value of mo'éhno'ha:

> The warrior horses and the buffalo horses were very valued animals and special care was devoted to them. The war horses received ceremonial painting and ornaments of feathers. They always seemed to trot with great pride. A warrior on a good horse was a combination hard to beat. He was breathtakingly fearless and so was his horse.⁴⁰

In no time, the Cheyennes developed into the Plains Indian equestrian culture and the horse became a valuable trade item, thrusting the Cheyenne economy into an era of wealth and status. The Cheyenne bands expanded in territory and grew in population. Before the Cheyennes had horses, the total population of the Cheyenne Nation never surpassed 4,000 people.⁴¹ Theoretically the population of the Cheyenne Nation should have increased dramatically after they secured horses, since the animals allowed them to become more efficient in hunting and moving. But the Cheyenne traditional beliefs of kinship and balance of population and with nature prevented them from outgrowing their buffalo-dependent lifestyle. Horses also revolutionized peacemaking as trade items and as common forms of compensation in civil disputes. However, the horse proved to be a blessing with uncertainties since it also led to more expansion and conflict with other nations. With the exception of a few nations, most Indian nations did not dramatically increase their populations because of the horse. Small nations, like the Cheyennes, that occupied large areas of land and sometimes contested hunting grounds with enemy nations, were conscious of the boundaries of their homelands and rarely traversed outside to overtake the lands of others. Nonetheless, encroachments onto enemy tribal lands became more common, especially when the horse came to dominate the cultures of Indians on the plains.

Aseehe, the moving of camp, was primarily done in accordance with cultural and spiritual laws that prevented people from residing in one area for too long and contaminating the environment. Even before the horse, aseehe allowed old campsites to regenerate and recover from the presence of humans. Resting in one area was unsanitary for the ground, water, and even the air and this uncleanliness was conducive to disease and sickness.[42] When horses were added into the equation, campsites became unsanitary sooner and the people responded by camping in places for shorter time periods. The people's consciousness of hygiene and constant moving allowed them to remain physically healthy, as described by Stands In Timber: "They roamed all through that country. They did not stay close together in one bunch. They would starve that way, because too many would hunt over the same place. And they moved often. They say they never camped on one place more than five days."[43]

Aseehe was a unified act and had to be done in an orderly way, which is why the act was spiritually driven to "move" the people forward. Moving hundreds to thousands of people, young and old, their property, horses, and dogs required much discipline and coordination, since the people were the most vulnerable to attack on such occasions.[44] Aseehe required everyone to pack up and move together toward a particular destination previously mapped out by the Véhoo'o. Spiritual leaders, especially for sacred journeys, planned the people's aseehe. The Notaxeo'o kept order to ensure that nobody got out of line during the aseehe because any problems could potentially befall the entire village. The Véhoo'o proclaimed to a selected society:

> You are the leaders today. Make all of the people obey you. Make them stay in their proper places. If any of them disobey our ordinary rules of travel you may pony-whip them, you may shoot their horse, you may kill their dogs, you may break their guns or their bows, you may punish them in any way that seems to you best, except you are not allowed to kill any Cheyenne.[45]

Aseehe required all citizens to take part in the move, even women and children. Their first task, after the Véhoo'o and warriors announced the move, was to disassemble the entire household and pack all items and the lodge itself into bundles on numerous travois, which were pulled by both horses and dogs. When the mobile village approached steep cliffs or creeks, all nonpatrolling warrior citizens, women, and children made temporary bridges from brush, branches, and earth, much like beaver dams.⁴⁶ The Véhoo'o stopped at places of good water, plenty of firewood, and thick grass for horses to set up temporary camps for one night. Here they mapped their movements, while a warrior society was ordered to hunt for the entire village. The women and other citizens set up temporary lodges, and by evening time the hunters returned to divide their game among the entire camp. By nightfall the entire village was asleep and as soon as the sun rose, a crier announced that the people pack up and begin the move to their destination. The laws of aseehe included the following:

1. No person was allowed to shoot a rifle while traveling.
2. The Véhoo'o designated a warrior society to police the move.
3. The designated warrior society also managed hunting and scouting while on the move.
4. No person was allowed to ride outside of the designated areas under the protection of the on-duty warrior society.
5. If scouts reported a threat, the Véhoo'o assigned a different warrior society, or multiple, to investigate and possibly engage the threat, while the moving camp departed.
6. If a person or family fell behind, they had to camp out of sight so as to not leave a trail for other people to follow; they were not exiled but they were on their own until they rejoined.

Every citizen was part of the aseehe, which is why the move had to be swift. The move was also to be a joyous occasion, since everyone worked together in harmony, to achieve a common goal: to traverse and arrive at a new campsite with renewed lands and fresh waters. Very few broke the laws associated with the aseehe because breaking a law could lead to enemy attacks or the stampeding of herds of buffalo. Wooden Leg explained his experience after violating the laws of the aseehe:

> We rode forward from our proper place in the procession and went on out to a hilltop, there to have a look over the country, as every Indian naturally likes to do. Four Crazy Dog warriors were right after us. They were riding fast. The other two boys got away, but my pony played out on me. I had to stop and dismount. I was frightened to distraction, but my mind was made up to take bravely whatever punishment they might inflict. Nevertheless, I became mentally upset when four determined-looking Fox warrior policemen dashed up to me. "Do not whip me," I begged. "Kill my horse. You may have all of my clothing. Here—take my gun and break it into pieces." But after a talk among themselves they decided not to do any of these penal acts. They scolded me and said I was a foolish little boy. They asked my name, and I told them. That was the last time I ever flagrantly violated any of the laws of travel or the hunt.⁴⁷

As the people traversed through their homelands and hunting grounds, young warriors explored their surroundings, especially those who may have recently come of age and were first-time travelers. While assigned warrior societies were determined in scouting and protecting the mobile village, young men looked for adventure and exploration. It became custom for smaller parties of young men to explore, with the approval and sometimes the guidance of the older warriors. The young men, sometimes in parties of only four, took long journeys to experience something new, or "to see or hear something" they never saw or heard before, such as springs, ponds, caves, rock formations, or other mysteries of nature.[48] Young men on these expeditions had more experiences with the supernatural than with other Indians, and these exploits were retold as prolific ghost stories filled with mystery and humor.[49] The mobile cultures of Plains Indians facilitated the exploratory opportunities, which is why these small groups became critical in developing early Plains Indian warfare. Young warriors went on expeditions as male-bonding experiences and to promote camaraderie and brotherhood. They endeavored to engage enemies even though the vastness of the Great Plains rarely yielded an opportunity for fights. When engaging enemies, however, young warriors did not have a desire to entirely destroy them or their people. Their goal was to outsport opponents through displays of gallantry, athleticism, and courage by counting coup or hand-to-hand combat. The killing of enemies was a common result, but both parties expected to meet their enemies again, in another challenge, on another day. The manifestation of a new style of Plains Indian warfare could not have been achieved without the introduction of the horse, the journeying of small parties of young men, and a profound respect for worthy enemies and the art of war.

CHAPTER 10

Ho'óhomo'eo'o: The Lakota Nation

The Cheyenne gave them horses and other gifts. That practice is still in vogue. When they visit they always give each other presents.

—Coyote (Northern Cheyenne)[1]

The Cheyennes always maintained friendly relationships with friendly nations they encountered. Relying on principles of ováná'xaetanohtôtse (peace) and héveseonematsestôtse (brotherhood), the Cheyennes expected the same treatment from other nations. Through the oral tradition, the history of peacemaking memorialized partnerships between nations even though they had different languages and customs. Divisions and intertribal conflicts were not one-dimensional disputes; likewise, unifications were not based on shallow similarities. While the Cheyenne's unification with the Só'taeo'o depended on shared language, customs, and histories, the Arapaho unification depended heavily on a shared sacred site. The amalgamation with the Lakota Nation (Sioux), however, proves that the Cheyenne unification process transcended the unifying principles of earlier unifications, since the two peoples differed significantly in language, custom, culture, and place of residence and origin.

The United Lakȟóta Nation (Sioux) comprises subnations called the "Seven Council Fires": the Mdewakanton, Sisseton, Teton, Wahpekute, Wahpeton, Yankton, and Yanktonais. The Teton Lakota, or "dwellers of the plains," were the largest subnation and comprised seven autonomous bands: the largest was the Oglala (Scatter or Pour Among Themselves); second was the Brulé (Burned Thighs); then the Hunkpapa (To Camp at the Entrance of the Circle); the Minneconjou (Plants Near the Water); the Oohenumpa (To Boil Two Kettles); the Sihasapa (Black Moccasins or Feet); and the Itazipo, or Sans Arcs (Without Bows).[2] The first two bands to cross the Missouri River into Cheyenne territory were the Brulé and Oglala.[3] In the following story, the Lakota recall how their first bands came to Cheyenne country.

| 181 |

PART III : NÉSTAXEO'O: ALLIES

How the Sioux Nation Was Born

М any, many winters ago when the world was young, a great flood visited the western plains. Many tribes came to the "hills of the prairies" to get away from the rising waters. These hills are near the present towns of Pipestone, Minnesota, and Flandreau, South Dakota. In the lands of the rising and setting suns, nations were destroyed from the earth. The water continued to rise on the hills until it covered all the people. Their flesh and blood was turned into red pipestone, say the wise old grandfathers. While the tribes were drowning, a big, bald eagle flew down so that a beautiful maiden could catch hold of its feet. The eagle carried her away to the top of a great tree on a high cliff above the water. Up on this cliff, when the water went down again, the girl had twins and their father was the war eagle! They began a new tribe that was strong and brave. It was in this manner that a great nation was born. The pipestone which was the flesh of their ancestors is smoked as a symbol of peace. The eagle's feather is worn on the heads of Sioux braves. The land of the pipestone still belongs to all tribes alike.[4]

The Cheyenne homeland was the Black Hills, and Lakota winter counts show that Brulé bands fought the Cheyennes in sporadic and inconclusive battles in the later part of the 1700s.[5] Nonetheless, "the Cheyennes have no recollection of ever having been at war with the Sioux," since they never considered them enemies as they did the Hóheeheo'o, who were especially aggressive toward the Só'taeo'o.[6] If any conflict with the Lakota continued into the 1800s, none were significant enough to completely change the relationship between the two nations, both of which consented to a long-lasting peace.

According to Cheyenne national history as told by Bent, Wolf Chief, and American Horse, the second nation that the Cheyennes met was a band of Lakota called the Moiseyu.[7] This first meeting was not the one that secured the long-lasting peace, but the Cheyennes remember the meeting as part of the Sweet Medicine legacy. In the story, the Cheyennes brought to the Moiseyu the Buffalo Ceremony. Old She Bear told the story, but included horses, which is inaccurate because each meeting with the Lakota occurred before the Cheyennes had horses:

Sweet Medicine, by Old She Bear

They were going to move camp. The old woman told the boy, "Go after those two horses over there." Some black birds were sitting on the horses' backs. The boy [told] the old woman to make 4 arrows so he could shoot the black birds. He went towards the horses. She was watching him. Everybody was busy packing up camp. When she looked up he had disappeared. The two horses were hobbled. They came back by themselves to the old woman. At the foot of the hill there was a big flat rock. They went over where the boy was last seen. They found his tracks.

They couldn't find him. He must have gone inside the hill. Nobody could lift that stone. The boy had gone in. The hill was a tipi inside. He saw a man and woman sitting down. They put him in the back of the lodge (an important place). The man and woman gave him instructions [on] what he should do when he got out in the world so he could help the people. While he was given instruction, they told him how people were going to live in the future and how he had been thrown away; that they would have buffalo again and have a happy hunting ground. They gave him this name Matsí'íov, and told him that he should tell all the people that was his name so that all nations would know it. They gave him a buffalo robe with horns and hoofs on. It was painted red. And they told him to go out into the world; to go back to his home; to help all the Indians. After he got out, a big herd of buffalo was sent out too. "You will find the Arapahos first, next Sioux, next Pawnees, fourth you shall find your own people, the Cheyenne. And your name shall go over all the nations." He started off on his journey. He went over the hill and sat down, took a smoke, looked down, saw the tipis in a circle. And he was told not to stop at any of these places but to keep on his journey. He passed hills. He looked down and saw a river. Everything looked blue. He saw the Sioux camped in a circle. He saw no one playing hoops, so he thought they were Sioux. Next he saw everywhere down the river camps. He thought they were not his people.[8]

The Cheyennes and Moiseyu lived in peace for some time, until the Cheyennes decided to move deeper into the Plains. The Moiseyu evidently were unaccustomed to killing buffalo and reverted to hunting small game, fishing, and farming. The Cheyennes did not formally unify—sanctioned and consecrated through the covenant bundles—with the Lakota until a later time.

According to Badger, his people, the Só'taeo'o, met a Lakota band first, on the Missouri River, then the Cree, and then the Cheyennes.[9] Badger's emphasis on the Só'taeo'o-Lakota unification, above others, probably resulted from the significance of the transference of the Hoxéheome (Medicine Lodge) ceremony from the Cheyennes to the Lakota as part of the unification. When horses arrived, the Só'taeo'o were not too fond of them and enjoyed walking instead of riding. They continued to hunt antelope and buffalo in their traditional manners, even though they slowly began to rely on horses for traveling.

A Só'taeo'o version of the Lakota unification, told by White Frog, occurred when a party of Só'taeo'o were out on a buffalo hunt on the Missouri River. The hunters came across a different group of people who were also on foot, hunting the same herd. The Só'taeo'o spotted these people right away but noticed that they were not their enemies, the Hóheeheo'o (Assiniboine) or Brulé. On the other side, the new people saw the Só'taeo'o and noticed that they were not enemies, the Cree or Pawnee. At a distance the two groups of people waved to one another and signaled peace and friendship. According to the customs on the plains, any friendly gestures warranted friendly treatment. Nevertheless, the people were suspicious of each other, so a Só'taa'e hunter shot an arrow high into the air as a sign of peace, and afterward a hunter from the other party did the same. Each party retrieved the arrows belonging to their counterpart, and this satisfied the leaders that they could depart without a fight. The arrows were symbolic and meant each party could return home to their people to inform them honestly of the event.[10] The Só'taeo'o named these people Ho'óhomo'eo'o, "arriving at a place people," because they arrived at the homeland of the Cheyennes as friendly people, and this first meeting between the Só'taeo'o and Lakota took place around 1760. The name Ho'óhomo'eo'o applied to all Teton Lakota.

The Tsétsêhéstâhese band histories, however, recall the meeting with the Lakota in a different light than do the Só'taeo'o. Yet there are some similarities: White Eagle, for example, believed that the Sioux came from Canada about the same time the Cheyennes were at war against the Hóheeheo'o.[11] Apparently, a small group of the Lakota made their way to the territory of the United Cheyenne Nation. They were half-starved hunters and were on foot when they met a band of Tsétsêhéstâhese. The Tsétsêhéstâhese warriors deliberated on whether or not to kill them because they spoke a language similar to that of the Hóheeheo'o, who were traditional enemies.[12] Eventually a peace agreement was made when two of the strangers did something daring, as Stands In Timber recalled:

Merger of Groups

One time when the ice was on the Missouri River, a bunch of Sioux followed a buffalo trail across the river, and two of them kept on until they came to the end of the place where the snow was on the ground. The rest of them went back, but the two kept on going; they could see the buffalo tracks. It didn't say how many days, they come to this Cheyenne village, and one morning they saw smoke [rising] from the valley. They were on top of a high hill, and they came down and close to examine the place. They found that the camp was there and made kind of a circle-shaped village, and they noticed there was a tepee towards the center. And these two told the story of when they come into it—both sides told the story: They went back down someplace and found a pool of water, not in the creek but on the prairie, like sometimes caught after a heavy rain; and it was in the springtime, when the ice was beginning to break out along the river—that was why the rest of them went back across.

These other two came on, and one of them stripped himself and went into this pool of water, and they had white clay and painted his body with that all over. The other went out to look for a buffalo skull, and he brought one and put a string on it. And this guy who was painted packed that head on his back and had his hair loose, and came out in front of the camp circle walking toward that tepee set out in front of the others. And everybody came out and looked, watched; they didn't know who he was and thought maybe one from the village did that for some purpose. They do something like that when they offer hides. They used to offer hides instead of cloth, when they give to the priest.

Well, this man walked slow, and the Keeper of the Arrows came out, watched him, and gave him room and opened the door for him. He went in, and the Keeper followed him in, and he took the buffalo skull and set it back of the tepee. And people started talking to him in Cheyenne, and the stranger began using sign language and made them understand he was not Cheyenne, but from another tribe. They did not know what tribe he was, but he made them understand he came from across the Missouri. The Cheyenne law is that, even [if] a fight goes on in the village and the enemy steps inside that medicine tepee, everything stops—that means no harm will be done. And they even go on to adopt that tribe that step inside the tepee.

And they come to find out that he was a Sioux, and [the] reason I tell this is after he washed himself, they all kind of shook hands with him (there was no shaking of hands at that time, when they meet they just hold themselves for a second or two; that is customary with the Cheyennes and they still do that). I have seen them here last year or so when the Southern Cheyennes come up and meet relatives and just lock themselves, you know, and let go, and that was the way they did. And they waited till the Missouri River froze again, and moved down there, planning to send him back where they came from. And they gave him a horse, and [an] extra one, and packed a lot of stuff on this extra one; he led it across and went back to the Sioux tribe. And the following year some more came back across on foot when the ice was frozen, and this time they took many horses back to their tribe. And the story has been told that the first one that brought the horses to the Sioux, they all got scared when he came in on an animal, and leading one of them, and all the pack stuff on the horse. And after a while they came up and told him, "These animals are owned by another tribe across the Missouri River." And the old Indians, all of them sat there watching those horses, and even towards evening they sat there, saying, "Let's see how much longer he will eat before he fills himself with grass." Some of them, you know, fill the pipes and point at that horse and call the horse god and pray to him. And that's how they receive horses.[13]

A spiritual law of the Tsêhéstanove forbade anyone to harm a person who finds sanctuary in the lodge of one of the covenants, even an alien or enemy. The Lakota (Sioux) man was protected when the Tséá'enôvâhtse (Arrow Keeper) welcomed and invited him into the lodge of the Maahótse. Horses were significant in establishing peaceful relations and the story highlights how the Lakota first received the horses as gifts of peace. Coyote also recalled the first meeting with the Lakota:

> Years after horses came into existence, the Sioux evidently knew where the Cheyenne were encamped but the Cheyenne were not aware that the Sioux were in the country. The Sioux evidently must have come from the north, for they only had dogs, while the Cheyenne were already well supplied with horses. The horses were found in the south by the Cheyenne. The Sioux came unannounced, without formalities. They were also recognized as friends thereafter. The Cheyenne gave them horses and other gifts. That practice is still in vogue. When they visit they always give each other presents. Then after a time the Sioux moved northeast from the Cheyenne. From then these 4 peoples [Tsétsêhéstâhese, Só'taeo'o, Arapaho, Lakota] allied, became powerful and fought with other tribes.[14]

Traditional Cheyennes believe that the first unified Teton Band of Lakota were the Oglala, and the Tsétsêhéstâhese named these people Hotóhkéso, which translates to "little star people." The Tsétsêhéstâhese believed that the Oglala came from the fallen star that the old people had followed worlds earlier (see chapter 1 in *A Sacred People*). If these Hotóhkéso were from that fallen star, then it was believed that their unification was predetermined and the two nations were destined to be allies and help one another in this current world. As is customary in unification, the Oglala named the Cheyennes Shyela (Red Talkers) and the Arapahos, Blue Clouds.[15]

Over the course of trade and interaction, the Cheyenne-Oglala peace agreement grew into a complete unification.[16] The Cheyennes believe that, as is custom in unification, they ceremonially gave the Oglala the Sun Dance ceremony, which they adapted to fit their traditions. The Oglala then gave the Sun Dance ceremony to the other bands of the Teton Lakota Sioux, since the Cheyennes did not ceremonially give the Sun Dance to any other band. In Stands In Timber's story, the Sioux man's ceremonial white paint, hairstyle, and use of the buffalo skull became central elements to the Lakota Sun Dance. The sacred laws, philosophy, and principles of the Lakota Sun Dance, regardless of band, are similar to those of the Cheyenne, as Standing Bear (Oglala) explained:

> According to our legend, the red man was to have this dance every summer, to fulfill our religious duty. It was a sacrificial dance. During the winter if any member of the tribe became ill, perhaps a brother or a cousin would be brave enough to go to the medicine man and say, "I will sacrifice my body to the Wakan Tanka, or Big Holy, for the one who is sick." Or if the buffalo were beginning to get scarce, some one would sacrifice himself so that the tribe might have something to eat.[17]

Lame Deer (Minneconjou) highlighted the significance of the Sun Dance of his people:

> The sun dance is our oldest and most solemn ceremony, the "granddaddy of them all," as my father used to say. It is so old that its beginnings are hidden as in a mist. It goes back to an age when our people had neither guns, horse nor steel—when there was just us and the animals, the earth, the grass and the sky....Thus in the old days the sun dance was not all sacrifice but also a happy time when the choke cherries were ripe, the grass was up and the game plentiful—a happy time for meeting old friends.... Among other things the sun dance also stood for the renewal of life—new plants shooting up, mares foaling, babies being born....Buffalo fat had been placed inside the pit which was waiting to receive the sun-dance pole. The fat was an offering to the Buffalo nation asking their help to feed the tribe in the coming year.[18]

Eastman, who was a descendant from the Mdewankton and Wahpeton bands, also explained elements of the Sun Dance that were in line with Cheyenne ways:

> In the old days, when a Sioux warrior found himself in the very jaws of destruction, he might offer a prayer to his father, the sun, to prolong his life. If rescued from imminent danger, he must acknowledge the divine favor by making a Sun Dance,

according to the vow embraced in his prayer, in which he declared that he did not fear torture or death, but asked life only for the sake of those who loved him. Thus the physical ordeal was the fulfillment of a vow, and a sort of atonement for what might otherwise appear to be reprehensible weakness in the face of death. It was in the nature of confession and thank-offering to the "Great Mystery," through the physical parent, the Sun, and did not embrace a prayer for future favors. The ceremonies usually took place from six months to a year after the making of the vow, in order to admit of suitable preparation; always in midsummer, and before a large and imposing gathering. They naturally included the making of a feast and the giving away of much wealth in honor of the occasion.[19]

The oral tradition of the Teton bands includes elements of the origin of the Sun Dance that are quite similar to the story of the Só'taeo'o culture heroes Ho'ehêvêsénóóhe (Standing On The Ground), his wife Ésevona'e (Buffalo Woman), and Heovéstáe'e (Yellow Top-to-Head Woman). Crow Dog explained the significance of White Buffalo Woman, the woman prophet who brought the Sun Dance to the Brulé: "This holy woman brought the sacred buffalo calf pipe to the Sioux. There could be no Indians without it. Before she came, people didn't know how to live. They knew nothing. The White Buffalo Woman put her sacred mind into their minds."[20] During the Brulé Sun Dance, a "mature and universally respected woman" was selected to represent the White Buffalo Woman. She also brought the pipe as a covenant to the Sun Dance, as told by Lame Deer (Brulé) in 1967. Like the differing stories across the ten bands of the United Cheyenne Nation, there are likely differing stories across the seven bands of the United Lakota Nation, each highlighting universal and national principles. Lame Deer recalls:

> She spoke once more to all the people: "The pipe is alive; it is a red being showing you a red life and a red road. And this is the first ceremony for which you will use the pipe. You will use it to keep the soul of a dead person, because through it you can talk to Wakan Tanka, the Great Mystery Spirit. The day a human dies is always a sacred day. The day when the soul is released to the Great Spirit is another. Four women will become sacred on such a day. They will be the ones to cut the sacred tree—the canwakan—for the sun dance."
>
> She told the Lakota that they were the purest among the tribes, and for that reason Tunkashila had bestowed upon them the holy chanupa. They had been chosen to take care of it for all the Indian people on turtle continent.
>
> She spoke one last time to Standing Hollow Horn, the chief, saying, "Remember: this pipe is very sacred. Respect it and it will take you to the end of the road. The four ages of creating are in me; I am the four ages. I will come to see you in every generation cycle. I shall come back to you."
>
> The sacred woman then took leave of the people, saying: "Toksha ake wacinyanktin ktelo—I shall see you again."
>
> The people saw her walking off in the same direction from which she had come, outlined against the red ball of the setting sun. As she went, she stopped and rolled over

four times. The first time, she turned into a black buffalo; the second into a brown one; the third into a red one; and finally, the fourth time she rolled over, she turned into a white female buffalo calf. A white buffalo is the most sacred living thing you could ever encounter.

The White Buffalo Woman disappeared over the horizon. Sometime she might come back. As soon as she vanished, buffalo in great herds appeared, allowing themselves to be killed so that the people might survive. And from that day on, our relations, the buffalo, furnished the people with everything they needed—meat for their food, skins for their clothes and tipis, bones for their many tools.[21]

The Cheyenne national history also adapted and converged, as some storytellers recalled that the Sioux entered the lodge of the Ésevone (Buffalo Hat) and not the Maahótse (Medicine Arrows), which reinforces that the Sun Dance was the unifying ceremony in the unification.[22] Some bands also adapted the story of Old Woman's Spring and the Two Young Men, replacing the story as the amalgamation of the Cheyennes and Lakotas instead of the Tsétsêhéstâhese and Só'taeo'o, or of the Heveškêsenêhpåhese (Aortas) and Ohmésêhese (Eaters) (see chapter 1 in *A Sacred People*).[23] The Lakota sacred history also converged with the Cheyennes' by including elements of Tsétsêhéstâhese culture and philosophy into narratives of White Buffalo Woman and the Sacred Pipe covenant, as told by Standing Bear (Lakota):

Then instruction was given regarding health and rules of clean living; also the use of herbs and roots for healing. When the woman came to the four most important moral commandments she shouted them in a loud voice:

"You shall not kill!
You shall not lie!
You shall not steal!
You shall not commit adultery!"

Then the Holy Woman presented the people with the Pipe of the Calf to symbolize prayer and a Holy Arrow to symbolize protection. The Pipe shall always be carefully kept by the Lakotas but the Cheyennes are today guarding the Holy Arrows. The last commandment to the people was to hold the sacred ceremony of the Sun Dance once every year, and this they faithfully did until oppressed by another people.[24]

The Lakota oral tradition is strikingly similar to that of the Tsétsêhéstâhese, the prophet Motsé'eóeve, and the sacred laws of the Maahótse and the Ésevone. Fools Crow (Lakota) also recalled the events preceding the arrival of the White Buffalo Woman, which included the origin of the Sacred Pipe of the Lakota and the Medicine Arrows of the Cheyennes. His story, which is incomplete, was recorded as the following:

Their tale began with a warrior who, while out hunting in ancient times, came upon a cave in Devil's Tower, a huge pillarlike formation in Wyoming. In this cave he found some arrows and a pipe bundle. Somehow, he knew he could take only one of the two back to his people, and he chose the arrows. Stanley [Orval Looking Horse's Father] did not identify the man's tribe, but it was probably Cheyenne, and his discovery would then have something to do with the origin of that tribe's sacred arrows.[25]

In a short time, the United Cheyenne Nation and the seven bands of the United Teton Nation became close allies, amalgamated by the blessing of the Maahótse and the Ésevone. As a sanctified and unified nation, the Hotóhkéso returned to the Tsétsêhéstâhese several times to acquire more horses through trade.[26] Through association, the Arapaho also became allies of the Oglala and other bands of the Teton Lakota. All nations united and frequently camped together, intermarried, and sustained close political, social, and spiritual relationships, frequently holding ceremonies together. Part of the reason for such successful unifications across peoples of different languages was that each shared a Plains Indian lifestyle that resembled the others as horse and buffalo peoples, as described by Wooden Leg:

> The Sioux tribes had ways closely resembling those of the Cheyennes. We traveled and visited much with them, particularly with the Ogallalas, sometimes with the Minneconjoux. The Sioux tribal governments were almost the same as ours. Each of them had numerous tribal chiefs, each had various warrior societies and chiefs of them. Their warriors dressed for death in battle, all of their people dressed for death in time of peace, according to the same customs among us. Their warrior training by precept and by discipline was similar to our system. They fought their battles as a band of individuals, the same as we fought ours, and the same as was the way of all Indians I ever knew. They had war dances and medicine dances differing only a little from our ceremonies of this kind. So when white people learn the ways of the Cheyennes they have learned also a great deal of the ways of the Sioux and of other Indians in this part of the world.[27]

Unifications endorsed by either one of the two highest covenants (the Maahótse or the Ésevone) were the most sacred of unions because every citizen of the entire Cheyenne Nation honored the agreements. The unification stories were then passed down to later generations as sacred history. This type of alliance building was more than a political merger; it was a deep, spiritual commitment for two nations to truly become partners in perpetuity. It was the ultimate exertion of Indigenous nations' sovereignty. After each unification beginning with the Great Unification, the unifying nations always reestablished, re-created, or converged existing sacred histories to safeguard the peace so it lasted for generations. Furthermore, each nation adopted the ceremonial and cultural practices of others. Learning each other's language also united the nations, as Wooden Leg explained:

> The Cheyennes during my youth associated much with the Ogallala Sioux, the Arapahoes and the Minneconjoux Sioux. Many Cheyennes learned the speech of these other tribes, and in turn they had many members who used ours. Most of my outside mingling was with the Ogallalas. By the time I was full grown to full stature I could talk Sioux about as well as I could talk Cheyenne.[28]

Even after the establishment of the reservation, it was common for Cheyennes to be fluent in multiple Indian languages.[29] The unifications were true and earnest commitments to lasting peace and friendship.

Because of the small population of the Cheyenne Nation, it was beneficial for them to make alliances with much larger nations like the Lakota. The Cheyennes had already proven themselves a worthy nation, holding their own territory and military presence despite small numbers. As the history of the West unfolded, the Cheyenne-Lakota proved to be one of the strongest intertribal coalitions in American Indian history. By 1800 this coalition was a military and geopolitical powerhouse, whose territory covered much of the Great Plains. And by 1870 the united Indigenous nations of the Cheyenne-Arapaho-Lakota alliance constituted one of the last forces standing in the way of US expansion.

According to inter-Indigenous national law, all Plains Indian nations, even enemies, were potential allies to the Cheyennes. Not only did these nations share the Great Plains as a permanent and aboriginal homeland but they relied on the sacred buffalo for sustenance. Peacemaking and making alliances were essential to the survival of these nations, while warfare was employed primarily for national defense. History reveals that while the Cheyennes and their allies continued to engage in sporadic warfare with their neighboring nations, they continued to make long-lasting peace agreements.

CHAPTER 11

Xamaevo'êstaneo'o Ho'emanestôtse: Indigenous Nations Law

In the old days, some Indian tribes had a special tribal ceremonial pipe that was only smoked when it was necessary to make a truce between enemies. Sometimes a pipe like this was placed on the ground between two enemy groups as a pledge of peace during trade talks.

—Fools Crow (Lakota)[1]

The Cheyenne term xamaevo'êstaneo'o means "ordinary people," and it applies to only the Indigenous peoples of the known lands. The Cheyennes held a degree of respect for all Indigenous peoples because any Indigenous nation could become an ally to the Cheyenne Nation. In fact, all of the nations viewed one another as potential allies under a set of unified Indigenous Nations Law (INL). This relationship, however, was not racially exclusive to Indigenous peoples, since the Cheyennes and other Indigenous nations also viewed whites, whom the Cheyennes believed to have belonged to another Indigenous nation, as potential allies. Discussion on the relations between the Cheyennes and whites, however, is for another time, since this chapter focuses on the foundation of exercises of Indigenous nation sovereignty under INL.

From the Cheyenne perspective, nótseo'o (enemies) were those peoples who were not necessarily full-fledged enemies but rather noncitizens of the Cheyenne Nation. The term nótseo'o is also applied to members of allied nations, probably because at one point these nations were once enemies to the Cheyennes. Nonetheless, the term nótseo'o is applied primarily to those people who were from former and current enemy nations, which indicates that "enemies" may not be a proper translation. "Foreigners" or "foreign peoples" is a better translation.

From the Cheyenne perspective, all xamaevo'êstaneo'o, even foreigners, held universal rights that the Cheyennes respected in accordance with INL of the Great Plains, especially the laws of peace and war. According to Plains INL and custom, all Plains Indian nations were expected to follow the law of the land, which included laws of war, rules of engagement, and establishing peace. Failure to adhere to these laws could lead to the "outlawing" of an entire nation, meaning that other nations labeled them as unreasonable, irrational, unworthy of respect, and untrustworthy. Breaches of such laws were rare, since no Indian nation wanted to be considered an enemy to all other Indian nations. Violations of Plains INL included (1) acts of war that were inhumane, (2) the failure to keep a peace agreement, (3) the failure to treat visiting and peaceful Indians kindly, and, in extreme cases, (4) the mass murdering of innocent women and children, which was unheard of until wars with whites. Severe crimes against humanity on the plains could potentially lead to the annihilation of an entire nation, but this was prevented because all Plains Indians held true to the Plains INL of war and peace. Few conflicts ever resulted from revenge, since the death of warriors in battle was a widely accepted fate. Few warriors went into battle to seek out a specific enemy who had killed a relative or friend.

The Plains Indian war customs were made for the sport of war, the thrill of victory, and not necessarily for a political end. Such customs were similar to the etiquette of the knights' codes of chivalry during the Dark Ages in Europe, the difference being that Indian warriors served no monarch and their warrior ways involved a high degree of spiritual development. The Plains Indian warrior code was more akin to bushido, the ways of the Japanese samurai. Inter-Indigenous fights and skirmishes were insignificant and resulted in fairly low death tolls, especially when compared to the wars fought between European nations. Skirmishes rarely took place when one party outnumbered another, since smaller groups were careful not to be spotted and often fled before any fighting ensued. Once a group of warriors was found, they became targets for military engagement, even if they were outnumbered. The purpose of most fights was to showcase athleticism and gallantry, as two opposing teams jousted and dodged each other's blows from arrows, spears, coup sticks, and clubs. If one side advanced, the other retreated and regrouped to charge back.[2] Numerous retreats and advances from both groups likely occurred before one withdrew entirely or until they were all killed.

Death was always a possible outcome in this type of warfare, but participants, who were primarily young men in their prime, did not fear it. Death in warfare was an honor to all who abided by the laws of the plains, as described by Standing Bear: "Sometimes, however, a Lakota deliberately chose to make himself conspicuous to the enemy just to show how brave he was, and putting on his regalia and headdress dared them to make of him a mark. Then, occasionally a warrior got a premonition that he would be killed, so he put on his finery so that he might die all dressed up."[3] Dying in a fight was a glorious part of the warrior way, and even enemies honored those who perished while displaying courage. Luther Standing Bear's father before a fight instructed him how to die: "I will be proud of you. But if the enemy is ready to shoot you (as they nearly always are) and you fall in their midst, keep your courage. That is the way I want you to die. I will be with you, my son."[4]

If a warrior was killed wearing a war shirt or war bonnet, he was to remain untouched, for it was considered an honor to be killed by an enemy who possessed the power to do so. When the enemy looked upon the slain body, it ended a spiritual path that both combatants ultimately shared, philosophically and spiritually. Such laws were understood as part of the art of war; other laws associated with the Plains Indian warrior ways were as follows:

1. Encroaching onto another nation's land was trespassing and violators were fair targets for military engagement. The first major law of war was that citizens had to remain conscious, aware, and respectful of the boundaries of the nation. They had to know where the borders were so they did not accidently cause a fight between enemies who may be simply on their own territory. Any trespass onto enemy territory, without consent from the chiefs or the on-duty warriors, could lead to unwanted fights or attacks on the main village. Rivers and mountains typically divided territories. Sometimes warriors or entire villages under the instruction of the leaders may deliberately encroach on the lands of another nation, as told by Northern Cheyenne Wooden Leg:

   > Our tribe during my growing years moved here and there throughout the region between the Black Hills and the Bighorn mountains and Bighorn River. We never went north of the Elk river (the Yellowstone) except on two occasions when some of the tribe went across for only a few days each time. The places of crossing were just above and just below the mouth of the Bighorn. Only one time was the camp circle made west of the Bighorn river. We considered that country as belonging to the Crows. Our war parties went there, but our campings were eastward from this stream. I do not know why we crossed to that side on this occasion. We had been having a series of ceremonial dances at successive camping places, and it may be that this invasion of Crow land was intended as a challenge.[5]

The rivers and mountains were major sources of game and the Plains Indians often held ceremonial dances in these places because of the bountiful flora and fauna. Crossing these boundaries was done as a deliberate affront, which was common for Plains Indian nations to do to one another as part of the art of war.

2. Groups of enemy warriors, scouts, or hunters were fair targets for military engagement.
3. Large-scale assaults on enemy villages could only be done at the will of the proper authorities, typically band or head chiefs.
4. Intermediary nations and/or members acting as messengers, mediators,

envoys, or diplomats were not to be harmed; intermediaries did not have to choose sides.

5. Only band or head chiefs could secure peace agreements.

6. Requests for peaceful meetings before a potential fight were to be honored.

7. When meeting peaceably, no lies could be told and all promises had to be kept.

8. All warriors were to adhere to the conditions of peace reached by their respective leaders.

9. Grown men of fighting age, warriors, could be killed on sight.[6] Bent (Southern Cheyenne) described this law: "The battle customs of the Indians all originated in the old-time intertribal wars. In the old days a warrior never surrendered; if he could not make his escape he died fighting, and this was why Indians never tried to take full-grown men prisoners in battle. When the wars with the whites came, the Indians stuck to the old custom, asking no quarter and never giving it."[7] Wrapped Hair claimed there was "no custom of adopting captive men to take the place of a son slain in battle," a custom among eastern woodland nations.[8]

10. No child should be killed in a fight. Captive children were treated with respect because they could potentially become relatives.[9] Iron Teeth Woman explained: "Indians did not kill each other's women and children. They captured them, to add them to the tribe of the captors." Captive women and children belonged to their captors and were adopted or married into the band of their male captors. Non-Cheyenne captives and their children became members of the man's band. Immoral and criminal by today's standards, intertribal kidnapping was an unfortunate but common practice among Plains Indians. Once two nations made peace, capturing women and children and other hostilities ended. The end of intertribal kidnapping was a blessing that came with the end of intertribal wars.

11. Women should never be mistreated or sexually abused by their captors. Since captive women were to become members of their captor's nation, they were treated as potential wives, sisters, cousins, mothers, or daughters. Any mistreatment was disgraceful and hazardous to the future of adoptees and their families.

12. No prisoner should be tortured or harmed. This was probably the most important law of war among Plains Indians. The law that protected prisoners was universal since the repercussions could damage the reputation of an entire nation, which could lead to more violence. Bent described the law against torture: "Cheyenne Indians never torture prisoners.

Harsh treatment of prisoners by captors was considered a disgrace to the tribe and was always resented as such. In a fight, the Cheyennes always killed the men at once, taking no prisoners except women, girls, and young boys, all of whom were invariably well treated and adopted into the tribe."[12]

Violators of Plains INL of war and peace typically were met with violence and eventually killed in war, but few Plains Indian nations violated the laws. Before the wars with whites, eastern nations were the common violators of Plains Indian etiquette. In one instance, a group of Cheyennes and Lakotas came upon some Delaware hunters. When Cheyenne chiefs High Backed Wolf and Standing On The Hill tried to approach the hunters in a friendly manner to talk of peace, the Delaware hunters fired upon them. The Cheyenne and Lakota warriors did not want to fight, but after four failed attempts for peace, they attacked the hunters and eventually killed them all.[13]

Plains Indian nations did not and could not differentiate among eastern nations. Before the coming of white people, the Cheyennes grouped the Delaware, Shawnee, Potawatomi, Sac and Fox, and Iroquois as one people, because they shared similar dress and appearance, which was indistinguishable from the Cheyenne standpoint.[14] Eastern Indians did not follow the same war etiquette as Plains Indians did. Some Cheyennes had witnessed a group of Eastern Indians cut open the chests of their fellow Cheyenne tribesmen to reach inside and pull out their hearts. The easterners placed the organs into their bullet pouches and then smeared the blood over their own faces. This frightened the Cheyenne witnesses, who turned away and ran for their lives.[15] The Cheyennes would not see anything like this until the late 1800s when the white presence increased and violence spread throughout the Plains, changing the war etiquette of all nations. The Cheyennes believed that white people significantly influenced the eastern Indians, after they saw whites commit atrocities against them at fights like the Sand Creek Massacre.

The warfare of the Plains also changed in response to the introduction of more advanced firearms. Before then, Plains Indian nations had developed and practiced a style of war that valued war honors above killing. When killing became easy, with the use of rifles, warfare on the Great Plains was further developed to value war honors, since warriors knew it did not take much athleticism, courage, or intelligence to simply pull a trigger and kill an enemy. The new adaptations allowed for the old war customs to remain as prominent codes of war. For example, counting coup increased in value, since rifles made their acquisition much more dangerous and difficult for warriors. Plains Indian warfare developed in sophistication when killing became outdated and progressed into an art of war without killing. By the mid-1800s the Plains Indians had mastered an art of warfare that honored counting coup over the killing of an enemy.[16] By comparison, the American philosophy of war was rooted in brutality so common in European rifled wars, which valued killing above anything else. For the

Cheyenne, taking an enemy's spirit through humiliation in the heat of battle was the honorable method of defeating an enemy. Warriors and warrior societies sanctioned counting coup as the prime means of acquiring status, but killing of the enemy also became part of the art of war. All Plains Indian nations engaged in counting coup as a form of combat, as warfare became a sport that benefited individuals rather than a politically charged act to benefit an entire nation. Such laws of war include the following:

1. When going to war, men should not think or talk of their wives or sweethearts. They should also refrain from using profanity, vulgar language, or anything sexual about women.[17]

2. A war-bonnet wearer should never ask for mercy in battle and expect to die.

3. Counting coup—that is, touching or striking an opponent—on a live enemy in the heat of battle is more honorable than killing him. Killing an enemy was never the goal in defeating him in battle. If a warrior did kill an enemy, he should have been spiritually blessed and prepared to do so under the guidance of his adviser. If a warrior killed an enemy without first making medicine, then he would have to be cleansed upon returning home.[19]

4. Taking a live enemy's gun is equivalent to a coup.

5. Taking a live enemy's horse is a coup.

6. Taking a live enemy's war implement (shield, spear, knife, hatchet) is a coup.

7. Touching a fallen warrior is a coup. A fallen warrior may still be alive but injured, so touching a supposed dead warrior counts as a coup. Successive touches are of lesser value.[20]

8. Killing a worthy enemy in combat is an honor, while killing unworthy ones is shameful.

9. When a horse is shot out from under a warrior, he must keep cool and calm and retrieve the bridle from the fallen horse to show proper warrior etiquette.[21]

10. Property taken during and after a fight belongs to the possessing warrior. Bent explained: "It was the custom that the first warrior to touch any animal or other sort of property became the owner of the plunder, and the warriors were always very eager to be the first to touch or count coup."[23]

11. Carrying a lance is more honorable than carrying a bow and arrow; a hatchet or war club more honorable than a lance; a coup-stick more honorable than a hatchet or war club.[24]

12. Rescuing a fellow warrior or an ally is a high honor. Leaving him is a disgrace.
13. Shooting an enemy warrior from a distance is fair but not honorable.
14. A warrior should die looking his best and wearing his best clothing.[25]
15. After a worthy victory, the entire village celebrates.
16. After a traumatic loss, the entire village mourns.
17. Upon returning from a fight, warriors must tell their stories to their superiors honestly under the strict principle of hetómestôtse (truth). Lying about war deeds or dishonesty in diplomacy was a considerably vicious crime, and those who told lies were branded as unworthy warriors. Lies about war and diplomacy directly contributed to more conflict between two nations. Those who were branded as liars could potentially bring harm to their own nation. The Plains Indians held a high degree of respect for their enemies in this regard, despite the violence each inflicted upon one another from time to time. Stands In Timber emphasized: "You cannot pretend to be the one [who counted coup]; you have to swear and have someone that saw you. The priest would tell him that men lying there [and it] is the same as a spirit [that tells of lies]; you must tell the truth."[26]

    One failure to tell the truth in war occurred in 1822. Bear Feathers, as a young Cheyenne warrior, was brave enough to enter into a Pawnee village to steal some horses while on an expedition. An older, stronger Pawnee and his wife caught him, but they quietly told him, through sign language, to enter into their big lodge. Here Bear Feathers realized he was in the lodge of a great man of the Pawnee Nation. The chief's wife fed Bear Feathers and the chief decided to give the Cheyenne warrior a mule with a saddle and other gifts. This was an honorable act of the Pawnee chief, but when Bear Feathers returned to the Cheyennes, he told his superiors that he risked his life to steal these items from a Pawnee chief. The people believed his war story and thought he was a brave warrior. Bear Feathers's lie kept the Cheyennes and Pawnee divided, eventually leading to more conflict between the two nations.[27] The Sun Dance and war dances were proper venues for a warrior to tell of his war exploits, as Mack Haag explained: "Recently at a sun dance an old man counted 3 coups. The biggest coup is getting into a tipi. Those who can brag of this are getting scarce. Next in line: if one of the war party falls within the foe's lines—another Cheyenne picks him up—puts him on a horse."[28]

18. Meeting an enemy to die and under uneven circumstances is not suicide; it is the most honorable way to die since such acts of bravery are the pinnacle of life. There was no shame in death as it was not considered

losing if a warrior died fighting. Sometimes a warrior vowed to fight to the death to sacrifice his life as part of a ritual.

Outright violations of Plains INL of war and peace always contributed to further resentment and animosity between Indian nations. Very few conflicts, if any, resulted from personal grievances, bitterness, or revenge vendettas, but a nation could choose to declare outright war against another nation if an enemy nation violated Plains INL. Inhumanity in war was punished. Sometimes warring nations would carry much animosity toward one another for generations, not because of blind hatred but because of repeated violations of the laws of war and failed diplomacy. A nation would then formally and ceremonially declare war on another nation. After such acts, small fights and skirmishes among warriors were no longer done for sport but became catalysts for major assaults and battles.

TSETOENOMÓSANÉO'O: OFFERING THE PIPE

Many Plains Indian nations sought earnest and long-lasting peace. Peacemaking was a serious ceremonial process secured by the universal emblem of truth and sincerity on the Great Plains: the peace pipe. From a modern perspective, the peace pipe was the universal emblem of a nation's sovereignty and nationhood. Those who earned the right to carry a pipe and use it in peacemaking, whether internally or externally, were responsible for protecting the nation and its sovereignty.

When nations united to secure peace, their leaders ceremonially smoked a pipe and gave generously of material wealth and horses to seal the peace. The ritualized agreement restored balance between two nations that had likely been at war for a number of years and throughout had inflicted violence upon one another, stealing each other's children and women and personal property. Reaching a peace agreement required leaders to forgive these acts of war and aggression, sometimes those directly responsible. The sacred ritual of peace absolved and reconciled past depredations and reestablished a new course of action through which the agreeing nations could move forward in harmony.[29] After the creation of an inter-Indigenous national peace agreement, the people created a new kinship system that included the new allies. Standing Bear (Lakota) explained:

> Peace—that ideal which man may some time reach—was symbolized in the Pipe of Peace and, under the society of the pipe, or codes symbolized by the pipe, native man made the most effectual effort at arriving at peace ever made on this continent. It was but a start, perhaps, but its strength lay in the fact that under the Great Peace, women had begun the necessary foundational work for the elimination of war by raising sons who could participate only in pursuits of peace. War was excluded from the existence of a certain portion of the male population and in this move the Indian mother pointed the way and the only road to the realization of peace between all men. The acceptance of a kinship with other orders of life was the first step toward humanization and the second was the dedication of sons to peace.[30]

Smoking the pipe was the best method to prevent deception between Plains Indian nations because all held it sacred. Upon a peace, new oral histories were created and/or old ones converged to ensure that children honored the peace, much like those converged stories already highlighted.

Breaking an oath endorsed by a ceremonial pipe was punishable by death.[31] The pipe was so highly respected that envoys that formally carried the pipe for peace to another nation were welcomed and protected by the warriors as they marched toward the appropriate authorities. Any person, enemy or ally, who attempted to or succeeded in inflicting harm upon the pipe-bearers was sentenced to swift and immediate death. The pipe was truly the instrument that united the Plains Indian nations. After a peace agreement, the leaders who smoked had the duty to ensure that their people upheld the sacred agreements; otherwise, they as the leaders would be held responsible and subject to retaliation. Such occurrences were rare.

From time to time, a Plains Indian nation formally declared war on another. Such declarations escalated from the conflicts between small groups of warriors into full-scale war between larger forces and over a longer period of time. Declaring war was a delicate matter, since the authorities, chiefs, and spiritual leaders knew of the fairly trivial rewards and potentially dire consequences of such decrees. Declaring war was therefore done in a ceremonial manner because full-scale war was considered an act by which humans could cause imbalance among other humans and in nature. Fools Crow (Lakota) explained the balance between the peace pipe and the war pipe:

> In the old days, some Indian tribes had a special tribal ceremonial pipe that was only smoked when it was necessary to make a truce between enemies. Sometimes a pipe like this was placed on the ground between two enemy groups as a pledge of peace during trade talks. Pipes were sent around villages to gather warriors for a horse raid or war party. The one who led the raid carried the pipe to the tipis of those he wanted to go with him. And war party leaders usually carried a small pipe that was specifically blessed by a medicine man. The warriors smoked it along the way, and if circumstances permitted, celebrated a short ritual with it just before the enemy was engaged.[32]

Just as serious as negotiating for peace, declarations of war through the war pipe involved ritual, thought, and lengthy discussion among the highest officials. Red Cloud explained:

> During these early wars any disaster, such as the destruction of a war-party or the killing of a prominent man, was sure to lead to a great gathering of the camps and a movement in force against the enemy. The customs that were observed on these occasions were fixed and were about the same among both the Tetons and the Cheyennes. The expedition did not set out as soon as news was received that a party of their warriors had met disaster; the people waited "one winter" and during that time the relatives of the dead men took the war-pipe to neighboring camps where they publicly mourned their dead and pleaded with the people to help them. In each camp the leading men

held councils and decided whether their chiefs should accept the pipe or reject it. The pipe was nearly always accepted, and when it had been smoked by the chiefs the camp was pledged to take part in the forthcoming expedition.[33]

The Cheyennes called both processes of declaring war and securing peace tsetoenomósanéoʼo, "offering the pipe," which was the same concept and principle used in resolving internal conflict. "Offering" a pipe of war typically began at the lowest ranks of warriors. One or several may load a ceremonial pipe with tobacco and together march to their society headmen to ask for military assistance. If, for example, a small group of young men, while hunting or exploring, engaged a party of enemies and were severely beaten, survivors could take the fight to their respective warrior society and petition the headmen to pursue their enemies further.[34] Typically, young warriors who wanted to gain war honors by stealing horses for status formally offered the pipe to set out on an expedition of ten to twenty warriors into enemy territory. The headmen either rejected the offer by not smoking or accepted by lighting the pipe and smoking with the petitioners. The Cheyenne custom was for consenting individuals to smoke four visible breaths of pipe smoke to consent to conditions of war, and the same was done when consenting for peace.[35] A young warrior would sometimes offer gifts to influence his superiors' decision, but acceptance was typically granted to encourage young men to fight. A headman may hold a ceremony to prepare the young man and his brothers for honor or death, and he will give instructions, critical spiritual advice, and "medicine" to help them in their efforts.

If the petition required a larger number of warriors than usual—for example, thirty to fifty men— then the headmen may hold a meeting to discuss the idea and decide on the next course of action. At this point, there were only two circumstances that could have stopped a plan for war: the first related to the current political state of the Cheyenne Nation, whether they were at war with this particular enemy or not; and the second related to the current spiritual state of the nation, if the Maahótse were renewed for the year or not. If both requirements were met, then a society could pursue its fight.

Sometimes petitions for war started new conflict between the Cheyenne Nation and another, and on those occasions the headmen may have taken the matter to the Véhooʼo. A headman prepared the society pipe and marched with the society members to the lodge of the chiefs to hold council to discuss the matter. The Véhooʼo would only consent to declare war in the event of outright violations of Plains INL of war and peace. The following circumstances warranted decrees from the Véhooʼo:

1. If innocent women and children were slaughtered.
2. If a chief or a prominent man was killed.
3. If a war party was annihilated. Warring parties often fought until one gave up and half of their survivors were let free to return home.[36]

4. If a formal peace agreement was broken.
5. If it became necessary to completely expel enemies from the homeland.
6. If an allied nation offered the war pipe against an enemy nation.

If the Véhoo'o accepted the petition, then they began a new formal process to initiate war. The assault on the enemy would not occur until a year later so that the people had time to prepare. Other Plains Indian nations followed the same protocols, as declarations of war were never done in haste.

Warriors prepared for large-scale attacks months or years ahead of time, by participating in the big ceremonies or smaller ones to improve their spirits through sacrifice and self-torture.[37] Some made new weapons for battle and all ensured they had the best clothing to die in. Warrior societies recruited new young fighters. The Véhoo'o may also decide to ask for the assistance of another allied nation, so they also had to have time to prepare.[38] After a year, warriors from the requesting society were sent out to offer the war pipe to allies in distant camps to formally ask for help. The chiefs from the allied nations consented to pursue the course of action by smoking the war pipe, but they did not always have to.[39] Consenting to war meant that the first consenting nation would take the lead, as Bent explained: "This was the custom, that when a war pipe was sent around, to ask aid in making war, the tribe that smoked first, thus promising

Woir-Oqtuimanists (Man on a Cloud) with Peace Medal and Headdress; Unidentified Man Nearby. 1892, James Mooney, 1861–1921, National Anthropological Archives, Smithsonian Museum Support Center, Suitland, Maryland.

their aid, was the tribe that was given the lead in all moves. The chiefs who smoked the pipe first had to be treated with respect, and so they were given the lead in all movements."[40] To be an ally in war meant more than reaping the benefits; it demanded leadership, dedication, and discipline from the entire nation. War is one of the exercises of sovereignty that today no American Indian nation engages in, at least not in the traditional, pre-reservation sense. Only when individual American Indians enlist in the US armed forces do they engage in war. In doing so, they represent and defend the United States, which has been interpreted from the Indian perspective as defending "Indian Country." This view holds true even though outsiders do not perceive that American Indian soldiers represent their respective nations. The old Indigenous Nation Laws of war have to a large degree vanished, yet those that do remain provide a spiritual foundation for American Indian veterans as they "heal from war."

CHAPTER 12

Tsėhéstanove and War

There is one stringent law given by Sweet Medicine. It is a general rule for all warriors; one who is able to be man enough to make success must carry out the rule of Old Man Charm.

—Stands In Timber (Northern Cheyenne)[1]

The war and peace pipes were universal symbols for Plains Indian war etiquette, but each nation also had its own body of laws and customs that directly related to national security and international diplomacy. The ten bands of the United Cheyenne Nation frequently clashed with other nations when they first arrived on the Great Plains, but they also developed a sophisticated system of war based on a highly spiritual dedication to fighting. Interestingly enough, there is no single word for "war" in the Cheyenne language, although it has been used as an adjective (e.g., war shirt, war club, war deeds). The term that is commonly used for war translates to "fight," which can have two meanings: (1) a small fight between two individuals, like a boxing match or game; or (2) a more aggressive fight, like the style of warfare that applies to Plains Indians. Nonetheless, "war" for the Cheyennes does not necessarily mean the same thing as "war" in the English language and culture, which primarily means all-out war with intent to annihilate. Despite this challenge, I will use the English term "war" and apply the Cheyenne definition of it in this chapter.

In fights with worthy adversaries the Cheyennes embraced honorable deaths from its citizen warriors, despite the trauma endured by their kinfolk afterward. Death, as recognized in the Cheyenne worldview, was inevitable for all humans—it was a supernatural law that no living organism could escape—but to die in the heat of battle was to achieve the highest level of spirituality that any human could reach. Beyond death, the human spirit enters into the afterlife and travels through the Vonoʼomēēʼe to be among the mysteries of the universe. Every year the Cheyennes held ceremonies to affirm the mysteries of death and the

PART III : NÉSTAXEO'O: ALLIES

universe, because the only way a Cheyenne citizen could prepare for this pinnacle was to bring himself or herself to the brink of death. And since no Cheyenne could kill another Cheyenne, hunting buffalo and the art of war were the only chances for citizens to die gloriously. In other words, they could experience the feeling of the mysteries of the universe, if only for a moment. They understood that like being born, a man could die only once. One might say that the Cheyennes were obsessed with death as a phenomenon of mystery, sacredness, and the human spirit. The héstanovestôtse, living-nation, seemed to respond by developing numerous rituals and customs that centered a warrior's chivalry and honor in the Cheyenne art of war.

A supreme law of war of the Tséhéstanove was that no war expeditions or declarations of war could be made until after the completion of the Maahéome (Arrow Lodge) ceremony.[2] Since war was considered a deliberate effort to cause imbalance among other peoples, the Cheyennes had to ensure that they were worthy enough to proclaim the authority to do so. The Maahótse represented the health and well-being of the entire nation, and if the nation suffered from suicides or homicides, then these tragedies had to be ceremonially cleansed before any citizen deliberately put himself or herself in danger. The consequences of entering into fights without the protection of the Maahótse could entail more harm inflicted upon the people. Those who petitioned for war, society headmen or warriors, may be advised by the Véhoo'o or the Arrow Keeper to wait an entire year or until after the next Maahéome before pursuing their war plans. The scratched plans were not rejections of the petitions but actions of proper protocol. If the Maahéome was not yet performed that year, sometimes the petitioning warrior and his society may sponsor the ceremony to expedite their request. The request was fair in accordance with custom, and a war expedition may depart a week after the ceremony. The Keeper of the Arrows held considerable authority in war matters, especially if the nation had already secured a peace agreement with the potential enemy. In the event that petitioning warriors were the first to request that year, before the Maahéome, then they would directly petition the Maahótse keeper.[3]

Probably the most infamous violation of the Maahéome law of war occurred in 1837, when the Bowstring warriors rushed to go to war against a band of Kiowa.[4] The warriors pushed to go to war before the Maahéome, although the keeper, White Thunder, did not wish to hold the ceremony until the time was right. The warriors became angry and eventually inflicted physical harm on the seventy-seven-year-old keeper. White Thunder consented to hold a Maahéome, but warned the Bowstrings that he saw that warriors would suffer a great loss. Forty-two Bowstrings went on the war expedition after the ceremony. While on the prairie one morning, they were spotted by a Kiowa scout, whom they fired upon, wounding his horse. The scout returned to the camp and rallied numerous Kiowa and Comanche warriors, who easily surrounded and trapped the Bowstrings, and the Bowstrings quickly ran out of arrows and bullets. All forty-two of the warriors were annihilated. Some fought valiantly with only their knives and clubs, but all were killed in what is remembered as a war expedition doomed to fail from the outset.

In the 1700s, the Hóheeheo'o killed numerous Só'taeo'o because they had the advantage of loud firearms, which were undeveloped but frightening and gave more of a psychological advantage than a technological one.[5] In that era, an Indian could have shot twenty arrows in the time it took to load and fire a rifle.[6] The Só'taeo'o can recall the horrific war customs in which, after a battle, the Hóheeheo'o scalped a number of their fallen men.[7] This was the first time they saw such practices. Scalping did not originate among the Plains Indians but was introduced by nations that had French and British influence from the east. The Só'taeo'o adopted the practice but limited scalping to only worthy warriors. The Ésevone bundle has several scalps from the best warriors of enemy nations and is evidence that the Só'taeo'o believed scalping to be a method to honor the spirits of defeated enemies, especially those who were exceptional. Stands In Timber explained: "The Cheyenne law was it had to be a scalp with braids or loose hair and it was taken to the Hat tepee and kept there; they would not accept a white man's scalp. That is why they didn't use them. All the scalps in their possession today have long hair. I don't know how many they have but there are five special ones for ceremonies."[8] Contrary to popular belief, however, Cheyenne warriors acting individually after the more common small skirmishes only took a small piece of the scalp and used it as evidence of bravery when telling their story or celebrating a victory. Women, either wives or mothers, became the primary owners of the scalps and used them only during and after a victory dance to honor the deeds of their son, father, or husband. Afterward the scalps were thrown in a big fire. The rule was never to accumulate scalps. Scalping, however, is an example of how Europeans, who took scalps as bounties and trophies, influenced Cheyenne warfare. Disappointing to the egos and lore of whites, the Cheyennes did not scalp whites because they did not find any value in white scalps.[9]

Women, especially wives, held prominent roles in warfare, since they were instrumental in preparing their men, as described by Tall Bull:

> The battle preparation made by the woman for the warrior was to make sure his pipe and food were packed and the fine quilled or beaded buckskins that he would wear into battle were placed in his war bag. The woman often went out into the horse herd and chose the warrior horse that would carry her husband or son into battle. She placed the saddle upon the horse and led it to her husband or son who was waiting at the lodge. She did this to honor them as she knew they might not return and she would be left without a husband to provide for her. At this point she would reassure him that everything would be fine until his return. She did her best to take care of the family while the warriors were away. Many prayers were said for their success in battle and their safe return.[10]

Women were the creators of exquisite war clothing including the popular Plains Indian war shirts, which were made for those warriors who counted a certain number of coups. Wearers of such shirts were obligated to be the first in an advance and the first to pick up a fallen comrade; otherwise, their rights and privileges as a "shirt wearer" could be revoked, meaning that they would no longer be leaders among their peers.[11] Society sisters would also join expeditions to cook meals for warriors, since war medicine required warriors, especially lead warriors, to avoid handling flesh and blood. Society sisters were also important in nursing wounded warriors. Although uncommon, women could also join men in fighting, sometimes winning war honors and respect among their peers and from their superiors. Women also became the owners of property taken in battles and were the primary caregivers of captives. The most well-known Cheyenne woman warrior is Buffalo Calf Trail Woman, who saved Chief Comes In Sight at the Rosebud Battle in 1876. This battle commemorating her deed is named "Where the girl saved her brother."

The Cheyennes in warfare, like all Plains Indians, did not have a military system that was like that of whites. Warriors fought as a group of individuals, since the primary purpose was to earn individual war honors. Stands In Timber explained: "Sometimes when a brave warrior takes the lead into action they all follow him; they were not appointed. Each man is on his own. They are all seeking to count coup. The Cheyenne Chiefs were supposed to stay back. But one might go in with the rest of the warriors. The younger chiefs did."[12] He continued: "The Cheyenne rule instructed each member of the warrior band not to wait for anybody or orders, not to try to do like the rest; he should do all he could for himself, and fight privately. He can retreat if he wants to but he would be criticized by many people who watched the battles."[13]

The Cheyennes and Lakotas had a custom where a warrior made a vow of death. The entire philosophy can be compared to the World War II kamikaze (divine, spirit wind) attacks by Japanese pilots, the philosophy originating from the Samurai Bushido code. The Plains Indian warrior code was "death before dishonor." Stands In Timber describes the Cheyenne philosophy behind this custom: "There is one stringent law given by Sweet Medicine. It is a general rule for all warriors; one who is able to be man enough to make success must carry out the rule of Old Man Charm."[14] The concept highlighted a young man's desire to be remembered as a brave and handsome warrior in death rather than to grow old and be forgotten, hence the custom was known as "Old Man's Charm." A pledger of the vow chose a sponsor or a painter, someone who had a fine military record, to prepare the young man for death. They put up a "Dying Dance" and announced the young warrior's wish to commit. After the ceremony, the young warrior fought without fear, and his prowess had a reverse effect, making him seem invincible and able to withstand pain and terrifying situations in the face of death. If a young warrior succeeded and was not killed, he gained a near godlike reputation. If, however, he died, the young warrior was memorialized as a brave warrior who reached the pinnacle of life. There were numerous pledgers of the Old Man's Charm custom, which has been inaccurately referred to as an act of suicide from "suicide warriors."[15] Stands In Timber explained: "The Cheyennes would not be so brave without that custom. Most of the tribes say the Cheyennes were the bravest. The Crows say they are not brave, just crazy. They have no fear; they want to get a hold of and kill everybody."[16]

While the Cheyennes had general laws of war, the Nótâxeo'o each had society laws of war. The Hotamétaneo'o (Dog Men) were particularly astute in the art of war. "If they saw a stream, no matter how deep, they must cross it with clothes on."[17] If their camp was attacked, every warrior was demanded to give up his horses to women and children while the Dog Men remained behind to fight on foot.[18] In the heat of battle, their best warriors would tie themselves to a stake, pinned to the earth, where they literally stood their ground until they were killed or were rescued by a society brother.[19] Wolf Chief elaborated: "The pegged soldiers of the Dog Soldiers had headdresses straight up, were painted black all over, and had a rawhide rope about a half inch wide and 10 feet long, with a pin on it to peg them. They slipped the rope over their head, passing it under their right arm and over their left soldier. It was for every brave man."[20] According to Bent, "The custom of wearing these ropes was very old, dating back to the time when the Indians had no horses and fought on foot."[21]

When attacked, "it was custom for a man to mount the first horse he came to, no matter who it belonged to. The owner could not prevent this, but the rule was that if a man riding a borrowed pony captured anything in the fight the captured articles became the property of the owner of the horse which the warrior was riding."[22] Cheyennes did not honor or recognize the coups of murderers or outcasts but counted those of allies.[23] When counting coup, a warrior had to yell to proclaim his feat to avert any discrepancies, since an enemy could only be touched three times. Sometimes coups and property were settled after a fight over a bonfire in the presence of the chiefs.[24]

When a brave warrior died, it was proper etiquette for enemies to ensure that the slain body was laid facedown. This was done out of respect so the enemy could later have a proper burial and so his spirit would not follow the living to their home. Such painstaking diligence and respect did not apply to whites in later years.[25] Cheyenne warriors believed that if they died in a great battle, their bodies should be covered with only a robe, for it was an honor to have their flesh eaten by eagles, wolves, and other animals of great power, and that their bodies be scattered throughout the land. Cheyenne warriors often left the bodies of their fallen comrades on the side of a hill so enemies could see the finely dressed warrior.

MOVING ARROWS

Although rare, sometimes conflicts between the Tséhéstáno and other nations escalated to full-scale military actions requiring a full declaration of war.[26]

PART III : NÉSTAXEO'O: ALLIES

Decrees of war were called "Moving the Arrows" and could only come from the Arrow Keeper and after the annual Maahéome (Arrow Renewal) ceremony. The first move is remembered as part of the Great Unification between the Tsétsêhéstâhese and Só'taeo'o, when Motsé'eóeve and Vóetsénae engaged in their epic dual (see the story of Lime in *A Sacred People*). White Bull/Ice (Southern Cheyenne) described the ritualized warfare strategy of Moving the Arrows:

> The reason the medicine of Mattsioiv was so powerful was because he had a small piece of medicine which he had obtained from heaven. When they wanted to go to the enemy whoever carried the bundle opened this medicine and pointed directly where the enemy was and blew the medicine through the bundle towards the enemy. As soon as that was done the whole camp charged on the enemy and exterminated them. The last attempt was made near the Black Hills when they were warring against the Crow Indians. There were two hundred and fifty lodges belonging to the Crow which were wiped out by the Cheyennes. That's why so many Crow women have been brought up with the Cheyenne.[27]

When the Cheyennes moved the arrows, all bands of the United Cheyenne Nation took a year to prepare for an assault on an enemy nation. This allowed for the Véhoo'o to send messengers to offer the war pipe and formally ask their allied nations to join in the fight. Moving the arrows meant that the Arrow Keeper would ceremonially shoot the Maahótse towards enemies to spiritually kill them before physically killing them. The entire nation would then move their camp, as described by Bent (Southern Cheyenne):

> These fights in which the entire Cheyenne tribe took part with the women, children, and old men formed up in a circle in the rear to watch the battle, were very formal affairs and full of ceremonies. In fact they were modeled on the old-time battles in which everyone fought on foot and the medicine men used magic to strike the enemy helpless and make their own warriors invulnerable. In these formal engagements the Cheyennes were drawn up in two divisions; in front of the first wing the Medicine Arrows were carried, and in front of the other the sacred Buffalo Cap. These two great medicines protected all who were behind them from wounds and death and rendered the enemy in front helpless. In such a fight a medicine man was always selected to carry the Medicine Arrows tied to the end of a lance.[28]

The entire nation camped a short distance from their foe, then all able-bodied adults were expected to fight, as the entire affair was ritualized not only to unify the nation but also to ensure that the attack was successful. First the warriors attacked and then the women entered the camp on foot to kill any remaining adult men and women. They were typically the first to claim children for adoption, horses, and other spoils.

The Tséhéstáno moved the arrows six times: against the Shoshone in 1817; the Crows in 1820; the Pawnees in 1830; a Kiowa-Comanche-Apache coalition in 1838; the Shoshone in 1843; and the Pawnees again in 1853.[29] The last attempt to move was done in haste against General Ranald MacKenzie's attacking white soldiers and Indian scouts in the Bighorn Mountains in November 1876. Not every move was successful, but each move typically led to a peace agreement between the warring nations. The success of a battle depended on the spiritual state of being and belief in the righteousness of the fight. Moving the arrows meant each Cheyenne person was going to fight, but this did not ensure victory.[30]

The most successful peace agreement was with the Kiowa, Comanche, and Apache in 1840, which was never broken. After the killing of the forty Bowstring warriors who rushed into war in 1837, the Tsêhéstáno along with their Arapaho allies moved the arrows against the Kiowa-Comanche-Apache coalition the following year in another successful campaign. In northwestern Oklahoma, the Cheyenne-Arapaho camped thirty miles from their foes on Beaver Creek. All men, women, and children, even the horses and dogs, traveled in a ritualized march toward the enemy camp. The Cheyennes killed any and all enemies along their way toward Wolf Creek, even young men and women who were out among the trees or who were digging for roots or berry-picking. When they arrived, the warriors rode directly into camp to count coup and kill all enemy men. Meanwhile, the women and children went another direction to view the battle from a hillside, but the Cheyenne dogs barked and alerted the Cheyenne women of a hiding Kiowa woman. Medicine Snake Woman rushed up to the Kiowa, caught her, and yelled to the other Cheyenne women: "Come help me; she is very strong." The other Cheyenne women ran up and killed her with knives. When the Kiowas and Comanches saw the Cheyenne women and children on the hill, they panicked, believing that another wave of warriors were going to attack. Their fear was legitimate, since Cheyenne women were expected to fight just as fiercely as men, especially when moving the arrows. The roles of women in war among the Cheyennes significantly changed on moves, since enemy women could be killed, but probably because Cheyenne women were also expected to fight. The Kiowa-Comanche-Apache village suffered great losses, and the Cheyenne-Arapaho withdrew, but White Thunder, the Arrow Keeper, was among their few casualties.[31]

In 1840, two years later, the Kiowa-Comanche-Apache coalition petitioned for peace with the Cheyenne-Arapaho alliance. A ceremonial peacemaking camp was set up for all parties to come together so the leaders could discuss the long-term conditions of peace. Under the leadership of Cheyenne Chief High Backed Wolf, the head chiefs representing the consenting nations ceremonially smoked and declared that all military engagements between all nations would cease. War expeditions against one another would be neither petitioned nor sanctioned. Following the ceremony the people feasted and exchanged gifts to solidify the unification among the citizenry. They sang and danced to celebrate the unification in the customary manner and the peace between all participating nations was never broken. Such peace agreements typically followed decisive fights, since all nations, their leaders, and their citizens desired to live in peace.

PART III : NÉSTAXEO'O: ALLIES

NÓTSEO'O (ENEMIES)

The Cheyennes memorialized the teachings of the prophet Sweet Medicine, which also included language about intertribal wars: "A time is coming when you will meet other people, and you will fight with them, and will kill each other. Each tribe will want the land of each other tribe, and you will be fighting always."[32] The Cheyennes knew their enemies and, more important, if the enemy wanted to fight or was a threat. Location and dress were primary identifiers, but obvious differences in speech, regalia, and weaponry were also identifiers.[33] Until peace was secured, enemy nations were also memorialized in war stories and other parts of the oral tradition.[34] One of the longest-standing conflicts was with the Hóheeheo'o (Assiniboine), who were the first serious foes of the Cheyennes and who are remembered in the oral tradition as the first to use rifles. Bitter conflict remained through the 1800s. In 1805 the Cheyenne tried to secure peace with the Hidatsa by offering a peace pipe of truce and even holding an adoption ceremony, but twelve Hóheeheo'o arrived in the peace village during the negotiations. The Cheyenne delegates wanted to kill the Hóheeheo'o, but the Hidatsa protected their guests, resulting in a botched peace agreement.[35] As the years progressed and as the Tséhéstáno became more powerful, conflict with the Hóheeheo'o eventually ended with the Fort Laramie Treaty of 1851, known as the Great Peace of Horse Creek.

With the widespread use of horses, the Great Plains were getting smaller and the Cheyennes could no longer sustain a strong presence in the vast grasslands and buffalo-hunting grounds as they did before. The Heévâhetaneo'o (Rope-hair-people), the Southern Cheyenne bands, competed with their three primary adversaries for a number of years: the Ho'néhetaneo'o (Wolf people or Pawnee); the Vétapâhaetó'eo'o (Greasy wood people or Kiowa); and Šé'šenovotsétaneo'o (Snake people or Comanche). In the north, the Northern Cheyenne bands called the Ôhmésêhese (Eaters) had two nations that were the most adversarial: the Óoetaneo'o (Crow) and the Sósonee'o'o (Shoshone). The Northern Shoshone and the Comanche of the south were kinfolk, but the former was not part of the 1840 peace agreement. From about 1800 to 1870, the Cheyennes continually fought with the Shoshone and moved the arrows against them twice, in 1817 and again in 1843. Disputes often escalated to all-out fights in which each nation lost numerous warriors. Peace with the Shoshone was not realized until 1896, after the establishment of reservations. The Cheyennes frequently returned to the Wind River Indian reservation to visit onetime enemies, the Shoshone, as well as their longtime allies, the Arapaho, who were placed on the same lands.[36] Today they continue this practice. The Cheyennes also engaged in war with the Mo'ôhtávêhetane (Black people or Ute) and did not secure peace until 1894.[37] All enemy nations were respected for their prowess and warrior etiquette, since each were potential allies. Most pre-reservation international conflicts between the Cheyennes and Nótseo'o ended in peace agreements, but some clashes carried on through the wars with whites, who proved to be clever and ambitious to exploit and capitalize on such intertribal divisions.

Old She Bear recalled intertribal war as part of the Sweet Medicine legacy and apparently after the Cheyennes made peace with the Pawnee: "He told the people the future life, and their enemies: 'Take prisoners to scalp,' he told them. The Cheyennes, Arapahos, Sioux, Pawnees, were all friends and all the other Indians against."[38] Unfortunately, a Pawnee-Cheyenne peace agreement could never be reached, for a number of reasons. One reason had to do with the Pawnees' relationship with the Lakota. Since the time the Lakota first arrived on the Great Plains from the east, around 1750, they had gained Cheyenne allies but established a hostile relationship with the Pawnee.[39] This occurred even though the Cheyenne-Pawnee conflict did not begin until 1820.[40] The fights of the Cheyenne-Pawnee conflict escalated as each annihilated one another's war parties until the Cheyennes moved the arrows in 1830. The move was disastrous because the Pawnee captured the Medicine Arrows, completely devastating the hearts and minds of the Cheyennes. The Cheyennes could not renew their world and also could not declare war. For a short time, the sanctity of the Tséhéstáno seemed in limbo and without happiness or cause.

The Pawnee victory proved to be a curse for that nation, however, since they faced numerous catastrophes over the next generation. In 1832 alone, the Skidi band of Pawnees endured significant losses against the Comanche, a smallpox epidemic that wiped out half of the population, and a great loss in a fight against the Minneconjou Lakota. Later a Cheyenne-Arapaho force surrounded and annihilated Pawnee war parties on two occasions. Delawares also attacked and burned an unguarded village of the Grand Pawnee. The effort for revenge was foiled by the US peace agreement, which inevitably opened Pawnee lands to eastern Indians. In 1833 the Skidi Pawnees captured a Cheyenne woman and sacrificed her, despite US government efforts to intervene.[41] The killing of the Cheyenne woman, while the Pawnee possessed the Maahótse, was considered an outright violation of traditional Cheyenne law as well as Plains Indian international customary law, and the Cheyennes attributed the Pawnee misfortune to their inability to properly care for the Maahótse and their failure to uphold and follow its associated sacred laws. Nonetheless, both nations tried to reach a resolution in 1835, requiring the Pawnee to return the Medicine Arrows. But the Pawnee returned only one of the four arrows. The Tséhéstáno recovered another arrow in 1837 from their allies, the Brulé Sioux, after they captured a Pawnee village, but the failure of the Pawnee to return the last arrows only prolonged bitterness. The spiritual leaders eventually made replacement arrows to continue the ceremonial cycle and renew the Cheyenne world.

Numerous fights followed, especially between the Pawnee and Oglala-Brulé Lakota, which only contributed to more violence. By 1860, the Pawnee had sought refuge on reservation lands and the protection of the United States, which employed Pawnee warriors as scouts in the Southern Cheyenne-Arapaho war and the Powder River Expedition against the Lakota, Arapaho, and Cheyenne from 1861 to 1866. Pawnee scouts killed twenty-seven Cheyenne warriors, further infuriating the leaders of the Cheyennes and their allies.[42] One day in 1873, an Oglala-Brulé coalition of about one thousand warriors attacked a village of seven hundred Pawnees, half of whom were women and children. The Lakota massacred nearly one hundred Pawnees and burned their village to the ground.[43] The Pawnees and Cheyennes would not acquire peace until both were confined to reservations. The Pawnees had the same right to protect their homelands and way of life as did any other Indigenous nations, but when whites were thrown into the mix all Plains Indians became subject to their long-term colonial agenda regardless of whether they were allies or enemies.

To the north, enemies frequently attacked villages of the Ôhmésêhese, but Northern Cheyenne warriors often took the offensive by knowingly challenging worthy combatants. In 1819, before the Cheyennes had guns, a party of thirty-four Crazy Dog warriors went on foot from the Black Hills to steal horses from a Crow village.[44] They were outnumbered and trapped atop a hill known as Crow Standing Butte, located in the northwestern part of what is now Nebraska. When the Cheyennes ran out of arrows, a Crow medicine man charged the Crazy Dogs, who were easily overtaken and killed by their spears, knives, and other weapons. Not long after, a mass of horse-mounted Crows annihilated all thirty Cheyennes. In 1820, the next year, the Cheyennes, along with a small number of their Lakota allies, moved the arrows against the Crows, deliberately entering into Crow country in the Bighorn River valley. A large party of Crow warriors was sent out to intercept the Cheyennes but missed them and left the Crow village unprotected. The Cheyennes easily captured the village, killed all the men, and captured or destroyed Crow property. Over one hundred Crow women, boys, and girls were captured and adopted into the Cheyenne and Lakota nations.

Years after the successful move, the Cheyennes captured another Crow village, but they violated international law by killing some of the adopted captives. The violence was considered unjust, unlawful, and unrighteous—in complete violation of Cheyenne traditional law because the adoptees were accepted as Cheyennes and protected by the sacred law preventing intratribal murder. In 1827, the Crows and Cheyennes sought a peace agreement, petitioned by a Crow chief through Arapaho intermediaries. But their motives were not pure. The Crows planned an ambush. The Arapahos and Gros Ventres warned the Cheyennes of the Crow chief's plans, thus preventing entrapment and massacre.[45] The entire affair was a violation of Plains Indian war etiquette since the Crow chief deceived the consenting Cheyennes under the guise of peace. As the years progressed, the fights continued and each nation became equally responsible for continuing the conflict, even after formally agreeing to the Great Peace of Horse Creek in 1851.

The Cheyennes reached their tipping point when the Crow sided with the United States to confiscate traditional Cheyenne homelands and their sacred Black Hills. The war of 1876 was the culmination of the conflict, even though the Crow scouts did not necessarily represent their entire nation. Bitterness prevailed years after the Little Bighorn battle, as expressed by Wooden Leg at the thirty-year anniversary: "Their actions made me angry. I let loose my tongue: 'You—Crows—you are like children. All Crows are babies. You are not brave. You never helped us to fight against the white people. You helped them in fighting against us. You were afraid, so you joined yourselves to the soldiers. You are not Indians.'"[46] The last fight occurred after the establishment of the reservation, in 1886, when a small Crow war party failed to capture Cheyenne horses; only two got away and the rest were killed.[47]

The Northern Cheyenne and Crow nations eventually secured a long-lasting peace, and old warriors frequently reunited to tell of their fights. Today both honor their indigenous pasts and share the challenges of living in their lands now colonized and dominated by whites and white culture. Both continue to struggle to hold on to their traditions, protect their indigenous identities, and remember the old ways of living on the plains. I have personally made many Crow friends; some have become relatives, and we, as descendants of great warriors, frequently discuss both the struggles and advantages of our current time.

The same can be said about the Cheyenne-Pawnee conflict. The Southern Cheyennes and Pawnees eventually secured peace even though the Pawnees retain one of the original arrows of the Maahótse. The Cheyennes have no desire to retrieve it out of respect for the Pawnees; the arrow has become part of the Pawnee sacred nation and ceremonial cycle. Today the Cheyennes and Pawnees continue to sing and dance together at traditional intertribal celebrations. They also share war stories, historic and modern. I have made several Pawnee friends and we are happy to share our culture and history. Old enemies of the Cheyennes, even those who allied with the whites, share the same modern challenges.

CONCLUSION

Intertribal Plains Indian wars were not politically driven, nor were they racially charged where one nation's people believed themselves superior to another. As history has shown, peace was always an option and the typical end result of war. Enemies and enemy nations were seen as potential allies and captives were potential relatives, but this did not mean that warring factions were immune to human error. Although conflicts intensified, the violence rarely reached a point where a nation lost its humanity and completely disregarded the universally accepted codes of war. Violations did occur. If and when a nation violated these Indigenous Laws of war, they were still able to regain their honor by securing peace agreements. If done wholeheartedly, under the sacred laws of the peace pipe and according to international customary law, perpetual peace was achieved. Achieving long-lasting peace is the ultimate exercise of Indigenous nation sovereignty.

The Tsėhéstáno in particular secured peace agreements employing ancient customs. So long as these customs survived in the oral tradition, then peace remained. One of the gifts that the Cheyennes ceremonially gave to new allies was the Hoxéheome (Medicine Lodge) or Sun Dance ceremony and associated laws. According to oral tradition, those nations that continue to practice their adapted version of the Sun Dance were historical allies to the Cheyennes and as long as they continue to practice the ceremony, they remain as allies to the Cheyennes. This rule also applies to the Crows, who did not receive the ceremony from the Cheyennes but from their Shoshone allies. The Shoshones acquired the Sun Dance from the Arapahos when they were forced onto the same reservation in the Wind River valley. Today the Sun Dance has become a widely practiced ceremony, but the Cheyennes claim that they hold on to the oldest form. Traditional Só'taeo'o believe that their Hoxéheome is the original that comes from the associated covenant the Ésevone. Some Cheyennes believe that the Sun Dance is a gift to those nations that sincerely and seriously wish to uphold its traditional teachings and sacred laws. The ceremony is considered to be an enduring legacy of the Cheyenne way.

PART IV

Colonizing the Tsėhéstáno

There shall come from the place the sun rises from men who shall destroy all the buffalo and take the land from the Indians. The cow and calf shall take the buffalo's place. They shall be all over the place. The white men shall come thick as bugs. They shall be all over the land. You shall give up your fighting.

—Motsé'eóeve[1]

American Indians held their own perceptions of colonization. They also had their own views of whites. It would be unfair to assume that American Indians viewed whites through a lens that was no different from the one that whites used to view American Indians. This section is an effort to uncover the Cheyenne perspective of colonization as well as how they viewed their colonizers at various stages in history. As I revealed in *A Sacred People*, these views are not necessarily the same simplistic racial views of others; instead the Cheyennes had known of white foreigners long before their arrival. The Cheyennes preserved a record of these views in the oral tradition.

One early account of how the Cheyennes viewed whites can be found in a time long before the Cheyennes ever met these foreigners. The linguist Rodolphe Petter, a white man, described: "There is a half forgotten tradition that a white being or brother would come from the east. If the Ch[eyenne] were of the last Indians to begin spilling the blood of a white man and starting warfare with him, it was because of their reverence for beings coming from the east and looking white."[2] This is the only account of such a belief and should be taken with some speculation because of how Petter continued to describe his personal experiences. He claims the Cheyenne women revered him, as they "fell before him in an attitude of worship," because he spoke the Cheyenne language. Petter, a missionary, also highlighted that the Indians became excitable and inclined to view white people with superstition when discussing the oral tradition. Nonetheless, the "half forgotten tradition" was completely forgotten over the course of history, and probably because of the mistreatment of the Cheyennes at the hands of whites and the US government. Through warfare, failed diplomacy, and genocidal policies of assimilation, the whites had proven that they were not brothers to the Cheyennes and that there was little, if anything, to revere. As the Cheyennes begin to rebuild their nations from the ashes of colonization, they must know what was destroyed and how the destruction took place from their perspective.

CHAPTER 13

Vé'hó'e: The White Man

In 1851, an estimated ten thousand Indians from the Arapaho, Crow, Shoshone, Lakota, Assiniboine, Hidatsa, Arikara, and Cheyenne nations met for treaty negotiations with the United States at Fort Laramie. From the Indian perspective, this treaty-making process was a celebration of the unification of the Plains Indian nations as they endeavored to reach the common goal of peace. From their perspective, the highest exercise of sovereignty is not achieved by success in war; it is achieved in securing lasting peace. The Cheyenne Nation arrived with the entire political and ceremonial body of leaders, including the keepers of the two covenants: the Maahótse (Medicine Arrows) and the Ésevone (Sacred Buffalo Hat). The Cheyennes referred to this meeting as "The Big Issue."[1] "There were parades of warriors in full regalia (four thousand Sioux riding four abreast; several hundred Cheyennes in their own martial display), all-night dances, intertribal hosting at ceremonial feasts, exchanges of gifts, and mutual adoption of each other's children among the tribes."[2] The Cheyennes, as with other Indigenous nations before, ceremonially unified with the United States under the leadership of High Backed Wolf, the Sweet Medicine Chief and Keeper of the Chiefs' Bundle. The Council of Forty-four Chiefs was in the forefront and they met with the whites for the treaty negotiations and signing, and then the keeper of the Maahótse held the Arrow Renewal Ceremony, as dictated by traditional law.

After the 1851 treaty, the Cheyennes re-created a story, adapting their oral tradition, as part of their unification process to ensure that the peace survived. The story of the first white man also includes elements of trade.

The First White Man

Once long ago a man in a starving condition wandered into the camp. When they saw him, the people said to one another, "This is one of the persons that Sweet Medicine told us we should meet," for the man had hair all over his face and his skin was white. The Cheyennes took him into a lodge, gave him food and clothing, and nursed him back to health. He remained with them for a long time—so long that he learned to speak their language—and explained that he had been with two or three other men in a boat which had upset and that his companions had been lost. He told them that his home was far off toward the sunrise and that he wished to return to it, but he said, "Some day I will come back and will bring you things that will be useful to you."

The man went away, and one day, a long time afterward, the people heard a noise like thunder—the report of a gun. Everyone went out from the camp in the direction from which the sound came to see what it was, and there they saw, coming, this white man and others with him. He had with him guns, knives, flint-and-steel, needles, and many other things which he gave them in exchange for skins.

With pieces of iron that he brought, he made arrow-points which they at once saw were better than theirs of stone or bone, so that all who could procure it used the iron for arrow-points. With these arrows they could kill animals much more easily than with those made of stone. They, therefore, threw away their stone points.

This man who had first come among them remained with the Cheyennes until he became old, and at last he died. Sometimes he made journeys to the east and took back with him in a boat the furs for which he traded.[3]

After unification, as evidenced by the story, the Cheyennes believed that the white man was going to become a long-standing trade partner and, in the end, a brother to the Cheyenne people. The story also highlights the prophet Motsé'eóeve and how the white man improved Cheyenne arrows, which speaks to a cultural influence that the white man had on the philosophies of the Maahótse covenant. The story is evidence that the Cheyennes prepared to secure a lasting peace with whites, even incorporating their technological advancements into the sacred nation. The 1851 treaty with the white man was itself representative of the sincerity of the forged peace and an affirmation of Cheyenne sovereignty. Furthermore, the treaty was the only agreement, at the time and since, in which the Cheyennes' traditional protocol for unification was completed. No other treaty or agreement since, between the Cheyennes and the United States, was done in accordance with Cheyenne law, which required the blessing of the keeper of the Maahótse. Unfortunately, the treaty was short-lived and so was the peace.

As history has taught us, the whites and their government officials could never keep peace with the Cheyennes. Conflict was inevitable, but full-scale war seemed to be the first resort for whites, even though it was traditionally a last resort for the Cheyennes. From the Cheyenne perspective, the failure to keep peace meant that the whites never really saw the Cheyennes as true allies after the unification. From the white perspective, the primary goal for treaty making was to acquire land and not to "unify." The Cheyennes had unified with other nations before and treated the whites no differently, but the whites did not see the Indians as equals, not as brothers, nor as relatives. An important attribute of

American values in the colonization of the West—one that every historian misses when studying Indian treaties—is that the Indians and whites had fundamental differences when it came to peacemaking. Whites did not fully comprehend the Indian concept of peace, which was based on three principles. The first was brotherhood. The second was the merging or converging of sacred histories so the peace and brotherhood would last in perpetuity. The third was the means or desire to adopt the languages, customs, rituals, and ceremonies of other peoples after making peace. This is not to say that individual whites did not make peace following these principles, as there are numerous such accounts, but the "White Tribe" as a nation proved that it was incapable of keeping peace in accordance with traditional Indigenous laws. Lakota scholar Vine Deloria Jr. asserts:

> Never has America lost a war....But name, if you can, the last peace the United States won. Victory yes, but this country has never made a successful peace because peace requires exchanging ideas, concepts, thoughts, and recognizing the fact that two distinct systems of life can exist together without conflict. Consider how quickly America seems to be facing its allies of one war as new enemies.[4]

Shortly after the 1851 treaty, the population of whites increased in the lands of the Lakota, and individual whites began to reveal trickster antics and unpredictable behavior. For example, in 1854 the shameful Mormon cow incident plunged the Lakota into war with the whites after High Forehead (Minneconjou) shot a cow. In response, US Lieutenant Grattan and his infantry attacked a peaceful village, killing Chief Whirling Bear. The Lakota responded by annihilating the white soldiers and the wars began. The whites proved to the Lakota that they would go to war over a cow.

In 1856, the whites revealed their trickster behavior to the Cheyennes after four warriors returned stray horses to a white man who claimed the horses were stolen. When the four boys tried to return the horses, a fight ensued and in the fray, one boy was killed, another jailed, and two boys escaped, including Little Wolf, who warned his people of the incident. The people abandoned the village and not long after the white soldiers looted and burned it. The whites proved to the Cheyennes that they would go to war over a few stray horses.

In 1858 gold was discovered in the Colorado mountains and hordes of whites invaded Cheyenne lands. The town of Denver was established and became a city of white men searching for riches, women, and a fight. The Cheyennes did not know how to view the whites, since they seemed to belong to no nation. Bent described:

> The Indians watched these mad proceedings of the whites with astonishment, but they were still further amazed, and alarmed, when the real rush began in the spring of '59. Even before the snow was melted on the plains and the ice had broken up in the streams, parties of eager gold-seekers began to make their appearance....Old Cheyenne men have told me, the Indians found many a white man wandering about, temporarily insane from hunger and thirst. The Indians took them to their camps

PART IV: COLONIZING THE TSÈHÉSTÁNO

and fed them. They did not understand this rush of white men and thought the whites were crazy.[5]

From the Cheyenne perspective, the invasion of whites came to represent a singular truth about colonization: it straddled white man's greed and white man's unpredictability. The Cheyennes were not met by the elite and wealthy whites who valued American core values of freedom, democracy, and progress. The Cheyennes did not meet citizens who were of the same stature or discipline as those in the treaty proceedings. Instead, the Cheyennes were met by the relentless forces of impulsive whites who became more hostile and ruthless toward Indigenous rights and sovereignty as the years progressed. The Cheyennes witnessed their lands overrun by the hordes of foreigners who all shared the same selfish ends: to get rich at the expense of the Indigenous people's lands, rights, and lives. Bent elaborated on the "mad proceedings" as whites made more "discoveries" of gold:

> The plains swarmed with hurrying bands of gold-seekers; the buffalo were frightened off, the last of the timber in the big groves along the streams was cut down, and the Indians did not know where to turn. The newcomers wished to get rid of the Indians and began to talk of putting them on reservations and letting them take their choice between farming and starving. The tribes were discontented at the invasion of their hunting grounds but were overawed by the great inrush of white men. They had never dreamed there were so many men in "the whole white tribe" as they had seen crossing the plains in the last two years. Some of the younger warriors were restless and wished to go to war on the invaders, but the chiefs and older men knew what the result of such an undertaking would be and held the hotheads in check. Then the Civil War, and the Cheyennes and all their friends were drawn into the great struggle.[6]

The Cheyennes were being invaded and there was nothing they could do but respond to the invasions with an equal force of resistance, which led to violence. After the "Mormon cow incident" and the "stolen horse incident," the Cheyennes and their allies were forced into wars with the whites, which never ceased until all of the Cheyenne lands were taken. The Southern Cheyennes suffered immensely, especially after the horrific massacre at Sand Creek. In the 1870s, the sacred Black Hills were invaded and the same story of colonization and greed played out for the Northern Cheyenne bands. Towns like Deadwood and Rapid City sprouted up, and these cities, like Denver, came to represent the repulsiveness of white civilization; their residents earned reputations for treating Indians, especially Indian women, with hostility and violence. Since white settlement of Cheyenne lands, the Cheyennes referred to the whites as vé'hó'e, tricksters, and this name remains part of the Cheyenne language and culture.

THE WHITE MAN'S WAYS

The Plains Indian wars, with all of the broken treaties, massacres, and thieving of Indian land, is representative of America's inability to achieve lasting peace with Indigenous nations. From the Indians' perspective, colonization and the settlement of their lands was viewed not as failed diplomacy but as failed humanity. For example, the unification story "The First White Man"—which spoke of peace, trade, and brotherhood—was rendered useless and replaced with factual narratives of violence and massacre. The whites earned for themselves a reputation that they were not to be trusted and Cheyennes had every right to meet these enemies with an equal force of violence. Wooden Leg told of an event from the 1876 war that can easily represent the new story of the first white man.

The First White Man, Decolonized

At Tongue river we stopped for a daytime rest. Our horses were picketed out to graze. After a while they began to show signs of alarm. A Cheyenne went out to look. He saw a lone white man afoot among the herd. Indian horses were afraid of white people, so they were snorting. The Cheyenne approached the white man and called out:
"How!"
"How," the white man responded.
    They shook hands. The Cheyenne got his own horse, mounted it, and asked the white man to go with him to the other Indians. They set off, the Cheyenne on horseback, the white man afoot. The stranger had a six shooter in a scabbard at his belt, but he made no offer to use it. He appeared friendly. He was thin and hungry-looking. His clothing was very ragged. The other Cheyennes got their horses, and they all gathered about the newcomer. Some of them mounted their horses, others stood afoot holding them.
    "Who are you?" a Cheyenne signed.
    The white man could make signs, but not very well. He made us understand him, though. He said he had been a soldier, but he got lost from them. He told us he had not fought us, as he had been lost before that time. He said the ragged clothing he had on was taken from a dead Sioux, as he did not want to be seen with soldier clothing. One Cheyenne kept saying, in our language, "Let's kill him."
    But nobody agreed with him. Finally he jerked up his rifle and fired. The white man fell dead. Others then cut him and beat him, so that no one man could have the blame nor receive the honor.
    Robbing the body was the next step. About all he had was the six shooter, some cartridges for it, and a little package tied to his belt. It had meat in it. It was horse meat and had been cooked in an open blazing fire. We threw it away.
    This man was killed not many miles down the Tongue river from my present home place. The exact spot is on a ranch where now lives a white man named Wolf. The place is on Tongue river below the present town of Ashland, Montana.[7]

Although the Cheyenne people endured challenges before colonization and their society adapted and changed, as evidenced in the early chapters of this book and in *A Sacred People*, colonization was perceived as a force that was more destructive than starvation, sickness, floods, and conflict with other Indian nations. White Bull/Ice (Northern Cheyenne) explained the contradictions of colonialism:

> The white man is so bad, Black robe. God came to the Indians and also to the whites. The former received him with reverence and love; He gave them buffaloes and reindeer in abundance and they were very happy. The whites on the contrary took Him and crucified Him. Seeing that the Pale Faces were so bad, the Great Spirit left the earth never to return, and fixed his abode in heaven. On account of this the Indians who are now unhappy, deprived of game, and their lands are conquered by the white man, who plunders and steals everything, and strive to exterminate the Indian.[8]

THE EARLY RESERVATION

The Plains Indian wars should be regarded as America's first foreign wars, in the creation of an empire by conquest, no different from the British, French, Spanish, and Belgian empires as they invaded and colonized the lands throughout the world.[9] Stolen Indian land, especially that secured through treaty, should be regarded as contested land, and the early Indian reservations regarded as refugee camps. After the violent and destructive wars with the vé'hó'e over the land, the Cheyennes were forced to live on confined reservation lands: the Southern Cheyenne along with the Southern Arapaho in Oklahoma and the Northern Cheyenne in southeastern Montana. Here the mental, spiritual, and psychological colonization ensued, creating a dysfunctional culture of people who were neither Cheyenne nor white. Sweet Medicine predicted such an outcome: "At last those people will ask you for your flesh (he repeated this four times), but you must say 'No.' They will try to teach you their way of living. If you give up to them your flesh (your children), those that they take away will never know anything."[10] Conrad Fisher (Northern Cheyenne) describes the Cheyenne perception of the reservation: "The time of the reservation is still known to the Cheyennes as Tse-se-emomáta'eotse, 'the time when the people were still mad.'"[11] Simply put, the Indian reservation as a confined land and as a concept epitomizes the colonization of Native America.

The greatest threat, by far, to Cheyenne sovereignty and nationhood was the invasion of the foreign whites. Although the US government engaged in government-to-government relations through treaty making, however unsuccessful, white citizens generally had no interest in building any relationships with the Cheyennes. This went against custom and Indigenous Law, which dictated that upon unification, peoples from differing nations should adopt each other as brothers and also adopt elements of each other's culture, language, and spiritual ways. History shows that the separatist attitudes of whites was commonly held toward all Indians, since whites rarely welcomed Indian people, cultures, languages, and spiritual ways. In fact, history reveals the exact opposite. Whites did not want separation; they wanted Indians to assimilate, adopting white culture, language, and religion exclusively.

VÉ'HÓ'E: THE WHITE MAN

MENTAL AND PSYCHOLOGICAL COLONIZATION

The reservation system was initially created to keep the white and Indian peoples separated, but US policy also sought to erase Indian cultures, languages, and spiritual ways. Before the Tongue River Indian Reservation was established for the Northern Cheyenne in 1884, a Catholic soldier contacted Bishop James O'Connor, who then contacted the Jesuits in Helena to "help" the Cheyennes by establishing a church.[12] In 1883, a horde of Catholic priests came to the Tongue River to set up a mission in what became Ashland, Montana (located on the eastern boundary of the reservation). Not long after, on January 17, 1884, a Catholic Mission was established and named after St. Joseph Benedicte Labre, who was a saint who dedicated his life to poor people. The namesake of the mission seemed fitting considering the dire state of the Northern Cheyenne people, at least in the eyes of the Jesuits. Before the reservation, the Véhoo'o operated under the principle of compassion and gave gifts to those in need. Christian pity was something that was new to the Cheyennes, who only knew the Cheyenne concept of compassion. The Christian concept and practices of pity had devastating effects on Cheyenne society, as it introduced and fostered dependence.

The Catholic Mission provided food, medicine, clothing, blankets, and of course biblical and secular teachings. Eventually the mission opened a boarding school and Cheyenne children were forced to attend. St. Labre has been credited with "saving" the Cheyenne people because the powers at hand believed that they had no other alternatives. Wooden Leg's daughters attended the mission school:

> Both of my daughters went to school at the Tongue river mission [St. Labre Mission]. They lived there during the school months. Each Sunday we were allowed to take them to our home. At other times we might go to the mission and see them for a few minutes. Later, I built a house only a quarter of a mile from the Mission, and on a sloping hillside above it. We could look from our front door and see the children at any time when they might be outside of the school buildings. My wife and I were pleased at their situation in life. "They will have more of comfort and happiness than we have had," we said to each other.
>
> But the younger daughter fell into an illness when she was about fourteen years old. We expected she soon would be herself again, but she grew worse instead of better. She became so weak she could not stay any longer at the school. She continued to go on downward after we brought her to our home. Finally, her spirit went back to the Great Medicine.
>
> All of our love now was fixed upon the other daughter. She advanced to full young womanhood. She could read the white man books, and she could write letters to our friends far away. But she too became ill, the same as her younger sister. During all of one winter she gradually wasted away. Every afternoon her body burned with fever.

Every night her bed was soaked with the sweating. Every morning she coughed almost to strangling. Neither the medicines of the agency physician nor the prayers of our own medicine men could help her. Just when the spring grass was coming up, she was buried in our mission cemetery.

My heart fell down to the ground. I decided then that the white man school is not good for Indian children. I think they do not get enough of meat at the boarding schools. I think too that they are kept in school too much during each year. They ought to be out and free to go as they please during all of the good weather of the autumn and the spring. It may be that white children can stand it to be in school most of the year. I do not believe, though, that Indian children can stand it. It is not good sense to have the whites and the Indians living by the same rules.[13]

The US government provided funding for St. Labre Catholic School for twenty years, until Tongue River Boarding School was opened in 1904 in Busby, Montana (located on the western boundary of the reservation).[14] The first generation of Cheyennes who went to boarding schools also sent their children to the same schools. These two generations of Cheyennes who lived from 1884 to 1935 had the burden to carry on the Cheyenne culture with greater responsibility than any previous generation because assimilation meant erasure. The pain and psychological trauma from forced assimilation and shame also began with these children. For the young people, it was hard enough just surviving. While some boarding school attendees may have had good experiences, the majority succumbed to the forces of shame, ridicule, and abuse. Parents had no control as the Bureau of Indian Affairs agent withheld rations if they did not send their children to school.[15] There was nothing that anybody could do to stop the mental destruction and spiritual colonization.

Boarding and mission schools were commonplace on Plains Indian reservations, and the system facilitated the wholesale destruction of Indian cultures and languages using the minds and spirits of Indian children. Mary Crow Dog (Lakota) recalled the principles of colonization that were outlined on a poster that the missionaries made her grandfather post on his wall while at a mission boarding school:

1. Let Jesus save you.
2. Come out of your blanket, cut your hair, and dress like a white man.
3. Have a Christian family with one wife for life only.
4. Live in a house like your white brother. Work hard and wash often.
5. Learn the value of a hard-earned dollar. Do not waste your money on giveaways. Be punctual.
6. Believe that property and wealth are signs of divine approval.
7. Keep away from saloons and strong spirits.

8. Speak the language of your white brother. Send your children to school to do likewise.
9. Go to church often and regularly.
10. Do not go to Indian dances or to the medicine men.[16]

As history has shown us, many of these rules applied exclusively to Indians, as the colonial system was designed to control them and not the vé'hó'e in power. One unforeseen goal of the assimilation scheme, which was also beneficial to oppressing future generations of Indians, was that Indian children learned deception, manipulation, corruption, abuse, and greed from their white and assimilated matrons.

For the Northern Cheyenne, the Catholic Mission school, St. Labre, gained power throughout the Tongue River Indian Reservation and sustained its presence until the modern era. From the traditional Cheyenne perspective, the mission was just another tool of the colonizer that provided neither restitution nor resolution to the problems of the Northern Cheyenne people. Eventually St. Labre established a high school. Today the mission has been quite successful in winning over Cheyenne converts, raising money, and maintaining an image as a beacon of pity. Few Cheyennes are willing to discuss their boarding school experiences, but some have publicly blamed St. Labre and the Tongue River Boarding School for destroying the Cheyenne language, culture, family unit, and kinship system. These "radical" Cheyennes, like the old Cheyennes who did not go to boarding school, assert that assimilating Cheyenne children eventually led to the creation of dependent adults, who lacked Indian virtues and were inveigled into white-man vices that destroyed the purity of heart.[17] If there ever was a threat to the Cheyenne cultural way of life and to future generations of Cheyenne people, the boarding schools were second only to the US government.

COLONIZING LEADERSHIP AND CITIZENSHIP

Outside of the schools, the early reservation Cheyennes lived in poverty, disease, alcoholism, and the dictatorship of the BIA agent. The Indian agent wielded all of the political power over the reservation and he ran it like a personal business. In 1886, the first agent assigned to Tongue River Indian Reservation was named Robert L. Upshaw. His main goal was to introduce farming and a wage economy to "enable the Cheyennes to achieve a degree of self-sufficiency," which was a fancy way of enforcing assimilation policies.[18] Until 1935, the Northern Cheyennes knew of numerous BIA agents because their turnover rate was high, but it mattered little to the Cheyennes since they all represented US dominance and bureaucracy.

The Northern Cheyenne people maintained the covenant ceremonies, cultural practices, and spiritual teachings, even as agents held the power and authority over them. Traditional leaders could not function, since the system of government and way of living under principles of balance and brotherhood had come to a "standstill": the colonial powers rendered the Véhoo'o powerless.[19] Ultimately the position of the agent of the BIA had the final say on all decisions on the reservation, and his police system assaulted and broke down traditional concepts of sovereignty.[20] The agent exerted power using fear tactics and threats of violence and often withheld food and clothing rations from the impoverished Cheyennes. Sometimes the agent met and discussed decisions with the Council Chiefs, but his consultation was not at all necessary.[21]

The agent often appointed a Cheyenne person to be the spokesperson for BIA decisions and policy: a token, a person who was not considered a leader according to the customs and traditions of the Cheyenne people, but who was Indian enough to validate decisions from the vé'hó'e. The agent fostered a culture of dysfunction, abusing his power, playing petty politics, and even embezzling tribal funds: a style of leadership endured for nearly two generations, but its lasting effects persisting into the modern era and into every reservation institution, even traditional ones. The white BIA agent's style of leadership was rooted in paternalism, thrived on dependency, and was sustained through corruption and greed; this is the legacy that dominates today, even years after the creation of the new Northern Cheyenne tribal government under the Indian Reorganization Act (IRA).

The BIA established a police force, commanded by vé'hó'e and composed of ex-warriors who had previously been scouts for the army. The "Indian police" enforced laws and demands of the agent. By 1889, the Courts of Indian Offenses (CIO) had been set up, and the agent appointed judges to preside over the court. Both the Indian police and the court enforced the laws and the colonial ways of the white man while ignoring Cheyenne law and custom. While the Indian agent and his court and judges undermined the Council of Forty-four Chiefs, the Indian police undermined the warrior societies and changed the structure and traditional function of what it "meant to be a warrior."[22]

The Nótåxeo'o, meanwhile, were still organized despite the Indian police, and they still practiced their sacred duties to some degree. Their warrior spirits remained strong: for example, as Stands In Timber discussed, when Blackfeet warriors came and tried to steal Cheyenne horses, groups of Cheyenne warriors wanted to fight even though they had surrendered to the United States and were not allowed.[23] The Nótåxeo'o also organized for ceremonial purposes but were not compatible with the sedentary reservation life. Their services could not be utilized because camp was never moved and there were no more large-scale buffalo and antelope hunts. The power further diminished when the traditional law and order system, the Véhoo'o, and the keepers of the covenants also lost power.

VÉ'HÓ'E: THE WHITE MAN

In 1884, there was one instance in which a white settler tried to shoot the hat off the Cheyenne Council Chief Black Wolf. The bullet hit Black Wolf directly in the head while he was riding a horse. The old chief survived, but the white culprit and his party fled the scene, expecting the worst. When Black Wolf was able to return to his camp, wounded and in disarray, he told of what happened and a small contingent of warriors organized to execute justice on behalf of the old chief. The crime, according to Cheyenne law, was attempted murder of a chief, which was traditionally punishable by death and which could have started a full-scale war according to Indigenous Nations Laws. The warriors wanted to go to the settlement and punish the criminal. Stands In Timber recalled:

> They sent word to the upper village, and those men all came down and organized a war party. By the time they got to the ranch it was deserted, so they rode in close and shot the windows out, and then broke in and took everything they wanted and set the house afire. They burned the whole ranch down—all the buildings and improvements, even the hay stacks and corrals. When they got through there was not much left.[24]

Not long after Cheyenne justice was served, a column of soldiers was sent to apprehend the warriors. Four were tried for acts of war and then taken to Miles City where they were imprisoned. They were Stands Different, Howling Wolf, Ax Handle, and Yellow Cook. Ax Handle died in prison and Yellow Cook died not long after his release. The four were nearly starved to death while held in solitary confinement. Meanwhile, the white man got away with assault and attempted murder. Northern Cheyenne Keeper of the Sacred Hat, Allan Jo Black Wolf, is a direct descendent of Chief Black Wolf, who survived the attempted murder. Alan Jo Black Wolf discussed the major changes of warriors during the time of the so-called Indian police:

> That's where [the Cheyenne men] were disappointed. But it also played into that he didn't have to do very much either. He was real important back then [before the reservation]. He represented the father upstairs. He did the hunting. He gathered the food and the main stuff. After the stores came, he got shut down. After the police came, he got shut down again. So that's why we kind of lost the importance of how the dad [was] supposed to be there [for his family]. So that's where Ma'heo'e was adjusting this, and we are still in an adjusting phase.[25]

The Indian police was one of several federal institutions that aided in the deterioration of the Cheyenne identity, in particular the Cheyenne male identity and Cheyenne concepts of manhood. Women maintained sacred roles of Cheyenne womanhood primarily by running the household and raising children, but Cheyenne men could no longer do anything to gain any prestige or earn any rank. The reservation ration system crippled warriors as providers, and traditional forms of leading and policing were extinguished. It would not be long before the ceremonial realm was attacked. Cheyenne men could not be

PART IV: COLONIZING THE TSÉHÉSTÁNO

hired for any skilled labor, and many sought comfort from injustice by drinking cheap liquor, another one of Sweet Medicine's prophecies fulfilled.

The Cheyennes could never understand the colonial justice system of the whites. At times it seemed that the whites could do no wrong, and anytime a Cheyenne man did something wrong, he was severely punished along with others. Without the traditional means of conflict resolution or justice, the Cheyenne people were at the mercy of the whites and their colonial laws of injustice, which were enforced with threats of violence.

Probably the most terrorizing actions by the US government were when a column of soldiers was sent into the reservation to detain tribal members or suppress any dissent. In one case a small uprising took place at the Crow Agency, some fifty miles west of the Tongue River, and the trouble was somehow linked to the Northern Cheyenne reservation and the Cheyenne people were blamed.

Once again soldiers were deployed and the white settlers organized as a posse; the vé'hó'e desired to instigate any fight with any Indians. There was fear from both the Cheyennes and the whites, but the Indians knew the erratic behavior and impulsiveness of the vé'hó'e, especially when armed and in search of a fight. The deployment of soldiers truly frightened the Cheyennes as they remembered the massacres of Sand Creek and Washita, and the brutal war of 1876, as well as the Wounded Knee Massacre of 1890, as Stands In Timber recalled: "They had had enough of being shot up in their villages at places like Sand Creek. It was the one thing they always feared when trouble started, that the white people would come in and attack the villages."[26] Such use of violence was successful in terrorizing the Northern Cheyennes into submission for whatever cause or purpose that served the agent and his colonial agenda.

SPIRITUAL OPPRESSION

For nearly two generations after the Northern Cheyenne people were forced onto a reservation they were further pressured to follow an alien way that had foundational principles rooted in ruthlessness and deception. The end of the buffalo-hunting economy left the Cheyenne with no other choice but to buy into the very system that cheated them out of their land, resources, and way of life. The cycle of internal oppression can easily be traced to this early reservation era. Ultimately, this system created a culture of corruption and dysfunction. This culture remains evident in modern reservation life. Arguably this culture has crept into almost every facet of modern Cheyenne life: the schools, the community, and even the circles of traditional practices like powwows and ceremonial practices. The Cheyenne concept of sovereignty, which emphasized responsibility, was nearly destroyed and replaced with a new concept that emphasized power and authority over land, property, and resources. This is the concept that remains.

The Tséhéstanove (Cheyenne way) was colonized when the US government declared war on the covenant ceremonies. While the Hoxéheome has proven to be one of the greatest unifying and spiritual ceremonies of the Great Plains, the vé'hó'e labeled it primitive and barbaric and said it had to be stopped. Commissioner of Indian Affairs John S. Collier provided a description of how the Sun Dance was suppressed on the plains:

> First, in the Sioux country, the Army crushed the Sun Dance with armed force. Then the missionaries influenced the Bureau of Indian Affairs to impose regulations against not only the Sun Dance but all "pagan" ceremonies which, they believed, impeded the progress of Indians toward Christian civilization. The Interior Department framed a criminal code forbidding Indian religious practices and established penalties. Enacted in 1884 and enriched in 1904, this code stood in force and effect until 1933.[27]

Like their traditional Lakota allies, the Northern Cheyennes of the Tongue River Agency were suppressed in a similar manner. Since the entire governing structure of the Cheyennes relied on the practice of the big ceremonies like the Medicine Lodge, suppression of the Sun Dance meant suppression of the entire Cheyenne way of life and a complete destruction of the sacred nation. We can assume that the suppression affected other Indian nations the same way. Collier continued: "Among the Plains tribes, the very nature of the Sun Dance, and of successor religions to the Sun Dance, made forcible suppression easy. The Sun Dance was a merging of every individual with the annually resurrected tribe in a social-cosmic worship. Merely to forbid the tribe to meet together at all was to kill the Sun Dance."[28]

Whether the BIA understood the intricacies of the traditional Cheyenne governing structure or not, their policies strategically undermined the fabric of the Cheyenne identity, the Hoxéheome. The exact date of the official ban on the Sun Dance is not known for certain and there are no Tongue River Agency records that reveal the date; however, the generally accepted date was 1897.[29] Nonetheless, the oppression of spiritual ways began as soon as the reservation was established. In the fight to preserve the Cheyenne spiritual identity, warriors and spiritual leaders rose to protect the Cheyenne way of life, sometimes threatening naysayers with violence, especially those who spoke adamantly against the covenant ceremonies.[30]

A Mennonite-Cheyenne conflict rose to the point where Superintendent Buntin had to call a meeting with all of the ceremonial leaders: about thirty Cheyennes arrived; some were members of various warrior societies while others were escorted by their society brothers. At the meeting, a Christian Cheyenne woman gave testimony of the nature of Cheyenne ceremonies emphasizing the degradation of women involved as well as customs and practices that were considered unhygienic and barbaric. The superintendent expressed these concerns to the Cheyenne spiritual leaders and outlined the legal consequences if a medicine man were to cause the unwarranted death of a patient in his care. Presented here are a number of rules established by the superintendent that the Cheyenne spiritual leaders had to abide by:

1. New doctors could not be initiated into the practice.
2. No money or property could be charged for medical or spiritual attention.
3. Ceremonies that involved the "debauching" of women were prohibited.
4. Doctors were prohibited from speaking against stock-raising, farming, placing children in schools, or "anything else which will prevent Indians from progressing or becoming self-supporting, respectable people."
5. No more than three dollars could be spent on medications or medical assistance (i.e., herbs, water, cleansing materials).
6. The use of a rattle was prohibited.
7. The singing of songs was prohibited.
8. Sucking or spitting on the body of a patient was prohibited.[31]

The strict suppression of the Sun Dance among the Plains Indian nations endured from the 1890s through the 1920s, yet the Cheyennes held sporadic ceremonies in secret. The ban on the Sun Dance was not officially lifted until 1935. It was enough to bring the nation's spirit to its knees, especially since the nation did not fully recover from the previous decades of war and massacre and the effects of the assimilation policies. The secret Hoxéheome, however, allowed for the Véhoo'o, the Nótâxeo'o, and the covenant keepers to sustain a degree of spiritual influence and exert Cheyenne sovereignty by upholding the duties and responsibilities bestowed upon them by the sacred beings. Altogether, the four branches of the traditional governing system fought to keep the Hoxéheome alive, which is why it remains strong today.

COLONIZATION THROUGH REORGANIZATION

From the 1880s to the 1930s, the US government's ruthless control over the Cheyenne people's destiny crippled the Tsėhéstáno, nearly destroying it forever. During this early reservation period, the leaders of the Northern Cheyenne Nation in particular were stripped of their responsibilities over their own people and affairs. The Northern Cheyenne Nation had no self-determination, authority, or sovereignty; basically it had been reduced to a primitive "tribe" in the image of the whites. During this time, the BIA and the Indian agent, acting on behalf of the US government, held the ultimate control over the lives and futures of the Cheyenne people. Traditional leaders struggled to maintain their presence in the face of oppressive, assimilation-based policies that directly assaulted the Tsėhéseamanėö'o and the Tsėhéstanove. The Cheyennes were to become farmers under the new policies, but even this would prove nearly impossible, since corruption and paternalism dominated the very program designed to help the Cheyennes. What resulted instead was the creation of a new class of Cheyennes who were privileged by the assimilationist system and who were entrusted to lead the rest of the Cheyennes into white civilization. In order for this transition to succeed, however, the Cheyennes would have to abandon their sacred nation and covenants to it, which they had depended on for centuries.

In 1934, Congress passed the IRA. This act was to be the "Indian New Deal" and was meant to address the problems outlined in the Meriam Report: health, economic development, education, and pervasive corruption and mismanagement of Indian agents.[32] Commissioner Collier, supporter of the "Wheeler-Howard Bill," was determined to change federal Indian policy and empower Indian nations and, in the act, outlined several guiding principles for reorganization. Among them was sovereignty: that "Indian societies must be given status, responsibility, and power."[33] Collier was championed as a hero for Indian rights, but some Indians still perceived the bill as another paternalistic policy aimed at assimilating Indians into mainstream America.[34] The IRA also addressed the failure of the Dawes Act (allotment policy) and the suppression of traditional Indian ceremonies and practices. The long-term goals, however, were to eventually absorb Indian nations into the capitalist machine of the American political economy, another form of assimilation.[35]

The IRA provided Indian nations a means to harness the American capitalistic system by allowing "tribes," the term used in the policy, to organize under a corporate model, with an executive and governing council. From the perspective of whites, strengthening Indian communities through self-governance was better understood under a business model.[36] After adoption, Indian nations were to transition from leaderless and colonized peoples to constitutional governments, which had the authority to sell leases for natural resource development like coal, oil, timber, and gas. Under the IRA, Indian "tribes" were also better protected from outsiders and corporations that could take advantage of Indian lands without following proper legal procedures in acquiring mining and leasing rights. The IRA constitutional governments allowed "tribal members," the term established during the early reservation period, to elect leaders to make decisions about their lands as representatives of their people. The "tribal members" were the voters, and membership was determined, for the first time, using blood quantum, which continues to contribute to problems with identity, social status, and politics. Ultimately, the goals of the IRA were to lead "tribes" down different social and political paths than in the previous system where the BIA and Indian agent held ultimate power. Theoretically, the IRA model made sense and was the solution to the problems created by the BIA.

Of the 258 "tribes" in the United States who voted whether to adopt the provisions of IRA, 181 accepted while 77 rejected the new policy.[37] Wilkins outlined several controversies that arose around the passing of the IRA, among them being the burden placed on members to vote against it; if they did not, their vote counted in favor. This flaw worked against Indian nations, like the Northern Cheyennes, who held utter contempt for the BIA, which represented the suppression of traditional governing systems. One of the greatest flaws, however, was that IRA governments were subject to the veto power of the US secretary of the interior. Such a provision cloaked unelected, and non-Indian, non-member officials with power and in positions higher than any elected tribal official. The IRA allowed BIA paternalism to continue under the guise of "democratizing" Indian nations.[38] The system also allowed the BIA to interfere with tribal affairs and politics, proving that the IRA was another form of paternalism and colonialism. Some tribes fared better than others upon adopting the IRA constitutional form of government, but the majority that did not want it in the first place, did not succeed. In particular, the Indian nations that endured harsh assimilation policies and brutal treatment from the Indian agent merely replicated the dysfunctional culture of bureaucracy and egotism with the IRA form of government. In the end, the IRA-style constitutional governments were at odds with traditional Indian cultures, systems of government, and especially concepts of leadership, citizenship, and sovereignty. The IRA has arguably proved to be generally unsuccessful to the Northern Cheyennes and their allies, the Oglala Lakotas, as these nations struggle with ongoing political challenges amidst social and spiritual ones.

On October 11, 1935, Harold L. Ickes, the secretary of the interior, approved the first draft of the Northern Cheyenne Constitution and Bylaws. It was assumed that the BIA superintendent, W. R. Centerwall, adapted a boilerplate constitution to fit the Northern Cheyennes. On November 2, 1935, the Northern Cheyenne people voted to adopt the new constitution and bylaws: 394 for, 53 against. Collier and Ickes approved the decision of the Northern Cheyennes, and tribal business commenced. The traditional Northern Cheyennes consented to the new government. According to Northern Cheyenne spiritual leader Gilbert White Dirt, the Véhoo'o delegated its power to the new government: "The Chiefs said, 'we will give authority to a council, they're going to help us. We'll give them authority over our ways.' And that must be about that time when we started losing our respect."[39] Chief Leroy Pine (Northern Cheyenne) also described how the government transition occurred: "As history goes, not too long ago, with the consent of the people, the Chiefs delegated governing authority to a tribal council. They established an IRA government. Now today we have a President and a Council."[40]

According to oral accounts, the Véhoo'o and spiritual leaders consented for the BIA to create a new government under the assumption that they, the Véhoo'o, could take it back at a later date, if need be. However unrealistic, the sentiment of such Indigenous sovereign thinking remains part of the conversations of traditional Cheyennes. From the BIA perspective, however, the Véhoo'o and spiritual leaders revoked all of their authority, without any provision or desire to reinstate the chiefs or any spiritual leaders in the future.⁴¹ During the voting, most traditional Cheyennes, who still believed in the sanctity of the traditional government, opposed the new IRA style of government and chose not to vote, but their abstaining votes did not count against it.⁴² Today the Northern Cheyenne people continue to live under two governments: the IRA constitutional government and the traditional one that includes the Véhoo'o, the Nótåxeo'o, and the keeper of the Ésevone. The traditional concepts of sovereignty and nationhood remain, while citizens struggle to remain true to the Tsėhéstanove.

CONCLUSION

Decolonizing the Tsėhéstanove

The final chapter in this story has not been written and, it is hoped, never will be. That is how it is when great Nations keep their word.

—Suzan Shown Harjo (Cheyenne and Hodulgee Muscogee)[1]

Throughout history, the Tsėhéstáno endured a number of traumatic events, but the Cheyenne people survived. Despite the harsh early reservation era, the Cheyennes held onto their traditional ways: the Tsėhéseamanēõ'o and the Tsėhéstanove. The Cheyenne cultural and spiritual ways of life, however, were forever changed from the lasting effects of the Plains Indian wars and the fragmentation and disruption of the ceremonial cycle.

The Cheyennes of the tumultuous eras of colonization and assimilation were burdened with the duty to ensure that the next generations remained Cheyenne and that the Cheyenne Nation survived. The era of war and assimilation was the time that Cheyennes had to make a conscious effort to speak their language, live by their cultural values, and practice rituals and ceremonies. In essence those Cheyennes who survived the wave of colonization had to make a choice either to continue to be part of the living-nation or to assimilate. Against the odds a body of traditional Cheyennes challenged the laws of the BIA and the wishes of assimilationist Cheyennes. These traditional Cheyennes resisted by continuing the legacy of their sacred nation by exercising their sacred sovereign rights and by keeping their sacred promises, but they could only resist to the degree that the new life allowed. They were confined on the reservation and subject to the laws and culture of whites, and therefore they had to navigate new challenges. The Cheyennes, like all Native peoples, have remained trapped and dependent on a system that has never really worked in their favor.

For a significant portion of time, the power and authority rested exclusively and absolutely in the hands of white BIA reservation agents. They created a political culture of competition, corruption, and paternalism. These agents remained in power even after the Northern Cheyenne drafted and adopted a formal constitution in 1935. The effects of colonization remained and political and social dysfunction exists in Cheyenne communities today. "Tribal sovereignty" rests in the hands of the tribal governments, yet there is still a large population of Cheyenne people who remain distrustful and contentious toward the primary institution that represents their interests. Probably more distrustful are the populations of people who continue to take advantage of the flawed political system to reap short-term benefits at the expense of Indigenous unity and Indigenous nation sovereignty. The flawed system allows for reservation politics to remain central to modern governance.

Despite the dysfunction, traditional Cheyenne duties, responsibilities, and concepts of traditional law and leadership still have value in the reservation. This does not mean that Northern Cheyenne and other Indian nations are not in need of good leaders. In fact, the utility and sanctity of traditional values are tested every day as modern leaders and citizens come to rely on the Tsėhéstanove and the Tsėhéseamanėō'o in trying times. The Véhoo'o also remain as central figures in Cheyenne daily life. They continue to represent the cultural and spiritual realms of Cheyenne life, and they maintain sacred relationships to the omnipresent sacred Cheyenne Nation. They lead based on traditional principles, and the Council of Forty-four continues to function even if it is not the federally recognized government. Furthermore, the keepers of the Maahótse and Ésevone continue to hold onto their sacred authority in the ceremonial realm, which means the Tsėhéstáno is alive. But threats to the sacred nation continue to devour Cheyenne concepts of personhood, family, and community.

Since the establishment of the IRA Constitution of 1935, the Northern Cheyennes have continued to struggle to reach their potential and find a means to regain the levels of sovereignty, autonomy, and self-determination needed to heal and promote a healthy nation. Many of today's challenges can be traced to the direct and indirect effects of colonization and assimilation, yet the primary internal threats to sovereignty are abstract and unseen. These threats manifest among leaders and citizens as jealousy, hate, and resentment, and they eventually surface through corruption, bullying, and unwise decision-making. Any efforts to confront these internal threats are met with vicious and emotional retaliation. The Cheyennes and other Indians are finding out that these challenges are not exclusive to them, nor are they exclusive to Indian country. Such social and political challenges seem to be commonplace among all peoples and societies past and present. The major difference, however, is that with every internal conflict, the Cheyenne Nation is further diminished, and this specific sacred nation loses a piece of itself. The Cheyenne Nation remains unhealed from external assaults, yet the pain inflicted internally endures. This is no way for a nation to survive and it is no way for a people to live.

Throughout the history of the United States, Indigenous nations have retained and managed to regain their inherent rights to self-determination and autonomy. Today Indian tribes have control over their own destinies more than they did during the colonization of their lands. Their problems are not exclusively in the system, but also in the ability of the people to exercise sovereignty, their ability to control their destiny, and their ability to make and keep promises to themselves and others. Achieving this end is easier said than done, since a significant portion of Plains Indian communities and people live in poverty and prioritize daily life struggles, like buying food and paying bills. Significant populations of Northern Cheyennes also confront social, mental, and personal issues that resulted from generations of abuse and disenfranchisement. Meanwhile, the elite class, which comprises primarily assimilated and mixed-blood Cheyennes, continues to benefit from white privilege and assimilative privilege: the privilege or advantage that a person possesses by being more assimilated (i.e., speaking perfect English, owning material wealth, and practicing the Christian religion). The Cheyennes desire unity, but the divisions have become so deeply embedded in daily life that every action is criticized for being an oppressive act to one person or group of people. When every action is politicized, the culture of apathy dominates because even sincere citizens are eventually disempowered. The time for change is long overdue, since these divisions will inevitably lead to the further diminishment of the sovereignty, and the ultimate end, of the Tsėhéstáno. To decolonize means to be able to make and keep promises to a sacred nation.

DECOLONIZING THE SACRED NATION

The Cheyenne people can take several actions to decolonize and revive their cultural and spiritual ways of living. "Knowing history" is not enough. The Cheyenne "tribal governments" also have several actions available to decolonize and indigenize their tribes to reawaken their nations. All of these actions could revive the Tsėhéstanove and the Tsėhéseamanēö́o but alone may not necessarily revive the Tsėhéstáno. Such a task requires much planning and spiritual preparation. The goal of the Cheyennes, like most Indigenous peoples, is to confront the challenges of colonialism and assimilation to achieve a level of stability, sovereignty, and good and healthy living. The ultimate goal is to build their nations by building their communities. These are basic challenges that seem nearly impossible to reach because Cheyenne communities are still trying to heal and unite.

The proposed decolonization projects I present here provide a foundation for any efforts in sacred nation building. I must assert that simply knowing traditional ways is not enough to heal the broken Cheyenne Nation; instead, the Cheyennes must act by drawing from traditional knowledge to take ownership and responsibility for their situation, and then creating new and effective ways to solve long-standing problems. And they must do so in a non-toxic and sincere manner, with love and compassion.

PART IV: COLONIZING THE TSÈHÉSTÁNO

I. Reintroduce the Concept of a Sacred Nation

The Cheyennes, like most Indians, need to shed their identities that are based on race and color and begin to see themselves as part of a sacred nation. The concept of a sacred nation should not be framed from a colonial, mainstream perspective, which tends to view one's belonging as membership to a club or an elite class. Belonging to a sacred nation is certainly exclusive but not discriminatory or oppressive. When one chooses to belong to a sacred nation, he or she chooses a set of unifying principles to live by, not those based on race, color, or blood quantum. All Cheyennes who believe and live by the Tsėhéstanove and Tsėhéseamaneōʹo belong to the sacred nation, the Tsėhéstáno. They make a promise or covenant to the sacred nation. Their belonging establishes a relationship that each individual must sustain by contributing to the Tsėhéstáno, that is, by contributing to their community.

II. Reintroduce Communal Ceremonies

Community events that accomplish this goal already exist in Cheyenne communities, like traditional powwows, feasts, celebrations, and other events. Communal ceremonies, however, were traditionally designed to provide the opportunity for creating and sustaining spiritual connections. Traditionally the community events built and fostered healthy relationships, which built and fostered a healthy nation. This can be done by using existing traditional events and adapting them to be more inclusive and encouraging participation from all community members, not just a select few or an elite group.

Recently the Cheyennes have begun to introduce traditional dances, which has proven to be successful. A challenge may be in reintroducing communal hunting rituals because the Cheyennes no longer depend on hunting for survival. They could, however, reestablish adapted rituals and ceremonies that highlight and focus on the purpose of the communal hunts without actually hunting. For example, the Antelope Pit Ceremony has guiding principles that promote unity and foster the healthy development of the next generation. Although the Antelope Pit Ceremony is long gone, it does not mean that the Cheyenne spiritual leaders cannot re-create a ritual fitting for today's modern challenges. These ceremonies revive old promises that the people have to the natural elements and each other. Part of belonging to a sacred nation is participating in the community rituals and events, because these events are traditionally viewed as exercising sovereignty.

III. Protect Covenant Ceremonies

The extant ceremonies of the Cheyenne Nation have survived the tests of time, yet the major threat against these ceremonies comes from the Cheyennes themselves in the form of exploitation and toxic traditionalism. I have witnessed on several occasions Cheyenne people aiding in the exploitation of Cheyenne ceremonial practices, cultural resources, and history for personal gain. There have been instances in which the traditional laws have been applied to one person but not to others. Sometimes traditions are used to inflict pain on others, through either shame or ridicule. It should not hurt to learn of traditional ways, especially for those who wish to reclaim their Cheyenne language and identity. There have also been times when non-Cheyennes have made their way into our ceremonies for selfish purposes. The Cheyenne tribal councils could pass laws to prevent exploitation by Indians and non-Indians, but the ultimate power to protect these ways is in the hands of Cheyenne citizens and traditional practitioners. In the end it is up to citizens to protect intellectual property. After all, these ceremonies are primarily for the citizens, especially those who rely on them for spiritual, mental, physical, and emotional healing. Citizens can also reintroduce or reinforce healthy living standards based on ceremonial practices: healthful eating, exercise, emotional support, and mental health through prayer and meditation. Healthy citizens and healthy families build healthy nations.

IV. Reintroduce the Concept of Ma'heónetanohtôtse

The sacred way of thinking is a concept that can be easily taught and reinforced. It simply means that people should be mindful of their decisions and actions. Children can easily pick up this way of thinking and carry it into adulthood. This book provides the basic principles of the sacred way of thinking, which can be adopted and reinforced by any organization without involving any protected traditional knowledge. All Cheyennes have the chance to reintroduce the ma'heónetanohtôtse at the individual and family levels because there are a lot of Cheyennes who still believe and live by the principles of the ma'heónetanohtôtse. Reintroducing the basic principles of ma'heónetanohtôtse may be challenging because not everyone will see value in these ways.

Yet, the Cheyenne sacred way of thinking should not be perceived as in contention with the Christian way of thinking, nor should the ma'heónetanohtôtse be equated with Christianity. The Cheyenne way of thinking should not be reintroduced as a set of rules to be followed or forced upon others; they should be used for positive reinforcement and people should rely on them when appropriate. The sacred way of thinking allows for individuals to make and keep promises to themselves.

V. Reinvigorate and Strengthen the Cheyenne Kinship System

Probably the most immediate action that Cheyennes can take is to begin to use kinship terms in the nuclear and immediate family. Traditional kinships have survived among traditional Cheyenne families, but with each passing generation and as more Cheyennes marry non-Cheyennes, the traditional kinship system is diminished. The traditional kinship system is the foundation of all traditional laws, band membership, and Cheyenne national citizenship. The family is the place where a person learns to be Cheyenne and to follow traditional Cheyenne customs, laws, and behaviors. Ceremonial knowledge is often passed down to family members and blood relatives. By actively and consciously establishing and sustaining traditional kinship roles, Cheyennes strengthen their nation and establish and reinforce kinship responsibilites. After all, a strong nation is made of strong families.

VI. Reinstate Traditional Cheyenne Family Laws

A large population of Cheyennes live by the Tsėhéstanove and the Tsėhéseamanėö'o, but they do not wear it on their shoulders as a badge of status. Many Cheyennes sincerely believe in "the old ways" but do not advise anyone or speak out against inappropriate behavior out of fear of criticism or the appearance of being know-it-alls. The time has come for the Cheyennes to begin setting standards for themselves and their immediate family members. Cheyennes need to hold their family members accountable when they violate any of the customs or traditions, and they need to do so out of love, not anger. Family members also need to hold one another to a standard of honor by helping and advising one another on proper behavior and in finding ways to reconcile when a family member makes a mistake. The reinforcement of proper conduct should be done with compassion and not shame. It should be done with grace and without the intention to humiliate or embarrass one another. The purpose of traditional family laws was to preserve balance and harmony, not to generate pain and resentment. For too long the Cheyennes have been shamed by people who are not of their family and who do not necessarily have the authority, moral or otherwise, to tell people how to live. This creates a vacuum of distrust since a learner sees only hypocrisy. This cycle must be broken but it will not happen overnight.

VII. Revive and Reinstate Marriage Customs

The Cheyennes have rich traditions that promote healthy relationships and that foster the proper courtship and marriage customs. The Cheyennes can begin to revive these customs to promote healthy sexual relationships and prepare young people for marriage commitments and parenthood—should they wish to marry and become parents, that is. Young people need cultural and social spaces in which to date as well. These spaces and places should be safe environments, free of drugs and alcohol. Young people need to prepare for healthy relationships so they can have healthy marriages later in life. Healthy marriages build healthy families, which build healthy communities. These traditions and customs can and should be taught in the household and in schools so that young adults gain a healthy perception of courtship and marriage. The Cheyennes can also revive puberty ceremonies, which some traditional households continue to hold. Much of the rituals and customs of the Cheyenne way do not require strict teachings or stringent guidance from the highest ceremonial leaders or keepers.

The Cheyenne communities have numerous cultural experts who can facilitate the introduction of minor rituals and customs without requiring the approval or consent of the spiritual leaders. The ultimate goal is to promote healthy family and social lives.

VIII. Reintroduce the Peacemaking Pipe Ceremony

The peace pipe continues to play a significant part in the Cheyenne way of living; unfortunately, it is not part of modern law and order. The tribal councils can include the pipe ceremony as part of their daily functions as decision makers and to facilitate conflict resolution. There are numerous Cheyenne "pipe carriers" who have the sacred responsibility of keeping the peace. While the Véhoo'o are the ultimate peacekeepers, Cheyenne pipe carriers are also knowledgeable and spiritually and mentally qualified to make peace at the family and community level. The mainstream punitive system of justice often creates more problems than solutions. Conversely, traditional peacemaking has yet to prove itself simply because the Cheyennes have not given it a chance. As a pipe carrier myself, I believe that traditional peacemaking can be effective in conflict resolution in most cases as an alternative to imprisonment or the creation of petty feuds.

IX. Build Relationships with Other Indigenous Nations

Following the old traditions of peacemaking and alliance building, the tribal councils and traditional leaders can begin reaching out to other Indian tribes to build strong cultural and spiritual relationships, not just political ones. Every year during the celebration of the Battle of the Little Big Horn and the Rosebud Battle, numerous families from the Oglala and Rosebud Sioux nations travel to the Northern Cheyenne Indian Reservation to take part in cultural and ceremonial events. These events are proof that the Cheyenne-Lakota alliance has not been forgotten. I think that the Cheyennes could also build alliances with other Indian tribes and Indigenous nations throughout the United States and the world. For example, the First Nations peoples of Canada, the Maori of New Zealand, and the Indigenous peoples of Central and South America all have shared interests in protecting sovereignty, nationhood, and indigenous rights. Building alliances at the local and global levels will further strengthen the sacred Cheyenne Nation, and it will also broaden the minds and spirits of Cheyenne leaders and citizens.

X. Reinstate Decolonized Inter-Indigenous-National Laws

The Cheyenne customs to aseehe (move camp) and Move the Arrows required all Cheyennes to take part. These events were the ultimate exercises of sovereignty. This same philosophy and custom can be harnessed to encourage all Cheyenne citizens to take part in a particular initiative or to combat social ills, health issues, and other problems. The philosophy of the "move" and not the actual ceremonial process is of importance; however, should the need to conduct a ceremony to sanction a move be necessary, then the move becomes of greater significance. How effective would a move to reduce suicide rates be? Such moves would be a united effort against a common enemy, whether abstract or tangible. Other moves can be aimed to combat violence against women and children, or ending drug and alcohol dependency. For a sacred sovereign nation, the limits are endless.

Another inter-Indigenous national custom that the Cheyennes can reinstate is the act of petitioning and declaring war. American Indians serve in the United States military at a higher rate per capita than any other ethnic group. The Cheyennes (both the Northern and Southern) also have a record of sending their sons and daughters to serve in the line of duty at high rates. Traditionally, a Cheyenne warrior could not go to war unless he petitioned his superiors. At each level he was allowed to engage in a certain type of warfare, ranging from horse raiding, scouting, and war parties to all-out war. The Cheyennes are still able to practice a fundamental custom of war, offering the war pipe: the process of asking permission to engage potential enemies. While the Cheyenne Nation no longer declares war, it can certainly make peace. Most people desire peace above anything else. The Cheyenne Nation is a sacred nation. Part of being sacred is being at peace. Right now, it appears that the Cheyenne Nation is at constant war with itself. The nation and its people need a declaration of peace. This will make both sacred again.

HÉVESE'ONEMATSESTÔTSE

While the Tsėhéstáno has endured centuries of pain and suffering, the core of the Tsėhéstanove exists because the Cheyenne ceremonial cycle remains intact. It is a form of resistance. Every year the major ceremonials take place, renewing and reviving Cheyenne hearts and minds, rekindling Cheyenne kinship roles, and strengthening the Cheyenne identity. Yet the threats of destruction have become more complex and are disguised as avenues for the Cheyenne people's potential economic prosperity, like natural resource development. Persisting internal conflict is also a threat to sovereignty and nationhood, but I believe the Cheyennes are at the forefront of a new time and place as a reemerging sacred nation.

As I reflect on the purpose of this book, I must reassert that *A Sovereign People* is by no means the one and only perspective on traditional Cheyenne worldviews. It is most certainly not a complete study either. This book serves as an example of how the Cheyennes viewed themselves and how they viewed the world. It is a glimpse of what was, and can be a guide to help build and rebuild a Cheyenne Nation in a manner that the Cheyenne people will actually have ownership over it. Today the Northern Cheyenne people in particular live under a concept of sovereignty that is fraught with flaws and operates in a system that is at best stable enough to help the Cheyennes merely "get by" on the reservation.

The law and legal system in place is effective, but as far as healing and promoting healthy living, a new way of thinking must emerge. A truly sovereign Indigenous nation should provide more for its people, but this can only be done if the people provide more for their nation. That is, the people must heal and then they can begin to effectively heal their nation. The Tsėhéstanove and the Tsėhéseamanēō'o belong to the Cheyennes; it is time that we give them a chance.

Notes

INTRODUCTION

1. Robert Odawi Porter, "John Mohawk, On Sovereignty," in *Sovereignty, Colonialism, and the Indigenous Nations: A Reader* (Durham, NC: Carolina Academic Press, 2005), 140. This essay originally appeared in *Akwesasne Notes* 1, nos. 3–4, Dec. 31, 1995.

2. See Barker, *Sovereignty Matters*.

3. Kristofic and James, *The Hero Twins*; Taube, *Aztec and Maya Myths*; Newmark, "Reclaiming Dene Womanhood in Our Stories."

4. Kovach, *Indigenous Methodologies*, 28.

5. Wilson, *Research Is Ceremony*, 15.

6. "Sacred scholars" is an adaptation of the Mohawk scholar Taiaiake Alfred's idea of a "sacred protector": "those who carry the burden of peace." See Alfred, *Wasáse*, 79. Sacred scholars have a "sacred responsibility to Indian nations and peoples undertaken for the sake of cultural survival." See Riding In, "Editor's Commentary."

7. A challenge in authoring this book was in decolonizing and indigenizing the Cheyenne people's view of themselves in history, then reconstructing and applying a new lens to view history and interpret concepts like sovereignty and nationhood. To accomplish this, I utilize Smith's Kaupapa Maori research model and apply it to the study of Cheyennes. See Graham Smith, "Kaupapa Maori Theory: Theorizing Indigenous Transformation of Education & Schooling."

8. I obtained approval from the sovereign entity, the Northern Cheyenne Tribe, through tribal council resolution, NCTC Resolution #DOI-159 (2011), to publish this history.

9. Coffey and Tsosie, "Rethinking the Tribal Sovereignty Doctrine," 191–221; Tsosie, "Introduction: Symposium on Cultural Sovereignty," 1–14.

10. Robert B. Porter, "The Meaning of Indigenous Nation Sovereignty,"

NOTES

75–112; Robert B. Porter, "Two Kinds of Indians, Two Kinds of Indian Nation Sovereignty," 629–56; Tsosie, "Sacred Obligations," 1615–72.

CHAPTER I

1. The editors of Akwesasne Notes, *Basic Call to Consciousness*, 1–6.
2. Lewis, Clark, et al., "1st of October Monday 1804" entry, "Part 5: Missouri River Miscellany, undated, winter 1804–5" entry, "Friday 22nd August 1806" entry in *The Journals of the Lewis and Clark Expedition*.
3. See Philip J. Deloria, *Indians in Unexpected Places*; Berkhofer, *The White Man's Indian*; Williams, *Like a Loaded Weapon*.
4. Alfred, "Sovereignty," in Salisbury and Deloria, *A Companion to American Indian History*, 460.
5. Alfred, *Peace, Power, Righteousness*.
6. See Barker, *Sovereignty Matters*, and Alfred and Corntassel, "Being Indigenous."
7. Getches et al., *Federal Indian Law*; Williams, *Linking Arms Together*; Austin, *Navajo Courts and Navajo Common Law*.
8. Alfred, *Peace, Power, Righteousness*, 79.
9. Wilkins and Stark, *American Indian Politics*, 60.
10. See Lee, *Navajo Sovereignty*, and Lerma, *Guided by the Mountains*.
11. Robert B. Porter, "The Meaning of Indigenous Nation Sovereignty," 75–112.
12. Ibid., 101.
13. Ibid., 102.
14. Holm, Pearson, and Chavis, "Peoplehood," 7–24.
15. Other Indigenous peoples have similar concepts to those of the Hopis. See Hongeva, "Contention through Education," and Kaye, "An Examination of Hopimonmngwit." Also see Figueroa Helland, "Indigenous Philosophy and World Politics."
16. See Killsback, "Indigenous Perceptions of Time."
17. Petter, *English-Cheyenne Dictionary*, 238.
18. Ibid.
19. Grinnell spells it Nĭ-ŏm-a-hé-tăn-iu in "Some Early Cheyenne Tales," 169. Stands In Timber spells it Ni-oh-ma-até-anin-ya and translates it to mean "Prairie People" in Stands In Timber and Liberty, *Cheyenne Memories*, 15.

20. See Andrée et al., *Globalization and Food Sovereignty*; and "Indigenous Food Sovereignty."
21. See McNab, *Earth, Water, Air and Fire*; Salmón, *Eating the Landscape*; Dennis, "Starving for Justice."

CHAPTER 2

1. NAA MS 2828-f1, 1–3.
2. Marquis, *Wooden Leg*, 144.
3. NAA MS 2822, f1-f, 2.
4. Ibid.
5. NAA MS 2822, f1-g, 1–2.
6. NAA MS 2822, f1-h, 3.
7. Stands In Timber and Liberty, *A Cheyenne Voice*, 158, 192, 272–74.
8. Grinnell, "Coup and Scalp among the Plains Indians," 306–10.
9. NAA MS 2684-a, 42.
10. Leman, *Cheyenne Texts*, 6–8.
11. Grinnell, *By Cheyenne Campfires*, 257.
12. NAA MS 2799, f1, 1–2.
13. Stands In Timber and Liberty, *A Cheyenne Voice*, 16–17, 73, 93.
14. NAA MS 2704-b, 6; NAA MS 2828-f2, b, 1–4.
15. Penney, "Sweet Medicine and Standing-on-the-Ground," in *Tales of the Cheyennes*, 15–25; Grinnell, "Some Early Cheyenne Tales," 181–90.
16. Stands In Timber and Liberty, *Cheyenne Memories*, 84–86; Stands In Timber and Liberty, *A Cheyenne Voice*, 18–20; Grinnell, *Cheyenne Indians*, 1:277–90; Hoebel, *Cheyennes*, 68–70.
17. Schlesier identifies her as Mukije (Short Woman) in *Wolves of Heaven*, 54. I have also heard elders simply refer to her as kâse'éehe (young woman). See Leman, *Náévóo'ôhtséme*, 251–63.
18. Leman's informant Albert Hoffman identifies the animal as a deer, while Hoebel identifies the animal as a buffalo. Leman, *Cheyenne Texts*, 53–55; Hoebel, *The Cheyennes*, 45–46.
19. Tall Bull and Weist, *Winter Hunt*.
20. Marquis, *Wooden Leg*, 87.
21. Leman, *Náévóo'ôhtséme*, 93–94.

22. Hoebel, *Cheyennes*, 69.
23. Stands In Timber and Liberty, *A Cheyenne Voice*, 18–21; Grinnell, *Cheyenne Indians*, 1:277–90.
24. Schwartz, *Last Contrary*, 67.
25. Leman, *Náévóo'óhtséme*, 95.
26. Grinnell, *Cheyenne Indians*, 1:280.
27. Marquis, *Wooden Leg*, 88, 90.
28. Grinnell, *Cheyenne Indians*, 1:288; Hoebel, *Cheyennes*, 70.
29. Petter, *English-Cheyenne Dictionary*, 194.
30. They are known as "buffalo drives." NAA MS 2796, f2-d, 3.
31. Grinnell, *Cheyenne Indians*, 1:336–37; Grinnell, *By Cheyenne Campfires*, 271–74; Stands In Timber and Liberty, *Cheyenne Memories*, 37–38.
32. Schlesier, *Wolves of Heaven*, 55.
33. Stands In Timber and Liberty, *A Cheyenne Voice*, 16–17, 73, 92–93, 216–18, 252–53. Stands In Timber claims that the Buffalo Ceremony is of "Suhtai origin," since they were the first to acquire the flat, circular pipestone talisman.
34. Wolf Chief, White Eagle, White Buffalo, and Old She Bear each have versions of the origin of the Buffalo Ceremony. Respectively: NAA MS 2822, f1-c, 6–8; NAA MS 2811, f3, 4–7; NAA MS 2811, f4, 8–16; NAA MS 2811, f1, 5–11.
35. NAA MS 2822, f1-c, 6–8.
36. NAA MS 2811, f3-4 to f3-7.
37. NAA MS 2811, f4, 8–16.
38. NAA MS 2811, f1, 5–11.
39. Stands In Timber and Liberty, *A Cheyenne Voice*, 216–18.

CHAPTER 3

1. Erdoes and Ortiz, *American Indian Myths and Legends*, 34.
2. Ibid., 94–96, 110–11, 241, 409, 412–13, 416.
3. "Keepers" is a term that I chose to use for such highly ranked ceremonial positions. Other scholars (Hoebel, 1961; Grinnell, 1972; Llewellyn & Hoebel, 1941; Moore, 1996; Powell, 1969; Schlesier, 1987) refer to these sacred positions as "priesthoods" and thus refer to the "keepers" as "priests." "Priests" has a definition rooted in Christian cultures, and

NOTES

I did not want to perpetuate this or any other misinterpretation. Since the highest-ranking spiritual leaders of the Cheyenne people are called "keepers" (e.g., Hat Keeper, Medicine Arrow Keeper) it seems only appropriate that lower ranking spiritual leaders be referred to as such, especially the ancient ones.

4. Marquis, *Cheyennes of Montana*, 140.
5. Stands In Timber and Liberty, *Cheyenne Memories*, 100.
6. Grinnell, "Some Early Cheyenne Tales II," 270.
7. Stands In Timber and Liberty, *A Cheyenne Voice*, 179.
8. Schwartz, *Last Contrary*, 78.
9. Hoebel, *Cheyennes*, 14–18.
10. Stands In Timber and Liberty, *Cheyenne Memories*, 35–39; Grinnell, *Cheyenne Indians*, 2:368–69; Grinnell, *By Cheyenne Campfires*, 274–76.
11. Nóvávóse is the Cheyenne word for Bear Butte, which roughly translates to "where sacrifices are made and where gifts are given." George Bent refers to the mountain as "Medicine-pipe Mountain." Hyde and Lottinville, *Life of George Bent*, 53, 242.
12. Penney, *Tales of the Cheyennes*, 30.
13. Stands In Timber and Liberty, *A Cheyenne Voice*, 251, 310 (quote).
14. NAA MS 2799, f1-21 to f1-23.
15. Petter, *English-Cheyenne Dictionary*, 59–60.
16. Hoebel, *Cheyennes*, 17.
17. Grinnell, *Fighting Cheyennes*, 70; Grinnell, "The Great Mysteries of the Cheyenne," 542.
18. The Strangeowl family, in Erdoes and Ortiz, *American Indian Myths and Legends*, 203.
19. Marquis, *Wooden Leg*, 140.
20. Stands In Timber and Liberty, *A Cheyenne Voice*, 317.
21. Powell, *Sweet Medicine*, 43.
22. Dorsey, *Cheyenne: Sundance*, 11.
23. Michelson noted: "A sucking doctor will be the keeper of the medicine arrows or sun dance in general; in particular the keeper of the arrows is maihitan arrow man." NAA MS 3343, 14.
24. Stands In Timber and Liberty, *Cheyenne Memories*, 87.

25. Dorsey, *Cheyenne: Sundance*, 11–12.
26. Marquis, *Wooden Leg*, 141–42.
27. Dorsey, *Cheyenne: Sundance*; Powell, *Sweet Medicine*; Stands In Timber and Liberty, *A Cheyenne Voice*, 140–42, 202–5.
28. Marquis, *Wooden Leg*, 142–43.
29. Hoebel, *Cheyennes*, 18–23.
30. Stands In Timber and Liberty, *A Cheyenne Voice*, 140–42, 297, 409–11.
31. Ibid., 27–30.
32. NAA MS 2704-d, 7–10.
33. Stands In Timber and Liberty, *A Cheyenne Voice*, xxxvi.
34. Erdoes and Ortiz, *American Indian Myths and Legends*, 34–37.
35. Petter, *English-Cheyenne Dictionary*, 209.
36. Grinnell, *By Cheyenne Campfires*, 257–63.
37. Weist, *Belle Highwalking*, 41.
38. Stands In Timber and Liberty, *Cheyenne Memories*, 74.
39. Ibid., 74–75.
40. Grinnell, *Fighting Cheyennes*, 71.
41. Petter, *English-Cheyenne Dictionary*, 1028–30.
42. Michelson, "Narrative of a Southern Cheyenne Woman," 9.
43. Grinnell, *Cheyenne Indians*, 2:211–84.
44. Schwartz, *Last Contrary*, 70–77.
45. Happiness can be measured among American Indians based on decision-making styles and traditionalism, among other variables. See Beckstein, "The Relationship between Decision-Making Style and Self-Construal and the Subjective Happiness of Native Americans."
46. Petter, *English-Cheyenne Dictionary*, 804.
47. Stands In Timber and Liberty, *A Cheyenne Voice*, 31.
48. Hoebel, *Cheyennes*, 18–23; Stands In Timber and Liberty, *Cheyenne Memories*, 74–78.
49. Grinnell, *Cheyenne Indians*, 2:285–336; Schlesier, *Wolves of Heaven*, 88–109.
50. Kroeber, "Cheyenne Tales," 179–81; Grinnell, "Some Early Cheyenne Tales," 169–94.

NOTES

51. Penney, *Tales of the Cheyennes*, 8.
52. NAA MS 2684-a, 31–34.
53. Grinnell, "Some Early Cheyenne Tales," 169–94. Grinnell's spelling is Ē-hyōph'-sta.
54. Grinnell, *By Cheyenne Campfires*, 257.
55. Schlesier, *Wolves of Heaven*, 43.
56. Grinnell, *Cheyenne Indians*, 2:285–336.
57. Schwartz, *Last Contrary*, 67–70.
58. Stands In Timber and Liberty, *Cheyenne Memories*, 100–103.
59. Schlesier, *Wolves of Heaven*, 82; Grinnell, *Cheyenne Indians*, 2:335.
60. Schlesier, *Wolves of Heaven*, 99.
61. Stands In Timber and Liberty, *A Cheyenne Voice*, 71.
62. Petter, *English-Cheyenne Dictionary*, 335–36.
63. NAA MS 2684-a, 22.
64. Weist, *Belle Highwalking*, 40–41.
65. Ibid., 39–40.
66. NAA MS 2704-d, 10.

CHAPTER 4

1. Marquis, *Wooden Leg*, 123.
2. Stands In Timber and Liberty, *A Cheyenne Voice*, 51, 158.
3. Leman, *Náévóo'ôhtséme*, 210.
4. Ibid., 10.
5. Ibid., 775.
6. Ibid., 212.
7. Marquis, *Wooden Leg*, 37–39.
8. Petter, *English-Cheyenne Dictionary*, 627.
9. Marquis, *Wooden Leg*, 130.
10. Ibid., 137.
11. Ibid., 55.

CHAPTER 5

1. Stands In Timber and Liberty, *Cheyenne Memories*, 40.

NOTES

2. Grinnell, *Cheyenne Indians*, 1:102–26; Moore, *The Cheyenne*, 245–65 and *Cheyenne Nation*, 287–312; Hilger, "Notes on Cheyenne Child Life."
3. Leman, *Cheyenne Dictionary*; NAA MS 2684-a, 8–10; NAA MS 3188-b, 22.
4. Stands In Timber and Liberty, *A Cheyenne Voice*, 307. Other scholars have recorded that the Cheyennes had attributed unfavorable behavioral traits to "white blood," but this is a discussion for another time. See Straus, "Northern Cheyenne Ethnopsychology," 336.
5. NAA MS 3336.
6. NAA MS 2684-a, 40.
7. NAA MS 3218, 8.
8. NAA MS 2684-a, 50.
9. NAA MS 3218.
10. NAA MS 2684-a, 50.
11. Black Wolf provided some basic kinship rules that use teasing in NAA MS 2684-a, 11.
12. "In the Cheyenne system, a cross sibling-in-law is a man's brother's wife, man's wife's sister, woman's sister's husband, or woman's husband's brother. It can also be a man's sister's husband's sister." Leman, *Cheyenne Dictionary*, 355.
13. Ibid., NAA MS 2684-a, 39–40.
14. NAA MS 2684-a, 39–40.
15. NAA MS 3188-b, 31–32.
16. NAA MS 2684-a, 6.
17. Stands In Timber and Liberty, *A Cheyenne Voice*, 307.
18. NAA MS 3218, 23.

CHAPTER 6

1. NAA MS 3220-j, 9.
2. Robert Odawi Porter, *Sovereignty, Colonialism, and the Indigenous Nations*, 3.
3. Ibid.
4. Lyons, "Law, Principle, and Reality," 209.
5. Williams, *The American Indian in Western Legal Thought*; Echo-Hawk, *In the Courts of the Conqueror*; Echo-Hawk and Anaya, *In the Light of*

Justice; Wilkins, *American Indian Sovereignty*; Getches et al., *Federal Indian Law*.

6. Stands In Timber and Liberty, *A Cheyenne Voice*, 306.
7. NAA MS 3188-b, 70–71.
8. I provide some laws based on my own knowledge as a practitioner of ceremonies and member of ceremonial guilds and societies but also provide some recorded by previous authors. See examples from Moore, *Cheyenne*, 324–25.
9. NAA MS 3220-j, 9.
10. NAA MS 3343, 13.
11. NAA MS 3218, 17–18.
12. NAA MS 3220-j, 1.
13. Marquis, *Wooden Leg*, 3–4.
14. Marquis, *Wooden Leg*, 3–4.
15. Marquis, *Cheyennes of Montana*, 171; Marquis, *Wooden Leg*, 372–73.
16. NAA MS 2684-a, 43.
17. Ibid., 42.
18. Marquis, *Wooden Leg*, 3.
19. Hyde and Lottinville, *Life of George Bent*, 297.
20. Hoebel, *Cheyennes*, 98.
21. Marquis, *Wooden Leg*, 74.
22. Grinnell, *Cheyenne Indians*, 1:129–31; Grinnell, "Cheyenne Woman Customs," 13–16.
23. NAA MS 2684-a, 43.
24. NAA MS 3338, 5–6.
25. NAA MS 3188-b, 71–72.
26. Grinnell, *Cheyenne Indians*, 1:121–22.
27. Marquis, *Wooden Leg*, 76–77.
28. NAA MS 2684-a, 44.
29. Bonnerjea, "Reminiscences of a Cheyenne Indian," 134–35. Red Eagle had a Cheyenne mother and a white father. His English name was Thomas Otterby.
30. Grinnell, *Cheyenne Indians*, 1:91

31. Hyde and Lottinville, *Life of George Bent*, 335.

CHAPTER 7

1. NAA MS 3218, 18–23.
2. Marquis, *Wooden Leg*, 215.
3. Grinnell, *The Cheyenne Indians*, 1:125.
4. Hyde and Lottinville, *Life of George Bent*, 76.
5. NAA MS 3338, 2.
6. Grinnell, *Cheyenne Indians*, 1:116–20.
7. Ibid., 1:66; Petter, *English-Cheyenne Dictionary*, 729.
8. Stands In Timber and Liberty, *A Cheyenne Voice*, 13. In this work, Stands In Timber uses an offensive word used to degrade Indian people, starting with the letter "s."
9. Ibid., 47, 306.
10. NAA MS 2822-f1, f, 3.
11. NAA MS 3355, card 39; NAA MS 3338, 3.
12. NAA MS 3188-b, 66.
13. NAA MS 2684-a, 5.
14. Stands In Timber and Liberty, *A Cheyenne Voice*, 116–19.
15. Grinnell, *The Cheyenne Indians*, 1:131–37.
16. NAA MS 2684-a, 50.
17. Ibid., 5.
18. Grinnell, *The Cheyenne Indians*, 1:137–53.
19. NAA MS 3188-b, 48.
20. Michelson, "The Narrative of a Southern Cheyenne Woman," 4–5.
21. Weist, *Belle Highwalking*, 13.
22. Marquis, *Wooden Leg*, 94–95.
23. Grinnell, *Cheyenne Indians*, 1:92–96; Moore, *Cheyenne Nation*, 251–85.
24. NAA MS 3218, 18–23.
25. Marquis, *Wooden Leg*, 92–94.
26. Michelson, "Narrative of a Southern Cheyenne Woman," 6–7.
27. Ibid., 8.

28. NAA MS 2822, f1-f, 4–5.
29. Weist, *Belle Highwalking*, 14.
30. NAA MS 3338, 3–4.
31. Stands In Timber and Liberty, *A Cheyenne Voice*, 45–46, 148.
32. Bonnerjea, "Reminiscences of a Cheyenne Indian," 138.
33. NAA MS 2811-f1, 14.
34. NAA MS 2684-a, 6–7.
35. NAA MS 2822, F1-f, 3.
36. NAA MS 2684-a, 38.
37. Marquis, *Wooden Leg*, 95.
38. Grinnell, *Cheyenne Indians*, 1:95–96.
39. Marquis, *Wooden Leg*, 366–69.
40. Grinnell, *Cheyenne Indians*, 1:153–54; Hoebel, *Cheyennes*, 34, 101–2; Llewellyn and Hoebel, *Cheyenne Way*, 186–87.
41. Llewellyn and Hoebel, *Cheyenne Way*, 187.
42. NAA MS 3188-b, 33.
43. Ibid.
44. Marquis, *Wooden Leg*, 96. Wooden Leg states, "Her husband might inflict some penalty. That was permissible, but he was not conceded the right to kill her. I knew one man who cut a great gash in his wife's forehead because of her going with another man." Modern spiritual leaders, men and women, all agreed that the physical harm of women was completely unacceptable.
45. Bonnerjea, "Reminiscences of a Cheyenne Indian," 141.
46. Marquis, *Cheyennes of Montana*, 62.
47. Marquis, *Wooden Leg*, 96–97.
48. NAA MS 3218, 112.
49. Leman, *A Reference Grammar*, 155. Hoebel, *Cheyennes*, 44.
50. Llewellyn and Hoebel, *Cheyenne Way*, 201–2.
51. Stands In Timber and Liberty, *A Cheyenne Voice*, 148; Marquis, *Wooden Leg*, 97; NAA MS 2822, f1-f, 3.
52. The original translation is fragmented. I pieced it together. NAA MS 2798, 4–11.

NOTES

CHAPTER 8

1. Told by the "Strange Owl family in Lame Deer, Montana in 1967," recorded in Erdoes and Ortiz, *American Indian Myths and Legends*, 204.
2. The most popular studies of Cheyenne law are fraught with abrasive interpretations and racist implications. Many of these studies, although commendable for their ethnohistorical record, utilize mainstream methods and interpretations through white perspectives of law, history, and cultural studies. My approach is rooted in the Cheyenne worldviews, oral traditions, and spiritual teachings discussed in previous chapters. Despite the flaws of earlier studies, they do provide some insights of significant value, especially to the goals of this chapter. See Llewellyn and Hoebel, *The Cheyenne Way*; Hoebel, *Cheyennes*; Hoebel, *Law of Primitive Man*.
3. Marquis, *Cheyennes of Montana*, 147–48.
4. As in the case of Lone Wolf in Llewellyn and Hoebel, *Cheyenne Way*, 153.
5. Marquis, *Wooden Leg*, 80.
6. Hoebel, *Cheyennes*, 46.
7. Llewellyn and Hoebel, *Cheyenne Way*, 61, 321.
8. Marquis, *Wooden Leg*, 103.
9. Ibid., 97.
10. Brown, *The Sacred Pipe*; Williams, *Linking Arms Together*.
11. Petter, *English-Cheyenne Dictionary*, 422.
12. Penney, *Tales of the Cheyennes*, viii.
13. Lame Deer and Erdoes, *Lame Deer, Seeker of Visions*, 273–78.
14. NAA MS 2822, f2-e, 1–3.
15. Nearly every author of Cheyenne studies elaborated on the complexities and sanctity of the law. See Llewellyn and Hoebel, *Cheyenne Way*, 130–66; Hoebel, *Cheyennes*, 16, 55; Grinnell, *Cheyenne Indians*, 1:349–58.
16. Stands In Timber and Liberty, *A Cheyenne Voice*, 110–11.
17. Marquis, *Wooden Leg*, 102–3.
18. Ibid., 110.
19. Ibid., 110–11.
20. Llewellyn and Hoebel provide examples of accidental murders resulting from imbibing alcohol (*Cheyenne Way*, 137–38). Alcohol

NOTES

overconsumption became a major problem for the Cheyenne. Wooden Leg's examples do not involve alcohol, which reveal the consistency and thought that the chiefs employed when making rulings in such cases.

21. Marquis, *Wooden Leg*, 111–13.
22. Ibid., 104.
23. Stands In Timber and Liberty, *Cheyenne Memories*, 44.
24. Marquis, *Cheyennes of Montana*, 88.
25. White Bull/Ice was wrongfully expelled from Crazy Dogs for his uncle's accidental shooting, in which no one was killed. He later joined the Crooked Lance or Bone Scraper Society. Hyde and Lottinville, *Life of George Bent*, 336.
26. Stands In Timber and Liberty, *Cheyenne Memories*, 44.
27. Stands In Timber and Liberty, *A Cheyenne Voice*, 25, 98.
28. Marquis, *Wooden Leg*, 105–7.
29. Grinnell, *Cheyenne Indians*, 1:254–55.
30. Llewellyn and Hoebel, *Cheyenne Way*, 149.
31. Grinnell, *Cheyenne Indians*, 1:356
32. Llewellyn and Hoebel, *Cheyenne Way*, 165–68.
33. Marquis, *Wooden Leg*, 115–16.
34. Ibid., 9–12.
35. Llewellyn and Hoebel, *Cheyenne Way*, 9–10.
36. Hoebel, *Cheyennes*, 58–59, 69; Llewellyn and Hoebel, *Cheyenne Way*, 112–13.
37. Marquis, *Wooden Leg*, 67–68.
38. Ibid., 67.
39. Ibid., 69.
40. The origin and lesson of the practice is found in a traditional story told by Laura Rockroads in Leman, *Náévóo'óhtséme*, 264–74. Also see Weist, *Belle Highwalking*, 8–9 and NAA MS 2134, 14–7.
41. NAA MS 2134, 14–17.
42. NAA MS 3219, f2, 20–23.
43. A single recorded incident of an alleged abortion is recorded in Llewellyn and Hoebel, *Cheyenne Way*, 118–19. The old Cheyennes knew of a plant that induced miscarriage in case of rape and incest; however, the

practice of abortion was a private and personal matter and was likely performed in secrecy with the assistance of the older women, possibly medicine women.

44. Llewellyn and Hoebel, *Cheyenne Way*, 178–79.

45. Ibid., 206–8.

46. Ibid., 202–8.

47. Llewellyn and Hoebel, *Cheyenne Way*, 202–10.

48. Ibid., 209.

49. Only recently have there been studies published that examine sexual violence in Native America and provide practical solutions to persisting challenges. See Deer, *The Beginning and End of Rape* and Fulton, "Ending Sexual Violence Against American Indian Women."

50. Hoebel, *Cheyennes*, 102.

51. Llewellyn and Hoebel, *Cheyenne Way*, 210. Grinnell also indicated that the concept was evident in wars against other nations, in particular as a means to expunge bad luck as when Long Chin "pledged to give a woman to be passed on the prairie" as a remedy to his blunder in breaking a tie on the Sacred Hat while he prepared for war against the Pawnees in 1853 (Grinnell, *Fighting Cheyennes*, 92). This is the only account of such a pledge, which leads me to believe that the account is untrustworthy.

52. Ibid., 202–8.

53. Hoebel, *Cheyennes*, 102.

54. NAA MS 3342, 15.

55. Cheyenne words that end in –oom and –om denote "the place covered, surrounded by, a precinct, sphere, region, area, time period." See Petter, *English-Cheyenne Dictionary*, 666.

56. Straus, "Northern Cheyenne Ethnopsychology."

57. NAA MS 3188-b, 72.

58. Grinnell, *Cheyenne Indians*, 2:91–92.

59. Petter, *English-Cheyenne Dictionary*, 534.

60. Marquis, *Wooden Leg*, 98–101.

61. Schlesier, *Wolves of Heaven*, 4–11; Hoebel, *Cheyennes*, 87–88. Both authors provide their own description of the Cheyenne worldview using similar concepts.

62. Petter, *English-Cheyenne Dictionary*, 543.

NOTES

63. Marquis, *Wooden Leg*, 155.
64. Ibid., 374.
65. Stands In Timber and Liberty, *Cheyenne Memories*, 87.

PART III

1. NAA MS 2811, f-1, 2–5.

CHAPTER 9

1. Marquis, *Wooden Leg*, 159.
2. NAA MS 2704-b, 6; NAA MS 2828-f2, b, 1–4.
3. Marquis, *Wooden Leg*, 159.
4. NAA MS 2822, F1, e, 1-2
5. Ibid., e, 1–2.
6. Ibid., f1, c, 12.
7. Ibid., 20.
8. NAA MS 2822, f1, c, 18.
9. Ibid., a, 21.
10. NAA MS 2811, f3, 9–11.
11. NAA MS 2822, f1, c, 20–21.
12. Ibid., f1, c, 18–19.
13. Ibid., 21.
14. Ibid., 11.
15. Ibid., 18.
16. Sutter, *Tell Me, Grandmother*, 70.
17. Ibid., 6.
18. Stands In Timber and Liberty, *A Cheyenne Voice*, 192.
19. NAA MS 2822, f1, c, 21.
20. Ibid., 19.
21. NAA MS 3218, 4–6.
22. Stands In Timber and Liberty, *Cheyenne Memories*, 89; Stands In Timber and Liberty, *A Cheyenne Voice*, 250.
23. Stands In Timber and Liberty, *Cheyenne Memories*, 81; Stands In Timber and Liberty, *A Cheyenne Voice*, 73.

NOTES

24. NAA MS 3218, 6–7.
25. Dorsey, *Arapaho Sundance*, 23.
26. Stands In Timber and Liberty, *A Cheyenne Voice*, 202–3.
27. Marquis, *Wooden Leg*, 143.
28. Stands In Timber and Liberty, *Cheyenne Memories*, 99.
29. Sutter, *Tell Me, Grandmother*, 70–71.
30. Grinnell, *Fighting Cheyennes*, 5.
31. Bass, *The Arapaho Way*, 3.
32. Grinnell, *Cheyenne Indians*, 1:354.
33. Stands In Timber and Liberty, *Cheyenne Memories*, 40, 117; Grinnell, "Some Early Cheyenne Tales," 319–20; Leman, *Náévóo'ôhtséme*, 6–7; Leman, *Cheyenne Texts*, 4–5.
34. Stands In Timber and Liberty, *A Cheyenne Voice*, 98.
35. Hyde and Lottinville, *Life of George Bent*, 21.
36. Stands In Timber and Liberty, *A Cheyenne Voice*, 311.
37. Hyde and Lottinville, *Life of George Bent*, 33–34.
38. NAA MS 2811, Grasshopper (f1, c, 18), White Eagle (f3, 1–2).
39. Stands In Timber and Liberty, *Cheyenne Memories*, 117–18; Stands In Timber and Liberty, *A Cheyenne Voice*, 73, 75–76.
40. Tallbull, "We are the Ancestors of those yet to be Born."
41. Moore, *Cheyenne Nation*, 130–31; Mooney, "The Aboriginal Population of America North of Mexico," 13.
42. Petter, *English-Cheyenne Dictionary*, 627.
43. Stands In Timber and Liberty, *Cheyenne Memories*, 125.
44. Marquis, *Wooden Leg*, 78–79.
45. Ibid., 61.
46. Petter, *English-Cheyenne Dictionary*, 627.
47. Marquis, *Wooden Leg*, 65–66.
48. Petter, *English-Cheyenne Dictionary*, 627.
49. Leman, *Cheyenne Texts*, 32–38.

CHAPTER 10

1. NAA MS 3218, 7–8.

NOTES

2. Mails, *Fools Crow*, 14–15.
3. Hyde, *Spotted Tail's Folk*, 4.
4. *Legends of the Mighty Sioux, Compiled by Workers of the South Dakota Writer's Project, Work Projects Administration* (Chicago: Albert Whitman & Company, 1941), 45–46.
5. Hyde, *Red Cloud's Folk*, 24.
6. Hyde and Lottinville, *Life of George Bent*, 22.
7. Hyde and Lottinville, *Life of George Bent*, 13; NAA MS 2822, f1, c, 1, 12.
8. NAA MS 2811, f-1, 2–5.
9. NAA MS 2828, a-2.
10. Grinnell, *Cheyenne Indians*, 1:32.
11. NAA MS 2822, f1-1; f3, 1–2.
12. Stands In Timber and Liberty, *Cheyenne Memories*, 119–20; Grinnell, *Cheyenne Indians*, 1:32–33.
13. Stands In Timber and Liberty, *A Cheyenne Voice*, 71–72.
14. NAA MS 3218, 7–8.
15. Neihardt, *Black Elk Speaks*, 10.
16. Stands In Timber and Liberty, *A Cheyenne Voice*, 213, 332–33, 354.
17. Standing Bear, *My People the Sioux*, 113.
18. Lame Deer and Erdoes, *Lame Deer, Seeker of Visions*, 199, 201, 204.
19. Eastman, *Soul of the Indian*, 56–57.
20. Erdoes and Ortiz, *American Indian Myths and Legends*, 47.
21. Ibid., 51–52.
22. Stands In Timber and Liberty, *A Cheyenne Voice*, 355.
23. Ibid., 254.
24. Standing Bear, *Land of the Spotted Eagle*, 222–23.
25. Mails, *Fools Crow*, 255.
26. DeMallie, *The Sixth Grandfather*, 315.
27. Marquis, *Wooden Leg*, 121–22.
28. Ibid., 13.
29. Leman, *Náévóo'óhtséme*, 382–83.

NOTES

CHAPTER II

1. Mails, *Fools Crow*, 55.
2. Grinnell, *Fighting Cheyennes*, 357.
3. Standing Bear, *Land of the Spotted Eagle*, 185.
4. Standing Bear, *My People the Sioux*, 75–76.
5. Marquis, *Wooden Leg*, 18–19.
6. Hyde and Lottinville, *Life of George Bent*, 221.
7. Ibid., 296.
8. NAA MS 2684-a, 43.
9. Stands In Timber and Liberty, *A Cheyenne Voice*, 244.
10. Marquis, *Cheyennes of Montana*, 60.
11. NAA MS 2684-a, 42.
12. Hyde and Lottinville, *Life of George Bent*, 296.
13. Hyde and Lottinville, *Life of George Bent*, 90–92; Grinnell, *Fighting Cheyennes*, 75–78.
14. Grinnell, *Fighting Cheyennes*, 94.
15. Ibid., 96.
16. Stands In Timber and Liberty, *A Cheyenne Voice*, 265.
17. Marquis, *Keep the Last Bullet*, 64.
18. Marquis, *Wooden Leg*, 85; Marquis, *Keep the Last Bullet*, 64.
19. Marquis, *Keep the Last Bullet*, 61–62.
20. Ibid., 59–60.
21. Marquis, *Wooden Leg*, 199.
22. Ibid., 91.
23. Hyde and Lottinville, *Life of George Bent*, 189.
24. Grinnell, *Cheyenne Indians*, 2:30–31.
25. Marquis, *Wooden Leg*, 245.
26. Stands In Timber and Liberty, *A Cheyenne Voice*, 266.
27. Hyde and Lottinville, *Life of George Bent*, 47–48.
28. NAA MS 3336, 17.
29. Williams, *Linking Arms Together*, 40–47.

30. Standing Bear, *Land of the Spotted Eagle*, 202–3.
31. Marquis, *Wooden Leg*, 322; Lame Deer and Erdoes, *Lame Deer, Seeker of Visions*, 271.
32. Mails, *Fools Crow*, 55.
33. Hyde, *Red Cloud's Folk*, 32.
34. Grinnell, *Cheyenne Indians*, 2:6.
35. Grinnell, *Fighting Cheyennes*, 102.
36. Marquis, *Keep the Last Bullet*, 67.
37. Grinnell, *Cheyenne Indians*, 2:12–13. Sometimes warrior society leaders had to endure self-torture and ceremonial practices before setting out on a war party.
38. Ibid., 10–11.
39. Hyde, *Red Cloud's Folk*, 32.
40. Hyde and Lottinville, *Life of George Bent*, 168.

CHAPTER 12

1. Stands In Timber and Liberty, *A Cheyenne Voice*, 91.
2. Ibid., 72.
3. Moore, *Cheyenne*, 90.
4. Hyde and Lottinville, *Life of George Bent*, 72–75; Grinnell, *Fighting Cheyennes*, 45–48.
5. Grinnell, *Cheyenne Indians*, 2:3.
6. Jablow, *Cheyenne in Plains Indian Trade*, 18.
7. Grinnell, *Cheyenne Indians*, 1:29.
8. Stands In Timber and Liberty, *A Cheyenne Voice*, 353.
9. Ibid., 264.
10. Tall Bull, "We are the Ancestors of those yet to be Born."
11. Grinnell, *Cheyenne Indians*, 1:58–59.
12. Stands In Timber and Liberty, *A Cheyenne Voice*, 378.
13. Ibid., 354.
14. Ibid., 91.
15. Ibid., 86, 264, 366–67, 378–82, 440–42, 455–58.
16. Ibid., 381–82.

17. NAA MS 2684-a, 3.
18. Hyde and Lottinville, *Life of George Bent*, 339.
19. Ibid., 334.
20. NAA MS 2684-a, 4.
21. Hyde and Lottinville, *Life of George Bent*, 339.
22. Ibid., 140.
23. Grinnell, *Cheyenne Indians*, 1:32.
24. Marquis, *Wooden Leg*, 91.
25. Hyde and Lottinville, *Life of George Bent*, 296.
26. There were several accounts of the Cheyennes "moving the arrows" against enemies. See Grinnell, "The Great Mysteries of the Cheyenne," 542.
27. NAA MS 2704, a, 9.
28. Hyde and Lottinville, *Life of George Bent*, 50.
29. Grinnell, *Fighting Cheyennes*, 72.
30. Moore, *Cheyenne*, 133–34.
31. Grinnell, *Fighting Cheyennes*, 45–62; Hyde and Lottinville, *Life of George Bent*, 78–82.
32. Grinnell, *By Cheyenne Campfires*, 277.
33. Marquis, *Wooden Leg*, 70–73.
34. For war stories see Grinnell, *By Cheyenne Campfires*, 3–77.
35. Jablow, *Cheyenne in Plains Indian Trade*, 47–49.
36. Stands In Timber and Liberty, *Cheyenne Memories*, 142, 158.
37. Petter, *English-Cheyenne Dictionary*, 480.
38. NAA MS 2811, f1, 12.
39. Hyde and Lottinville, *Life of George Bent*, 138.
40. Hyde, *Pawnee Indians*, 174.
41. Hyde, *Spotted Tail's Folk*, 31; Hyde, *Pawnee Indians*, 180–87.
42. Grinnell, *Fighting Cheyennes*, 206–7.
43. Hyde, *Pawnee Indians*, 313–14.
44. Stands In Timber identifies these warriors as Crazy Dogs, while Bent identifies them as Bowstrings, and Grinnell identifies them as Crooked Lances. Modern Northern Cheyenne informants assert that whatever

the society, it was completely annihilated and reestablished some forty years later. Stands In Timber and Liberty, *Cheyenne Memories,* 128–30; Hyde and Lottinville, *Life of George Bent,* 24–26; Grinnell, *Fighting Cheyennes,* 25–26.

45. Hyde and Lottinville, *Life of George Bent,* 28–30.
46. Marquis, *Wooden Leg,* 354–55.
47. Stands In Timber and Liberty, *Cheyenne Memories,* 136–37.

PART IV

1. NAA MS 2811, f3, 11.
2. Petter, *English-Cheyenne Dictionary,* 424.

CHAPTER 13

1. Stands In Timber, *Cheyenne Memories,* 161.
2. Hoebel, *The Cheyennes,* 108–9.
3. Grinnell, *The Cheyenne Indians,* 11, 33–34.
4. Vine Deloria Jr., "A Redefinition of Indian Affairs," 312.
5. Hyde and Lottinville, *Life of George Bent,* 106–7.
6. Hyde and Lottinville, *Life of George Bent,* 108–9.
7. Marquis, *Wooden Leg,* 172–74.
8. Schrems, "The Northern Cheyennes," 27.
9. Vine Deloria Jr., *Custer Died for Your Sins,* 51. See also Chamberlain, *Decolonization.*
10. Grinnell, *The Cheyenne Indians,* 2:381.
11. Conrad Fisher, in Killsback, *The Chiefs' Prophecy* (DVD).
12. Weist, *History of the Cheyenne People,* 106.
13. Marquis, *Wooden Leg,* 371–72.
14. Marquis, *Cheyennes of Montana,* 107.
15. Ibid., 239–40n6.
16. Crow Dog, *Lakota Woman,* 31.
17. Marquis, *Cheyennes of Montana,* 239.
18. Weist, *History of the Cheyenne People,* 107.
19. Conrad Fisher, in Killsback, *The Chiefs' Prophecy* (DVD).
20. See Stands In Timber, *Cheyenne Memories,* 270n1.

21. Weist, *History of the Cheyenne People*, 123.
22. Fisher, in Killsback, *The Chiefs' Prophecy* (DVD).
23. Stands In Timber and Liberty, *Cheyenne Memories*, 244–49.
24. Ibid., 243.
25. Allan Jo Black Wolf, in Killsback, *The Chiefs' Prophecy* (DVD).
26. Stands In Timber and Liberty, *Cheyenne Memories*, 250.
27. Collier, *Indians of the Americas*, 137.
28. Ibid.
29. Powell, *Sweet Medicine*, 1:320.
30. Threats were made against Enemy Captive and his wife for speaking out against traditional Cheyenne spiritual practices. Powell, *Sweet Medicine*, 1:346.
31. Butin to Commissioner of Indian Affairs, March 17, 1919. Cited in Powell, *Sweet Medicine*, 1:349.
32. See Taylor, *The New Deal and American Indian Tribalism*.
33. Deloria and Lytle, *The Nations Within*, 59.
34. Calloway, *First Peoples*, 446.
35. Rusco, "The Indian Reorganization Act and Indian Self-government," 50–52.
36. Wilkins and Stark, *American Indian Politics*, 66–68.
37. Ibid., 64.
38. Ibid.
39. Killsback, *The Chiefs' Prophecy* (DVD).
40. Ibid.
41. Pommersheim, *Braid of Feathers*, 65.
42. Champagne, *Social Change and Cultural Continuity*, 294.

CONCLUSION

1. Harjo, *Nation to Nation*, 11.

Bibliography and Suggested Readings

The editors of Akwesasne Notes. *Basic Call to Consciousness.* Summertown, TN: Native Voices, 2005.

Alfred, Taiaiake. *Peace, Power, Righteousness: An Indigenous Manifesto.* 2nd ed. New York: Oxford University Press, 2009.

———. *Wasáse: Indigenous Pathways of Action and Freedom.* Toronto: University of Toronto Press, Higher Education Division, 2005.

Alfred, Taiaiake, and Jeff Corntassel. "Being Indigenous: Resurgences against Contemporary Colonialism." *Government and Opposition* 40(4): 597–614.

Andrée, Peter, Michael J. Bosia, Jeffrey McKelvey Ayres, and Marie-Josée Massicotte. *Globalization and Food Sovereignty: Global and Local Change in the New Politics of Food.* Toronto: University of Toronto Press, 2014.

Austin, Raymond D. *Navajo Courts and Navajo Common Law: A Tradition of Tribal Self-Governance.* Minneapolis: University of Minnesota Press, 2009.

Banyaca, Thomas. "Essence of Hopi Prophecy." Unpublished manuscript, 1994. http://tierra-y-vida.blogspot.com/2007/12/hopi-declaration-of-peace-essence-of.html.

Barker, Joanne, ed. *Sovereignty Matters: Locations of Contestation and Possibility in Indigenous Struggles for Self-Determination.* Lincoln: University of Nebraska Press, 2006.

Bass, Althea. *The Arapaho Way: A Memoir of Indian Boyhood.* New York: Clarkson N. Potter, 1966.

Beckstein, Amoneeta. "The Relationship between Decision-Making Style and Self-Construal and the Subjective Happiness of Native Americans." PhD dissertation, Arizona State University, 2015.

Berkhofer, Robert F., Jr. *The White Man's Indian: Images of the American Indian from Columbus to Present.* New York: Random House, 1978.

Berthrong, Donald J. *The Cheyenne and Arapaho Ordeal: Reservation and Agency Life in the Indian Territory, 1875–1907.* Norman: University of Oklahoma Press, 1976.

———. *The Southern Cheyennes*. Norman: University of Oklahoma Press, 1986.

Bonnerjea, Biren. "Reminiscences of a Cheyenne Indian." *Journal de la Société des Américanistes* 27, no. 1 (1935): 129–43.

Brown, Joseph E., ed. *The Sacred Pipe: Black Elk's Account of the Seven Rites of the Oglala Sioux*. Norman: University of Oklahoma Press, 1989.

Bureau of American Ethnology, Smithsonian Institution. *Annual report of the Bureau of American Ethnology to the Secretary of the Smithsonian Institution, 1895*, vol. 24 (1902–03), 442–43. http://archive.org/stream/annualreportof-bu24smit/annualreportofbu24smit_djvu.txt.

Calloway, Colin G. *First Peoples: A Documentary Survey of American Indian History*. 5th ed. New York: Bedford/St. Martin's, 2016.

Chamberlain, M. E. *Decolonization*. 2nd ed. Malden, MA: Blackwell, 1999.

Champagne, Duane. *Social Change and Cultural Continuity among Native Nations*. Lanham, MD: Altamira Press, 2007.

The Chiefs' Prophecy: Survival of the Northern Cheyenne Nation, DVD. Directed by Leo Killsback. 2009, Tucson, AZ: Arizona Public Media.

Coffey, Wallace, and Rebecca Tsosie. "Rethinking the Tribal Sovereignty Doctrine: Cultural Sovereignty and the Collective Future of the Indian Nations." *Stanford Law and Policy Review* 12, no. 2 (2001): 191–221.

Collier, John. *Indians of the Americas: A Long Hope*. New York: New American Library, 1975.

Cook-Lynn, Elizabeth, and James Riding In. "Editors' Commentary," *Wicazo Sa Review* 19, no. 1, American Indian Encounters with Lewis and Clark (Spring 2004): 5–10.

Crow Dog, Mary, and Richard Erdoes. *Lakota Woman*. New York: Harper Perennial, 1991.

Deer, Sarah. *The Beginning and End of Rape: Confronting Sexual Violence in Native America*. Minneapolis: University of Minnesota Press, 2015.

Deloria, Philip J. *Indians in Unexpected Places*. Lawrence: University Press of Kansas, 2004.

Deloria, Vine, Jr. *Custer Died for Your Sins: An Indian Manifesto*. Norman: University of Oklahoma Press, 1969.

———. *Evolution, Creationism, and Other Modern Myths: A Critical Inquiry*. Golden, CO: Fulcrum Publishing, 2002.

———. *God Is Red: A Native View of Religion*. Golden, CO: Fulcrum Publishing, 1992.

———. *Red Earth, White Lies: Native Americans and the Myth of Scientific Fact.* Golden, CO: Fulcrum Publishing, 1997.

———. "A Redefinition of Indian Affairs." In *Image and Event: America Now.* David Bicknell and Richard Brengle, eds. New York: Appleton-Century-Crofts, 1971, 303–15.

Deloria, Vine, Jr., and Clifford Lytle. *American Indians, American Justice.* Austin: University of Texas Press, 1983.

———. *The Nations Within: The Past and Future of American Indian Sovereignty.* Austin: University of Texas Press, 1984.

DeMallie, Raymond J., ed. *The Sixth Grandfather: Black Elk's Teachings Given to John G. Neihardt.* Lincoln: University of Nebraska Press, 1985.

Dennis, Matthew R. "Starving for Justice: Reading the Relationship between Food and Criminal Justice through Creative Works of the Black Community." Master's thesis, Arizona State University, 2017.

Diné Bi Beenahaz'áanii (1 N.N.C. §§ 201-206), http://www.navajocourts.org/dine.htm.

Dorsey, George A. *The Arapaho Sundance: The Ceremony of the Offerings Lodge.* Field Columbian Museum Publication 75, Anthropological Series, vol. 4 (June 1903).

———. *The Cheyenne: Sundance.* Anthropological Series 9, no. 1. Chicago: Field Columbian Museum, 1905.

Driver, Harold. *Indians of North America.* 2nd ed. Chicago: University of Chicago Press, 1975.

Eastman, Charles A. *The Soul of the Indian: An Interpretation.* Boston: Houghton Mifflin Co., 1911

Echo-Hawk, Walter R. *In the Courts of the Conqueror: The 10 Worst Indian Law Cases Ever Decided.* Golden, CO: Fulcrum Publishing, 2010.

Echo-Hawk, Walter R., and James Anaya. *In the Light of Justice: The Rise of Human Rights in Native America and the UN Declaration on the Rights of Indigenous People.* Golden, CO: Fulcrum Publishing, 2013.

Erdoes, Richard, and Alfonso Ortiz, eds. *American Indian Myths and Legends.* New York: Pantheon Books, 1984.

Fanon, Frantz. *The Wretched of the Earth.* New York: Grove Press, 1963.

Fields, Jerry, and Barbara Mann. "A Sign in the Sky: Dating the League of the Haudenosaunee." *American Indian Culture and Research Journal* 21, no. 2 (1997): 105–63.

Figueroa Helland, Leonardo E. "Indigenous Philosophy and World Politics:

Cosmopolitical Contributions from Across the Americas." PhD dissertation, Arizona State University, 2012.

Fisher, Eugene, interpreter. "Cheyenne Indian Lore Related by Holy Bird and Yellow Nose, Tribal Historians." Conference between Grant A. Solberg and Members of the Cheyenne Indian Tribe. September 28, 1939. Unpublished manuscript.

Fulton, Madison. "Ending Sexual Violence Against American Indian Women: A Diné Woman's Perspective on Renewing Concepts of Justice on Tribal Lands." Master's thesis, Arizona State University, 2015.

Getches, David, et al. *Federal Indian Law: Cases and Materials.* 7th ed. St. Paul, MN: West Academic Publishing, 2017.

Grande, Sandy. *Red Pedagogy: Native American Social and Political Thought.* Lanham, MD: Rowman & Littlefield, 2004.

Green, Candace S., and Russell Thornton, eds. *The Years the Stars Fell: Lakota Winter Counts at the Smithsonian.* Lincoln: University of Nebraska Press, 2007.

Green, Jerome A. *Battles and Skirmishes of the Great Sioux War, 1876–1877.* Norman: University of Oklahoma Press, 1996.

———. *Lakota and Cheyenne: Indian Views of the Great Sioux War, 1876–1877.* Norman: University of Oklahoma Press, 2000.

———. *Morning Star Dawn: The Powder River Expedition and the Northern Cheyennes, 1876.* Norman: University of Oklahoma Press, 2003.

———. *Washita: The U.S. Army and the Southern Cheyennes, 1867–1869.* Norman: University of Oklahoma Press, 2008.

Grinnell, George Bird. *By Cheyenne Campfires.* Lincoln: University of Nebraska Press, 1962.

———. *The Cheyenne Indians.* 2 vols. Lincoln: University of Nebraska Press, 1972.

———. "Cheyenne Woman Customs." *American Anthropologist*, New Series, vol. 4, no. 1 (1902): 13–16.

———."Coup and Scalp among the Plains Indians." *American Anthropologist*, New Series, vol. 12, no 2 (1910): 296–310.

———. "Early Cheyenne Villages." *American Anthropologist*, New Series, vol. 20, no. 4 (1918): 359–80.

———. *The Fighting Cheyennes.* Lincoln: University of Nebraska Press, 1955.

———. "The Great Mysteries of the Cheyenne." *American Anthropologist*, New Series, vol. 12, no. 4 (1910): 542–75.

———. "Some Early Cheyenne Tales." *Journal of American Folklore* 20, no. 78 (1907): 169–94.

———."Some Early Cheyenne Tales. II." *Journal of American Folklore* 21, no. 82 (1908): 269–320.

Harjo, Suzan S. *Nation to Nation: Treaties Between the United States and American Indian Nations*. New York: National Museum of the American Indian and Smithsonian Books, 2014.

Harry, Debra. "Biocolonialism and Indigenous Knowledge in United Nations Discourse." *Griffith Law Review* 20 (2011): 702–28.

———. "Indigenous Peoples and Gene Disputes." *Chicago-Kent Law Review* 84 (2009–2010): 147–96.

Hedren, Paul. *Fort Laramie and the Great Sioux War*. Norman: University of Oklahoma Press, 1998.

———. *The Great Sioux War, 1876–77*. Lincoln: University of Nebraska Press, 1991.

Hilger, Sister M. Inez. "Notes on Cheyenne Child Life." *American Anthropologist* 48, no. 1 (1946): 60–69.

Hoebel, E. Adamson. *The Cheyennes: Indians of the Great Plains*. 2nd ed. New York: Harcourt Brace, 1988.

———. *The Law of Primitive Man: A Study in Comparative Legal Dynamics*. Cambridge: Harvard University Press, 1961.

Hoig, Stan. *The Battle of the Washita: The Sheridan-Custer Indian Campaign of 1867–69*. New York: Bison Books, 1979.

———. *The Peace Chiefs of the Cheyennes*. Norman: University of Oklahoma Press, 1980.

———. *Perilous Pursuit: The U.S. Cavalry and the Northern Cheyennes*. Boulder: University Press of Colorado, 2002.

———. *The Sand Creek Massacre*. Norman: University of Oklahoma Press, 1974.

Holm, Tom J., Diane Pearson, and Ben Chavis. "Peoplehood: A Model for the Extension of Sovereignty in American Indian Studies." *Wicazo Sa Review* 18, no. 1 (Spring 2003): 7–24.

Hongeva, Justin. "Contention Through Education: From Indian Education to Hopi Education." Master's thesis, Arizona State University, 2014.

Hyde, George E. *The Pawnee Indians*. Norman: University of Oklahoma Press, 1974.

———. *Red Cloud's Folk: A History of the Oglala Sioux Indians*. Norman: University of Oklahoma Press, 1987.

———. *Spotted Tail's Folk: A History of the Brulé Sioux*. Norman: University of Oklahoma Press, 1974.

Hyde, George E., and Savoie Lottinville, ed. *Life of George Bent: Written from His Letters*. Norman: University of Oklahoma Press, 1968.

"Indigenous Food Sovereignty." *Indigenous Food Systems Network*. Working Group on Indigenous Food Sovereignty. http://www.indigenousfoodsystems.org/food-sovereignty.

Jablow, Joseph. *The Cheyenne in Plains Indian Trade Relations, 1795–1840*. Lincoln: University of Nebraska Press, 1994.

Kappler, Charles J., ed. "Treaty with the Cheyenne Tribe, 1825, July 6, 1825. 7 Stat., 255. Proclamation, Feb. 6, 1826." *Indian Affairs: Laws and Treaties*, Vol. *11*. Washington, DC: Government Printing Office, 1904. http://digital.library.okstate.edu/kappler/Vol2/treaties/che0232.htm.

Kaye, Cliff. "An Examination of Hopimonmngwit: Hopi Leadership." Master's thesis, Arizona State University, 2016.

Killsback, Leo. "Indigenous Perceptions of Time: Decolonizing Theory, World History, and the Fates of Human Societies." *American Indian Culture and Research Journal* 37, no. 1 (Winter 2013): 119–47.

———. "The Legacy of Little Wolf: Rewriting and Righting Our Leaders Back into History." *Wicazo Sa Review* 26, no. 1 (2011): 85–111.

———. Review of *The Cheyenne Exodus in Memory and History*, by James N. Leiker and Ramon Powers. *American Indian Quarterly* 38, no. 3 (2014): 396–99.

———. Review of *White Man's Water: The Politics of Sobriety in a Native American Community*, by Erica Prussing. *Wicazo Sa Review* 27, no. 2 (Fall 2012): 128–34.

Kovach, Margaret. *Indigenous Methodologies: Characteristics, Conversations, and Contexts*. Toronto: University of Toronto Press, 2009.

Kristofic, Jim, and Nolan Karras James. *The Hero Twins: A Navajo-English Story of the Monster Slayers*. Albuquerque: University of New Mexico Press, 2015.

Kroeber, A. L. "Cheyenne Tales." *The Journal of American Folklore* 13, no. 50 (1900): 161–90.

Lakota Winter Counts: An Online Exhibit. National Anthropological Archives, Smithsonian National Museum of Natural History. http://wintercounts.si.edu/index.html.

Lame Deer, John (Fire), and Richard Erdoes. *Lame Deer, Seeker of Visions: The Life of a Sioux Medicine Man*. A Touchstone Book. New York: Simon &

Schuster, 1972.

Lee, Lloyd. *Navajo Sovereignty: Understandings and Visions of the Diné People.* Tucson: University of Arizona Press, 2017.

Legends of the Mighty Sioux, Compiled by Workers of the South Dakota Writer's Project, Work Projects Administration. Chicago: Albert Whitman & Company, 1941.

Leman, Wayne, ed. *Cheyenne Texts: An Introduction to Cheyenne Literature.* Occasional Publication in Anthropology, Linguistic Series, no. 6. Greeley: Museum of Anthropology, University of Northern Colorado, 1980.

———. *Náévóo'óhtséme/We Are Going Back Home: Cheyenne History and Stories Told by James Shoulderblade and Others.* Algonquian and Iroquoian Linguistics, Memoir 4. Winnipeg, Manitoba: Algonquian and Iroquoian Linguistics, 1987.

———. *A Reference Grammar of the Cheyenne Language.* Busby, MT: Cheyenne Translation Project, 1991.

Leman, Wayne, et al. *Cheyenne Dictionary.* Lame Deer, MT: Chief Dull Knife College, 2004–2006.

Lerma, Michael. *Guided by the Mountains: Navajo Political Philosophy and Governance.* New York: Oxford University Press, 2017.

Lewis, Meriwether, William Clark, et al. "1st of October Monday 1804" entry, "Part 5: Missouri River Miscellany, undated, winter 1804–5" entry, "Friday 22nd August 1806" entry. In *The Journals of the Lewis and Clark Expedition.* Edited by Gary Moulton. Lincoln: University of Nebraska Press, 2005. http://lewisandclarkjournals.unl.edu/index.html.

Llewellyn, Karl N., and E. Adamson Hoebel. *The Cheyenne Way: Conflict and Case Law in Primitive Jurisprudence.* Norman: University of Oklahoma Press, 1941.

Lyons, Oren. "Indian Self-Government in the Haudenosaunee Constitution." *Nordic Journal of International Law* 55 (1986): 117–21.

———. "Law, Principle, and Reality." *New York University Review of Law and Social Change* 20, no. 2 (1993): 209–15.

———. "Sovereignty and Sacred Land: Bardie C. Wolfe, Jr., Keynote Address." *Thomas Law Review* 13 (2–2001): 19–28.

Mails, Thomas E. *Fools Crow.* Garden City, NY: Bison Books, 1990.

Mankiller, Wilma. *Every Day Is a Good Day: Reflections of Contemporary Indigenous Women*, Memorial Ed. Golden, CO: Fulcrum Publishing, 2011.

Mann, Henrietta. *Cheyenne-Arapaho Education, 1871–1982.* Niwot: University

Press of Colorado, 1997.

Manuel, George. *The Fourth World: An Indian Reality.* New York: Free Press, 1974.

Marquis, Thomas B. *The Cheyennes of Montana.* Algonac. MI: Reference Publications, 1978.

———. *Keep the Last Bullet for Yourself: The True Story of Custer's Last Stand.* Algonac, MI: Reference Publications, 1976.

———. *Wooden Leg: A Warrior Who Fought Custer.* Lincoln: University of Nebraska Press, 1962.

Marquis, Thomas B., and Ronald H. Limbaugh, eds. *Cheyenne and Sioux: The Reminiscences of Four Indians and a White Soldier.* Stockton, CA: Pacific Center for Western Historical Studies, 1973.

McNab, David T., ed. *Earth, Water, Air and Fire: Studies in Canadian Ethnohistory.* Waterloo, ON: Wilfrid Laurier University Press, 1998.

Michelson, Truman. "The Narrative of a Southern Cheyenne Woman." *Smithsonian Miscellaneous Collections* 87 (5): 534–47. Publication 3140. Washington, DC: Smithsonian Institution, 1932.

Mihesuah, Devon A., ed. *Indigenizing the Academy: Transforming Scholarship and Empowering Communities.* Lincoln: University of Nebraska Press, 2004.

———, ed. *Natives and Academics: Researching and Writing About American Indians.* Lincoln: University of Nebraska Press, 1998.

Miller, Susan A., and James Riding In, eds. *Native Historians Write Back: Decolonizing American Indian History.* Lubbock: Texas Tech University Press, 2011.

Mooney, James. "The Aboriginal Population of America North of Mexico." *Smithsonian Miscellaneous Collections* 80 (7): 1928.

———. "The Cherokee Ball Play." *The American Anthropologist*, Old Series, vol. 3, no. 2 (1890): 105–32.

———. "The Cheyenne Indians." *American Anthropological Association*, Memoirs, I, part 6 (1905). Reprint; Whitefish, MT: Kessinger Publishing, 2009.

Mooney, James, and Father Peter J. Powell, eds. *In Sun's Likeness and Power: Cheyenne Accounts of Shield and Tipi Heraldry.* Lincoln: University of Nebraska Press, 2013.

Moore, John H. *The Cheyenne.* Malden, MA: Blackwell, 1996.

———. "Cheyenne Names and Cosmology." *American Ethnologist* 11, no. 2 (1984): 291–312.

———. *The Cheyenne Nation: A Social and Demographic History*. Norman: University of Oklahoma Press, 1987.

———. "Cheyenne Political History, 1820–1894," *Ethnohistory* 21, no. 4 (Autumn 1974): 329–59.

———. "The Developmental Cycle of Cheyenne Polygyny." Special Issue: American Indian Family History. *American Indian Quarterly* 15, no. 3. (1991): 311–28.

———. "Evolution and Historical Reductionism." *Plains Anthropologist* 26, no. 94, Part 1 (1981): 261–69.

———. "Native Americans, Scientists, and the HGDP." *Cultural Survival Quarterly* 20, no. 2 (1996): 60.

———. "The Reproductive Success of Cheyenne War Chiefs: A Contrary Case to Chagnon's Yanomamo." *Current Anthropology* 31, no. 3 (June 1990): 322–30.

———. "Review: *The Wolves of Heaven: Cheyenne Shamanism, Ceremonies, and Prehistoric Origins*." *American Anthropologist*, New Series, vol. 90, no. 2 (1988): 450.

Morris, Irvin. *From the Glittering World: A Navajo Story*. Norman: University of Oklahoma Press, 2000.

Neihardt, John G. *Black Elk Speaks: Being the Life Story of a Holy Man of the Oglala Nation*. Lincoln: University of Nebraska Press, 1961.

Nequatewa, Edmund. *Truth of a Hopi*. Radford, VA: Wilder Publications, 2007.

Newmark, Mahalia. "Reclaiming Dene Womanhood in Our Stories." Paper presented at Western Social Science Conference, Reno, NV, 2016.

"Northern Cheyenne Vision Page." *Northern Cheyenne Tribe: Official Site of the Tsististas and So'taa'eo'e People*. http://www.cheyennenation.com/vision.html.

Penney, Grace J. *Tales of the Cheyennes*. Cambridge, MA: The Riverside Press, 1953.

Petter, Rodolphe. *English-Cheyenne Dictionary*. Kettle Falls, WA, 1913–1915.

Pommersheim, Frank. *Braid of Feathers: American Indian Law and Contemporary Tribal Life*. Los Angeles: University of California Press, 1995.

Porter, Robert B. "The Meaning of Indigenous Nation Sovereignty." *Arizona State Law Journal* 34, no. 75 (2002): 75–112.

———. "Two Kinds of Indians, Two Kinds of Indian Nation Sovereignty: A Surreply to Professor LaVelle." *Kansas Journal of Law and Public Policy* 11, no. (2001–2002): 629–56.

Porter, Robert Odawi. *Sovereignty, Colonialism and the Indigenous Nations: A Reader*. Durham, NC: Carolina Academic Press, 2005.

Powell, Peter J. "Ox'zem: Box Elder and His Sacred Wheel Lance." *Montana: The Magazine of Western History* 20, no. 2 (Spring 1970): 30–41.

———. *People of the Sacred Mountain: A History of the Northern Cheyenne Chiefs and Warrior Societies, 1830–1879, With an Epilogue, 1969–1974*. 2 vols. San Francisco: Harper & Row, 1981.

———. *Sweet Medicine: The Continuing Role of the Sacred Arrows, the Sun Dance, and the Sacred Buffalo Hat in Northern Cheyenne History*. Norman: University of Oklahoma Press, 1969.

Randolph, Richard W. *Sweet Medicine and Other Stories of the Cheyenne Indians*. Caldwell, ID: The Caxton Printers, 1937.

Riding In, James. "Editor's Commentary: An American Indian Studies Paradigm Statement." *Wicazo Sa Review* 26, no. 2 (Fall 2011): 5–12.

Rusco, Elmer. "The Indian Reorganization Act and Indian Self-government." *American Indian Constitutional Reform and the Rebuilding of Native Nations*. Austin: University of Texas Press, 2006.

Salisbury, Neal, and Philip Joseph Deloria. *A Companion to American Indian History*. Malden, MA: Blackwell, 2004.

Salmón, Enrique. *Eating the Landscape: American Indian Stories of Food, Identity, and Resilience*. Tucson: University of Arizona Press, 2012.

Schlesier, Karl H. *The Wolves of Heaven*. Norman: University of Oklahoma Press, 1987.

Schrems, Suzanne H. "The Northern Cheyennes and the Fight for Cultural Sovereignty: The Notes of Father Aloysius Van Der Velden, S.J." *Montana: The Magazine of Western History* 45, no. 2 (Spring 1995): 27.

Schwartz, Warren E. *The Last Contrary: The Story of Wesley Whiteman (Black Bear)*. Sioux Falls, SD: The Center for Western Studies, 1991.

Segar, John H. *Early Days among the Cheyenne and Arapahoe Indians*. Norman: Oklahoma University Press, 1979.

Smith, Graham. "Kaupapa Maori Theory: Theorizing Indigenous Transformation of Education & Schooling." Paper presented at the International Education Research/AARE-NZARE Joint Conference, Auckland, New Zealand, December 2003. http://www.aare.edu.au/03pap/piho3342.pdf.

———. "Theorizing, Transforming & Reclaiming 'Our Indigenous Selves.'" Paper presented at the American Anthropology Association Conference,

San Jose, CA, November 19, 2006.

Smith, Linda Tuhiwai. *Decolonizing Methodologies: Research and Indigenous Peoples*. 2nd ed. New York: Zed Books, 2012.

Standing Bear, Luther. *Land of the Spotted Eagle*. New Edition. Lincoln: University of Nebraska Press, 1960.

———. *My People the Sioux*. New Edition. Lincoln: University of Nebraska Press, 1975.

Stands In Timber, John, and Margot Liberty. *Cheyenne Memories*. New Haven, CT: Yale University Press, 1967.

———. *A Cheyenne Voice: The Complete John Stands In Timber Interviews*. Norman: University of Oklahoma Press, 2013.

Straus, Anne S. "Northern Cheyenne Ethnopsychology." *Ethos* 5, no. 3 (1977): 326–57.

Sutter, Virginia. *Tell Me, Grandmother: Traditions, Stories, and Cultures of the Arapaho People*. Boulder: University of Colorado Press, 2004.

Tall Bull, Henry, and Tom Weist. *Cheyenne Legends of Creation*. Billings: Montana Council on Indian Education, 1972.

———. *Cheyenne Warriors: Stories of the Northern Cheyenne*. Billings: Montana Council on Indian Education, 1983.

———. *Mista!* Billings: Montana Council on Indian Education, 1971.

———. *The Rolling Head*. Billings: Montana Council on Indian Education, 1971.

———. *Winter Hunt*. Billings: Montana Council on Indian Education, 1971.

Tallbull, Bill (Wolf Feathers). "We are the Ancestors of those yet to be Born: Northern Cheyenne History of the Battle of 100-In-The-Hands (the Fetterman Battle)." *Fort Phil Kearny/Bozeman Trail Association*. Last modified March 22, 2004. http://www.philkearny.vcn.com/fpk-tallbull.htm.

Taube, Karl. *Aztec and Maya Myths (The Legendary Past)*. 3rd ed. Austin: University of Texas Press, 1997.

Taylor, Graham D. *The New Deal and American Indian Tribalism: The Administration of the Indian Reorganization Act, 1934–45*. Lincoln: University of Nebraska Press, 1980.

Tom, Naomi. "Protecting Tribal Nations Through Community Controlled Research: An Analysis of Established Research Protocols Within Arizona Tribes." Master's thesis, Arizona State University, 2015.

Tsosie, Rebecca. "Introduction: Symposium on Cultural Sovereignty." *Arizona State Law Journal* 34, no. 1 (2002): 1–14.

———. "Sacred Obligations: Intercultural Justice and the Discourse of Treaty Rights." UCLA *Law Review* 47, no. 6 (1999–2): 1615–72.

Wallace, Paul. *White Roots of Peace: The Iroquois Book of Life*. Santa Fe, NM: Clear Light Publishers, 1994.

Weist, Katherine M. *Belle Highwalking: The Narrative of a Northern Cheyenne Woman*. Billings: Montana Council for Indian Education, 1979.

Weist, Tom. *A History of the Cheyenne People*. Billings: Council for Indian Education, 1977.

Wilkins, David E. *American Indian Sovereignty and the U.S. Supreme Court: The Masking of Justice*. Austin: University of Texas Press, 1997.

Wilkins, David E., and Heidi Kiiwetinepinesiik Stark. *American Indian Politics and the American Political System*. 3rd ed. Oxford: Rowman & Littlefield, 2011.

Wilkinson, Charles. *Blood Struggle: The Rise of Modern Indian Nations*. New York: W.W. Norton, 2005.

Williams, Robert A., Jr. *The American Indian in Western Legal Thought: The Discourses of Conquest*. New York: Oxford University Press, 1990.

———. *Like a Loaded Weapon: The Rehnquist Court, Indian Rights, and the Legal History of Racism in America*. Minneapolis: University of Minnesota Press, 2005.

———. *Linking Arms Together: American Indian Treaty Visions of Law and Peace, 1600–1800*. New York: Routledge, 1999.

———. *Savage Anxieties: The Invention of Western Civilization*. New York: Palgrave and Macmillan, 2012.

Wilson, Shawn. *Research Is Ceremony: Indigenous Research Methods*. Black Point, NS: Fernwood, 2009.

Wooden Legs, John. *A Northern Cheyenne Album: Photographs by Thomas B. Marquis*. Edited by Margot Liberty. Norman: University of Oklahoma Press, 2007.

Yazzie, Ethelou, ed. *Navajo History*. Rough Rock, AZ: Navajo Curriculum Center, 1982.

BIBLIOGRAPHY

NATIONAL ANTHROPOLOGICAL ARCHIVES (NAA), SMITHSONIAN INSTITUTION

NAA MS 2134., NAA MS 2684-a., NAA MS 2704. , NAA MS 2790., NAA MS 2796., NAA MS 2798., NAA MS 2799., NAA MS 2811. , NAA MS 2822. , NAA MS 2828, folder 1., NAA MS 2828, folder 2., NAA MS 3188-b., NAA MS 3218., NAA MS 3219., NAA MS 3220., NAA MS 3336., NAA MS 3338., NAA MS 3342., NAA MS 3343., NAA MS 3355.1.

Index

Page numbers in *italics* represent figures, photographs, and tables.

Aä'ninĕna (White Clay People), 171
Aanu'hawa, 171
abortion, 259–60n43
adoption/adoptees, 93–94, 96–97, 98, 106, 107–9, 131, 142, 194–95, 208, 212, 219. *See also* captives
adultery, 130–31, 257n44
afterlife. *See* death
alcohol, 128, 143, 227, 244, 258–59n20
Alfred, Taiaiake, xxii, 247n6
Algonquians, 172
All night dance. *See* Leaving the camp dance
alliance, 6, 17–19, 170, 189–90, 209, 243. *See also specific federations*; peacemaking; spiritual alliance; unification
allies. *See* Néstaxeo'o
allotment policy. *See* Dawes Act; reservation
American bison. *See* American buffalo
American buffalo, 7, 15, 66, 188. *See also* hōtōw'ëanä'ō; Vóhaenóhónestôtse
American Horse
    dances identified, 22, 23, 24
    encounter with Ho'óhomo'eo'o, 182
    first encounter with Arapaho, 172
    Indigenous nations identified, 164, 167, 169
    Red Rocks people, 165
"animal calling," 27
Animal Dance, 39
Animal Lodge. *See* Måséháome
Antelope Creek (Black Hills), 30, 32
antelope hunting ritual. *See* Vó'kaehénooné
Antelope Pit Ceremony. *See* Vó'kaehénooné
Antelope River (Black Hills), 30
Antelope Singing. *See* Vó'kaehénooné
Aortas. *See* Heveškèsenêhpåhese
A'ó'tonóóma (Into-the-ground realm), *155*, 157
Apache, 161, 164, 168, 208–9
Aquqavenuts (Crossed Feathers), *109*

Arapaho. *See* Hestóetaneo'o
Arikara, 168, 169, 219
arranged marriage. *See* marriage, arranged
arrow lodge. *See* Maahéome
Arrow Keeper. *See* Maahótse Tséá'enövâhtse
Arrow Renewal, 39, 40, 208, 219
Arrow Worship, 38
The Arrows of Sweet Medicine story, 43–45
aseehe (the moving of camp), 176–80, 228, 243
Ashland, Montana, 223, 225
assimilation
    Christian teachings, 137–38
    destruction of family unit, 128
    devaluation of sovereignty, xxv
    loss of language/cultural practices, 16, 73, 224–27
    survival of covenant ceremonies, 40, 237–39
    US government policies, 66, 219, 232–34
    See also colonization
Assiniboine. *See* Hóheeheo'o
Átonoome (underworld), *155*, 157
Ax Handle (Cheyenne), 229
Ba'achinĕna (Red Willow Men, Blood-Pudding Men, Mother People), 171, 173, 175
Baä'sawunĕ'na (Wood Lodge Men), 171
Badger (Só'taeo'o)
    encounter with Lakota, 183
    medicine buffalo hunt origin story, 27
Baldwin Twins, Amitsehei, *83*
Baldwin Twins, Nakai, *83*
Baldwin Twins, Oivit (Scabby; keeper), 47, *83*
Ball Ceremony, 24
band chief, 7, 11, 106–7, 170
band system
    alliance building, 17, 170
    Arapaho, 171–76
    band-kinship system, 92–94
    described, 7–8,
    Lakota Sioux, 181–90
    ten band camp circle, 11, *11*, 165, 167
    unity, 105, 161

INDEX

See also specific band
Bare Legs. See Öttō ha nĭh'
Bear Butte, South Dakota, 53
Bear Feathers (Cheyenne warrior), 197
"Bear Mountain." See No'awús'
Bear Rope, 147
Begging Men. See Hitu'něna
Bent, George (Southern Cheyenne)
    Bowstrings attempt to take Crow horses, 266–67n44
    captives in war, 194
    consenting to war, 201–2
    description of gold seekers, 221–22
    encounter with Moiseyu, 182
    hetanévestôtse, 116
    laws against torture, 194–95
    Medicine-pipe Mountain, 251n11
    moving camp, 208
    pegged soldiers, 207
    property and war, 196
"Berdaches," 25
berry dance, 23
BIA. See US Bureau of Indian Affairs
The Big Issue, 219
Big Sister. See Voestaehneva'e
Bighorn Mountains, 24, 193, 209
Bighorn River, 193, 212
bison. See American buffalo
Black (Southern Cheyenne)
    The Buffalo Bones, 145–46
Blackfeet Nation. See Sihasapa
Blackfoot Confederacy. See Blackfeet Nation
Black Hills, 27
    Cheyenne homeland, 27, 161, 172, 173, 182, 193, 213
    Ma'xema'hĕŏ'e, 73
    Motsé'eóeve's travels to, 43
    moving the arrows, 208
    Standing Horns story, 50–51
    Vó'kaehénooné, 32
    white invasion, 222
Black Moccasins Nation. See Sihasapa
Black Mountain (Black Hills), 54, 56
Black Wolf (chief)
    extended family, 87
    kidnapping, 151
    kinship list, 82, 86, 88, 90
    wounded by white settler, 229
Black Wolf, Allan Jo, 227
"blanket courtship," 117–18. See also marriage, courtship
Blood Bachelor, 108
Blood-Pudding Men. See Ba'achiněna
blood quantum, xxiii, 233, 240

Bloods, 164, 167
"Bloody Bits." See Bloods
Blue Cloud Indians. See hitáni noS e'yo'U
Blue Wing, 151
boarding schools, 80, 225–27
"Boat Rowers," 167
Bone Scraper Society. See Crooked Lance Society
bow and arrow, 196
"Bows and Arrows" people, 165
Bow String Society Dance, 23
Bowstring warriors, 204–5, 209, 266–67n44
breathing, art of, 72
brotherhood. See hévese'onematsestôtse
Brulé (Burned Thighs) Lakota Sioux, 164, 165, 181, 182, 183, 187, 211–12
buffalo. See American buffalo
Buffalo Bones (Mrs. High Walker), 146
The Buffalo Bones (Black), 145–46
Buffalo Ceremony. See Vóhaenóhónestôtse
buffalo dance. See Vóhaenóhónestôtse
buffalo drive, 250n30
Buffalo Hat. See Ésevone
Buffalo Hump, 147–48
Buffalo Lodge. See Måséháome
The Buffalo Lodge story (John Stands In Timber), 37–38
Buffalo Woman (sister of One Eye's wife), 151
Bull Thigh
    Keeper of Sacred Arrows, 49
    The Sacred Arrows story, 45
    Sweet Medicine's powers, 27
bundle/bundle keeper. See sacred bundle/bundle keeper
Buntin, Superintendent, 229–30
Bureau of Indian Affairs. See US Bureau of Indian Affairs
Burned Thighs. See Brulé Lakota
"Burners." See Haudenosaunee
Busby, Montana, 226
Bushido code, 192, 206
Calf Woman, 151
camp, moving. See aseehe
"Canoes" (people), 164, 165
captives, 96–97, 106, 108, 147, 194–95, 208. See also adoption/adoptees
Carries the Arrows, 151
case law, 134, 258n2
catlinite, 29, 135
Catlinite, 165
Centerwall, W. R., 234
ceremony
    apprentice, 42, 66
    arrow lodge, 45–47

INDEX

communal, 21–38, 240
covenant, 39–64, 226, 240–41
cycle/calendar, 3, 19, 20, 25–26, 26, 42
decline, 174
Ésevone Tséá'enövâhtse, 55–56
farming, 66
Hoxéheome, 48–55
leaders, 41–42
Maahéome, 43–45
Maahótse Tséá'enövâhtse, 47–48
Mâséháome, 58–64
medicine hunts, 25–29
medicine lodge, 56–58
protocols, 21–22
recreation of world and universe, 20
ritual laws, 105–7
sacred sovereignty exercise, 19–20
sacrifice, 68–69, 72
"tests," 66
Vóhaenóhónestôtse, 33–38
Vó'kaehénooné, 29–33
See also specific ceremony
Charcoal Bear, 115
chastity belt, 120
Cheyenne Nation. *See* Tséhéstáno
The Cheyenne Way (Llewellyn and Hoebel), 134, 148–49
Chief Dull Knife College, xxvii
Chiefs' Lodge. *See* Véhooneome
Chiefs' Renewal Ceremony. *See* Véhooneome
Chippewas, 167
chivalry, code of, 192
Christianity, 16, 40, 73, 137–38
CIO. *See* US Bureau of Indian Affairs
citizenship, 91–94, 105, 225–28
Civil War, 222
Clark, William, 6
Collier, John S., 231, 233, 234
colonization
    assimilationist policies, xxv
    decolonizing sovereignty, xxiii–xxiv, 8–10, 237–45
    destructive force, 223–24
    internal, xxii–xxiii
    leadership and citizenship, 225–28
    mental and psychological, 227–29
    reorganization, 230–33
    spiritual oppression, 230–32
    white man, 219–35
Comanche Nation. *See* Šé'šenovotsétaneo'o
Comes In Sight, 147
communal ceremony. *See* ceremony
Contraries, 24
Contrary Dance/Dancers. *See* Hohnóhka

Contrary Society. *See* Hohnóhka
Corn Dance, 23
corn farming, 21, 24, 26, 51, 66, 165, 171
Corn Tassel, 151
Council of Forty-four Chiefs. *See* Véhoo'o
counting coup, 29, 162, 180, 195–96, 207. *See also* war
coup-stick, 196
Courts of Indian Offenses. *See* US Bureau of Indian Affairs
courtship. *See* marriage
"covenants of sovereignty." *See* Ésevone; Maahótse
Coyote (Northern Cheyenne)
    Arapaho unification, 172–73
    arranged marriage, 122
    divorce customs, 130
    first meeting with Lakota, 185
    nuclear family description, 88
    treatment of visitors, 104–5
Coyote Man, 59, 61
crazy, acting, 60
Crazy Dog Dance, 23
Crazy Dogs, 143–44, 179, 212, 259n25, 266–67n44
Crazy Lodge Ceremony. *See* Mâséháome
Cree. *See* Vóhkoohétaneo'o
crime, 135–36. *See also* sexual norms/taboos
crimes against humanity, 192
Crooked Lance Society, 259n25, 266n44
Crooked Nose Woman, 148, 149
Crow (good spirit), 153
Crow Dog
    significance of White Buffalo Woman, 187
Crow Dog, Mary (Lakota)
    principles of colonization, 226–27
Crow Nation. *See* Óoetaneoo
Crow Standing Butte (hill), 212
cultural law. *See* ho'emanestôtse
Custer, George Armstrong, 166
dances/dance societies, 22–25. *See also specific dance*
Dawes Act, 233
dead realm. *See* Naévóóma
Deadwood, South Dakota, 222
death
    accidental, 139–46, 258–59nn20, 25
    afterlife, 154
    drowning, 155
    embraced as part of life, 69
    in war, 192–95, 203–4
    strangulation, 156
    vow of —, 206–7

INDEX

See also murder; suicide; war
death penalty, 145, 147
decolonization. *See* colonization
Delaware people, 195, 211
Deloria, Vine, Jr. (Standing Rock Sioux), 8, 221
Denver, Colorado, 221, 222
depression, 68, 139–40, 153
Dirty Moccasins, 142–43, 148
divorce. *See* marriage, divorce/separation customs
Dog (informant), 151
Dog Men. *See* Hotamétaneo'o
Dull Knife Battle (Bighorns), 24, 208–9, 213
Dying Dance, 206
Eagle Bird, 142
ear-piercing ceremony, 109–10
Earth. *See* Éškemane
Eastman, Charles
    elements of Sun Dance, 186–87
Eaters. *See* Ohmésêhese
Elk Warriors society, 140
eloping, 121. *See* marriage, elopement
Enemy Captive, 268n30
environment, 3, 156. *See also* nature
Ésevona'e (Buffalo Woman)
    children playing, 93
    culture hero, 187
    The Great Medicine Dance story, 52–54
    marriage ceremonies/customs, 116
    union with Tomôsévêsêhe, 123
Ésevone (Sacred Buffalo Hat)
    bundle covenant of the Hoxéheome, 48, 50, 205
    Christian converts, 16
    covenant of sacred sovereignty, 14, *14*, 163, 171–70, 174
    kinship system, 92
    sanctity of laws, 55–56, 77
    social and political organization, 158, 219
    spiritual laws, 143, 145, 148, 152
    unification, 188–89, 214
    women's rights, 147, 260n51
Ésevone Tséá'enövâhtse (Sacred Buffalo Hat Keeper), 12, 55–56, 147–48, 158, 170, 219, 235
Éškemane (Mother Earth)
    laws originate from, 96–97
    life-giving powers, 137
    Medicine Hat law, 143
    principle of, 83
Everybody Was Starving story (Wrapped Hair), 58–59
Evevêšeevehó'nehe (Horned Wolf), 61
family, renewing, 20. *See also* nevo'êstanémaneo'o

farming. *See* corn farming
Fast Creek (Running Creek; Black Hills), 51
fatherhood. *See* héhe'estovestôtse
Feathered Wolf (Elk warrior), 143
"Fish Eaters," 164, 167, 168
The First White Man story, 219–20, 221
The First White Man, Decolonized story, 223
Fisher, Conrad (Northern Cheyenne) perception of reservation, 224
fishing, 24
Flandreau, South Dakota, 182
Following Dance. *See* Leaving the camp dance
food, 19, 61, 71, 100–101, 104
Foolish Dance Lodge. *See* Mâsêháome
Fools Crow (Lakota)
    arrival of White Buffalo Woman, 188–89
    declaring war, 199
forest realm. *See* Ma'táa'evóóma
Fort Laramie Treaty, 210, 219, 221
Fox people, 24, 165, 179, 195
"full-blood" label, xxiii
galloping buffalo-bull dance, 24–25
Gentle Horse (Cheyenne), 142
"geographical spirituality," 7
Ghost Dancers, 23
Giving Medal River, 142
Goes in Lodge (Arapaho), 175
    first meeting with Cheyenne, 171–72, 175
gold, discovery of, 221–22
"Goose Warriors." *See* Peigan
Grand Pawnee, 211
Grandmother Earth. *See* Éškemane
Grass Buffalo, 60
Grasshopper (informant), xxix–xxx
    Crees and Cheyenne, 169, 171
    first encounter with Arapaho, 172
    horses from Kiowa, 177
    Indigenous nations identified, 164, 167
Grattan (US lieutenant), 221
Greasy wood people. *See* Vétapâhaetó'eo'o
Great Medicine. *See* Ma'xema'hēō'e
The Great Medicine Dance story (Josie Limpy), 52–54, 111
Great Mystery Spirit. *See* Wakan Tanka
Great Peace of Horse Creek, 210, 212
Great Race, 33, 71
Great Unification. *See* unification, Só'taeo'o with Tsétsêhéstâhese
"Grey Blankets" people, 164, 165
Grey Wolf Lodge, 60–61

INDEX

Grinnell, George B., 24–25, 128, 142, 248n19, 260n51, 266–67n44
Gros Ventre. *See* Aä'ninĕna
guns, 18, 134, 161, 178, 196, 205, 212, 220
Haag, Mack (Southern Cheyenne)
    cultural laws, 99
    divorce customs, 129
    grandparents and teasing, 91
    Hoxéheome, 197
    kinship list, 82, 86, 88, 90, 92
    menstruation ritual laws, 112
    protecting woman's virtue, 117, 120
    universal laws, 153
"half-breed" label, xxiii
"Half-Civilized" people, 165–66
halfman-halfwoman gender, 25
Ha'nahawnena, 171
Háomóhtâhévêhanéhe (Sickness), 44
happiness, 57, 67, 73, 80, 89, 211, 252n45
hatchet, 196
Haudenosaunee (Iroquois), 166, 195
Hawk Feather, 58–59
healing, 67–68, 152–53
He'ämahéstanove (Above-world realm), 156
He'amo'omēē'e (Above-the-sky realm), 156
he'eévestôtse (womanhood) ritual, 110–13, 120–21, 144, 147–49
He'emanehe (half-woman man), 25, 115
Heévâhetaneo'o (Rope-hair-people), 177, 210
héhe'estovestôtse (fatherhood), 81, 83, 84, 85
Heovêsta'e'e (Yellow Top-to-Head Woman), 59, 93, 187
heške'estovestôtse (motherhood), 81, 82–83, 85
héstanovestôtse ("the life of the people"/"the living-nation"), 15–16, 171
Hestóetaneo'o (Arapaho; Cedar people)
    alliance, 6, 18, 162, 171–76, 181, 185, 189–90, 211–12, 214
    Cheyenne first encounter, 167, 169, 183
    horses, 177
    intertribal marriage, 109
    murder case, 142
    peacemaking, 209–10
    relationship with Pawnees, 212
    treaty negotiations, 219
hetanévestôtse (manhood) ritual, 113–14, 116–19
hévese'onematsestôtse (brotherhood)
    arranged marriages, 119
    decolonization, 244–45
    extended family, 87
    inter-Indigenous national peacemaking, 165, 167
    intratribal murder, 138
    sacred sovereignty, 10–11, 16–17, 93
    unification, 28–29, 173
Heveškėsenêhpåhese (Aortas), *11*, 17, 188
Hidatsa, 210, 219
high authority. *See* ma'xenėheto'stôtse
High Backed Wolf (Cheyenne chief), 195, 209, 219
High Forehead (Minneconjou), 221
High Walker, Mrs. (Southern Cheyenne), 146
Highwalking, Belle (Northern Cheyenne)
    "Buffalo Bones" story, 145
    Buffalo Dance, 61–63
    incest, 145
    women's challenges, 120–21
history and storytelling, xxvii–xxx
hitáni noS e'yo'U (Blue Cloud Indians), 172, 186
Hitu'nĕna (Begging Men), 171
Ho'e (Earth), *98*, 157
Hoebel, E. Adamson, 128, 134, 142, 148–50, 151–52, 258–59n20
Ho'ehêvêsénóó'e (Standing On The Ground)
    culture hero, 187
    Everybody Was Starving story, 59
    The Great Medicine Dance story, 52–54
    marriage ceremonies/customs, 116
    original corn covenant, 24
    The Two Young Men story, 28–29
    See also Tomôsévéséhe
Ho'ehêvêsénóóhe. *See* Tomôsévéséhe
ho'emanestôtse (law)
    cultural laws, 98–102
    described, 95–97, *98*
    evaluation of, 134, 258n2
    ritual laws, 105–7
    traditional laws, 102–5
Hoffman, Albert (informant), 249n18
Hóheeheo'o (Assiniboine), 161, 164, 177, 183, 184, 205, 210, 219
Hŏhēēū, 166
Hohnóhka (Contrary Society), 23, 60, 63
Holy Ear of Corn, 36
Holy Hat Woman, 147–48, 149
homicide. *See* murder
Ho'néhetaneo'o (Wolf people; Pawnee), 58, 169, 176, 177, 183, 197, 208, 210–13, 260n51
Ho'óhomo'eo'o (Lakota Nation; Sioux)
    access to guns and horses, 161
    alliance/unification, 6, 36, 161–62
    effects of colonization, 231
    horse worship, 66–67
    intertribal marriage, 93–94, 109
    relationship with Pawnees, 211–12
    relatives, 164

INDEX

treaty negotiations, 219
unification, 181–90
See also Oglala Lakota; Sioux
Horned Wolf. *See* Evevėšeevehó'nehe
Horns Standing Up, 52–55
"horse nation," 161. *See also specific nation*
Horse Medicine Ceremony, 24
Horse Worship Ceremony, 65–66, 177
horses, 65, 134, 161–62, 176–78, 185, 208
Hotamétaneo'o (Dog Men), 207
Hotóhkéso ("little star people"), 168, 186
hōtōw'ëanä'ö (buffalo jumps), 33
How the Sioux Nation Was Born story, 182
Howling Wolf (Cheyenne), 229
Hoxéheome (Medicine Lodge/Sun Dance)
    covenant ceremony, 39, 41, 175–76
    described, 40, 48–55
    effects of colonization, 230–32
    elements added, 57–58
    geo-spiritual practice, 7
    level of unification, 170
    Mȧséháome as sister ceremony, 64
    modern, 38
    spiritual alliance/laws, 15, 143, 145, 148
    unification, 174, 183, 186–88, 214
    universal laws, 153
    vows, 56, 152
    warrior's war exploits, 197
    women's rights, 147
Human-Flesh Eaters. *See* "Tonkawa" people
Human realm. *See* Vóto' sóoma
humor in kinship system, 89, 90–91
Hunkpapa Lakota (To Camp at the Entrance of the Circle), 181
hunting rituals. *See* medicine hunts
Ice. *See* White Bull/Ice (Northern Cheyenne)
Ickes, Harold L., 234
incest, 84–85, 90, 119, 127, 145–47, 259–60n43
"Indian police," 228–30
Indian Reorganization Act (IRA) government, 228, 233–35
Indigenous methodologies, xxvi–xxvii
Indigenous Nations Law (INL), 191–202, 224, 229, 243–44
"Indigenous Nation Sovereignty" model, 9–10
Indigenous People. *See* Xamaevo'ėstaneo'o
inhumane/unkind acts, 69–70
INL. *See* Indigenous Nations Law
in-laws. *See* nevo'ėstanémaneo'o
IRA government. *See* Indian Reorganization Act government, 228, 233–35
Iron Teeth Woman (Northern Cheyenne)
    divorce customs, 129
    war captives, 194

Iroquois. *See* Haudenosaunee
Itazipo (Without Bows; Sans Arcs), 181
Jesuit (Catholic order), 225
joking. *See* humor
ka'ėškónevestôtse (childhood), 84
kamikaze attacks, 206
Kamxwiwiyaxtah. *See* Wooden Leg
kȧse'ééhe (young woman). *See* Mukije
Kaw people, 164
Ke'ééhe (Grandmother), 55, 59, 93
keeper. *See* Tséá'enövâhtse
Keeper of the Pipe, 175
Kickapoo, 164, 165
kidnapping, 147–53, 194
Kiiwetinepinesiik Stark, Heidi (Anishinaabekwe), 9
Killsback, Hattie, 58
kinship. *See* nevo'ėstanémaneo'o
Kiowa. *See* Vétapâhaetó'eo'o
Labre, St. Joseph Benedicte, 225
Lakota (Sioux). *See* Ho'óhomo'eo'o
Lame Bear, 105–6
Lame Deer (Minneconjou)
    significance of Sun Dance, 186
    universal and national principles, 187
lance, carrying, 196
language, 7, 10, 16, 81, 171–74, 181, 189–90, 222, 224–27, 237 260n55
Last Bull, 151
law
    concept of, xxii–xxiii
    ho'emanestôtse, 95–114
    Western, 77
    See also ho'emanestôtse; Noóněho'emanestôtse
Leaving the camp dance, 24
Leman, Wayne
    Cheyenne Dictionary, 82
    extended family, 87
    kinship terms, 86, 88, 90, 92
Lewis, Meriwether, 6
Liberty, Margot, xxix
lightning, fear of, 63
Lime (culture hero). *See* Vóetséná'e
Limpy, Josie, 51–54, 111
Little Bighorn, Battle of the, 166, 213
Little Bird, 58–59
Little Sea Shell, 147–48, 149
"little star people." *See* Hotóhkéso
Little Wolf, 144, 221
Little Yellow Calf, 36
Llewellyn, Karl N., 128, 134, 142, 148–50, 151–52, 259–60n20
lodge. *See* ceremony

| 288 |

INDEX

Long Chin, 260n51
Looking Horse, Orval, 189
Looking Horse, Stanley, 189
Louisiana Purchase, 6
love, principle of, 89, 126
"love medicine," 118–19
Lyons, Oren (Onondaga), 95
Maahéome (Arrow Lodge), 26, 41, 43–47, 50, 138, 204, 208, 211
Maahótse (Medicine Arrows)
    adoption ceremonies, 108
    children becoming, 93
    Christian converts, 16
    covenant of sacred sovereignty, 14, *14*, 163–64, 172–73
    elements added to Hoxéheome, 57
    incest laws, 84, 145
    kidnappers/rapists/murderers, 152
    kinship system, 92
    law, 138–43, 188
    renewal and cleansing, 45–48
    sanctity, 77
    social and political organization, 158
    suicide, 153–54
    teachings, 45
    unifications, 173, 185, 188–89
    universal laws, 153
    white man's influence on arrows, 218
Maahótse Tséá'enövâhtse (Arrow Keeper), 12, 47–48, 158, 170, 185, 204, 207–9, 219–20
MacKenzie, Ranald, 208
Ma'eomene (Red Lodge), 30
Maheo (the Creator), 53–54, 229
Ma'heónehó'nehe (Sacred Wolf), 61
ma'heo'néstónestôtse (sacred covenants)
    communal ceremonies, 21–38, 240
    covenant ceremonies, 39–64, 240–41
    Ma'heónetanohtôtse (sacred way of thinking), 65–74, 241
    Ma'heónohéstanove (sacred nation), 5–20
ma'heónetanohtôtse (sacred way of thinking), 65–73, 241
ma'heónohéstanove (sacred nation), 5–20, 239–40
ma'hëö'o hesto'emanestôtse (sacred laws)
    described, 133–35
    Medicine Arrow law, 138–43
    Medicine Hat law, 143–44
    pipe and peacemaking, 135–38
    spiritual laws, 135
    universal laws, 153–56
    violence against women, 144–53
Mâhtamâhááhe (Old Woman), 28–29, 32. *See also* Voestaehneva'e
manhood. *See* hetanévestôtse
Man on a Cloud. *See* Woir-Oqtuimanists
The Man Who Turned into Buffalo Bones (Laura Rockroads), 145
marriage
    adoptees, 106, 194
    arranged, 119, 122, 123
    courtship, 113, 114, 115, 116–21
    divorce/separation customs, 125, 126, 127, 128–32, 148, 152, 257n44
    dowry, 119, 122, 127
    elopement, 121, 125, 149
    intertribal, 93–94, 109, 170, 171, 174, 176, 189
    polygamy, 116, 126–28
    refusal, 150, 152
    relationship acquired, 89
    revive and reinstate customs, 242–43
    ritual, 105, 121–26
    spousal abuse, 125–26, 257n44
    success, 126, 128
Mâséháome (Crazy Lodge), 23, 24, 41, 58–64
mass murder, 192
Ma'táa'evóóma (realm of the forest), 154
Matsīyōv. *See* Motsé'eóeve
Ma'xema'hëö'e (Great Medicine)
    Arrow Lodge, 45, 140
    pipe smoking, 137
    spiritual and physical worlds, 72–73, 157
    supreme power, 20, 97
ma'xenéheto' stôtse (high authority), xxx, 10, 12, *13*, 20, 73. *See also* sovereignty
Mdewakanton Lakota, 181, 186
Medicine Arrows. *See* Maahótse
Medicine Buffalo Hunt (Standing In The Morning), 27–28
Medicine Hat law, 143–44, 145, 152–53
medicine hunts, 25–29, 143
Medicine Lodge, 56–58, 174, 189. *See also* Hoxéheome
Medicine Lodges (people), 164
medicine man/woman, 42
Medicine-pipe Mountain," 251n11. *See also* Nóvávóse
Medicine Snake Woman (Kiowa), 209
medicine tipi, 53
menses, 110–13
"menstrual lodge," 110–13
Merger of Groups story (John Stands In Timber), 184–85
Meriam Report, 233
Michelson, Truman, xxix, 112, 153
Michelson collection, Truman, xxviii

INDEX

Miles City, Montana, 229
Milky Way. *See* Seánemeo'o
military alliance. *See* alliance
Minneconjou Lakota (Plants Near the Water), 181, 189, 211
miscarriage, 259–60n43
mission schools, 225–26
missions/missionaries, 225–27, 231
Missouri people, 169
Missouri River, 172, 177, 183, 184–85
Moiseyu (Lakota band), 182
Moktu'uahAtAn (Ute Nation; Black people; Mo'óhtávêhetane), 58, 169
Mo'óhtávêhetane. *See* Moktu'uahAtAn
Mormon cow incident, 221, 222
Mother People. *See* Ba'achiněna
motherhood. *See* heške'eestovestôtse
Motsé'eóeve (Sweet Medicine)
    adoption ceremonies, 107
    apocalyptic prophecies, 64, 230
    Arrow Lodge, 46
    Buffalo Ceremony, 33–37
    communal hunts, 27
    creation of warrior societies, 138
    culture hero, 60
    epic dual with Vóetséna'e, 208
    inconsistencies in stories, xxix
    intertribal war, 210
    kidnapping/sexual assault, 149
    killing other tribes, 169
    kinship laws, 91
    language about intertribal wars, 210
    legacy preserving starvation/suffering memories, 37
    Maahéome originator, 43–45
    marriage rules, 117
    meeting white man, 219–20
    Old Man Charm, 206–7
    Old Woman Spring story, 55
    on old people, 84
    Sioux nation, 182–83
    spiritual leader/spiritual powers, 5, 51, 172, 188
    The Two Young Men story, 28–29
moving camp. *See* aseehe
Moving the Arrows, 207–9
Mukije (Short Woman), 249n17
murder, 16, 137–44, 147, 148, 150, 152, 176, 192, 204, 212, 229, 258–59n20
Naévóóma (realm of the dead), 154
Ná'kasiněna (Sage Brush Men), 171, 174, 175
Naméhane. *See* Voestaehneva'e
naming ceremonies, 107
Nǎnǎhǎxwū (ceremonial age societies), 175

Nantowun (Arapaho), 142
"Nasty" village, 131–32
National Anthropological Archives, Truman Michelson collection, xxviii
nationhood, xxii–xxiii, 6–8, 20, 222
nature, 54. *See also* Noávóóma
Nawathi'něna. *See* Na'wuněna
Na'wuněna (Southern Arapaho), 171, 224
Né'ohma'ehétaneo'o (Sand Hill People), 17
Néstaxeo'o (allies)
    Cheyenne Nation and Indigenous Peoples, 163–80
    described, 161–62
    Ho'óhomo'eo'o and Cheyenne, 181–90
    Indigenous Nations Law, 191–202
    war, 203–14
    nevo'ėstanémaneo'o (family)
    described, 80–81, 97, 144
    extended family, 85, 86, 87
    immediate family, 81–85
    in-laws, 89–91
    kinship terms, 82, 86, 88, 90
    language as foundation of — system, 81
    nation of families, 91–94
    nuclear family, 87–89
    reinvigorate and strengthen, 239
    role of humor, 89, 90–91
    traditional laws, 79–80, 241–42
New Life Giving Lodge. *See* Hoxéheome
Night Dancers society, 23
Noávóóma (realm of nature), 154
No'awús' ("Bear Mountain"), 172
Nonóma'e (Roaring Thunder), 53, 54
nooného'emanestôtse (traditional law)
    described, 77–78
    kinship laws, 79–94
    marriage, 115–32
    sacred laws, 133–58
    way of life, 95–114
Northern Arapaho, 168, 171, 173, 175
Northern Cheyenne. *See* Tsėhéstáno
Northern Cheyenne Constitution and Bylaws, 234
"Northern Piegan," 167
North Ponca people, 164
nose cutting, 131
Nótåxeo'o (warrior society)
    aseehe, 178–79
    balance of power and authority, *14*
    communal ceremonies, 23
    counting coup, 196
    creation, xxix, 5
    dance societies, 23
    effects of colonization, 228–30, 232

INDEX

hetanévestôtse, 114
inter-Indigenous national peacemaking, 170
ma'xenéheto'stôtse shared with Véhoo'o, 12, *13*
"police force," 41, 136–37
preparing for war, 201, 265n37
sanctity, 77
self-torture, 57–58, 265n37
society laws of war, 207
system of governance, 5, 11–12, 234–35
war as sport, 161
warrior discipline, 46–47
Nótseo'o (enemies), 191, 210–13
Nóvávóse (sacred mountain in the Black Hills; Bear Butte), 43, 161, 172, 173, 251n11
O'Connor, James, 225
Oglala Lakota (Scatter or Pour Among Themselves), 18, 142–43, 181, 186, 189, 211–12, 234
Ohmésêhese (Eaters), *11*, 17, 188, 210, 212
Old Bear, 144
Old Man Charm, 206–7
Old She Bear (Northern Cheyenne)
    intertribal war, 210
    polygamy, 126
    Sweet Medicine story, 182–83
    Sweet Medicine Calls the Buffalo story, 36–37
Old Woman. *See* Mâhtamâhááhe
Old Woman's Spring story, 55, 188
Omaha people, 128, 164, 169
One Eye, 151
On-top realm. *See* Táxeto'vóóma
Óoetaneo'o (Crow), 58, 108, 169, 193, 207–8, 210, 212–13, 214, 219, 230, 266–67n44
Oohenumpa Lakota (To Boil Two Kettles), 181
oral tradition, xxviii–xxix, 66
orphans. *See* adoption/adoptees
ostracism, 16, 139, 141, 151
Otá'tavóóma (Blue-sky realm), *155*, 156
Otterby, Thomas. *See* Red Eagle
Ŏttō ha nĭh' (Bare Legs), 25
ována'xaetanohtôtse (peace)
    described, 17
    enemies, 210–13
    maintaining sovereignty, 16
    pipe carriers as peacekeepers, 136
    political and social alliances, 15, 169–76, 209
    reintroduce ceremony, 243
    Véhoo'o as peacekeepers, 137, 139, 161, 164, 167, 170, 194
    with United States, 219, 220–21, 223
    See also alliance; peace pipe; unification
Owl Woman, 151
pain and suffering, 67, 68
paint, 29, 56, 113
Painted Ceremony, 24
Paiutes, 167
Pawnee Nation. *See* Ho'néhetaneo'o
Peace Dance, 24
peace pipe, 15, 129–31, 135–38, 198–202, 243. *See also* ována'xaetanohtôtse
peacemaking. *See* ována'xaetanohtôtse
Penney, Grace J., 137
Petter, Rodolphe, 217
physical world, 72–73
Piegans (people), 164, 165, 167, 168
Pine, Leroy (chief; Northern Cheyenne), 234
Pipe Dancers. *See* Winnebago
Pipe of the Calf, 188
pipe smoke, 122, 104–5. *See also* peace pipe
Pipers, 164
Pipestone, Minnesota, 182
pipestone plate, 34, 37, 250n33
Plants Near the Water. *See* Minneconjou Lakota
Plover Wings story (Wolf Chief), 131–32
polygamy, 116, 126–28, 150
Ponca, 164, 165, 168, 169
Porter, Robert (Seneca), 9–10
Potawatomi people, 195
Pour Among Themselves. *See* Oglala Lakota
Powder River, 174, 212
practices, 18–19, 151. *See also* ceremony
priests, 250–51n3
profanity, use of, 89, 196
puberty rituals, 110–14
"Rabbit-Blankets." *See* Paiutes
Rabbit People. *See* Vóhkoohétaneo'o
race-based division, xxiii–xxiv
rape, 147–48, 152. *See also* sexual norms/taboos
Rapid City, South Dakota, 222
realms, 153–57
Red Bear, 67
Red Bird, 151
Red Buck, 107
Red Cloud
    declarations of war, 199
Red Eagle (Thomas Otterby, Southern Cheyenne), 113, 148, 255n29
Red Hair, 107
"Red Jackets," 166
Red Leaf, 148
Red Lodge. *See* Ma'eomene

| 291 |

INDEX

"Red People," 167
Red Rocks people, 164
Red Talkers, 186
Red Willow Men. *See* Ba'achiněna
Rees, 51, 177
Reservation, 225–235
    allotment policy, 233
    custom changes, 117
    destruction of family unit, 128
    early, 222, 224, 230
    impact on language, 190
    locations, 224
    peace among tribes, 210, 212, 214
    poor living conditions, 91
    ration system, 229–30
"rez," xxiv–xxv. *See also* reservation
rifles. *See* guns
ritual laws, 105–7. *See also* ceremony
Roaring Thunder. *See* Nonóma'e
Rockroads, Laura (Northern Cheyenne)
    The Man Who Turned into Buffalo Bones, 145
    power of thought, 71
Rocky Mountains, 172
Rope-hair-people. *See* Heévâhetaneo'o
running dance, 24
Sac people, 164, 195
The Sacred Arrows story (Bull Thigh), 45
Sacred Buffalo Hat. *See* Ésevone
Sacred Buffalo Hat Keeper. *See* Ésevone Tséá'enövâhtse
    sacred bundle/bundle keeper. *See* Tséá'enövâhtse
sacred covenants/promises. *See* ma'heónéstónestôtse
sacred due diligence, 22, 77
sacred due process, 22
Sacred Hat. *See* Ésevone
sacred laws. *See* ma'hëö'o hesto'emanestôtse
Sacred Medicine, laws of. *See* ma'hëö'o hesto'emanestôtse
sacred nation. *See* Ma'heónohéstanove
A Sacred People (Leo K. Killsback), 7, 15, 17, 41, 111, 149, 150, 161, 186, 208, 219, 223
Sacred Pipe, 175, 187, 188–89
"sacred protector," 247n6
sacred scholar/scholarship, xxvi–xxvii, xxviii, 247n6
sacred way of thinking. *See* Ma'heónetanohtôtse
Sacred Wolf. *See* Ma'heóneho'nehe
sacrifice. *See* ceremony, sacrifice
"sacrifice flag," 31, 32
Sacrifice Offering, 56

Sage Brush Men. *See* Ná'kasiněna
Sahaptin, 167
Sahée, 167
Sand Creek Massacre, xxix, 195, 222, 230
Sand Hill People. *See* Né'ohma'ehétaneo'o
Sans Arcs. *See* Itazipo
Santee, 164
Saötähön, 166
scalp dance, 24–25
scalping, 205, 211
Scatter Among Themselves. *See* Oglala Lakota
Schleisier, Karl H., 60
schools, 225–27
Seánemeo'o (Milky Way), 44, 154, 156
Séáno (happy hunting grounds), 154
seasons and ceremonial cycle, 3
Seicha (sacred pipe covenant), 175
Šé'šenovotsétaneo'o (Snake people; Comanche), 161, 167, 169, 176, 204–5, 208, 209–11
Sétóvóóma (Middle-of-the-water realm), 155–56
"Seven Council Fires," 181
sexual norms/taboos, 120–21, 144–53, 194
shame, 102, 111, 121, 127, 129, 141
Sharp Nose (Arapaho Chief), 171
Shawnee people, 195
"Short Hairs" people, 164
Short Woman. *See* Mukije
Sickness. *See* Háomóhtâhévêhanéhe
Shield (Bull Society) Dance, 23
Shipitan, 167
Shoshone Nation. *See* Sósone'eo'o
Sihasapa (Black Moccasins or Feet), 57, 167, 181, 228
Sioux, 6, 129, 142, 144, 151, 167. *See also* Ho'óhomo'eo'o
Sisseton Lakota, 181
Skidi Pawnees, 211
sky realm. *See* Otá'tavóóma
slippery dance, 24
Slow Bull (Southern Cheyenne)
    fundamental law of living, 104
    ritual laws, 105–6
smallpox, 211
Snake people. *See* Šé'šenovotsétaneo'o
Snakes of California, 166
Somers, A. E. (Southern Cheyenne)
    Story of Pipe and Smoke, 137–38
Sósone'eo'o (Shoshone), 58, 167, 169, 208, 210, 214, 219
Só'taeo'o, 25, 163, 182, 183–84. *See also* Tséhéstáno; unification, Só'taeo'o with

INDEX

Tsétsêhéstâhese
Southern Arapaho. *See* Na'wuněna
Southern Cheyenne, 39, 40, 94, 167, 210, 213, 222, 224. *See also* Tsêhéstáno
sovereignty
    in achieving peace, 214, 219
    concept of, xxii–xxiii
    decolonization, xxiii–xxiv, 6–7, 8–10
    Ma'heónohéstanove, 6–8
    sacred —, 10–14, 16–20
    success in peace, 16–17
    threatened by colonization, 222, 224, 228, 230
    use of term, 8
    Western versus Indigenous societies, 95–96
    See also ma'xenéheto'stôtse; tribal sovereignty
spear and hoop game, 28
sphere as place, 153–54
spiritual alliance, 15–16, 18. *See also* alliance
"spiritual death," 135
spiritual laws, 133, 135, 152–54, 268n30
spiritual relationships, 3
spiritual world, 72–73, 96, 137
Standing Bear, Luther (Oglala)
    death in warfare, 192–93
    Lakota Sun Dance, 186
    Tsetoenomósanéo'o, 198
    White Buffalo Woman and the Sacred Pipe covenant, 188
Standing Hollow Horn, 187
Standing Horns story (Tall Bull), 50–51, 64
Standing In The Morning (Só'taeo'o)
    The Medicine Buffalo Hunt story, 27, 28
    meeting other Indians, 163, 169
Stands Different Colors, 151
Stands In Timber, John (Northern Cheyenne)
    aseehe, 178
    The Buffalo Lodge story, 37–38, 250n33
    count coup, 206
    Crazy Dogs attempt to take Crow horses, 266–67n44
    cultural laws, 98–99
    Ésevone Tséá'enövâhtse, 55–56
    first encounter with Arapaho, 172
    importance of Tséá'enövâhtse, 158
    kinship laws, 91
    Maahótse Tséá'enövâhtse, 48
    marriages, 116–117
    Merger of Groups story, 184–85, 186
    Nótåxeo'o and colonization, 228

    old people, 84
    punishment for shooting Black Wolf, 229
    scalping, 205
    spiritual unification, 175
    war deeds, 197
    warrior's vow of death, 206–7
    Wounded Knee Massacre, 230
Standing On The Ground. *See* Ho'ehêvêsénóó'e
Standing On The Hill (Cheyenne chief), 195
Standing Rock Agency, 166
Stands Different (Cheyenne), 227
Sticks Everything Under His Belt, 143
St. Labre Catholic School, 225–27
Stockbridge people, 164, 166
Story of Pipe and Smoke (A. E. Somers), 137–38
storytelling, xxvii–xxx, 19–20. *See also specific stories*
Strong Eyes, 148
Stump Horn, 142
suffering. *See* pain and suffering
suicide, 69, 142, 153–54, 197–98, 204
suicide warrior, 207
Sun Bear, John (Northern Cheyenne), 141
Sun Dance. *See* Hoxéheome
Surrounding Buffalo. *See* Vóhaenóhónestôtse
Sutaiu, 50, 169, 250n33
Sweet Medicine. *See* Motsé'eóeve
Sweet Medicine Calls the Buffalo story (Old She Bear), 36–37
Sweet Medicine Calls the Buffalo story (White Buffalo), 35–36, 111
Sweet Medicine's Buffalo Songs story (White Buffalo), 34–35
Sweet Medicine's Buffalo Songs story (Wolf Chief), 34
Sweet Medicine story (Old She Bear), 182–83
Sweet Medicine story (White Eagle), 169, 176
Tall Bull
    horse's impact on Cheyenne society, 177
    Standing Horns story, 50–51, 64
    women's role in warfare, 205–6
Tall White Man, 142–43, 148
Tassel Woman, 151
Táxéto'vóóma (On-top realm), 154, 155, 156
teasing rules, 90–91
tepee. *See* tipi
Teton Lakota, 181, 184, 186, 189, 199
thoughts, powerful as words/actions, 70–71
"thunder nest," 57
tipi (lodge), 87–88, 141
To Boil Two Kettles. *See* Oohenumpa Lakota

INDEX

To Camp at the Entrance of the Circle. *See* Hunkpapa Lakota
Tomôsévêséhe (Erect Horns)
    apocalyptic prophecies, 64
    children becoming, 93
    culture hero, 60
    The Great Medicine Dance story, 50–55
    Old Woman Spring story, 55
    union with Ésevonae, 124
    See also Ho'ehêvêsénóó'e
Tongue River Boarding School, 225–27
Tongue River Indian Reservation, 225–27, 230–31
"Tonkawa" (Human-Flesh Eaters) people, 164
traditional law. *See* Noóneho'emanestôtse
tribal membership, xxiii
tribal sovereignty, xxiii, xxv–xxvi, xxx, 8–10, 233–35. *See also* sovereignty
tribe, xxiv, 233
Tséá'enövâhtse (keeper), 12–13, 41, 47, 56, 97, 135, 158, 175, 228, 250–51n3. *See also specific keeper*
Tsėhéema'heónetanohtôtse, principles of, 67–73
Tsėhéstáno (Northern Cheyenne Nation)
    alliance/unification, 6, 14, 15, 36
    aseehe, 178–80
    band. *See* band system
    birth, 18
    "buffalo culture," 66
    colonizing, 219–35
    communal ceremonies, 21–38, 240
    contempt for BIA, 234
    covenant ceremonies, 39–64, 239–40
    decolonization, 237–44
    grandmother as metaphor, xxiv
    ho'emanestôtse, 95–114
    Ho'óhomo'eo'o and —, 181–90
    horse economy, 161. *See also* horses
    "Indigenous Nation Sovereignty" form, 10
    Indigenous peoples and —, 163–80
    internal colonization, xxii–xxiii
    ma'heónohéstanove, 5–20
    Ma'heónetanohtôtse, 65–74, 241
    ma'hëö'o hesto'emanestôtse, 133–58, 258n2
    nation-state, 6, 7
    Néstaxeo'o, 161–62
    Nevo'êstanémaneo'o, 79–94, 240–41
    Nótseo'o, 210–13
    population growth, 177–78
    precontact autonomy, xxx
    reservations, 224
    sense of belonging. *See* citizenship
    Só'taeo'o teachings, 48
    starvation/suffering memories, 37, 52, 58–59
    studies research model, xxvii
    treaty negotiations, 219
    tribal conflicts, xxiii
    view as "nation," xxiv
    war, 191–202
    worldview, 153–56, *155*
    See also marriage; nationhood; sovereignty
Tsėhéstanove (spiritual way of life), 64, 79–94, 95–114, 230–32. *See* Tsėhéstáno; unification, Só'taeo'o with Tsétsêhéstâhese
Tsetoenomósanéo'o ("offering the pipe"), 135–138, 198–202, 243. *See also* peace pipe; pipe smoke
Tsis-tsistas, 54. *See also* Tsėhéstáno
"Turn Bloods" people, 164
"Turning Eyes" people, 164
The Two Young Men story, 17, 28–29, 188
unification
    ceremonial — with United States, 219
    Ho'óhomo'eo'o and –, 181–90
    inter-Indigenous national peacemaking, 167–76
    Só'taeo'o with Tsétsêhéstâhese (Great Unification), xxix, 17–18, 24, 57–58, 60, 161, 163, 169–70
    spiritual —, 175
    stories, 17, 93
    See also specific federations; alliance
United Lakhóta Nation (Sioux). *See* Ho'óhomo'eo'o
universal laws, 153–56
unkind acts. *See* inhumane/unkind acts, 69–70
Upshaw, Robert L., 227
US Armed Forces
    American Indian veterans, 202
US Bureau of Indian Affairs (BIA), 226, 230, 234
    agent, 227–28, 232, 233
    Courts of Indian Offenses (CIO), 228
US Court of Indian Offenses, 127
US Department of Interior, 231
Ute Nation. *See* Moktu'uahAtAn
Véhooneome (Chiefs' Lodge/Chief's Renewal Ceremony), 41, 170
Véhoo'o (Council of Forty-four Chiefs)
    aseehe, 178–79
    balance of power and authority, *14*
    choosing a Tséá'enövâhtse, 47

INDEX

colonization and powerlessness, 228, 232, 234–35
communal ceremonies, 23
creation, xxix, 5, 11, 111, 136
divorce customs, 129, 130
handing down judgments/punishments, 135
jurisdiction in murder cases, 138–43
ma'xenéheto'stötse shared with Nótåxeo'o, 12, *13*
peacekeepers, 137, 161, 167, 170, 230
polygamy, 127
sanctity, 77
seat on, 61, 133–34
sexual abuse, 147
strict laws, 97
unification, 173–75
war declarations, 200–201, 204
vé'šeeseo'o (medicine bundles), 25
véstomoó'hanestôtse (covenant or promise), 41
Vétapâhaetó'eo'o (Greasy wood people; Kiowa), 167, 169, 176, 177, 204–5, 208, 209
visitors, treatment of, 104–5
Voestaehneva'e (Naméhane; Big Sister)
children playing, 93
creator of Véhoo'o, 30
pipe and pipe smoking, 136
Só'taeo'o origins, 60
Vó'kaehénooné, 31
See also Mâhtamâháahe
Vóetséna'e (Lime; White Clay), 50–51, 59, 93, 163, 208
Vóhaenóhónestôtse (Surrounding Buffalo)
Buffalo Dance, 7, 61, *62*, 63
communal hunts, 143, 171, 175, 176, 204, 228, 230, 240
described, 33–38
Suhtai origin, 250n33
Vóhkoohétaneo'o (Crees), 161, 169, 171, 172, 183
Vó'kaehénooné (Antelope Singing/Antelope Pit Ceremony), 7, 29–33, 60, 143, 163, 176, 228
vonâhé'xá'e (talismans or relics), 25
Vono'oméé'e (Lost-in-time-and-space realm), 156–57, 203–4
Vó'oménéhotoa'e (White Faced Bull), 30, 31, 32
Vóto'sóoma (Human realm), 154
Wahpekute Lakota, 181
Wahpeton Lakota, 181, 186
Wakan Tanka (Great Mystery Spirit), 187
Walking Coyote (Ponca), 142
war
bonnet, 193, 196, *201*
clothing, 201, 206, 207
club, 196
codes/customs, 192–202
dance, 24, 115, 189, 197
death, 192–95, 203–4, 207
declaring, 161, 199–201, 204, 207–9
law of, 203–7
Nótseo'o, 210–13
preparation, 201–2, 260n51, 265n37
term for, 203
torturing/harming prisoners, 194–95
vow of death, 206–7
war prisoners, 194–95, 211
War Dance/Dancers, 23, 24
warrior society. *See* Nótâxeo'o
Washita massacre, 230
water, 43, 71–72, 155
wedding. *See* marriage, ritual
Wheeler-Howard Bill, 233
Whirling Bear, Chief, 221
White Buffalo (Northern Cheyenne)
challenges of inter-Indigenous peacemaking, 167, 169
dances identified, 22–24
list of Indigenous nations, 164
strategy of Moving the Arrows, 208
Sweet Medicine Buffalo Songs story, 34–35
Sweet Medicine Calls the Buffalo story, 35–36, 111
White Buffalo Woman
spiritual leader, 5, 187–88
White Bull/Ice (Northern Cheyenne)
contradictions of colonialism, 224
expelled from Crazy Dogs, 259n25
White Clay People. *See* Aä'ninĕna
White Dirt, Gilbert, 234
White Eagle (Dog Soldier; Southern Cheyenne)
dances identified, 22, 23
horses from Pawnees, 177
marriage practices, 117, 124–25
meeting with Lakota, 184
polygamy, 126–27
Sweet Medicine story, 169, 176
White Faced Bull. *See* Vó'oménéhotoa'e
White Frog
Lakota unification, 183–84
White man (Cheyenne trickster), 146
White Thunder (Maahótse Tséá'enöváhtse), 204, 209
Whiteman, Wesley, 43
whites
as Indigenous nation, 191

INDEX

as vé'hó'e (tricksters), 222–23
colonization, 212, 219–35
increase in violence, 195
invasion of, 143
mass murder, 192
military conflicts, 149, 213, 218, 222
scalping, 205
threat to sovereignty and nationhood, 224
trading partners, 218
unification versus land acquisition, 219
viewed as disease-ridden, 177
viewpoint, 217
white man's way, 222–24
Wilkins, David (Lumbee), 9, 233–34
Wilson, Shawn, xxvi
Wind River Indian reservation, 210, 214
Winnebago (Pipe Dancers), 164
Woir-Oqtuimanists (Man on a Cloud), 201
Wolf (white man), 223
Wolf Chief (Ôhméseheso; Northern Cheyenne)
    courtship process, 117
    Dog soldiers, 207
    encounter with Ho'óhomo'eo'o, 182
    kinship rules, 91
    marriage customs, 119
    Plover Wings story, 131–32
    polygamy, 126
    Sweet Medicine's Buffalo Songs story, 34
Wolf Dance, 23
Wolf Medicine, 140
Wolf people. See Ho'néhetaneo'o
Wolf Pup Ceremony, 24
Wolfvoice, Grover (Northern Cheyenne), 32
womanhood. See he'eévestôtse
women
    feminine in nature, 56
    Medicine Hat law, 144
    power of procreation, 111–12
    protecting virtue, 117, 120, 145
    role in warfare, 205–6, 209
    sacred place in culture, 111, 120, 130, 144, 229
    violence against, 142, 144–53, 194, 257n44
Wooden Leg (Kamxwiwiyaxtah; Northern Cheyenne), 166
    accidental deaths, 139–40
    adoption ceremonies, 108
    antelope meat, 32
    aseehe, 179
    courtship, 115
    crimes against Cheyenne, 142

    daughters' attendance at Catholic Mission, 225–26
    decline in ceremonies, 174
    divorce customs, 129–30, 257n44
    elopement, 121
    The First White Man, Decolonized story, 223
    healing, 67
    Hoxéheome, 48, 50
    importance of water, 72
    intervention by Nótâxeo'o, 136–37
    land encroachment, 193
    Little Bighorn battle, 213
    Maahéome, 138
    Medicine Hat law, 144
    naming ceremonies, 107
    polygamy, 127–28
    spiritual and physical worlds, 72
    unifications, 189–90
    universal laws, 157
    women's puberty and role of grandmother, 113
World War II, 206
Wounded Knee Massacre, 230
Wrapped Hair (Só'taeo'o)
    Berdaches, 25
    captive men, 194
    Everybody Was Starving story, 58–59
    he'eévestôtse, 120
    menstruation rules, 111
    polygamy, 127
    teasing rules, 90–91
    woman's "stone war club," 113
Xamaevo'êstaneo'o (Indigenous People), 164–76, 243. See also specific peoples
Yankton Lakota, 181
Yanktonais Lakota, 181
Yellow Cook (Cheyenne), 229
Youngest, adoption ceremonies, 107
Young Wolf Society, 60, 61

www.ingramcontent.com/pod-product-compliance
Lightning Source LLC
Chambersburg PA
CBHW022017280725
30246CB00024B/212